Reading
Strategies
And
Enrichment
Activities
For
Grades 4-9

Virgie M. McIntyre

Western Carolina University

CHARLES E. MERRILL PUBLISHING COMPANY
A Bell & Howell Company
Columbus   Toronto   London   Sydney

The Charles E. Merrill
COMPREHENSIVE READING PROGRAM

Arthur Heilman
Consulting Editor

This book was set in Times Roman.
The Production Editor was Cynthia Donaldson.
The cover was prepared by Will Chenoweth.

International Standard Book Number: 0-675-08453-9

Library of Congress Catalog Card Number: 76-51628

2 3 4 5 6 7 8 9 10 — 82 81 80 79 78 77

PRINTED IN THE UNITED STATES OF AMERICA

Preface

One interesting definition of reading which I saw recently stuck with me—a tumult of the brain. I wonder how many students in today's classrooms would agree with this.

As a teacher of reading, are you creating any tumult in the minds of your students? A stranger can walk into a classroom, stay for a few minutes, and tell whether or not learning is taking place. A teacher's job is to set up situations that challenge students, that lead toward success, and that invite them to come back tomorrow for more.

Many teachers and students admit that the reading period is the worst part of the day. How sad! It could and should be one of the most exciting and rewarding. How do you make it so? How do you individualize learning? How do you help students increase their vocabulary? When you recognize a student is in trouble because of poor reading achievement, what do you do? How can you teach him or her to read with comprehension? How can you coordinate reading groups and keep all students performing?

Hundreds of books have been written on how to teach reading. Reading for the primary, high school, the MR's, elementary school, diagnostic, developmental, corrective, etc.; but when we started looking for a specific textbook for our course, "Teaching Reading in the Middle Grades" (herein defined as Grades 4-9), it was like a no-man's land. So we developed our own course outline, incorporating in Part I, which became Chapters one and part of four and ten of this text, just enough theoretical background to initiate students, many who have never had a reading course, into the field.

Chapters two and three tell you how to "learn" your students so that you can efficiently teach them. The remaining chapters deal with specific topics which need to be utilized in all grades, but especially in the middle years where students are just developing into independent readers.

Today's students are inclined to doubt most of what adults tell them. We waste much time in talking and telling. There are other ways of doing it. By giving you activities, teaching procedures, practice exercises, and models, this book will tell you, show you, and suggest some ways you can adapt materials to fit the needs and levels of your groups. Though based on theory, it is not a theoretical book. Though many practice and reinforcement exercises are given, it is not a practice manual. I prefer to think of it as a resource book for busy people in search of different ideas.

This book has two unique features. First, it is specifically designed for the teaching of reading in the crucial middle grades; but could be used at any level, and it shows you how. Specific suggestions for putting theory into practice which have worked in some classrooms make up the bulk of the material.

A beginning teacher can understand and use this book. The in-service teacher can extend her thinking. In addition to the above features, statements and activities are included to provoke and stimulate teachers and prospective teachers to think about why they do what they do other than because some teacher's guide says so.

Over a period of years in all levels of classrooms from primary to college, and through in-service workshops, I've gained much inspiration and knowledge from students, teachers, and colleagues—how they study, how they learn, and how they react to each other. Encouragement from these people resulted in the compilation of this material. My ideas and biases, adaptations of ideas, and specific suggestions from other sources (credit given when used) have made the teaching of reading exciting for me. While it is virtually impossible to know where many thoughts and ideas come from, my philosophy of reading is definitely influenced by the Herber, Early, Green trio at Syracuse University, and from the other sources listed in the Bibliography.

Special acknowledgements go to Dr. George Maginnis and Dr. Al Kingston who encouraged me to write this text, to the many students and teachers who used the ideas in their work, to the girls who helped with typing, and especially to my family—Bryson, Teresa, and Dawn—who let me go my own way, making it possible for me to complete this work.

And a very special thinks to Fred Kinne, Cynthia Donaldson, and all other people at Charles E. Merrill Publishing Company who helped in getting this material into print.

V.A.M.
Western Carolina University

Contents

ONE

Reading as an Active Process: An Overview

THESIS: The activity of reading in grades 4-9, if practically and efficiently done, will function as a thought process, as a search for meaning from printed symbols, and as a skill to use daily in all areas of the curriculum.

PREMISE I: A teacher should know what he or she believes in, wants to do, and how much he is willing to put out before attempting any plan of action.

PREMISE II: Every teacher should do diagnostic teaching.

PREMISE III: In order to do diagnostic teaching, a teacher must first diagnose.

PREMISE IV: In the absence of specialists, funds for testing, teacher aides, and so forth, the regular classroom teacher can make her own tests and do her own testing.

PREMISE V: Teachers can meet the needs of students.

PREMISE VI: Given the know-how and the time, teachers will meet the needs of students.

PREMISE VII: The middle grades, here including grades 4-9, can be an exciting challenge which holds students in school rather than making dropouts of them.

Premise I and Some Definitions

As in the case of most disciplines dealing with words, definitions used in the field of reading are highly controversial, often unsatisfactory, and lead to different interpretations. When one begins to look for them, it is reminiscent of Humpty Dumpty's speech in *Through a Looking Glass,* "When I see a word, it means just what I choose it to mean—neither more nor less."

Definitions for terms in reading are as numerous as the people who talk and write about them. Some of the most prevalent general meanings leading toward the more complex are listed here. Which of these meanings can you defend?

Reading is
1. A small child   What I do in school
2. A prisoner   Escape
3. A blind person   Heaven
4. A reluctant reader   Hell
5. A bachelor girl   Life and romance
6. Some teachers   Decoding
                          Decoding, comprehending, and applying
                          Communication
                          Reaction
7. Hall, Mann, Huey, Stauffer   A thought-getting process (143, p. 10)
8. Reading is essentially a form of communication in which a reader interacts with an author.[1]
9. Reading is not a simple mechanical skill; nor is it a narrow scholastic tool. Properly cultivated, it is essentially a thoughtful process. However, to say that reading is a "thought-getting" process is to give it too restricted a description. It should be developed as a complex organization of patterns of higher mental processes. It can and should embrace all types of thinking, evaluating, judging, imagining, reasoning, and problem solving. Indeed, it is believed that reading is one of the best mediums for cultivating many techniques of thinking and imagining.[2]

From this inexhaustive list, is there any wonder that you have problems deciding which meaning you will accept and use as a basis for teaching? What models for reading can be built using these definitions? Berg's list (13) is comprised of: (a) word perception; (b) comprehension; (c) reaction, intellectual and whether to accept or reject; and (d) assimilation.

The components of a model depend upon one another. Comprehension of materials comes only if the reader perceives verbal symbols that represent an author's meaning. Valid reactions to and full integration of ideas can come about only if the reader accurately comprehends meaning. From the very first, children should be taught that reading means to interpret the message.

We have another definition which also plagues us: *comprehension*. What is it? What does it include? What are the processes involved? Most of us talk glibly about teaching the skills of comprehension. Books are written on the subject, but do we really know what we're talking about?

. . . Understanding a paragraph is like solving a problem in mathematics. It consists in selecting the right elements of the situation and putting them together in the right relations, and also with the right amount of weight or influence or force for each.[3]

. . . Reading comprehension, therefore, results from a constellation of many factors and the reading comprehension score actually reflects the behavioral response of the organism to a complex process.[4]

Most authorities will agree that comprehension is a complex process, not easily understood, and needs more study. However, it does include some things which can be listed and stressed by teachers. Comprehension is some form of meaning related to experience and to the items in question: ability to paraphrase, to abstract from content, to answer questions, to deal critically with material, to discover new meanings. Your job as a teacher is to set up classroom structures to lead students toward these skills. Problems in some areas, however, may not be reading problems per se. They may result from low intelligence, restricted language skills, and/or restricted experiences. Even the content of the material may lack interest and will not motivate.

William Gray, Thomas Barrett, Helen M. Robinson, Frederick B. Davis, Albert J. Kingston, Constance McCullough, and Jack A. Holmes are some individuals who have given models for reading and/or comprehension. Yet they all admit that these models are only attempts at understanding processes and further study and research are needed.

Suppose you believe you are doing a good job of developing the skills of word recognition and comprehension, yet the children come up with wrong answers? Perhaps that wrong answer for you was the right answer from the child's viewpoint. He used his thinking processes to arrive at the answer. Does this mean that his thinking processes are faulty?

The story is told of the teacher who was introducing the concept of *average* in arithmetic. She asked if anyone in the class knew the term. A little fellow in the back of the room raised his hand. When she gave him the chance to answer, he gave the meaning of average as a "hen's nest." Upon further questioning he explained that his father was a farmer who raised chickens. Many times he had heard his father tell people that his hens laid four eggs per week on the average.

Another teacher, this one in a Head Start class with ghetto children, had them quoting the Pledge of Allegiance to the flag. She explained where to place the hand over the heart. Each time they did the pledge, one little fellow placed his hand on his back hip. Again, she would explain, but he didn't hear. One afternoon she walked home with him. As they approached the house she saw an old, old man sitting on the porch. The boy ran up to his grandfather who put a shaky arm around the child and patted his back side saying, "Bless his little heart." The teacher no longer had to ponder the child's concept of the location of the heart. However, she did have to find a way to change it. Richard Samson (116) would say that these two children understood, at least as thoroughly as circumstances permitted.

Like the physical parts of our body, thinking and comprehension are developmental. Both include factors such as maturity of the reader, capabilities of the writer, and the purpose of the reader.

> Thinking is a process rather than a fixed state. It involves a sequence of ideas moving from some beginning, through some sort of patterns of relationships, to some goal or conclusion . . . It is possible to make a logical distinction between the materials of thinking (such as perceptions), the motives of thinking

(such as attitudes influencing it), the process of thinking (such as classifying), and the abilities of thinking which produce ease and precision in problem situations.[5]

A summation of many definitions of thinking might sound something like this: thinking is something that goes on in the mind as a result of sensory capacities, motivation from within resulting from past experiences and present stimuli, and brain waves going all directions with selective patterns chosen as a result of the purpose for which reading is done.

Action is the key to cognitive functioning. Your job as teacher is to set up tasks in order of difficulty levels so that they can be carried out successfully by students, see that they carry them out, and guide toward less and less teacher support by student internalization. If you help with developing language as a cognitive tool by improving vocabulary and problem-solving techniques, then you are helping students to expand, develop, and use their thinking capacity.

David Russell (114) claims that little can be done to change the reader's capacity to learn to read, but much can be done to stimulate and direct reading activities so as to insure maximum progress. Reading, thinking, developmental maturity, cognitive processes, comprehension, intelligence—these are all interrelated terms which must be dealt with in the classroom.

The teacher can lead students. You can suggest, hint, question, lead through phases of understanding, suggest reasons for existence of problems, formulate hypotheses for the solution of problems, and so on. You can assure them that thinking (learning) is an active process and does not always require set answers. By being a good model and by having an attitude of inquiry and suspended judgments, you can set the stage for thoughtful, purposeful reading. You can give instruction and practice in techniques for reading critically, give time and chance for discussion about what is read, and encourage students to relate their experiences to their reading.

As a teacher, you must also present students with reading situations where they experiment with ideas, ask questions and seek answers, manipulate things and ideas, reconcile what they find at one time with that of another time, and compare findings with those of others. An atmosphere where pupils are free to think and evaluate, to learn to have the strength of their own convictions, and the courage to deal with ideas, with the end products being the ability to examine, hypothesize, look for proof, hold off quick judgment and make decisions, will enhance the learning situation. Knowing is a process, not a product, says Bruner (24, p. 335). The whole brain works together to get the job done. Disturbance in one link affects the end product. Intelligence is becoming thought of as a problem-solving ability—a process of choosing from among unanticipated combinations those patterns which have significance in reality. If interest in a task requires an element of uncertainty, learning requires a disequilibrium to be created, then satisfied, and genius must go back to a child's creativeness to create, then how important the job of teaching reading as a thinking process!

Some other brief definitions as used in this text need to be stated here.

Diagnose	Find the strengths and weaknesses of students.
Objectives	What we want to accomplish.
Behavior	How we perform.
Assessment	Do we accomplish what we set out to do?
Teaching	Setting structure and/or classroom atmosphere where students are challenged and free to perform.
Intelligence	The ability to profit from instruction.
Study Guides	Questions, exercises, games, and/or other plans of guided study which the teacher prepares and students use as they work on materials.
Inquiry Training or Problem Solving	Students learn by doing in contrast to teacher spoon-feeding.
Developmental Reading	Continued growth in the acquisition of skills. These skills should become more sophisticated as students progress through school. Only the basic beginnings are developed in the primary grades. Middle-grade teachers must provide a definite planned reading program to continue development.
The Cognitive or Thought Process	Using the higher mental powers of interpreting and evaluating reading. We call it thinking. If this is what we want to develop, then as teachers we must know and understand what to do about some of the influences which develop or hinder the process.

What Affects Cognition?

1. Principles of learning
2. How the student perceives
3. Listening ability
4. Purpose for reading
5. Motivation
6. Concentration
7. Ego's function
8. Sociology
9. Intelligence and levels of understanding
10. How the student perceives the reading act
11. How the teacher perceives the reading act
12. Language

Relating Theory to Learning

If student and teacher effectiveness is expected in the classroom, a closer look at the items listed above is mandatory. How do each of these relate to, help, or hinder what goes on in the classroom?

1. The Principles of Learning.

William Palmer (107) says that the principles of learning plus *x* number of other things affect the cognitive processes. He stresses that intellectual functioning develops best if you, the teacher: (a) structure hierarchies of tasks from simple to complex; (b) build these tasks upon natural responses, which also lead toward maturity; and (c) listen to students, helping them weigh and see relationships. The student-teacher reaction and interaction is definitely an asset in cognitive thinking. The different activities, dialogue, intellectual and emotional atmosphere, the kinds of questions asked, and your response to student questions are assets, or not, according to practices engaged in.

Too many times teachers cut off a discussion just when it becomes interesting to the students. There is no faster way to "turn them off" to learning. The more vital, vibrant, and vigorous the interaction (not mechanical responses memorized from a textbook), the more likely that learning will take place.

When the student reads, can he create from himself these kinds of reactions? A teacher should know the student—his or her experiences, conflicts, state of mind, and limitations. Can he accept or is he blocked by what he reads? What are his expectations, his mind set? His responses—what do they reveal or hide? Are they relevant? Do they point toward growth in thinking?

2. How the Student Perceives.

Certainly how a student perceives—his/her tensions, fears, and past experiences as well as what he is looking for and how he interprets what he finds—affects his thinking on what he reads. You can't separate thinking from emotions. Personality and attitude, self-concepts, what he is willing to look at—these influence the reading process of building upon, adding to, and elaborating on what he already knows.

3. Listening and Thought.

From Paul Hollingsworth (76B), "Many of these research reports show that *through improvement of listening abilities reading can be improved.* Listening does have a positive effect on teaching a child."

The listening ability of students affects their thought processes. Listening is an intellectual task which includes discrimination, focusing (tuning out of other things), tracking, and remembering. It requires rejecting as well as processing. Selecting what to remember, organizing, internal accuracy, and speed are cognitive tasks which can be trained.

This author experimented with an eighth-year class of thirty-five students in a self-contained classroom. We began with six student-chosen quotations and read them orally (after silent student preparation) to the class. Then each reader asked one question about his or her quotation to which the class responded. Our purpose, which students knew, was to build listening power and recall. We did this twice weekly for six weeks. As they saw themselves growing, students were motivated to listen more carefully and by the end of that six weeks, most could respond 80 percent correctly to questions from sixteen quotations.

4. The Purpose for Reading.

According to Ruth Strang (138), "What the individual gets out of his mind depends upon the way in which ideas were put into it. By organizing and relating these ideas while reading, he will better be able to remember and communicate them." None of us knows all about this process we call reading, but we should give students a purpose for reading, explain how the skill we are attempting to develop will help them, and demonstrate its use. Along with purpose goes efficiency. Many people, including some adults, assume that fast reading is efficient reading. You must stress the fact that rate of reading depends upon purpose as well as the reader's interest and background in the subject matter.

5. Motivation.

Motivation sometimes stems from purpose. Students learn what they *want* to learn. Words inscribed on public utilities prove this. Even the disadvantaged little fellow who can't read or write in classroom activities can write and spell some words correctly.

There are different schools of thought on motivation. One says you can motivate students to want to learn. The other says motivation must come from within. Still another one says we are stupid to worry about motivation, that everyone is motivated toward something. The conflict arises as a result of divergent goals of teacher and student. Perhaps all of these have merit, yet the fact remains that the teacher is responsible for what goes on in the classroom. You must set the structure and/or situation that creates disequilibrium and the disquieting effects within the student, requiring that he do something about it. Hopefully learning occurs.

6. Concentration.

Benger (11, p. 120) argues that concentration is the most important trait of all in a student's capacity to understand reading. Certainly not many would deny that this trait is important. The best teacher in the world cannot reach someone who is mentally absent. The most exciting reading will not challenge if the student covers white space with his mind on last night's party or this morning's fight at the break-fast table.

Concentraton may need training. Students can learn to attend to tasks at hand just as they learn to tune in and out other things, such as voices, when they're listening to music, or one voice in a room of voices.

Huey (78) advises readers "to search diligently for meaning by examining carefully each word, phrase, and line. . . ." This calls for concentration on the task at hand.

7. Ego's Function.

Ego's function includes the neurological and psychological interwoven: perception, concept formation, memory, motility, language formation, cognition, thinking, integration, association, postponement of gratification, reality testing, and synthesis.

. . . Reading, being a complex process, may involve any or all of these aspects, with cause and effect being closely interwoven.[6]
. . . ego's functions play a crucial role in individual's adaptations to the learning situation.[7]
. . . One should never forget that the child is a physical organism functioning in a social environment in a psychological manner.[8]

Interference with one link in the system affects the end product of that system. A dictionary definition of ego might say something like this: the thinking, feeling, and acting self that is conscious of itself and aware of its thoughts and other operations.

Self-esteem, which can be a justifiable pride, may suggest a reasonable concept of self. Sometimes the self-esteem is used to denote an overestimate of self, thus a derogatory connotation.

A child who gives up easily, who says he can't; a child who rebels and creates her own diversions; a child who withdraws into self; and the child who is without love: these children are aware of the fact that they are different. They may feel insecure, alone, and emotionally tired of trying to cope. They may feel ashamed, guilty or "bad." Reading, as well as other school tasks, is just another activity at which they fail.

What can you do? (1) Carefully assess strengths and weaknesses. (2) Help students develop skills, concepts, and cognitive power. (3) Help them to realize they can do, but a healthy self-concept does not develop automatically or overnight. (4) Accept them as they are, language and all. (It works for them in their society.) (5) Create an atmosphere in class that is conducive to self-realization: materials they can handle successfully to satisfy needs of approval; involvement to stimulate needs and desires; and rewards so that the reading goals become the reader's goals. (6) You, the teacher, must realize that reading is a personal thing, part of the self and that some students must have tasks relevant to now, not some far-off remote college entrance test or job application. They want to know how to play a game, to construct a drag racer, or read the funny paper. To be most efficient, effective, and effortless, the student's reading tasks need an immediate purpose and pay-off which relates to self.

Reading is an ego function. Success builds self-esteem, failure reduces it. On the other hand, a student with a confident self-concept will probably find it easy to read, those with a low id will have a more difficult task.

8. Sociology.

Spache (131, ch. 7) points out that society influences cognition. Television, newspapers, radios, magazines, and films influence thinking; how or how much, we're not sure. Peers, community, school, the family, and cultural and socioeconomic factors affect how students react to the learning tasks of school. Is parent failure transmitted to the child? Some argue yes, others no. The little research that has been done indicates peers are more important than socioeconomic status. Some students from disadvantaged backgrounds are low achievers. Others may be in the top ten percent.

9. The I.Q. and Learning Ability.

    A. Some behaviorist theory suggests that I.Q. is independent of the ability to learn.

    B. Some has found certain types of learning directly related to intelligence while others are not.

    C. Still another theory states that all learning is related to intelligence.

Harry Munsinger (102) reported a study done by B. Eisman with simple discrimination using subjects with low, average, and high I.Q. scores. He used common objects such as jacks, hammer, and baskets and found no measurable differences in the three groups. The educable mentally retarded and normal groups developed new associations at about the same rate. He also looked at a study done by S. Harter—the effect of I.Q. on learning set formation. Harter gave children a series of ten problems and pairs of objects to connect in simple association. Problem solvers showed chance in early problems then climbed abruptly after several tries. The number of trials to reach criterion in learning decreased as I.Q. increased. Older children learned faster and so did brighter children. In the simple paired associations, learning was not affected by I.Q. or Mental Age. Kathlyn Benger (11) concludes that intelligence is significantly related to reading success in grade one but less than visual and auditory perception and personality traits.

Under superior instructional conditions, I.Q. and reading achievement tend to correlate—but not always. "Brightness does not insure high reading achievement. A low M.A. does not always indicate a limit to the child's reading achievement." (49, ch. 11)

In one study with 1,130 children in the sixth grade, Donald Durrell found that 29 percent had reading ages above their Stanford Binet scores, 15 percent were one or more years below, and 56 percent were within one year of their M.A.

One must look at the student's cognitive processes, level of functioning, and total personality—many facets not measured or susceptible to change by instructional techniques.

Is he a slow learner? Is he highly creative? Can she decode? Which modality is favored in her learning? Does he understand linguistic use of print? Can she do adaptive reading? Can she use reference and study skills? Can he recognize various cues? Can he make relationships? What are her interests and expectations?

If, as Thorndike suggests, learning is a matter of connections, all of these processes become very important.

10. How the Student Perceives the Reading Act.

Though scarcely mentioned in the literature, how the student perceives the reading act seems to have merit. When teachers work on teaching the reading and/or study skills, how can one separate them, should they help students reach some understanding of how these skills work to help them?

"For tomorrow, outline chapter ten in your textbook." How often an assignment such as this one is given students as they leave the room for the next class, especially in secondary schools. They try to comply. The next day outlines are turned in. Their reward: a big red D or F and the instructions to do the paper over.

Now, isn't that a ridiculous assignment? If they had known how to outline, they would have done it correctly the first time.

If you want students to succeed with the tasks you assign, it is your responsibility to see that they have the skill to perform the task. If not, teach it. You cannot assume that the overworked English or reading teacher has done the job. (More about this later.) You should discuss with your students the merits of outlining as a study skill, how seeing patterns of organization in material can make it easier to understand, and how these patterns will help them in remembering the information.

Second, and just as important for student mastery of the skill, is the process of *how to*. Go through the process of outlining with them. Give them a model to follow. This is your task. If students could do everything, they wouldn't need you.

11. How the Teacher Perceives the Reading Process.

How the teacher perceives the reading process is basic to efficient teaching and learning. Is it recognizing words, "parroting" back literal facts, or problem solving tasks where reacting to materials read is practiced? Instruction in the classroom will reflect your definition of reading. What happens between you and your students (instruction) makes the difference. The three-year study of first grades sponsored by the federal government several years ago concluded that the teacher was more important than either method or materials. Students learn sometimes because of you, but too many times, in spite of you.

12. Language and Reading as a Thought Process.

The relationship of language and learning is not fully understood, but may affect school learning experiences if a child cannot think and/or communicate or does not have the words in abstract form.

Language is a way of thinking, of responding, and of participating. These three processes are important in present day classrooms. Just as a good listener interprets the words of a speaker, a good reader interprets the language of an author (68). Translating the message he gets into his own language is a matter of relating the message to previous experiences with words, rearranging, seeing new relationships, and selecting certain meanings while rejecting others—all requiring complex mental processes which sound like what we typically call reasoning.

Your job is to challenge, aid, and guide students in extending their vocabulary (language). Just as the language-experience approach works in primary grades, it will work in building ideas and concepts for older students. Firsthand experiences facilitate acquisition of language better than any other method. If this is impossible, you can use the armchair traveling technique, audio-visuals, games, and similar approaches. Open discussion about emotional words creates interest. Why does a teen-ager resent being called "kid," "chicken," "boy," "freak," or most any label he doesn't make up himself? The extent to which one can associate meanings with written language is a matter of experience. So give experiences.

If you want students to really learn the new words (as concepts) after they have been introduced, then you must make sure they use them. A student who never sings will not be a singer. If one never puts on a pair of skates, he will never be a skater. If students don't use words, they will never be sesquipedalians. To build word power, let them read; let them write; let them talk.

> We must build upon the students own responses to reading even though such responses may be lacking in sophistication.[9]
> Unfortunately, many teachers lack competence in guiding students in momentary and central learning experiences. For too many teachers evade, restrict, and control genuine responses to reading experiences. . . .[10]

Since reasoning, intelligence, and language are all functions of reading, the teacher must realize that reading is a receiver-oriented task, that some stimuli may not be sufficient to challenge some individuals, and that the best teacher in the world can work day after day and no learning will take place if the student doesn't want to learn. The teacher's job is to guide responses toward maturity in thinking.

In one first grade filled with Head Starters, children were asking questions such as "Is it solid or liquid?" "Is it animal or mineral?" "Is it edible?" Their teacher had used the Surprise Box to stimulate questions. To find out what the box contained, the students had to question the teacher. At first they didn't ask too many questions, the teacher had to help with kinds of questions they might ask, but not for long. Reinforcement came when they figured out what the box contained. Double reinforcement came when it was something like bubble gum, balloons, or a turtle which they could keep in the classroom to watch and study.

Yes, language is the basis of speech, reading, and writing. Development comes from application. Let them talk. If they know something, they should be able to put it into words, if given the chance. Before they can put it into words, they must think it out internally. And before they can understand what the symbols mean (reading), they must think them out according to their backgrounds and individual understandings.

How Do Children Learn?

How do children learn? A four-year-old was watching a doodle bug hide in the sand. When the bug was out of sight the child stirred him up again. "You can't fool me," he told the bug. "You look like a brace and bit, but you're really a jet." I asked him why he said that. "Well, he looks like he's working with his head, but he's really doing the work with his back side. See! Look how it moves from side to side." I asked him how that was like a jet. "Oh, silly, you know. It gets its go from the back of the plane, you know, the white thing you see in the air." This child is one of the lucky ones.

From a linguistic point of view advanced by C. C. Fries (58), there are three stages in learning. 1. *Transfer stage.* A child can learn to read within a year after he has learned to talk if the teacher begins at the child's level with what he knows. It's simply transferring, a shift from talk (auditory) to graphic signs for the same signals. Fries then explains the linguistic way of doing this by beginning with the differentiation of letters.

2. *Productive stage.* From imitation and practice she can read visual signs automatically and no longer has to think about them. Then comes understanding beneath the symbols. She responds. Practice and small steps, telling her that "reading" is a substitute for "talk," leads to understanding.

3. *Vivid imagination and realization stage.* The symbols stimulate imaginative realization of vicarious experiences. Reading becomes equal with, or better than, live speech as a teacher.

Psychologists differ somewhat in their explanations, in specific steps, and in the theory of what learning is. But most of them, it appears, would agree that the first stage is relatively manipulative. Action. It begins as highly unstable and with single-track attention and is short-lived. There is little reflection involved. Sensations and skills in handling are practiced.

Then comes reflective thinking. Perceptional organization begins, some visual, some auditory, and some multisensory. Internal representation and images are organized or related to larger chunks of the environment than the immediate block in hand.

Third comes the language. A child considers words rather than objects. Symbolic operations become possible, and finally, the fusing of the knowledge of what he learns with previous knowledge.

Robert Gagne (61) says the important thing for education is the condition of learning. A teacher must know these conditions and set them up. He lists the sequence of learning from the simple stimulus- response, building progressively up toward understanding concepts, each step dependent on the one before.

Pressures to please, to cover materials, to conform, and to excel may block learning. Early learning surrounded by conflict and/or failure may block learning. The emotional conflict may become a greater problem to the child so that he shuts out or defends himself from learning.

While curiosity is essential to learning, it too may lead to distractibility. It must be channeled and controlled in order for the child to cope with schoolwork. He may have to solve a math problem when he would much prefer to watch the bird on the windowsill.

While sensations, images, percepts, memories, concepts, and generalizations are the key steps in most learning, there are children who can skip some steps and others who may have to take half-steps and not learn though guided in all. Each of these steps may be considered separately, but it seems that thinking or learning remains a whole and a mystery. Why can one group or one child grasp something quickly and another one slowly or not at all? Much has been done in the last decade to find some solutions to the problems, yet in attempting to set up the structure or classroom situations to meet the individual differences of personality, ability, motivation, and needs, questions remain.

The Linguists' Points of View

Linguists claim that the primary language function is speech. Writing and reading are secondary. Yet they have the same trouble with definitions and processes as others do. How the knowledge of linguistics relates to the reading progress varies from linguist to linguist. The point of introducing this view point is to substantiate the thesis that, though some people do not understand it this way, reading is a thought process.

The Phonologists:	This group attacks current methods of teaching phonics as irrational and distorted.
The Structural Linguists:	They say that sentence structure brings comprehension, and they attack the phonics and whole-word method of teaching reading.
The Semanticists:	This group emphasizes the importance of shades of meanings of words and their relation to a reader's background and experience.
The Psycholinguists:	Application of the techniques and concepts of psychology as applied to language development is stressed by these theoreticians who treat language as a thinking process.
The Descriptive Linguists:	This group emphasizes the structure of morphemes (combination of sound). Word structure, they say, is important to reading.

Some interesting facts about reading from the linguists should stimulate the teacher's thinking on the subject: (a) simple, normal power of speech is all a child needs as readiness for the act of reading; (b) reading is highly dependent upon auditory memories; and (c) comprehension depends upon the reader's ability to hear (think) the written word in sentences as he or she reads.

Definite research supports the significance of a child's comprehension and use of language for success in beginning reading. Spache (133) supports Fries and Bigson who seem to have some agreement on the question of reading. Fries (58) says that one can "read" insofar as he can respond to the language symbols represented by graphic shapes as fully as he has learned to respond to the same language signals of his code represented by patterns of auditory shapes. Response requires understanding.

Understanding Comprehension

What is your opinion of these summary statements of concepts from the writings of some of today's authors?

Bruner: A child can learn anything in some form. (24)

Durrell: Materials differentiated into levels of difficulty can be made to meet the needs of students. (49)

Fries: It isn't when you start, it's where. (58)

Herber: Any child can succeed at some level. (75)

Kingston: If the writer employs symbols which represent a cognitive level of abstraction comparable or identical to that of the reader, comprehension is likely to result. (84)[11]

What is comprehension? If we knew what it was, we would teach it. Webster says comprehension is the art of understanding, grasping with the intellect. Thus, the next question is, can we teach a child to understand what he reads? We have beautiful verbalizers who can't tell you a thing about what they read. It has been said that one way of meeting the individual needs of students and having them succeed is by giving guidance at the different levels of comprehension difficulty of the materials they work with.

If levels of comprehension is the answer, what kind of guidance do we give? In class lectures at Syracuse University, M. J. Early explains the levels thus: literal —what the author says; interpretative—literal plus deeper meaning involving infer-ence, drawing conclusions, reasoning, cause and effect, speculation on what happened between events, anticipation, association of personal experiences with content, and emotional reactions; and critical—any reading where thinking is done. The student passes judgment and evaluates.

Harold Herber has these steps: (1) literal level, what does the author say? (2) interpretative, what does the author mean by what he says? (3) applicative, how can students make use of the information?[12]

George Spache lists five steps in his explanation of comprehension: (1) Cog-nition—recognizes information; (2) Memory—he retains it; (3) Divergent pro-duction—logical and creative ideas; (4) Convergent production—draws conclu-sions and does inductive thinking; and (5) Evaluation—includes critical thinking and judging.[13]

Donald L. Cleland lists six steps in his construct of comprehension. Perhaps his four middle steps could be renamed interpretative:

1. Perception—meaningful response to words, more than simple recognition;
2. Apperception—refers to the process of relating one's background to experience in words;
3. Abstraction—selects facts relevant to his purpose;
4. Appraisal—estimates value to creating concepts;
5: Ideation—generalizing, drawing conclusions, reasoning, problem solving; and
6. Application—using ideas acquired.[14]

N. D. Marksheffel (95) believes that literal and critical reading cannot be differentiated. They both vary according to (1) reader's purpose, and (2) type of material. What is literal reading for one student may be critical for another whose purpose may be entirely different from the first reader.

A. J. Kingston, in his model of comprehension (84), indicates that other things are just as important to comprehension as levels of thinking. Relationships of speed, thought processes, personality structure, mind set, developmental stages of reasoning and organizing ability, language ability, and similar past experiences of both reader and writer—all these in addition to the mastery of the mechanics of reading are a part of the process of comprehension.

DeBoer and Dallman (37) agree with Kingston. They say that what a reader takes to the printed page determines what he will take from it. It is a matter of input and reflection.

After attempting to explain just what comprehension is, can we say we know? Actually, do we really know what these terms, which we use to describe it, mean? It's like looking up a word in the dictionary and the words in the definition are more difficult than the original. It becomes as Pelham Thomas, Math Department of Western Carolina University, tells his students. It's a "Whosit did Whatsit?" And we still don't understand.

Did Maria Montessori have the right idea when she intimated that we worry too much about something we know nothing about, and advised that we set up the materials and structure for learning by discovery and problem solving in the class-room, get out of the way, and let children learn?

In grades 4–9, it's imperative that the materials and structure center around problems, interests and everyday situations of the students. This is the transition stage, where they decide to stay with school or to drop out. Many thirteen-and fourteen-year-olds are just waiting for that magic number of sixteen when they can leave captivity and get on with the real world of living. Mentally, they often drop out before age sixteen, and we let them. A good teacher must capture the minds and imaginations of students. Attempting to understand how they function and then letting them do so on their own level, at their own unique speed, and in materials relevant to them, as prescribed in the remainder of this book, is one way to achieve it.

SUMMARY

One should always keep in mind that there are many and varied influences which affect how the human organism perceives and responds to anything. We cannot separate the cognitive from the physical, behavioral, or affective aspects of learning. Successful teaching strategies utilize each of these to enhance the others.

From the study of the whys and wherefores of reading and learning and from research, it seems safe to make the following observation. There really should be no controversy about the concept that reading is a necessary skill and that it should be taught from the beginning as a practical, necessary, communicative, thought-provoking, thought-getting process, by any method which works for the teacher and learner.

Questions to Stimulate Your Thinking

A. For Graduate Students: you spent five or six hours in the classroom today. Recall one lesson you taught and answer these questions about it.

1. Upon what definition of reading was today's performance based? Consider both teacher and student tasks.
2. How did you meet individual differences? Or did you require all students to act and respond the same way on the same level?
3. What did you do to create interest, set purpose for, and reinforce learning of the skill or concept in materials presented?
4. What linguistic principles, if any, did you use?
5. Were your students involved in active participation? Did they do some actual thinking or merely parrot facts memorized from a textbook?
6. How did you evaluate learning?
7. Think about the individual students in your class and recall the statement made by Jerome Bruner that a child can learn anything in some form. Discuss this with your peers.

8. After thinking about the issues raised in chapter one, would you change anything about the teacher and/or student performances in your classes?

B. 1. If you are an undergraduate, consider these points on the classes you sat through today:
   a. What type of teaching-learning situation did your professors set up?
   b. Did they take into consideration all four aspects of learning?
   c. Did they utilize the theories discussed in this chapter?
   d. Did they utilize in their own teaching the theories that they were advocating that you use in your future teaching?
   e. On which level of comprehension would their lectures force you to perform in your study? in class? on tests?

2. What is your personal perception of the reading act?

TWO

Diagnosis: A Personal Key to Classroom Success

PREMISE II: EVERY teacher should do diagnostic teaching.

QUESTION: How can you treat the patient without first knowing the problem?

What do you want to find out about this sixth-grade class assigned to you?

1. How well do they understand silent reading?
2. Can they perform orally?
3. What skills or approaches do they have for pronouncing and analyzing new words?
4. Can they use the textbook assigned to their class?
5. Do they have a method of study?
6. Can they work in groups?
7. How do they feel about school?
8. What are their personal interests, hobbies, and aspirations?
9. What kind of school environment has been their fare for the past five years? (Traditional, open, team teaching, parent tutors, and so forth.)
10. How much do they know about "books too good for them to miss"?

How many students answer their parent's question, "What did you learn in school today?" with "Oh, nothing. It was the same old stuff."

You will do more effective teaching later on, as well as save yourself and your pupils much time and anguish, if you spend a few days at the beginning of the year to find out what they can already do. Where should you begin? Where the students are is the obvious answer. How do you find out where they are?

Here outlined is one plan which any teacher can follow. Yes. It takes time and effort. Why fret? That's what we have—time to spend with these students—nine months. In fact, if spent wisely, this initial preparation will result in more efficient teaching and learning during the remainder of the year.

A Plan of Action

I. MAKE YOUR OWN TESTS. Only you know what you want to find out.
   A. *Phonics Skills Tests*. Can they hear sounds? Do they know syllabication techniques? (Give a test such as this only if you need to find out these things.)
   B. *Interest Inventory*. These are unique for each territory. An interest inventory made in California may not suit the needs of children in the hills of North Carolina.
   C. *Informal Skills Test on Using the Textbook*. Can they use this text assigned to this class? Do they know how to use the table of contents, the index, the glossary? Is the comprehension level too complicated?
   D. *Give an Informal Reading Inventory*. Again, some commercially made tests may not do what you want done and you would be better off to make your own tests.
   E. *Give an Inventory on Literature*. What have they read? Where are the gaps in their knowledge?
II. START A FILE to set on your desk—a card for each student. Record the results of the activities mentioned in number I. Also, record any observations you may make as you observe and listen to individual students.
III. STUDY THE CUMULATIVE RECORDS. Record pertinent information from these records on your cards. Do any test scores look questionable? How do they compare with what you've found? (Some experts advocate not looking at cumulative folders until after the first grading period. Whether or not you do will depend upon your preferences. Are you professional enough to look at them and not prejudge students?)
IV. Let the students WRITE AN AUTOBIOGRAPHY in which they include what they feel to be their strengths and weaknesses. Remember, however, they may not be honest with you at first. They don't know you and may feel threatened. If you can get an honest self-appraisal, it will be worth more than anything you can find out by tests.
V. MAKE A CLASS MATRIX. (See chapter 3.) Are other tests indicated? How does the achievement score match the potential score?
VI. SET UP INITIAL PLANS. How will you group in different subjects to meet the needs of individuals? Sam may be in the lowest reading class but at the top in the math group. Keep in mind that initial grouping may change as you move along.

Now, let's take a closer look at some of these suggested activities. Also, when you find out about your students, their strengths, and needs, thumb through this book and you will find prescriptive suggestions for almost any problem they may have.

Make Your Own Tests

One of the first tasks any reading teacher should perform in beginning to work with new pupils is to find out where they are, what they are interested in, and what kind of attitude they have toward school. Standardized test scores, cumulative records, and other prior appraisals are fine, but they are not enough. The teacher does not have to wait for a clinician, a supervisor, or a guidance counselor (who are all overworked and who may not get to help you for several months). He can make his own informal measurement for whatever tasks he is interested in measuring.

There are four basic steps in the making of a test.

1. *Objective*: Determine what you want to find out. No test should be given without a specific purpose.
2. *Directions*: Write directions for carrying out the task.
3. *Examples*: Make several examples to explain to students.
4. *Test Items*: Choose items you want included in the test to find out whether the student can perform the tasks.

Part of a sample Informal Test on Phonics is given here. The overall objective is auditory discrimination. Can the child hear the different items tested for? If he can't hear the differences in sounds, he certainly won't be able to see and read them. After a teacher goes through this type of activity with the student, he will know if there are trouble spots and what they are.

He can begin with what they know—their strengths—and work from there. For too long in the field of education we have accentuated the negative, played up weaknesses, deplored, despised, and defeated. Just like the song says, why not accentuate the positive? Let the student know that we recognize his knowledge, and we're going to help him know more. Look him right in the eye and make a believer of him. (Of course, you must believe it first. He'll know whether or not you are honest.)

Words for an instrument such as this can be adapted to any age level, and there should be enough items on each task to ensure student knowledge. Too few items is a limitation to the validity of many standardized tests. After teaching tasks are carried out, the same teacher-made instrument can be used to assess student learning.

INFORMAL TEST OF WORD-ATTACK SKILLS

Task I.   Number of syllables

    A. *Objective:* To determine if a child can hear the number of syllables in a word.

    B. *Directions:* Listen to each word as I pronounce it and write the number of syllables you hear. (Begin with familiar words so that he gets the idea, then move to nonsense words to be sure he hasn't memorized the words.)

    C. *Examples:* basement (2)   floor (1)   grandmother (3)

    D. *Test:*

1. squirrel	11. laydoctoo
2. ugly	12. mustoyday
3. boot	13. captabkle
4. summertime	14. skylake
5. boat	15. dopynoc
6. about	16. laphorse
7. tornado	17. aptosto
8. question	18. bloploflo

9. slide	19. astrofiddle
10. hospital	20. kockla

Task II.   Test for short vowel sounds
Task III.   Long vowel sounds
Task IV.   Long and short sounds—can they discriminate?
Task V.   Vowel digraphs
Task VI.   Blends
Task VII.   Initial consonant digraphs

   A. *Objective:* To determine if a child can write the appropriate letters for the initial consonant digraph clusters.
   B. *Directions:* Listen to the sounds of these nonsense words. Decide what the beginning digraphs are. Write the letters which make the sound.
   C. *Examples:* Shive—the first two letters make a sound different from what they say when each letter works alone. You should have written *sh.* thod—You should have written the letters *th.*
   D. *Test:*

1. choch	11. whack
2. shupe	12. shate
3. thupt	13. plock
4. whestle	14. thore
5. shawt	15. chuckle
6. chige	16. thime
7. whub	17. wheem
8. thub	18. cheeve
9. chucken	19. sheeb
10. shive	20. shabe

Task VIII.   Terminal sounds
Task IX.   Rhyming words

Caution: Give a test such as this only if the student is in trouble and you need to know these things about him or her. If you find that he needs help on initial, medial, or terminal sounds, if he doesn't understand how digraphs work together, can't syllabicate, and/or has trouble with long and short sounds, give help. However, if students are reading beautifully and with comprehension, why bother?

One of the most foolish inefficient things which many teachers do is to assign students page after page of workbook type activities on some of these tasks because the teacher's manual for some basal series suggests them—teaching the reading skills, they call it. These are the things students complain about and legitimately call busy work.

Rather than waste their time on meaningless drill which they don't need, why not let them read, thereby learn? School would be much more meaningful for them.

An Informal Skills Test
on the Textbook

Use a history, science, geography, or other textbook assigned to your class and make an informal test on the different parts of the book. Record the purpose for the task right on the paper so students will understand why you ask them to do the work. Inform them that it isn't a test and they will not be graded. You want to give them a chance to work with the different parts of the book to find out how well they use the tools the author furnishes.

As students work, you circulate among them with pencil and pad in hand, jotting down observations about how they handle the different tasks. What specific problems does Sarah have? How many times does John ask for help? How proficient are they with using different parts of the book? Do they know where to look for what? What specific weaknesses and strengths do you spot and what skills will you have to teach?

The comprehension section will give clues to the difficulty of the reading level of the book for these students. Do they need easier material in order to be able to handle the decoding and concept load? If the technical vocabulary and concept load is too difficult for them, they will have difficulty reading and succeeding with assigned tasks. You need to know this at the beginning of the year. Do they need easier books to succeed with the tasks you plan to assign? Remember, success with assigned tasks is one of the best motivators for learning.

The *cloze* test (see chapter 5) is another measure of readability of materials used by some systems to discover compatibility of material to the student.

Reading Interests

Children are more likely to read that which interests them. This interest, in part, is a result of background experiences. Students will stretch beyond their level on subjects they are interested (motivated) in. Many of you fail to capitalize on this fact. Classroom atmosphere should be conducive to creating purpose, to expanding, to giving a wide variety of tasks which call for reading which students want to do.

You know that successful completion of any task comes from within. If you know a student's *now* interests, you are in a better position to provide the stimulating environment he needs to expand them. By giving an informal interest inventory, you are attempting to discover his tastes and interests. This gives you a basis for conversation and for choice of initial reading materials.

In order to be able to give the help and guidance students need to build and expand these reading interests, you must know books and you must allow students freedom to read of their own choosing, not always that prescribed list of what you think they need.

When you know the child, when you know the books, and when you know what he's already read, you are in a position to be a humane, challenging guider of reading rather than that authoritative, coercive "Checker off of book reading lists" which produces dislike for reading. The Interest Inventory and Informal Inventory on Literature will help in the direction you need to go. A sample of each follows.

Remember, students may not be honest with you at first. They don't know you yet and may feel threatened. Also, older students (depending upon their attitudes) may consider some questions too elementary, some none of your business, or they've made a habit of not being truthful because it hurts too much.

INTEREST INVENTORY

1. Name: _____
2. Grade: _____
3. Birthday: _____
4. Number of brothers: _____
       sisters: _____
5. What is your favorite television program? _____
6. How long do you watch television per day? _____
7. Do you have a pet? _____ What? _____
8. Do you read newspapers at home? _____ Which ones? _____
9. Do you read magazines? _____ Which ones? _____
10. Do you have a record player? _____
11. Do you listen to it when you study? _____
12. Do you like to read? _____ Why or why not? _____
13. What is the very best book you've ever read? _____
14. About how many books do you own? _____
15. What is your favorite subject in school? _____ Why? _____
16. What is your least liked subject? _____ Why? _____
17. What is the thing you like most about teachers? _____
18. What is the thing you like least about teachers? _____
19. How could this school be improved? _____
20. What is the happiest word you know? _____
21. What is the saddest word you know? _____
22. What is your most favorite place in the whole world? _____ Why? _____
23. What place do you like least of all? _____ Why? _____
24. Do you like homework? _____
25. Do you have a quiet place at home to study? _____
26. Do you have a hobby? _____ What? _____
27. Does your father have time to do things with you? _____
28. Does your mother have time to do things with you? _____
29. Put a check mark beside the places you have visited:

A movie_____	Church_____	Public Library_____
A farm_____	Museum_____	Indian Reservation_____
A zoo_____	Circus_____	Washington, D.C._____
The mountains_____	Disneyland_____	The beach_____
A fair_____	A summer camp_____	

30. What city, state, or country have you visited that is the greatest distance from your home? _____
31. Would you like to go back? _____ Why or why not? _____
32. Do you eat breakfast before you come to school? _____
    Why or why not? _____
33. If you could change into someone else or something else, what do you think it would be? _____ Why? _____
34. If you could choose one partner in this class to work with, it would be _____
35. If you could choose someone to play with, it would be _____
36. What is one thing you would really like to learn about this year? _____
37. When people tell you to shut up, how do you feel? _____
38. When people tell you to speak up, how do you feel? _____
39. When people expect you to know things you don't know, how do you feel? _____
40. The greatest thing about school is _____

41. The school club you would most like to join this year is _____
42. If you could tell the principal one thing about how to make our school better, what would you tell him? _____

An Informal Reading Inventory

The informal reading inventory[15] is an individual or a group diagnostic testing method designed to be used by classroom teachers, corrective reading teachers, remedial teachers, and clinicians. The inventory may be based on any series of books, usually basal readers, with controlled vocabulary. The inventory consists of a silent reading passage with comprehension questions and vocabulary check plus an oral passage for checking word recognition.

When a teacher learns how to properly construct and administer the inventory, the results gained, along with teacher judgment, should be used for grouping students for instructional, corrective, remedial, and/or enrichment purposes. When a teacher gains competence in the use of the inventory, it can, in a short period of time, reveal as much or more about a reader as any one single evaluation instrument. Of course, students in serious reading difficulty will need more diagnostic testing.

Let's assume you want to make an informal reading inventory to use with your students. How would you go about it? The following is one way.

PURPOSE: To find the level on which a child should be instructed in reading.

MATERIALS NEEDED: Series of graded reading textbooks. (Some people argue that it is best if you use a series other than those used regularly for instruction. However, I prefer using the series I plan to use in my teaching. All series do not have the same readability level.)

PREPARATION:
A. *Silent Passage*
   1. Select a portion of a story in the front third of each textbook in the series you are using. Selections should consist of at least 100 words, but should not be too long due to time factor in administration.
   2. Select high interest stories which are unfamiliar to students.
   3. Prepare a few sentences of introduction or motivation for silent reading.
   4. Prepare a variety of types of questions including main idea, detail, organization, and/or inference. (At least one question should deal with thought beyond what is stated in the story.)
   5. A group of words from the story may be selected to check on student's vocabulary. Additional words related to the story may be used to check background of experience.

B. *Oral Passage*
   1. Select a second passage of approximately 100 words from the same section of the book.

2. Prepare brief introductory section with motivation for reading.

3. Prepare a general type comprehension question.

ADMINISTRATION:

A. Assemble books to be used. (Actual textbook or selection may be cut out or typed on index cards with questions posted on back.)

B. Choose passage difficulty on which you think child is likely to succeed.

C. Give quick introduction for motivation.

D. Let child read silently. Record any words on which he requests help. Note reading habits, any symptoms of poor reading. Record information.

E. When child has read, ask questions on the material. (He is not to look back to find answers.) Record answers in complete form if practical. If not, use some sign which shows discrimination for right and wrong. (Plus and minus or checkmark.)

F. Ask child the meaning of vocabulary words. Record answers.

G. Motivate for oral reading. Have child read. Record any errors, incorrect words, repetitions, omissions, and so on.

H. Determine if the child has comprehension and word recognition skills. If so, take next higher level and repeat from step C. If he fails, drop to a lower level. (A variation is to ask the question first. Then child reads silently to find the answer. When he finds it, he reads orally the sentence which contains the answer. Many students like this variation better than the preceding form.)

Now What?

After you have given the inventory, what do you do with it? Study and use results for placing your students in the correct book, supplementary materials, class, or level. Different people use different percentages of correct answers to find levels. These seem to approximate:

Instructional Level: *Comprehension:* Answers 75 percent of comprehension questions.

Word recognition: Misses not more than one of each twenty words he reads (95 percent of running words). Proper names and additional misses on same word are not counted.

The teacher's main concern is with this instructional level, but you should be aware of and familiar with the criteria for the other levels.

Independent Reading Level: Level on which a child can read successfully without help. Usually is one level below instructional level.

Criteria: Comprehension—90 percent

Word Recognition—98 percent

Frustration Level: Level on which skills break down; extreme difficulty occurs and signs of tension such as finger pointing and lip movement are evident.

Criteria: Comprehension—65 percent or below

Word Recognition—90 percent or below

Potential or Listening Level: Level on which child can understand and discuss what has been read to him. When this is above instructional level, specific reading skills can usually be taught to improve reading ability.
Criteria: Comprehension—75 percent or higher

Additional Comments

1. The potential level is very important in determining the needs of a child. He may be making A's on classwork, yet be reading and/or working below potential.
2. If the listening level is greater than the instructional level, the student has potential to do better and is a possible prospect for remedial reading.
3. In order that you may detect emotional and physical handicaps or characteristics, observe the student carefully as he/she reads.
4. Comprehension tests may not test comprehension at all. The child may have stored information in memory and does not have to read a test to make a good score on a subject she knows.
5. Look for recurring errors in letter sounds, words, and so forth, throughout test.
6. The independent level is the level of the book a child should take home to read.
7. The examiner must consider the number of words pronounced for the student and the effect this gives the comprehension check.
8. A test is as good as the teacher who constructs it.
9. Use the information found from the informal inventory to help place suitable books with students. A sixth-year student with a reading level of a third-year student will have trouble with basal textbooks issued to the sixth-grade class. The teacher must realize and use this fact, or we will continue to have students failing with textbooks.

Sample Section of an Informal Reading Inventory

The three "toughies" stared unbelievably at the neat arrangement of files, books, and records, all classics they found by examining them. Their one accomplishment in history class so far this year had been disruptive argument. How shocked they'd been when their teacher invited them to dinner.
Elias Rhoer, all 147 pounds of him, appeared in the doorway connecting the small kitchenette with the sitting room of his bachelor apartment. Though he was only 5'7" tall, as he crossed his legs and stretched one arm upward for support on the door jamb, to his young guests he towered ten-feet tall. Keen myopic eyes, one slightly crossed, crinkled in amusement. His smile made the fellows feel like real people.
"You guys want pepsi, milk or tea?" their host asked, breaking the silence.
"Beer," they yelled in unison.

Literal questions which could be asked to test recall:
1. How many boys came to visit?
2. How much did Elias weigh?
3. How did the boys feel about being invited to dinner by their teacher?

Deeper *comprehension* questions:
1. Did these boys like school? Explain your answer.
2. According to the information given here, what kind of relationships do you think the boys usually experienced with adults?

Inference question:
Why has the teacher invited the boys to have dinner with him?

Vocabulary questions:
1. Do you know the word *myopic?* What kind of eyes?
2. The boys were disruptive, the story says. Do you know how you would act in school to get me to call you disruptive?
3. What does the word *unison* mean?

An Inventory on Literature for Grades 4–9

One of the major reasons for students' lack of love for reading is that they do not know books nor book characters. One of your jobs as a teacher is to bring books and students together. *Remember:* Enthusiasm is caught, not taught.

At the beginning of the school year, you should share with students your interests and love for books. Also, you want to know what they are familiar with and where you should fill in gaps of their knowledge. Just as you give other kinds of inventories to find out where students are, give one here.

The following items make up a sample which you might use as a guide in making yours. It does not cover the field, nor does it claim to be a model of what students should read. It is simply what it claims: an example of some questions on some literature.

INVENTORY

Directions to student:
Read the questions and choices of answers. Choose the one of the three that best answers the question. (An answer key is included. Students may self-check or someone else can do it.)

LITERATURE
1. Bob Cratchit carries Tiny Tim through wintery London is a scene from which of these?
     a. *A Christmas Carol*
     b. *The Snow Queen*
     c. *Winter Night*

2. *The Hounds of Ulster* (a modern mystery) is thought to have as a basis some background in the earlier story of
   a. *Beowulf*
   b. Sherlock Holmes Mysteries
   c. *Iliad* and *Odyssey*
3. The dormouse is a character in
   a. *Alice in Wonderland*
   b. *Story of Mankind*
   c. *Door in the Wall*
4. One of the attractive things about the March sisters is that they are like the girls in the warm human family next door. Their story is described in the book
   a. *Jane Eyre*
   b. *Little Women*
   c. *Caddie Woodlawn*
5. Most of the action on *Durango Street* is
   a. stereotype
   b. portrayal of regional life
   c. grim gang violence
6. *The Edge of April* is a biography of
   a. Mark Twain, the humorist
   b. John Burroughs, the naturalist
   c. James Will, the Cowboy
7. Ben Franklin is known as
   a. that lively man
   b. a satirist
   c. the man who discovered jazz
8. *Madame Curie* is the biography of the discoverer of
   a. radium
   b. penicillin
   c. uranium
9. John Bunyan's *Pilgrim's Progress* discusses the life and loves of
   a. America's first Pilgrims
   b. a Christian striving for salvation
   c. the religious treks to the Holy Land
10. Many authors have tried but none have surpassed the story of life alone on a desert island as told by Daniel Defoe in
    a. *Robinson Crusoe*
    b. *Bounty*
    c. *Watch for a Tall White Sail*
11. *Moby Dick* is a description of
    a. whaling
    b. Civil War pirates
    c. adventure in the desert
12. In *The Prince and the Pauper* Tom Canty changes clothes with and for a time plays the part of
    a. Pope John of Italy
    b. Prince Rainier of Monaco
    c. Edward VI of England
13. Kit Tyler was a colorful, vivacious girl in a stern Puritan background. Her outgoing spirit and willingness to help others got her labeled as a

      a. devil

      b. witch

      c. bad girl

14. When Jethro Creighton had lived *Across Five Aprils,* he realized that
    a. some things which at first seem exciting and wonderful may in reality be heartbreaking and disruptive
    b. that a young news reporter may have many chances to correct a story
    c. sometimes in silence one can find a strange satisfaction

15. Sam Gribley escapes the pressures of crowded apartment living by
    a. spending a winter alone in the mountains
    b. going to sea as a stowaway
    c. working as a sheep herder in a lonely wilderness

16. Doing what he wanted to do or what was expected of him and how he grows in decision making is the theme running through the story
    a. *Shadow of a Bull*
    b. *Wheel on the School*
    c. *The Witch of Blackbird Pond*

17. Who went down the "great gray-green greasy Limpopo River" to find out what the crocodile had for dinner?
    a. Heidi
    b. The Elephant's Child
    c. Hansel and Gretel

18. Heidi lived in the hills of
    a. Chile
    b. Switzerland
    c. Holland

19. What race is depicted in the story of *Bright April* by Marguerite De Angeli?
    a. Negro
    b. Caucasian
    c. Indian

20. It was the sea Mafatu feared, and fear was shame for those early Polynesians. He faced the storm, fought a shark, overcame an octupus, escaped maneaters and proved to himself he had changed.
    a. *The Yearling*
    b. *Call it Courage*
    c. *Johnny Tremain*

21. *The Yearling* is the story of a lonely boy and his
    a. fawn
    b. dog
    c. calf

22. Meg saves her brother from a distant robot-like planet when she realizes she has something the power called *It* does not have. What does she have?
    a. courage
    b. blood
    c. love

23. Gilly Ground represents all youth; Kobalt represents evil; and the Hunter may represent love in this sinister unbelievable story. It is
    a. *Dorp Dead* by Cunningham
    b. *Tistou* of the Green Thumb
    c. *Hot Rod* by Felsen

24. Zeke was a lonely crippled boy living in Harlem. In his story the only thing that really talks his language is
    a. music
    b. animals
    c. the street gang
25. "The Daffodil Massacre" is the episode which starts the satirical tale of funny and pathetic modern life in
    a. *The Gate of Worlds*
    b. *The City Underground*
    c. *The Pushcart War*
26. Alec Ramsey and a wild black stallion are the only survivors of a shipwreck in
    a. *Smoky*
    b. *The Black Stallion*
    c. *King of the Wind*
27. Karana, the Indian girl who lived alone on an island for 18 years, was not lonely after she found a friend to talk to. This friend was
    a. Rontu, a dog
    b. An aleutian girl
    c. a priest
28. Mary Poppins is characterized by these items:
    a. hat and gloves, umbrella, and carpet bag
    b. umbrella, laughing gas, and flying carpet
    c. dog, cat, and magic bag
29. Daniel Bar Jamin takes the long dark journey of life and finds in *The Bronze Bow* that only
    a. hate is stronger than love
    b. evil overcomes good
    c. love overcomes hate
30. Edward and the *Matchlock Gun* save his family from Indians in a story of early America. This story is based on
    a. truth
    b. fiction
    c. folklore
31. *Amos Fortune, Free Man* tells about
    a. a great political leader
    b. a man who spent money freely
    c. common man who lived simply and gently
32. *I, Juan de Pareja*, won the coveted Newberry award and was the biography of
    a. a great political leader
    b. a man who spent money freely
    c. common man who lived simply and gently
33. Helen Keller judged the character of a person by his
    a. handclasp
    b. tone of voice
    c. warmth of personality
34. Agha, the deaf-mute Arabian boy, showed unequaled courage, loyalty and patience in *King of the Wind*. This is a story of a boy and his
    a. dog
    b. horse
    c. ship

35. In the story *Cress Delahany,* Cress is a young girl whose character
    a. shows how growing up presents difficulties
    b. reveals reincarnation
    c. shows the power of brain over muscle
36. *Twenty Thousand Leagues Under the Sea* has a setting in the year
    a. 1600
    b. 1800
    c. 2000
37. The *Great Heritage* shows the development of the United States in terms of
    a. its mechanization
    b. its political structure
    c. its natural resources
38. Captain Bligh's 3,600 mile trip in an open boat is based on tales of
    a. adventure
    b. authenticity
    c. fantasy

EPIC, BIBLE, AND MYTHOLOGY
39. The Hungarian legend of Hadur, god of the tribe, and the doubt in the souls of men
    is the basis for which of these stories?
    a. *Backbone of the King*
    b. *The White Stag*
    c. *The Golden Fleece*
40. King Midas was punished for his greed by which of these methods?
    a. his wings melted and he fell to the earth
    b. he had to perform heroic deeds with iron gloves
    c. everything he touched turned to gold
41. Shadrach, Meshac, and Abednego are heroes from
    a. Bible
    b. Greek Myths
    c. Modern day fable
42. *A Basket in the Reeds* (Saporta) is a book based on the happening in the life of
    a. Ruth
    b. Moses
    c. David
43. *The Iliad* is an account of the Trojan War fought by the Greeks to recover
    a. Paris, son of King of Troy
    b. Mother of Achilles
    c. Helen, most beautiful woman in world
44. *Beowulf* is an English epic which deals in adventure. Though there is horror in the
    adventure, the theme of the work is
    a. nobility, justice, and loyalty to friends
    b. the strongest survive
    c. revenge brings destruction
45. The quest for the Holy Grail is a theme running through the
    a. King Arthur Tales
    b. Robin Hood tales
    c. *Odyssey* of Homer
46. The hero who robbed the rich to give to the poor was
    a. Henry, the Navigator
    b. Tarzan
    c. Robin Hood

47. Over 100 years ago one of America's greatest poets captured in eleven lines the mood of an entire nation. This poem was
    a. "America"
    b. "I Hear America Singing"
    c. "America, The Beautiful"
48. In the poem, "I Meant to Do My Work Today," why did the speaker leave his work undone?
    a. He had no intention of doing the work.
    b. Nature beckoned and he could not resist.
    c. The other people influenced him.
49. The final inning of the baseball game found the Mudville team leading by two runs. If only mighty Casey could get up to bat once more! What happened?
    a. Casey got to bat and won the game for Mudville
    b. Casey's turn didn't come again and they lost
    c. Casey's turn came up and he struck out
50. Psalm 121 is a favorite of many people. The Psalm states that man's strength and help comes from
    a. the sun and moon
    b. the shade and man's ingenuity
    c. the hills and the Lord
51. Who said this: "All the world's a stage and all the men and women merely players. . . ."
    a. Robert Frost
    b. William Wordsworth
    c. William Shakespeare
52. "Old Ironsides," from which the poem by the same name was written,
    a. was dismantled and demolished after the War of 1812
    b. is a nickname for the U.S. ship *Constitution* and was dismantled in 1929
    c. is a national monument at dock in Massachusetts
53. The symbolic roads in Frost's poem "The Road Not Taken" relate to
    a. decision making
    b. an old man's reminiscences
    c. finding serenity
54. The poem "The Charge of the Light Brigade" deals with
    a. English-Russian War history
    b. English-French War history
    c. French-Russian War history
55. In Whittier's "The Barefoot Boy" the mood is
    a. nostalgia
    b. sarcasm
    c. irony

SUMMARY

This chapter has given you ways to get information about your students. Don't be the teacher who wastes time—yours and the students—waiting for a supervisor, curriculum consultant, or guidance person to do your work for you. It may be six weeks before they can get to you.

Standardized tests do not diagnose. They do not prescribe. In fact, they seldom measure a student's achievement. What test maker 1,000 miles away knows what you teach your students in that little four-room school in Caney Creek?

"Granpa's learned them kids a lotta common sense, but they don't show it on them hifalooting tests they give at school," one grandmother told me when I was discussing tests results of one of her bright grandchildren who lived with her. "Our kids could tell ye a lot about the varmits, the milk aphids, the plant lice, but they ain't got much use fer escalators, subways, er Micky Mouses."

If you go through the activities suggested in this chapter, you will know a great deal about each student's strengths and weaknesses. You have diagnosed. Is he healthy or does he have weak spots? What do you prescribe which will fit each unique personality?

The terms *diagnosis* and *prescription* are more than educational jargon. If used properly, they are keys to successful teaching. They enable a teacher to refrain from boring rehash or over-the-head frustration—two legitimate complaints made by many students who discuss teachers and their methods. Most important of all, let's remember that one good conversation across the table with a student may be more valuable than all the tests created.

Answers to the Literature Inventory Questions

 1. a. *Christmas Carol,* Charles Dickens (Lippincott, 1952).
 2. a. *The Hound of Ulster,* Rosemary Sutcliff (Dutton, 1964).
 3. a. *Alice in Wonderland,* Lewis Carol (Macmillan, 1950).
 4. b. *Little Women,* Louisa May Alcott (Crowell, 1955).
 5. c. *Durango Street,* Frank Bonham (Dutton, 1965).
 6. b. *Edge of April,* H. H. Swift (Morrow, 1957).
 7. a. *That Lively Man, Ben Franklin,* Jeanette Eaton (Morrow, 1948).
 8. a. *Madame Curie,* Eve Curie (Heinemann, 1958).
 9. b. *Pilgrim's Progress,* John Bunyan (1678). Many editions.
10. a. *Robinson Crusoe,* Daniel Defoe (Scribner, 1957).
11. a. *Moby Dick,* Herman Melville (1851). Many editions.
12. c. *The Prince and the Pauper,* Mark Twain (many editions).
13. b. *The Witch of Blackbird Pond,* Elizabeth Speare (Houghton, 1958).
14. a. *Across Five Aprils,* Irene Hunt (Follett, 1964).
15. a. *My Side of the Mountain,* Jean C. George (Dutton, 1959).
16. a. *Shadow of a Bull,* Maia Wojciechowska (Atheneum, 1965).
17. b. *The Elephant's Child,* Rudyard Kipling (Garden City Books, 1942).
18. b. *Heidi,* Johanna Spyri (many editions).
19. a. *Bright April,* Marguerite de Angeli (Doubleday, 1946).
20. b. *Call it Courage,* Armstrong Sperry (Macmillan, 1940).
21. a. *The Yearling,* Marjorie Kinnan Rawlings (Scribner, 1952).
22. c. *A Wrinkle in Time,* Madeleine L'Engle (Farrar, Straus, 1962).
23. a. *Dorp Dead,* Julia Cunningham (Pantheon, 1965).
24. a. *The Jazz Man,* Mary H. Weik (Atheneum, 1966).
25. c. *The Pushcart War,* Jean Merrill (W. R. Scott, 1964).
26. b. *The Black Stallion,* Walter Farley (Random House, 1941).
27. a. *Island of the Blue Dolphins,* Scott O'Dell (Houghton, 1960).
28. a. *Mary Poppins,* Pamela L. Travers (Harcourt, 1934).
29. c. *The Bronze Bow,* Elizabeth Speare (Houghton, 1961).
30. a. *The Matchlock Gun,* Walter D. Edmonds (Dodd, 1941).

31. c. *Amos Fortune, Free Man*, Elizabeth Yates (Dutton, 1950).
32. c. *I, Juan de Pareja*, Elizabeth Borton De Trevino (Farrar, Straus, 1965).
33. a. *Helen Keller Story*, Catherine Owens Peare (Crowell, 1959).
34. b. *King of the Wind*, Marguerite Henry (Rand McNally, 1948).
35. a. *Cress Delahany*, Jessamyn West (Harcourt, 1953).
36. c. *Twenty Thousand Leagues Under the Sea*, Jules Verne (Scribner, 1925).
37. c. *The Great Heritage*, Katherine B. Shippen (Viking, 1947).
38. b. *Mutiny on the Bounty*, Charles Nordhoff and James Hall (Atlantic Mo. Press, 1932).
39. b. *The White Stag*, Kate Seredy (Viking, 1937).
40. c. *The Golden Touch*, Nathaniel Hawthorne (many editions).
41. a. *Shadrach, Meshach, and Abednego*, Paul Galdone (Crowell, 1962).
42. b. *A Basket in the Reeds*, Raphael Saporta (Lerner, 1965).
43. c. *Iliad of Homer*, Alfred J. Church (Macmillan, 1935).
44. a. *Beowulf, The Warrior*, Ian Serraillier (Walch, 1961).
45. a. *King Arthur and His Knights*, Mabel L. Robinson (Random House, 1953).
46. c. *The Merry Adventures of Robin Hood*, Howard Pyle (Scribner, 1946, 1883).
47. b. "I Hear America Singing," Walt Whitman (many editions).
48. b. "I Meant to Do My Work Today," Richard LeGallienne (Dodd, Mead, 1913).
49. c. "Casey at the Bat," Ernest L. Thayer (many editions).
50. c. "Psalm 121," The Bible.
51. c. *As You Like It*, Shakespeare (many editions).
52. c. "Old Ironsides," Oliver W. Holmes (many editions).
53. a. "The Road Not Taken," Robert Frost (many editions).
54. b. "The Charge of the Light Brigade," Tennyson (many editions).
55. b. "The Barefoot Boy," Whittier (many editions).

Activities for the Teacher

1. Make an Informal Inventory of Skills on one of the textbooks you are currently using. Let the students work with it. Observe their actions and reactions. Do any of them need help? Which skills do you need to work on with them?
2. Did all students comprehend on a competent level?
3. If students showed specific weaknesses, plan some activities, job cards, or study guides to help them overcome their weak spots.
4. If you are interested, give your class the Inventory on Literature shown in this chapter. Does it create any interest in reading the books? Where are the gaps in their reading? (One group of sixth graders were so motivated by this inventory that they asked their teacher and librarian to get all of the books and put them in the classroom reading center.)
5. Choose three students from your group and give them an Informal Reading Inventory. (Different from the Skills Inventory in number 1.) Are they reading on an instructional level at their grade placement? How will you use the results of these inventories?
6. If you find that your students are weak in some of the word recognition or comprehension skills, look at the exercises located throughout this book and make up some exercises to give them practice.

7. If you are not currently working with a class, find textbooks being used in your state. Study two samples of inventories available in the Counseling Center, Reading Center, or Curriculum Lab of your school. Make a sample IRI on a Basal Reader series, an IRI of Skills on a content area text, and/or a sample Cloze exercise from one of the texts.

THREE

Practical Ways to Use Test Data as Basis for Instruction

For twenty years I've watched teachers give tests, list them from highest to lowest, average the scores, or talk about who did or didn't do well, then give a copy to the curriculum supervisor and file the other one in the principal's office. There it rested until the next testing date when it might be brought out to check whether Sam improved only two months while Mary went up two years and Tom actually regressed five months.

The whole testing program, as used by most individual teachers and school systems, is overrated, used for the wrong purposes, inhumane, and a waste of time. Most of you know how your student will score before you test. The primary principle governing a test should be, will it be used diagnostically? We should find out where students are strong and weak, whether they have learned what we attempted to teach, and whether or not they have the concept basic for the next step in our program.

QUESTIONS: 1. If only five people pass an arithmetic test, where is the failure?
2. What should be the teacher's attitude when 90 percent of the students fail a test?
3. If students take a reading skills test and 10 students make the same score, does this justify grouping that ten together for instruction?
4. If Susan rated only 40 percentile on an achievement test, does that mean that she should be failed?
5. How do you decide what achievement might be expected from students?

The Class Matrix

One way to get a quick picture of a new class is by use of a matrix. Using the scores available or your own scores from preliminary testing, plot a chart

35

showing whatever relationship you are interested in. One of the basic things we need to know about any student is whether or not he is working up to his measured potential. Comparing an intelligence test score (keeping in mind it may or may not be accurate) with an achievement test score is one example.

Using the scores given in table 1 from a fourth grade group who was tested on reading during the first week of school and I.Q. scores from a test given them in the second grade, let's plot a matrix to show the comparison of potential with achievement.

First: Rate students from highest to lowest according to I.Q. scores.

Second: Give students a number beginning with the highest score as number one. (Some teachers use names, but this is something you might want to keep around for handy use. Numbers are better on things which students may see.)

Third: Find the line where the reading score meets with the I.Q. score on the chart. Put the student's number at this point. See figure 3.1.

TABLE 1

Students and Scores:

		WISC	SAT-Reading	
1.	Ken	130	80	4.8
2.	Bob	127	90	5.7
3.	Betty	122	80	5.3
4.	Nancy	102	50	3.3
5.	Brenda	101	80	4.4
6.	Kevin	100	70	4.0
7.	Ronnie	94	30	2.3
8.	David	85	50	3.3
9.	Debbie	61	50	3.4
10.	Sammy	60	25	2.0

FIGURE 3.1

A class matrix showing potential and achievement

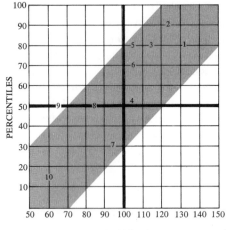

I. Q. SCORES

Ken has the highest WISC score so he will be number one. His achievement score is the 80th percentile. So find where the 130 I.Q. score (horizontal) intersects the percentile (vertical) line and put a number (1) at this spot. Continue this procedure until you have all ten numbers plotted on the matrix.

Now, study the chart. The shaded area represents a class with normal distribution, and it is expected that most students will fall into this area. The dark lines represent the midpoints around which most scores cluster.

This group is not far off. But there are three or four students whose scores indicate that they may need retesting. Number 9, Debbie, looks questionable. She may be an overachiever, her I.Q. may have changed since the second grade, or the tests' scores may be inaccurate. Number 7, Ronnie, needs study. If his I.Q. is really 94, he should be achieving better than 30 percent. Either one or both scores may be incorrect, or he may be an underachiever who needs remedial help.

Look at Nancy and Brenda. How do you explain these scores? What would you do about them?

The matrix is simply a picture of a class to be used for initial grouping at the beginning of the year. As further work, study, testing, and observation progress, changes may need to be made and students helped on individual skills.

The Checklist

When they diagnose students, university and public reading clinics use long involved checklists for their recordings. They can afford to do so, because they usually have two things which are needed but inadequate in the typical elementary school—time and personnel. The classroom teacher will use a much more simple one suitable for her purposes.

Before the tests discussed in chapter 2 are given, make a check sheet on which you will record observations about your students. It should be practical, easy to add to for comparison later on, and self-explanatory. Table 2 is one form you might use. The plus symbol means *no problems,* the minus, *needs help.*

The Expectancy Formula

How can we determine how well a child should be reading? What do we expect each individual student to do? Is he or she reading up to this expectancy?

Reading expectancy formulas of varying degrees of difficulty have been offered by concerned theoreticians. How reliable any of these are can be questioned. To test potential, the listening test makes more sense than depending upon an I.Q. score. Simply read something to the student and ask him some questions. How well does he understand what he hears? You may find comprehension adequate. The problem may be that he hasn't learned the mechanics of reading.

However, for the teacher who believes in and relies on measurement, it has its value. Here is one of the more simple formulas which any teacher can understand and use. Multiply the Intelligence Test Score by the number of years a student has spent in school and add one.[16] Look back at the list of scores for the fourth grade used on the matrix.

Ken: I.Q.—130. Grade level score on Reading—4.8

At the beginning of fourth year, he's been in school for three years. Use the formula:

$$130 \times 3 + 1 = R.E. \qquad 3.90 + 1 = 4.9$$

TABLE 2

Checklist for Student Performance

NAME_____ AGE_____ GRADE__4__ DATE_____ TEST_____

GRADE	4	5	6	7	8	9	10
Word Recognition							
beginning sounds	+						
medial sounds	+						
terminal sounds	+						
syllabication	−						
others							
Vocabulary							
sight	+						
in context	−						
structural parts	−						
meanings	−						
Fluency							
word-by-word	−						
points	+						
voices	−						
skimming	−						
punctuation used	−						
Comprehension							
follow directions	−						
recall of details	+						
reads for ideas	−						
organization	−						
others							
Habits							
reverses words	+						
omits words	−						
repeats words	−						
loses place easily	−						
works steadily	+						
others							
Attitude							
enjoys	+						
bored	−						
alert	−						
tense	−						
Grade Level Adequacy (IRI)	3						
Literature Score	D						
Main Interest	Cars						
Skills on Textbook	−						
Index	−						
Contents	−						
Maps	−						
Comprehension							

According to this formula Ken is one month behind expectancy level.

Ronnie: I.Q.—94. $92 \times 3 + 1 = 3.8$.

Ronnie's Reading score was 2.3 and his expectancy score 3.8.

According to this formula Ronnie is 1.5 behind where he should be.

Bob: $127 \times 3 + 1 = 4.8$.   9 months above R.E.   SAT Reading 5.7.

Now, you find Brenda's Reading Expectancy. Is she working up to level?

How about Debbie? Should she be retested? Is she an overachiever? What is your opinion?

Use the scores you have for the class you are now teaching. Work the formula on some of your students. Are they living up to expectancy? What can you do about it?

Like everything else in education, Reading Expectancy Formulas worked out by different people do not yield the same expectancies. The one by Bond and Tinker, illustrated above, is most simple. However, Harris (72, p. 215) says it overestimates the reading expectancy level for the low I.Q. and underestimates the high I.Q. For comparison, let's use the same three student scores and use both the Harris and Fry formulas.

The Fry Formula: [17]

$$\frac{\text{I.Q.} \times \text{C.A.}}{100} - 5.4 \text{ equals Mental Age Grade Expectancy}$$

Ken: $\frac{130 \times 9.2}{100} - 5.4$ equals $11.96 - 5.4$ equals 6.5

Ronnie: $\frac{94 \times 9.2}{100} - 5.4$ equals $8.6 - 5.4 = 3.2$

Bob: $\frac{127 \times 9.2}{100} - 5.4$ equals $11.68 - 5.4 = 6.2$

The Harris Formula: [18]

$$\frac{2\,(\text{MA}) + \text{CA}}{3} - 5.2 \text{ equals Reading Expectancy Age}$$

Ken: $\frac{2(13) + 9.2}{3} = \frac{35.2}{3} - 5.2 = 11.7 - 5.2 = 6.5$

Ronnie: $\frac{2\,(8.6) + 9.2}{3} = \frac{26.4}{3} - 5.2 = 8.8 - 5.2 = 3.6$

Bob: $\frac{2(11.6) + 9.2}{3} = \frac{32.56}{3} - 5.2 = 10.85 - 5.2 = 5.6$

Using the three different formulas, Ken has a Reading Expectancy age of 4.9 (Bond and Tinker); 6.5 (Fry); and 6.5 (Harris). Ronnie has a 3.8; 3.2; and 3.6. Bob comes up with a 4.8; 6.2; and 5.6.

Use the one you like best to get some estimate of what can be expected of a student based upon I.Q. and M.A. And always remember, scores vary from test to test, formula to formula, and day to day according to a student's physical, mental, psychological, and sociological state. It might vary as much as twenty points tomorrow.

Grouping

From the Bluebirds, Redbirds, and Robins in grade one to the college tracks in secondary school, no practice is more controversial, misused, despised by students, and cursed by parents, than that of the grouping of students for instruction.

Almost every college text on reading has a section on the subject. The Joplin, the Modified Joplin, Special classes for the Exceptional (both degrees), so-called homogenous groups by I.Q., reading achievement, chronological age, by tracks (college bound, terminal, technical schools), large television classes and/or lecture groups, peer groupings, skills, interest, buddy or big brother, individualized—the list is enormous. Then, of course, there are all kinds of combinations.

The reason for talking about grouping here is to uphold whatever method of grouping will work to produce the results you want for your students. What method of organization will best meet the needs of your talents, your students' needs, and the organization of the school program as a whole?

After the diagnostic testing suggested in chapter 2, and the results of your checklist suggested in this chapter, what is your prescription? What students need help with what skills? As they master a skill, the group changes, disbands, regroups. From your Informal Inventory on Skills, you find that only five students need help with reading the table of contents. Work with that five. Don't bore or waste the time of the other twenty-five. Let them work on what they need. In math, only seven students out of thirty-five seventh graders do not know how to find averages. Work with this seven. "But it's in the textbook," you argue? So what? Are you teaching a textbook or students?

There are times, of course, when you'll need to deal with the whole group—introducing a new concept, discussing plans of action, setting up new units. However, once this is done, use flexible scheduling and group work according to needs and interests. No plan is sacred. As soon as the tasks for which the group was set up are completed, disband and move on.

Tutorial grouping benefits three groups of people. At Sunnyview, a small mountain school in Polk County, North Carolina, reluctant weak readers in their seventh year were challenged to tutor second semester first graders. While an aide had the first graders outside for physical education, the teacher worked with the seventh graders, helping them to understand concepts, to organize materials, and to plan how to teach the first grader they would be working with. It wasn't long until they were taking time to plan on their own and asking the teacher if they could try out their own ideas. In the following weeks, one could often see little six-year-olds dash across the playground and grab the hand of their tutor. These older students developed a whole new concept of themselves and education.

Any type of classroom organization has its advantages and disadvantages. Choose the type which most nearly fulfills your requirements. And remember that the only reason you are there is to meet the needs of individuals, each one unique. Today's trend is toward the more humanistic, open, let-students-discover-for-themselves, types of activities with more student involvement and less teacher talk.

Gregg's Story

Gregg was in the sixth year of school, behind his classmates, but moving along at a pace comfortable for him. He had the fortune or misfortune to happen along just at the time of Special Education classes. Despite the fact that teachers complained that they had dozens of students who couldn't do their work, in Gregg's small school there really weren't enough mentally retarded students to set up a special class. However, the money and teacher were available, so a special education class was set up and peopled with discipline cases and slow learners, neither of which should have been there.

Neither Gregg nor his teacher wanted him moved into this class of fifteen problems from grades three to eight. Administration won and Gregg learned to count beans, make aprons, paint, and cook. He and his friends called him "Dumbie" and he lived up to this label. Two years later, in grade 8, Gregg was again shifted, this time back to his regular class much regressed and with a lower self-concept. It took me two years to restore in him the attitude that he could achieve. Grouping should be for the advantage of the students, not the administrators, and not for teachers wanting to get rid of discipline problems.

Scales of Readability

The purpose of this section is to introduce you to the concept of readability. How do you determine which book for which child? Graduate students learn about readability formulas and use them. Researchers work with them. In fact, they've been around a long time, but few classroom teachers actually use them.

Edgar Dale, Jean Chall, Edward Fry, Flesch, SRA, Klare, Spache, Botel, Smog: these and others have written about, worked with, and produced their own methods for measuring the difficulty of reading materials. If you're interested in going further into this concept, look up the works of any of these authors.

For our purpose here, we need only say that if we want to get the so-called right book to the right child, one way is to attempt to know reading comprehension and vocabulary levels of books. Some companies give approximate levels for their books, others do not. Most of you are not interested in technical complicated formulas and would not have the time to work with them. However, there are simple informal techniques which will give a quick approximation of the grade level of materials. Two of them will be shown here.

The difficulty of material for a given student depends upon many factors, some of which may not be measurable. These include (1) the purpose for reading, (2) the degree of understanding called for, (3) how much a student already knows about the subject, (4) vocabulary, (5) sentence structure and length, and (6) the student's interest in the material. Some may argue no to number six, but students often stretch for difficult material if they're interested in it.

Joy L. Keith [19] uses the following table to determine readability based on two factors: (1) number of syllables, and (2) number of sentences in a given one-hundred-word selection. She cautions that a chart such as this is for a quick classroom approximation of grade level of material and not for precise readability.

Readability: An Example

Syllables per line

By mid-afternoon her feet ached, her eyes stung, and her thoughts	14
fused. Nancy carelessly flung down her mink, kicked off her heels, and	15
dropped onto the bench. The obstinate line of her straight, chisel-	15
perfect back and the sharp thud as she snapped her book closed estab-	15
lished the fact that time for recalculation had arrived.	14
Though born in anger and heart-breaking frustration, her idea to	15
fight rather than give up was a commendable one. Yes. She would	16
fight them, use their own weapons. Knowledge of the arts, the latest	15
fashions, the current Broadway hits: she'd revel in all of them *and*	16
at the same time develop the art of polite conversation. No one in	135

New York could be more suave and impersonal than she.

Number of Syllables	135	Grade 7
Number of Sentences	7	Grade 5
		12

Readability: 12 ÷ 2 = 6   grade level of passage

TABLE 3

Keith's Readability Chart

KEITH'S READABILITY CHART			To determine readability:
Syllables	Grade	Sentences	1. Select a passage from the material.
118	1	14	2. Count 100 words and underline word 100.
120	2	11.5	3. Count the number of syllables occurring in the 100 words.
122	3	9.5	
123	4	8	4. Count the number of sentences occurring in the 100 words.
125	5	7	
128	6	6.5	5. Find the corresponding grade level for the number of sentences and syllables. If they differ, average.
134	7	5.5	
140	8	5	
145	9	4.5	
151	10	4.3	
155	11	4.2	
160	12	4.1	

Another readability measure which is easy to use is the graph by Fry, extended by Maginnis (figure 3.2). It, too, uses sentences and syllables. Choose three typical paragraphs from the book you are checking. Count off 100 words in these three locations. Count the number of syllables in each. Count the number of sentences in each. Average the three counts. Plot on the graph.

SUMMARY

You go to a medical doctor and tell him you're sick, he pulls down a bottle from the top shelf, takes your $20, and sends you home. But you don't get well. Your new class for the year comes to you. They are handed a set of textbooks issued from the administrative offices. You assign a lesson in each one and send the students home. But they don't learn. One side of this analogy is as stupid as the other. Yet, many teachers are guilty of such practices.

The class matrix, the checklist of student strengths and weaknesses, flexible grouping to handle the findings, expectancy formula results, reading, and scales of readability to get the right book to them: all of these data will help you decide what kind of instruction you will use with your new class.

Remember that test scores are often unreliable measures and you need observation, common sense, dialogue with students, and so forth, to help with instructional decision making.

FIGURE 3.2*

Fry's Readability Graph extended thru preprimer level
Average number of syllables per 100 words

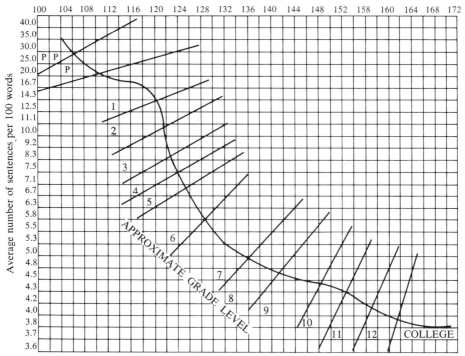

Activities for the Teacher

1. Using your present class, make a matrix. Is the picture what you expected?
2. Using one or more of the formulas given in this chapter, run a readability test on one of the textbooks you are using. What are the results?
3. Find the expectancy level for some of your students. Are they on target, over-achieving or underachieving? Do they need retesting?
4. If you haven't done so this year, make a reading checklist or use the one in this chapter and listen to several students read. Record their performances. What did you find? Plan remedial measures, if needed.
5. If you are not currently working with students, use the Fry and Keith formulas given in this chapter and, following the instructions, run a readability check on this textbook. What do you find? What does this say to you about your reading and understanding of the material?

---

* SOURCE: George Maginnis, "The Readability Graph and Informal Reading Inventories," *The Reading Teacher* 22 (March 1969). Note: For further information, see the April 1968 *Journal of Reading.*

FOUR

Vocabulary: Fifty-five Ways to Teach and/or Reinforce It

Lack of ability to read proficiently is one of the greatest deterrents to student and teacher success in the classroom. Reading is based upon a student's knowledge and manipulation of words. Can we help?

We have a built-in motor for learning—*curiosity*. Too many times this motor is turned off in the normal classroom. We talk of waste in our nation today—waste in manpower, in education, in natural resources. The greatest waste of all is the human mind. If most adults use only one-tenth of their capacity, how much less is used by students! Pressures to please, to cover materials, to conform, to excel: these may block teaching as well as learning.

There are attempts being made in classrooms (a small percentage in comparison to the whole) today to get stereotyped practices out—practices which bypass those who can't and frustrate those who could do more, thereby leading to mass-produced mediocrity.

QUESTIONS: 1. How can we be more effective teachers?
2. How can we make learning an integral part of living?
3. How does a student acquire language?
4. What factors influence how well a student learns words?
5. What can the regular classroom teacher do about vocabulary expansion?

Solving the Major Cause of Teacher Ineffectiveness in Reading

In an attempt to eradicate a part of the maglapolas of criticism (some justified, some not) hurled our way, without adequate preparation, training, materials, or facilities, many teachers have attempted to jump on the bandwagon of any fad which gets publicized. High pressure salespeople with scanty research hold fabulous claims for their methods and materials. Just recently, in a college setting for prospective teachers, I saw a beautifully done demonstration of a kit for non-readers which left the young hopefuls ecstatic: "Wasn't that something!" "Every school should have it." "Any student would learn with those materials and methods." It was nothing more than what good teachers have been doing for years—all in one colorful multimedia package and presented by a top-notch technician. Few of the inexperienced admirers would get the same results.

What were the main ingredients? Enthusiasm and know-how. A dull set of facts can be made into an interesting lecture by a person willing to put forth the time and effort.

One of this writer's pet peeves is the way many teachers (some rated by their peers and administration as top-notch in their field) teach new words. Each Monday morning the students are given a mimeographed list of 25 to 50 words, depending upon whether they are in the slow, average, or enriched class, told to look them up in a dictionary, learn a meaning, write a sentence, and be ready for a test on Friday. What happens? They memorize a meaning for each word for Friday's test and forget them Saturday morning. Why not? They never use them again. Next Monday they get a new list. Is there any wonder they complain, "I'm sick of words"?

If we want students to really learn new words, will more memorization of a vocabulary list do the trick? Can checking off multiple choice items on literal questions build or evaluate learning? Can sitting in straight rows, looking at books, or filling in blanks in workbooks, and never opening their mouths or questioning the material be profitable practice for students?

The list of factors which influence learning, briefly discussed in chapter one, major requirements if a student is to reach full potential for reading, might be summed up into three much simpler groups. He or she can absorb, emit, and feel. Perhaps a fourth item should be added to this list, especially when dealing with our middle-grade students. He/she is willing to do so.

Progress in recognizing words, understanding concepts, and reading is made by cognitive restructuring in search of answers. Even the early beginnings of visual and auditory discriminations are learned abilities. Learning requires thought. Thought can be stimulated, challenged, guided, and restructured by problem-solving tasks set up by teachers. A well-developed brain is active, curious, and perceives reading as a tool to help in the goals of acquiring and communicating information. Lev Vygotsky (150) claims that direct teaching of words and/or concepts is impossible and fruitless. If one follows this theory, then the teacher's obligation must be to structure situations and to give tasks which aid in the restructuring, reorganizing, and expanding of concepts already present. Gagne says set up structure. Bruner says structure. Montessori said it years ago.

If cognition concerns the recognition of knowledge (words, language) and development of intellectual abilities and skills (using these words), what can be done in a regular schoolroom to improve it? William Palmer (107) advocates (1) arranging cognitive skills in reading in a hierarchy, (2) letting tasks involve emotions and parts of the personality of which a student may not fully be aware, (3) building upon natural responses and leading toward sophistication and maturity in reasoning, and (4) letting there be student-teacher interaction, but not the usual cold-blooded analysis. He sums up by saying that in the society of today, teachers can no longer divorce thought from feeling nor emotion from behavior. Students must be given a chance to talk; to respond; to observe; to discuss and modify feelings, thoughts, and behaviors; and to see alternate choices. We need teachers who listen, weigh, and guide student responses, who consider both cognitive and effective domains, and can develop with students a kind of interaction which goes beyond simple memorization or passive acceptance of reading materials.

R. G. Stauffer (136) says that the teacher should be an intellectual agitator asking, "what do you think, why do you think so, and read the line that proves it." We can help to improve thinking by improving skill with words which leads to mental flexibility—the ability to invent, to innovate, and to have new ideas.

How Does a Student Acquire Language?

The linguists claim that the primary function of language is speech. Writing and reading are secondary. If normal speech is all that a child needs as readiness for the reading act, why do we have so many students who become poor readers?

The behaviorists follow the view of B. F. Skinner. The child imitates a model and is rewarded. The frequency with which he hears the model will affect language acquisition. We do know that in homes where children are played with, talked to, read to, and are given many concrete experiences, they seem to progress easier and faster in the school setting. The trouble here is that they may ignore the model and produce their own variations, and vocabulary is controlled in books.

The *nativistic* theory claims that language development is biologically determined. No other animals besides humans have language. Abnormal language (speech defects) may be the result of congential or environmental factors. Carol Chomsky (30) calls language the "universals of the mind." The problem here is how do we get from the child's innate knowledge to language performance?

The group of linguists which hold to the cognitive theory claim that the child takes an active role in learning the language. His or her thinking is a kind of information processing.

The transformational grammarians claim their theory models some of Piaget's views (109) on stages of cognitive growth. Stage I is perception centered. The child attends to one situation. Can he pick out a figure from a background, or distinguish between letters? Stage II moves toward "centration"—vision and sound simultaneously. If the child has the inability to deal with more than one thing at a time, trouble in reading may result.

Although all the theories claim to, none give an adequate explanation of "how" a child acquires language, but they are valuable in that they provide parts of information we need to know to understand language.

If the child enters the classroom equipped with a language and with the ability to learn language, the teacher must encourage this learning, make it possible, expose him/her to a rich variety of language inputs in interesting situations, and let the child read. One little fourth grader complained to this writer, "All day long she talks, talks, talks. She never gives us time to do or to think."

Chomsky (30) advises encouraging students to skim, skip, and get to the good parts. This way of reading is more close to nature than when everything is "controlled." If he wants it, is ready for it, he'll stretch to get it.

Little is known about the process by which a child learns language, but interest, amount of time spent on it, reading or hearing books read by good models, no put-down about dialects, and a classroom atmosphere of inquiry may contribute more to individual measures of reading acquisition than is now realized.

Understanding what one sees and hears is a complex process. It necessitates connecting words with certain conceptual patterns that exist in one's memory. The inference, the relations, the preceding inputs, the learned emotional reactions— all of these work together with the immediate input to process the information to produce reasonable replies. A correct response for one may be incorrect in another reference. This is proven when one discusses theories or ideologies with persons from a different cultural background. A compliment in one culture may be an insult in another.

What is the task of the teacher in guiding the building of concepts? Because acquisition of a language system involves a continuous reorganization of mental processes, constant meaningful communications with others, especially adults in power, is of decisive significance. A student's understanding of "words" must expand in accordance with his developmental maturation and expanding world. Upper-grade teachers criticize lower-grade teachers for not teaching reading when the students' difficulties in learning subject matter may not be due to their inability to read, but to the result of failure to learn to deal with these higher level unique skills, symbols, and concepts (words) of the material.

Since almost everything a student does in school, and life for that matter, depends upon his or her knowledge and manipulation of words, should we teachers not accept as ours the task of showing students how to build word power?

Vocabulary: How Do We Teach It?

Some experts claim that we do not need to be taught how to think, how to solve problems, how to spell, nor how to improve personality by the reading process. Others say even the skill of word recognition should be taught as a thinking process. There is reasoning involved in word recognition. For instance, look at the word *mesocephalic*. The student must know the key parts, recognize them, know they unlock meaning, then relate them to background experiences. To read a word is to recognize it, know what it means, and be able to use it. A cognitive process! Spache and Berg (131) agree with the second premise. A person cannot read on a higher level than his vocabulary skill. Words are the accurate tools of thought. In order to know, we must be able to say.

Before a teacher decides which technique to use in helping students improve in vocabulary, he/she must consider their needs, the purpose of the lesson, and overall class objectives. Also, especially if dealing with slower students, he must ask himself what are the causes of poor vocabulary?

Some Causes of Limited Vocabulary:

1. Low intelligence
2. Poor environment—lack of experience
3. Bilingual language spoken in home and/or a different dialect
4. Physical defects—hearing and speech
5. Little reading
6. Skipping of words or ignoring context clues
7. Attitude that you don't know words you don't know
8. Poor teaching methods—list for the week, books with too much too fast, no reinforcing from teacher, and lack of practice.

Students Must Understand:

1. That to know words is a must to learning.
2. They must use words to learn them.
3. They must relate them to life as they live it.
4. No word has meaning out of context.
5. Words can change in meaning.
6. Students themselves help to make words.

Vocabulary Building in Higher Grades

The acquisition of new words is a complex process. In any grade level the range of vocabulary is great. A new organization in a school which crosses grade lines (combination grades—ten fifth graders and fifteen sixth graders) will draw instant complaints from the traditional teacher. "I can't teach fifth and sixth graders in the same room." Isn't this ironic when we know that in the most structured grouping there will be a variety of levels of development in all areas of the curriculum. That so-called sixth grade reading group will probably have three to ten levels in some areas. Before you read on, think about these things. With which can you agree?

1. There is no such thing as homogeneous grouping.
2. The best way to improve vocabulary is to let students read.
3. Vocabulary expansion is the job of every teacher.
4. Most students are interested in words until some teacher kills that interest.
5. Incidental teaching of word meanings is good, but direct teaching of word meanings is imperative.

6. If all teachers taught concepts well, we would have fewer reading problems.
7. The teaching of words in isolation is a waste of time.

Fifty-five Techniques for Teaching Words

1. Words Change Meaning

A basic understanding students must have at the very beginning of learning is that words can change meaning with thought or context. Give them a model to study. After they think about the model, have them take a word and see how many meanings they can come up with.

Example 1: Take a symbol such as the number 13 and put it in various texts:

a game token	a horse in a race
amendment to the Constitution	a ball player
sum of 12 and 1, abstract value	13 Beaufort Street
size in clothing	a length of measurement
rank in a series	a car in a race
sign of bad luck	a weight in liquids or pounds

Example 2: run   (A simple word usually taught in the first month of a child's school life. Yet, Reader's Digest Encyclopedia Dictionary lists over 100 meanings. Simple?)

2. Labeling

Labeling for sight word vocabulary? Yes. Some middle- and upper-grade teachers may object because this sounds like a primary technique. It is. In primary school we label things, pictures, children's desks. In higher grades, we label the microscope, models, charts, maps, and graphs.

3. Flash Cards

This method, too, might be criticized. I can understand that. However, if you have never taught eighth grade nonreaders (I don't think there is such a creature) who want to learn worse than anything in the world, who don't care what method or material is used if it works, then you may not know that older students enjoy putting their skill against the quick flash. Programmed readers, television match games, puzzles, and such, have the same principle. The thing to remember is to adapt everything you do to the age and level of competency of the students. For slow or remedial readers, flash cards can work as reinforcers, even for older students. Try them.

4. Concrete Objects

If available, and many are if you will take the time to find them, concrete objects are a sure way to imprint something in a student's mind. The real thing is more impressive than merely talking about it. One of my favorite examples for third, fourth, and remedial students in higher grades is the word *miniature.*

Example 1: miniature

Assemble on the desk, table, or shelf a group of things, large and small, bottles, pencils, boxes, envelopes, toys, perfume bottles, drinking glasses, pins, leaves, and anything.

Then talk about them. Let students look, talk, and handle articles. Discuss other words they know for describing these things: large and small, little and big, tiny and huge, gigantic and minute, etc.

See if they can come up with the word you're discussing today. What other words do they know that begin like *miniature?* What do they mean? (Minute, minibike, miniskirt.)

I tried this with a group of special education students and it worked. The next day when we asked if they remembered the new word they had learned, one little fellow jumped up and pointing to his thigh said, "uh, uh, uh," his eyes shining because he had remembered it had something to do with miniskirt.

Example 2: opaque

How easy to use the opaque projector or the window panes.

5. Categorizing and/or Classifying

No group, including the teachers in in-service classes, has failed to enjoy the exercise of categorizing. We do it daily in all walks of life, why not in learning new words?

Example 1: In primary grades or remedial classes, use words such as bread, fruit, potato, ship, bird, insect, bug, bluebird, apple, mosquito, etc.

Example 2: In middle grades, use words from the materials you're working with. Words like carbon, starch, cellulose, amino acids, division, formula, multiplication, subtraction, science, etc.

Example 3: Name as many animals in thirty seconds as you can think of. Talk about results. Did they categorize into cats, dogs, wild, tame, zoo, etc.? Most will not the first time.
Do the same thing again, reminding them to categorize. Is there any difference in the number they get?

6. Compound Words

Many words can be recognized as two already familiar words or word roots.
Examples: birdhouse, bellhop, phonograph, grandparents

7. Dramatization, Puppet Shows, Pantomime, Charades, and So On

Teacher or student acts out new words for class. Class attempts to guess the word. This activity is popular with all ages, including adults. Some good words to use with grades 4–9 are wilt, dress, love, park, equal, and multiply.

8. Etymology

Many words have exciting, interesting, even bizarre histories. When presented by an enthusiastic teacher, they come alive in the minds of students. Drop a hint of mystery, or something a little shady or risque, in a word background and watch them start digging to find it. What possible connection can there be in the two meanings for the word *pupil:* student and the part of an eye? Where did we get these meanings? Are they reasonable?

Who is a *lizard scorcher?* Where was the word *berserk* first used? Was the word *Amazon* first used to describe a man, a woman, or a river? *Buccaneer, sandwich, neighbor, gerrymander,* are good words to get students interested in etymology.

Most libraries have at least one book on interesting words. One librarian told me that after one ninth-grade English teacher introduced her class to the word *etymology* (many of them had never heard of it) and used several of the students' names as examples, that the book on word origins, which before had never been checked out, became one of her most sought after books.

9. Structural Analysis

At the beginning of the year tell your students that you'll teach them 300 new words this year and as a result they'll know 3,000. Watch the disbelief register in their eyes. Proceed to show them.

Have them group themselves into threes or fours after which you'll give them a root and see how many words they can come up with in a specified time. I usually limit it to three minutes and ask for at least thirty words. The first time most groups come up with ten, fifteen, maybe twenty. They rarely reach thirty. (Before you read on, why not try this idea yourself? See how many words you can come up with in three minutes using the root *port.*)

Have them count their list. Discuss how well they did. Then ask how many categorized by prefixes, suffixes, and so on? Show them how they could have taken the root and come up with sixty or more in the three minutes. The list is endless.

Prefixes: de, re, im, ex, sup, pre, trans

Suffixes: s, ed, ing, ly, ate, ation, ee, er, ment, al, age, ance, able, ably, ive, liness, ability

Compound words: airport, jetport, seaport, davenport, porterhouse, port-hole, portfolio, port of call, port of entry

Proper Names: Newport, La Porte, Shrevesport, Portsmouth, Porte, Portia, Southport, Westport, Port Royal, Port Jackson, Portugal, Port Washington, Port of Spain

Foreign Words: portico, portiere, port-manteau, porte cochere, porte-mannaie

This is an ideal way to use that extra five minutes before lunch, the break, or picture taking. The activity prevents discipline problems and students enjoy it.

Then show how biped, photograph, telephone, malcontent, and such words meanings can be figured out by using this technique of structural analysis. How is the word made up? Do you know any of its parts? Does the context help to complete meaning?

Like all other techniques or approaches to meanings of new words for students, structural analysis will not always work. Some words have parts which might be an affix in one word and not in others. They must learn to look out for this. Some of these words are *malevolent, matriarch, mallet,* and *matrix.* In the first two words parts *mal* and *matri* help with the meanings. In the second two words they are parts of the words and do not help.

10. Word Lists That Belong to the Same Family

As a direct follow-up to teaching the skill of structural analysis, have students practice the skill by giving them a similar task of making lists of words that belong to the same family—words that are built from the same root, belong to the same category, are used in the same field—and have them use any sources available to add to their list.

Example: Name as many _____ as you can. (The blank word can be anything you're dealing with in the content of your courses: *trees, animals, rivers, sports, fruits, cars, movie stars.*)

Or if you're working with word parts—*phobia, press, biblio*—how many words do they know or can find with these parts? Reading, reference skills, spelling, writing, science, word recognition: all of these skills are practiced in an activity such as this one.

During one in-service course a teacher told me that her class had that last-month-of-the-school-year blues. Nothing she tried seemed to help. She got this idea from class, tried it the next day, and all of a sudden the last month of school became as interesting as the first for her and her students. One young fellow in her lowest reading group chose *rivers.* She said she hadn't seen him work that hard all year. His comment after he had found about seventy-five names of rivers, which he got from social studies books, maps, globes, and encyclopedias, was "Miss Smith, how come we didn't do this long ago? I didn't know geography could be so much fun. Say, do you think I can find 100?"

11. Trades

As new industries, new science projects, and new products are studied, discovered, or developed, new words are added to our vocabulary. Many of these words take the name or combination name of the product and what it does. Some examples are kodak, kleenex, astronaut, vegeburger, and hundreds of others.

Do a lesson with the students using current products on the market. See the lesson given on coined words (page 70).

12. Experience Charts

Most everyone realizes the value of experiences and the discussion, writing, and lessons which can be developed with young children. This approach for teaching new words (concepts) will work just as well for older students, especially those in trouble or with poor language backgrounds. See examples in other sections of this book.

13. Use the Thesaurus or Word-Finder for Finer Shades of Meaning

Example: Instead of using the word *good*, find specific terms to replace it in the following sentences.
  1. I had a *good* time at the party.
  2. The apple pie was *good*.
  3. You made an A. *Good* for you.
  4. That was a *good* play.
  5. *Good* living means steak every night.
  6. The doctor did a *good* job. I lived through surgery.
  7. If that teacher ever gives me a *good* word, I'll flip.
  8. *Good* jobs are hard to find.
  9. How many *good* rains have we had this year?

14. Audio-Visuals to Teach Vocabulary

Use pictures, filmstrips, movies, and other audio-visuals to show, explain, and demonstrate new words. Some words which could be effectively taught like this: module, mock-up, aerial, brainwashing, meandering, transparent, genocide, philanthropist, snow (TV), and freeway.

15. In Giving Directions

In giving directions, both oral and written, occasionally use a new term which students will need to know to comply with the directions. Let them work to find the answer. We tell too much. Like the television commercial says, "They'd rather do it themselves."

Example: Use four hardback and two current periodicals to find background information for tomorrow's reading. Then write a composition or essay on your subject. To make an A, your paper must be *succinct*.

16. By Example

Teach the words *labyrinth, boustrophedon, cyprinoid, pedestrian, tripod* or any other interesting word by showing or working with examples. Give them an alphabet puzzle of words dealing with sports, vegetables, synonyms. These can be made up by the teacher, found in magazines, bought at the supermarkets, or made by students. The Greeks had a two-directional type of writing called boustrophedon which is an interesting word to teach by example.

Boustrophedon: Make a sample and show it to the students. Let them use the discovery technique to figure it out. It looks like this.
The expansion of vocabulary if
fo eno si dediug ylevitaerc

the most exciting chores in
loohcs.

For reinforcement, let each student make a sentence in this pattern, exchange papers with his neighbor and figure out the message.
Other words good to show by examples:

pedestrian: The hall is full of them.

cyprinoid: Do you have an aquarium? If so, good. If not, get hold of a fish bowl and actually show fish.

tripod: probably you have one standing in the corner or in the supply closet. Use it. Discuss other words similar in meaning. triplets, tricycle, triangle.

Have students look for interesting words they can teach to the class by examples. Let them teach one. Was it interesting, a good word, one they want to remember? (Think of the skills students must use in this chore.)

17. Choral Reading to Teach Words and/or Concepts

Concepts can be taught, reinforced, and used in interesting and diverse ways through choral readings. From kindergarten throughout life, people enjoy being part of a group. Reading in a group is rewarding, good for fluency, should be used with shy children, and can teach words. Countless poems, prose selections, songs, and scriptures have been and can be arranged to be read in chorus. One of my favorites for grades 4–9 is given in chapter 13. (See page 288.)

18. Music

Use the music they sing, listen, and dance to and which is relevant to them, to teach words, ideas, and even grammar. By listening to and working with songs such as "Old MacDonald," "Shortnin Bread," and "Oh Dem Bones," a remedial reader can learn some basic vocabulary and sentence patterns. The repetition he needs, the melodious flow of word patterns, and the reading as he listens to it on a record, sings along, or does it as a choral reading is reinforcing. Use the cloze technique to see if he mastered the words. His spelling lesson for the day can be the new words he learns to recognize.

His grammar can be another verse added or a parody on his favorite selection. Students enjoy taking something someone else has done and making it their own.

Example: Parody on "Dem Bones" composed by a male student:

Chorus: Oh, the auto, the auto's a running thing.
Oh, the auto, the auto's a running thing.
Oh, watch it go.

Verse: The *carburetor's* connected to the *fuel pump,* and the *fuel pump's* connected to the gas tank.
Oh, watch it go!   (Chorus)

The *cylinder's* connected to the *piston* and the *piston's* connected to the rods; the rod's connected to the crankshaft.

Oh, watch it go!   (Chorus)

For other ideas using music, see pages 68, 127 and 231

19. Phonic Analysis

Despite the controversies which have raged off and on for decades, phonics are and usually have been used to some extent by most teachers to help students approach the pronunciation of new terms they meet in their reading. Memorizing forty-five phonic rules which may or may not work is not the way to give students the help they need. A few definitions, a few generalizations, a few practice exercises when the need arises may be the best ways to approach the phonic help students need. One thing which is known is that too much phonics turns most of them off and too early phonics, without understanding of or need for, slows up reading.

For anyone interested and wanting more help, there are many sources available. For our purpose here a few basic facts will suffice.

a. The phoneme is a sound unit. The word *run* has three phonemes: *r*, *u*, and *n*.
b. The morpheme is the smallest meaning unit. *Run* is one morpheme. It means one thing. *Runs* is two morphemes. *Run* and *s*. *S* adds to or changes the meaning.
c. The grapheme is a written symbol for words.
d. A blend (some of the new basals are calling it cluster) is two or three letters all sounded but working together. They are important because they are not separated when syllabication is used to get pronunciation of a word.

   *pl*ay   *spr*ing   *gr*ound   com*pl*ex
e. A consonant digraph (cluster) is two consonants working together, but making a different sound from either and usually not to be separated when syllabicating.

   *ch*urch   *sh*oe   tele*ph*one

   A vowel digraph is two vowels side-by-side. Usually the first one is pronounced with its long sound and the second one is silent, but there are many exceptions.

   g*oa*t   p*ai*d   st*ea*l   exception: p*ie*ce

   A diphthong is a vowel digraph with an exaggerated sound: *oi* in oil, *oy* as in boy, *ou* as in ounce, and *ow* as in cow.
f. Syllabication is the division into units for sounding out of a word for pronunciation. Each syllable has one vowel sound.

   hap py   pret ty   ra di o
g. Open syllable—when a vowel is on the end of a syllable it usually has its long sound: hi, no, na tion, why. Exception: do, to.
h. Closed syllable—when a vowel has a consonant following it the vowel usually is short: cat, hit, dad.

Many other terms, rules, and complex theories are involved. But for our purpose phonics are simply an aid to the pronunciation of words which, if in one's vocabulary, the context will verify. If not, we must go to the dictionary for verification.

Any generalization about sounds, syllabication, and so on, should be taught by using words already in the student's vocabulary and by the discovery method. See the sample lesson in chapter 13.

20. Analogies

One of the biggest problems students have on college boards and other standardized tests is that of dealing with word relationships. This is a result of never working with this kind of activity in classes.

First-grade teachers usually do a great deal with analogies when they are teaching concepts. English teachers sometimes use them when working with synonyms, homonyms, and so forth, but the average classroom teacher has an opportunity every day to have students work with some kind of word relationships.

Science, social studies and math terms are good ones to use to extend concept teaching by the use of analogy. Any kind of relationship can be used as illustration and practice. Try your luck with these.

Directions: Read the sentences. Study the relationships for the given terms. Then decide which word would fit in the blank space to show the same kind of relationship with the given word as the first two. Sometimes more than one term will work.

(These made to be used with the Bird Unit in chapter 8. For weak students, choices could be given. However, I believe even weak students need to work for themselves on certain tasks. One reason they're weak may be that we always give it to them and they need not work to succeed.)

1. Milk is to cow as egg is to _____.
2. Canary is to bird as bamboo is to _____.
3. Word is to sentence as sentence is to _____.
4. Birds are to air as moles are to _____.
5. Apiary is to bees as aviary is to _____.
6. Paleontologist is to fossils as ornithologist is to _____.
7. Baseball is to pitcher as football is to _____.
8. Oxpecker is to oxen as birds are to _____.
9. A _____ is to a king as the erectile crest is to Hoopoe.
10. The quetzal is to Guatemala as the _____ is to the U.S.
11. Sapsucker is to woodpecker as man is to _____.
12. Cock is to faucet as ovum is to _____.

Answers:
1. chicken, bird
2. tree
3. paragraph
4. underground
5. birds
6. birds
7. quarterback
8. plants
9. crown
10. eagle
11. Homo sapiens
12. egg

21. Job Card for Expanding Vocabulary Through Questions

Directions: Read the question. Decide upon the key word or words in each. Use the reference book which will give you the answer you're looking for in the shortest amount of time. Answer yes or no and explain your decision.

1. Does a kiwi lose its leaves in winter?
2. Is a bird fond of eating paleontologists?
3. Would a chicken lay an embryo?
4. Would your mother make soup from birdsnest?
5. Would an ornithologist be interested in conservation of rare birds?
6. If you wanted a bird for its beauty and chose the Bird of Paradise, would you choose male or female?
7. If your friend told you that he was going to build an apiary for his birds, would you help him?
8. Suppose your father told you that his salary was chicken feed. Does this mean you would have a generous allowance?
9. Your mother tells you if you don't start studying you're going to end up being a hawker. What does she means?
10. The eagle is described as a large duirnal bird of prey. Does this mean he prays before he dies?

Answers:

1. No. A kiwi might lose a hairlike feather or two. It's a bird.
2. No. But there was a movie where flocks of birds attacked people. A paleontologist is a fossil hunter.
3. No. It lays the egg which under favorable conditions will hatch into an embryo. (Your technical scientist may say yes.) Discussion good.
4. Yes. It is a secretion of certain Asian swifts, used in building nests and highly esteemed for making soup. A nest built by birds would be two words—bird's nest.
5. Yes. An ornithologist studies birds and would like that we don't kill rare ones.
6. The male. They are especially noted for the form and beauty of their plumage.
7. No. An apiary is a place of bees. Your friend should have said aviary.
8. No. Chicken feed is slang for small change or low wages. He would have little money to give you.
9. That I'll end up peddling in the street.
10. No. It means he catches other birds and does so mostly during the day.

22. Use the Chalkboard To Teach New Words

Put a new word in a prominent place on the chalkboard each day. Students learn to look forward to this new term and the many ways it may be used.

23. Be a Good Model

Students learn more by being shown than by being told. A teacher who uses new words in her own speech will encourage students to look for new terms. One teacher said she used an unknown word to refer to students when addressing or reprimanding them and watched them go for the dictionary.

24. Read to Students

Just as primary teachers do, so should teachers in grades 4–9 read to their students. There will be those who argue with this idea. (Then they don't know students, and how they listen to Rod McKuen read his poetry, or an actor impersonate Mark Twain.) As you read, you'll run across words new to your students, some perhaps even new to you. Talk about them and how they were used to create a certain mood, tone, or atmosphere for the story. How would another person state the same thing?

This is a good technique to use for that left over ten minutes, for getting students settled after a break, or just back from lunch. I used it to get eighth graders back to class from the lunchroom. There are always those laggards who play around, who take as long as they can to complete tasks that keep them out of class. I chose a book interesting for students, read a chapter per day, and always began at a certain time after lunch. Students knew this, and I had no problems getting my laggards in on time.

25. Games, Puzzles, Brainteasers, Riddles

One fun way to teach new words and get total class involvement in the activity is through such things as games, puzzles, brainteasers, and riddles. Try some of these. You'll find them scattered throughout this book where units and lesson plans are given.

26. Study Guides Using The Dictionary and/or Thesaurus

Very few people, including many teachers, know the extent of the information to be found in a good dictionary or that most of them have different pronunciation keys. Believe it or not, students (at least mine did) like this kind of dictionary play. Make a study guide, a job card, a puzzle, or a game for a learning center where the dictionary is the source book. Example given on pages 149, 268, 277, and 299.

27. Learn New Words by Association or Relationships with Words Already Familiar to Student

Give some words which have a familiar root meaning and ask the students to figure out the meanings.
a. elephantine _____
b. contractile _____
c. vaporizer _____

28. Paired Associates (Usually Go Together)

a. salt and pepper
b. cup and saucer

c. soap and _____
d. Flipper and _____
e. apogee and _____
f. Sonny and _____
g. bacon and _____
h. crime and _____

29. Complete the Series

a. bag, poke, carton, box
b. elephant, lion, zebra, monkey
c. nihil, nothing, annihilate, _____
d. abstract, absent, avert, _____
e. hydrophobia, claustrophobia, bibliophobia, _____

30. Descriptive Terms Associated with Some Category

Example: Sports (See chapter 14)
Have these terms used in creative writing, puzzles, reports, ask where they
would be used, and so forth.

31. Experiment with Words

Use the discovery technique to teach a new concept:
Use two eggs, one boiled, one raw. Number them 1 and 2 and spin. Students
watch what happens and ask questions of the leader to discover what word or
concept he or she is demonstrating. The word can be any that would be used in
the process he is carrying out. With the egg, it could be friction, rotation, gravity,
or motion.
Once they discover your term, then go into the other ways you could use the
same term. How many of them have used the process today? Talk about: its make-
up, begins with a blend, *tion* pronounced shun, letter *i* is short because, and so on.
Then lead into tomorrow's science lesson with a question you want answered.
When they have an idea of the concept they are to read about and a purpose for
reading the assignment, most of them will not resent it. It's those assignments they
have to do simply because the "teacher said so" which leaves them cold.

32. Collect Strange Words

Have students who are interested in and want to collect strange words, keep
a list of them, and occasionally share it with the class. A bulletin board might be
made to display them.

33. Notebooks and Vocabulary Cards

These old standbys—the vocabulary notebook, the vocabulary cards, the
individual dictionaries—are still good ways to keep words for study, review, and
reinforcement. However, if this is only a chore done by students because it is a

requirement, too often it is just that and little learning takes place. I've seen it work detrimentally even in college freshmen classes. Built-in motivation or want-to must be a part of this technique if it is to be worth the time it takes.

34. Programmed Kits, Workbooks, and Related Ideas for Vocabulary Building

Any commercial materials for vocabulary building or reinforcing are like the teacher-made materials—as valuable as the student sees them for his/her needs and purposes. If it is isolated drill, everybody on the same page the same day doing the same thing, chances are it's of little value. However, if the practice is needed by the individual, if he knows how it will help him, and if it has been pre-taught and will be evaluated, these aids are a big help to the busy teacher.

35. Meaningful Experiences Produce Growth in Vocabulary

An excursion to the site where a house or office building is under construction will lead children to observe materials, processes, and workers. They may increase vocabulary. Make a list of terms identifying and summarizing what they see. Some words listed by one group of sixth graders: floor, joist, studding, window sash, pitch, rafters, cornice, insulation, air conditioning, floor plan, carpenter, plumber, architect, builder, pouring concrete, laying bricks, bungalow, basement, linoleum, real estate, realtor, split-level, slate, stucco, contractor, heating plant, Venetian blind, and cellar.

36. Descriptive Terms To Build Word Power

Exercises in finding words that aptly describe a picture, selection or other word may be used to profitably promote clear thinking as well as develop vocabulary. The teacher may write a word on the board and ask students to give words suggested by it.

> *Noise:* bang, crash, shattering
>
> *Taste:* sweet, spicy, delicious
>
> *Halloween:* ghost, scary, pumpkin
>
> *Music:* soft, rhythmic, lullaby, sleepy
>
> *Squirrel:* flurry, scampering, chattering

Words in Context

A. Steryl Artley says by giving a student the skills of beginning sounds and using context clues, he can figure out most words in his reading.

Perhaps in a list dealing with vocabulary expansion, context clues should be listed first. It is placed last in this list because of its variety of clues, some of which may overlap in other methods of vocabulary expansion.

If students are given clues which authors use to help them (taught what to look for), they'll be more efficient readers with less word meaning problems.

Techniques 35 through 55 can all be listed under *how to teach words in context* clues. Students can be shown examples of how authors help them with new words, they can find examples in their textbook reading, and they can make some of their own.

37. The Synonym Clue

The new term is compared with a familiar one.

"If you were sitting on the roof of a house floating toward the sea, you'd probably wonder if the *deluge,* or rainstorm, would ever cease."

38. The Antonym Clue

The new term is contrasted with a familiar one.

"From the back patio of the palatial home, the *cool* ocean breeze belied the fact that on the streets the *torrid* wind burned one's eyes."

39. Author Uses Other Words To Explain New Terms

"One symptom of a drug overdose is the *torpor* of the victim. In other words, he may appear dull, lifeless, or apathetic."

40. Definition Is Given in the Text. (Similar to the Antonym Clue)

"As the show was about to begin, the actress found that her *mobcap,* the headdress for her costume, was missing."

41. Meaning of the Sentence Containing a New Term Is Restated

"When Susan came down the stairs dressed for the party, Bill thought she looked *foudroyant.* In fact he told her so. "Sue, Baby, I've never seen you look so striking!"

42. A New Word Is Compared with a Known Idea

"You do not have to *cogitate*; you can *fail.*"

43. Meaning is Inferred

"They call themselves Christian. They perform their pious deeds. What sanctimonious speeches they make on Sunday mornings! Yet, when they deal with their neighbors daily, how *intolerable* their acts."

44. Words in a Series Clue

Bob is a ballnut. He plays football, basketball, soccer, *lacrosse,* softball, handball, and tennis.

(Student knows category of series—here games using balls. Thus he will know that lacrosse is some kind of game which involves a ball).

45. Unknown Word Summarizes Several Ideas Which Precede It

"They operate in secret, are usually composed of criminals, are organized to control racketeering and peddling of illegal products, and operate throughout the world. Beware of the *Mafia*."

46. Word Meaning Derived from Linguistic Pattern of the Sentence

"As they sat in the twilight listening to soft music, Mary expected Bill to *propose* to her."

47. Tone or Mood Clue

Tell a story which is a frightening, somber, gay, satirical, or sad. The new word will probably follow a pattern created by known words.

48. A New Term Is Explained in Footnotes or Glossary

49. A Direct Explanation Is Given

"Social Studies should be an *interdisciplinary* subject. By this we mean that social studies should not be a separate subject in the classroom. It has overtones in math, health problems, economics, group living, geographic and historical arenas, and especially in reading."

50. Example Is Give in Text

"The price of a *commodity* depends upon its demand. For example, when we have plenty of money and everyone wants steak, the price of meat goes up."

51. Connotations

Vocabulary can be expanded by practice exercises where students figure out the different meanings for the same words. Despite the fact that most terms have more than one meaning, too many practices in the classroom still lead toward one meaning per word.

Examples: Take the simple word *can* and see how many different ways it can be used.

Mother will *can* the food.	preserve
The *can* of beans spoiled.	container
Can the chatter.	stop
He got put in the *can*.	jail
I *can* sing better than you.	am able to
You *can* go now.	have permission to
How many balls did he *can* today?	hit into cup

52. Stretch the Imagination by:

1. figures of speech
2. emotional reactions

3. sensory impressions
4. satire
5. irony
6. creative writing using the haikus

Figurative Language

Figurative language is a big problem for some students, especially those who are in trouble verbally. Yet, it is used daily, even by those students who do not recognize it as such. It is not my intention to go into depth here, nor is it needed. Many teachers have students memorizing all of these terms, trying to distinguish between them, and thoroughly despising English classes. Working with them as they occur in materials, calling attention to them in local speech, commenting upon how they are used by the news media to sway us: these are better approaches. Several practice exercises are given in lesson guides scattered throughout this book.

For our purposes, let's look at six types of figurative speech—speech used to evoke images or to show relationships different from their usual meanings.

1. *Metaphor:*

Shows comparison of two unlike objects with the words *like, as,* or *than* omitted.

Examples:

Grim fingers of death beckoned the speed freaks.
Baker's chevrolet was a speeding jet.
The racetrack was a sea of glass.

2. *Personification:*
Examples:

Gives animals and things the characteristics of a person.
Hot tires hugged the tracks.
Snap, snap, sang the axle as the car scraped the wall.
Debris whirled and danced across the tracks.

3. *Simile:*

Comparison of two things of unlikeness using *as, like,* or *than*

Examples:

When Pearson passed him on the last lap, Baker's smile melted like a snowflake in July.
My Porsche purrs like a kitten.

4. *Hyperbole:*
Examples:

Exaggerates
He drove until I thought he would die.
Fiberglass belts are just out of this world.
Turning laps at 195 mph is my idea of heaven.

5. *Idioms:*
Examples:

Short, local, sometimes vigorous expressions.
Accidents seemed to dog his footsteps.
His personality stood him in good stead on the race circuits.
Speed demons drive like bullets.

6. *Irony:*

Sarcastic or humorous, when one says one thing and means another.

Examples: His *best* friends applauded when champion Joe Smith's car careened into the sandbags.

"How exciting," Mary remarked when the race was rained out.

"One hundred twenty-five miles per hour. That's very good!" (At the tracks with average speeds up to 160 mph)

53. Build Words through Use of Syntax

Words mean nothing in isolation. Let students work with them in all kinds of interesting tasks. Let them discover for themselves that words get meaning from those around them—syntax—how they're arranged in relationships with other words.

Examples: 1. John *bowed* his arrow, aimed, and hit the bull's eye.
He *bowed* to the audience as it applauded his success.
2. Underline the describing words in this sentence, then add another relating sentence using these additional describing words: slippery and powerful.
"The teacher's dilapidated 1960 station wagon groaned its way through the snarled lines of snowbound new Mustangs."
3. See if you can beat the teacher at this game: Make sentences using as many similar phonemes as possible.
"The carsick carload of human cargo who had paid carfare to ride the Caracus streetcar wondered whether or not the carmine carcass on the cartoon was a message from the carman or the carhop."

54. Concrete Past-Experience Clues

Many of today's theorists advocate using the language and life of the young student to build reading power. The same thing will work with older students. Look at these two examples and how the past experience can help a student figure the meaning of the italicized words.

Susan Hayward cooed *sensually*. (Student is familiar with movies and her sensual voice helps to clarify meaning.)

The snake *slithered* quickly into the grass. (Past experiences with snakes might clarify the verb.)

Sylvia Ashton Warner (152) suggests organic teaching. She says ask the child what he wants to learn today. The words relating to his everyday life and world have intrinsic motivation. Because he wants to know them, he'll learn them.

55. Conversation for Vocabulary Development

"One hour's conversation across the table with a wise man is worth more than reading a thousand pages."

While we all know that one of the most enjoyable ways of building vocabulary is wide reading, this old Chinese proverb speaks clearly to the modern teacher. Repeatedly in education we claim that students learn by doing. Then they come into classrooms and sit and listen to teachers talk, talk, talk. And this talk is often one-sided (teacher does it all), repetitive, monotonous, uninteresting, and in a nagging tone. Why do we fail to practice what we know?

We've already said that teaching words in isolation is a waste of time. Words are to be used, not merely in written work, but orally. How can you, the teacher of vocabulary, encourage oral use of new language? Look at the following list:

1. Encourage students to use new words in conversation at least once daily until they become natural for them.
2. Back up your encouragement by giving them time to talk.
3. Games where conversation is required appeal to students.
4. Have planned sharing time, a talk show, a puppet show where students ad lib.
5. Have students go to lectures, plays, or demonstrations of new products, and return to class with interesting terms they hear.
6. Give merit points for every time you hear students use a new word correctly in regular conversation.
7. Occasionally tape conversations and in playback let students decide upon different ways to say the same thing.
8. In unit work, when students make reports, they often use new terms connected with their project. Call attention to these. List them on the chalkboard.
9. Use the world students live in to enhance their vocabularies. One teacher used these techniques:
   a. Resource people from the communities were invited to come to class and students interviewed them, much as a newspaper reporter or TV talk show does. They wrote up the interviews for newspapers and exposé type magazines.
   b. Another time the group used photography as the basis for vocabulary building. They took pictures of interesting faces on the street, at work in the school building, fellows loitering on the street corners, and an interesting study of human personality, emotions, genealogy, and race developed.
   c. A different group went to a nearby city on Saturday afternoon, casually listened to conversations from all kinds of people in all types of situations, listened for new words or expressions they could pick up, and reported to class. Students, themselves, evaluated this teacher as one of the best they ever had and the year as one of the most rewarding learning experiences.

Remediation of Vocabulary Difficulty

What do you do if you find a student is weak in reading because of a lack or a weakness in vocabulary? Many suggestions, games, exercises, and workbooks are available. A few specific suggestions might help. First of all a good diagnostic test, either commercial or self-made, should be administered.

Does the child miss all similar words: Utility words? For example: *when, where*. Teach these as sight words. Large words like *elephant* and *Christmas* can be taught with some other word attack approach.

Does the child need instruction in word discrimination? Programmed materials, closure activities, and experience charts can help here.

Do words missed represent abstract concepts: *this, and, if, these?* They must see these in context to make sense. Use them in the student's own sentences or stories. Phrase cards may help. They lose meaning with isolated word drills.

Does the child know a word in isolation, but not in context? Then the teacher must use it in context—highlight it, frame it, underline or mark it in a different color. Let students work together on learning. Let them make and exchange vocabulary cards, notebooks, lists of interesting words, demons, technical content words, but only if students want to. Otherwise, it is a waste of time. Students won't learn from the task by doing it simply because the teacher says to.

Can he pronounce words but see no meaning in them? This may be the result of too much preoccupation with phonic analysis or lack of background experience. Give him easy material to read. Let him paraphrase the author's words. Use the words in different contexts. Give an opportunity for group experiences in conversations. Use the dictionary, especially with older students.

Is the problem one where the student eventually pronounces the words, but with hesitations? Let him practice oral reading. Use the tape recorder, choral reading, timed and flashed exposure toward recognition, and echoic reading. The problem is to build up fluency and self-confidence.

A student who is having great difficulty with learning words can be and must be helped. Otherwise he turns into a disgruntled, unhappy person who may become your discipline problem, and who can blame him! An adaptation of Fernald's VAKT (Visual-Auditory-Kinesthetic-Tactile)[20] method is one way to help some of these students. To motivate, ask what words he/she would like to learn today. If they want to, they will. When you know what a student wants to learn:

1. show him the word;
2. have him say the word as he traces it;
3. after he has traced the word several times, have him attempt to write it without looking at it;
4. if he has it, add the word to his file, box, or notebook. If he doesn't know it yet, repeat the process; and
5. overlearn the word by reviewing and using it frequently.

Using all the senses reinforces the word tract in the student's mind. The idea is to get a written symbol associated with the spoken word. Here are some other ways to help a student who is in trouble.

a. Let him use the typewriter. He gets sequence, left-to-right practice of reading through the word, concentration on it, and reinforcement when he sees it typed.
b. Rhyme phrases help to build power with utility words:

bug under the rug	duck under a truck
mouse in the house	ball over the wall
frog on a log	Red Rover, Red Rover, let Jan come over.

c. Use the Language Master. With this machine the students get a visual and auditory picture, left-to-right mastery, repeated practice, and can produce models of words they are interested in.

d. Individual letter and word trays.

e. Games, games, games. Games stimulate, motivate, and reinforce the learning of words, hence language, and finally to reading. For instance: *Whingo*. This is a take-off from Bingo. One uses the *wh* words for playing. It teaches the *wh* digraph, cluster, sight words beginning with this sound, and eventually the sounds of vowels in the words. Use this game in a center for practice when the teacher is busy elsewhere.

f. Creative writing has been one of my best vocabulary builders with students who need special motivation to learn new words. Try this: *Today I'm Not Me. I'm a geometrid.* Student writes his description of what he thinks a geometrid might be, then checks dictionary to see how close he came to getting the correct definition. He remembers how close or how far off he was.

g. "Annie's Song" by John Denver is one of the teen-ager's favorites. Use it to motivate that remedial or reluctant student into vocabulary and reading skills practice. This song is very simple reading so most of them would have little trouble working with it. I suggest making task cards. Materials needed would be the task cards, copies of the words, a simplified copy of the music with autoharp chords, and an autoharp.

Task Card I.	Look at the words to this song. See how many you can find which fall under these categories.	
A. Naming words (nouns)	B. Action words (verbs)	C. Figurative language
night, mountain, love	love, like, walk	sleepy blue ocean

Task Card II.	Play around with the sounds of words in this song. See how many of the following categories you can find.	
A. Blends	B. Digraphs	C. Phrases which use small utility words (Prepositions)
*spr*ing, *st*orm	oc*ea*n, moun*tai*n	*like* the mountains

Task Card III. How many words in "Annie's Song" can you find which have more meanings than one according to the way they are used in context?

Example: *walk* a. People *walk* in the woods. (action)
b. Go for a *walk* in the woods. (naming something)
c. There are few paved *walks* in the mountains. (naming, but different from b.)

Task Card IV. Use the music sheet provided for you and play the song on the autoharp.

Task Card V. A more difficult task would be to rewrite the song substituting your own words for the ones given. Change all of the nouns to other appropriate ones. What happens?

Examples: a. like the fingers in a glove
                   b. like the perfume of a lilac
                   c. like ice cream in a cone

Students needing remedial help respond to activities such as these, even those so-called incorrigibles. Take a song popular with them right now and do something similar to this and watch their reactions.

For older students, a study of lexicography might be desirable and interesting. There are four levels of meaning for words: (1) concrete or physical; (2) abstract, names of things; (3) fictional or mental construct, such as beauty; and (4) metaphorical, such as jury box or arterial highway.

How we get words is also interesting for students. You might go into some of these ways.

1. generalizations: go from simple to broader meaning.
                         Once a *ship* meant carrying something over water by ship.
                         Today, it means most any way we send it.
2. specializations: opposite from generalization.
3. melioration: from Latin melior, meaning going up in meaning.
                         Early meaning of *marshall* was keeper of the horses.
                         Today, many meanings including honor place in parade.
4. pejoration: goes down in meaning—good to begin with, such as *boor* meant behavior. Today—bad behavior.
5. transfer: *priest* was an elder in the community,
                         by transfer came to be known as a *minister*.
6. acronyms: made from other words—a *jeep*—general purpose initials of something: NATO, PACE, UFO.
7. coinages: another name for trade words, such as *kleenex, kodak*.
8. port-manteau: two words blended to form new word:
                         chortle—blend of chuckle and snort;
                         smog—blend of smoke and fog.
9. usage: a word may be accepted because it is used—*ain't*.
10. idiomatic: words put together and having a different meaning from the original: (1) shy *chick* (2) *whale* of a good time.

In word study, of course, students should be taught the proper use of the dictionary, that there is no *one* meaning or dictionary, and that symbols, marks, and keys differ from one another. The efficient reader uses his other word skills first, and goes to the dictionary for verification of the correct word use, pronunciation, and/or spelling.

Context Clues Help in Word Recognition

STUDY EXERCISE

Directions: Below are sentences illustrating clues authors use to help students understand what they read. Some clues are listed. Read the sentences. Decide what context clue is illustrated by each of them, and write the letter beside the corresponding sentence number.

a. analogy
b. contrast
c. association
d. synonym
e. appositive
f. figurative language
g. example

h. antonym
i. comparison
j. meaning known from past experience
k. word meaning given in other terms
l. word known by linguistic pattern of sentence
m. no help given

Sentences:

1. An *apiary,* a place where bees are kept, was set up just inside the garden.
2. Birds are to air as moles are to *earth.*
3. You do not have to *cogitate:* you can fail.
4. The *contractile* quality of the dress made it an impractical purchase.
5. The snake *slithered* quickly into the grass.
6. She was much more *precocious* than her friend who showed lack of maturity in most everything she did.
7. One symptom of a drug overdose is the *torpor* of the victim. In other words, he will appear dull, lifeless or apathetic.
8. One reason given for poor comprehension is the *desultory* reading habits of the reader. It is sometimes said of such people that they walk around like a chicken with its head chopped off.
9. As they sat in the twilight listening to soft music, May expected Bill to *propose.*
10. PBTE has just completed a study which claims that a performance based teacher education program produces teachers who are more effective with their students than traditionally educated teachers.

Teaching Reading Using "Manufactured" Words

STUDY EXERCISE
1. Students will use manufactured words to develop and expand vocabulary.
2. Given a list of manufactured words, students will identify the word components, demonstrating their understanding of how the words are formed.
3. Given a selected list of brand names, the students will develop a hypothesis of why the product was given a particular name.
4. Students will identify the function of a product by its name.
5. In deciphering manufactured words the students will utilize structural analysis, configuration, sensory association and word meaning.

Techniques used in teaching manufactured words:
1. Structural analysis and word meaning of new words, with examples on chalkboard.
2. Teaching word meaning and descriptive clues through use of rhymes and charades.

    Example: It wiggles, it squiggles,
                    It tastes good, too.

It's nourishing and flourishing,
And good for you. What is it?

Wipe out the odor,
Keep it fresh and clean.
Hold your nose no longer,
Air freshener's on the scene.

3. Utilizing sensory association by letting students taste, smell, feel, see, and hear the product.

Below is a list of manufactured words to choose from for your teaching:

Twigs	Snowdrift	Bugles	Tang
Enfamil	Borateem	Blistex	Fasteeth
Scotkins	Jello	Renuzit	Mop and Glo

As a follow up or review for teaching manufactured words, let the students look for some in a magazine and bring them to school. If they don't have magazines at home, they can go to the library, find a manufactured word in a magazine, and draw a picture of the product to share with the class. They then have fun doing the following exercise.

FUN QUIZ: Match the manufactured word from the list on the left with its correct description on the right. (Composed by Marietta Cloud, Graduate Student. Western Carolina University.)

1. Cheez-Willikers	Bio-Enzyme
2. Onyums	Decaffinated coffee
3. Chipsters	Numbs the guys
4. Twigs	Maximum flight
5. Pream	Refrigerator Cold air
6. Cocoa Krispies	Oregon plus Idaho potatoes
7. Puffa Puffa Rice	Play plus school
8. Tame	Stops nail biting
9. Bugles	Horned shaped snacks
10. Ruffles	Civilizes your hair
11. Enfamil	Sanitary commode cleaner
12. Biz	Alkali plus effervescent
13. Sani-Flush	Wears forever
14. Scotkins	Gelatin dessert
15. Endust	White shortening
16. Snowdrift	Tart flavored instant drink
17. Tang	Scott napkins
18. Fasteeth	Infant milk
19. Congespirin	Potato chips
20. Lolli-Pops	Cheese flavored snacks
21. Pampers	Stops dust
22. Alka-Seltzer	Quick dry
23. Mop and Glo	Onions plus yummy
24. Borateem	Coffee cream
25. Wearever	Wipe and shine
26. Renuzit	Holds teeth fast

27. Jello	Electric dishwasher solvent
28. Jet-Dry (Water Spot Preventer)	Ridged potato chips
29. Bisquick	Puffy cereal
30. Frigidaire cold air	Pants plus diaper
31. Electra-Sol	Borax teams with detergent
32. Ore-Ida	Aspirin plus congespirin
33. Woolite	Dog biscuits
34. Playskool	Wool plus bright
35. Num-Zit	Quick biscuits
36. Stopzit	Freshens air
37. Maxfli	Crisp, chocolate flavored cereal
38. Decaf	Stick-shaped snack

Vocabulary Building in Higher Grades
Name as Many _ _ _ _ _ as You Can, Fun with Words

One way to review the words that you know is to write them. Here is one way to review them. Think about the category. Begin writing those you think of. As you write others will probably come to your mind. When you have written all that you think of, use the encyclopedia to find others to add to your list.

Name as Many Fruits As You Can

1. fruits
2. vegetables
3. kinds of fish
4. birds
5. reptiles
6. mammals
7. kinds of rocks
8. insects
9. planets
10. kinds of weather conditions
11. minerals
12. oceans
13. lakes
14. seas
15. mountains
16. islands
17. continents
18. directions
19. presidents
20. southern states
21. northern states
22. western states
23. kinds of cars
24. types of power
25. holidays
26. kinds of homes
31. units of measure
32. garden tools
33. kitchen appliances
34. carpenter tools
35. types of boats
36. types of planes
37. kinds of relatives
38. rooms of a house
39. athletic games
40. famous buildings
41. coins
42. bills
43. sewing materials
44. colors
45. shapes
46. articles of clothing for a boy
47. articles of clothing for a girl
48. musical instruments
49. communication
50. objects in this room that are made of wood
51. kinds of snakes
52. rivers
53. movie stars
54. rock singers
55. types of dances

27. trees
28. flowers
29. kinds of cloth
30. words that answer the question when

56. races of people
57. games
58. names of colleges
59. magazines
60. names of books

Vocabulary Building as a Cognitive Activity (Used with a unit on "time")

A teacher cannot teach all of the new words in any lesson. If he tried to do so, there would be little time left for anything else. Three or four words should be well taught and the others called to their attention and pronounced.

1. Words that must be known for students to understand the concepts of material they are to read.
2. Words with utility value, those which will be used many times during a life-time.
3. Words according to the students' present competency. What do they already know? What do they need? (21, 75)

Working with the words is the only way to insure permanent learning—practice or reinforcement in all kinds of situation. Try this one with your students.

Activity: MATCHING
Directions: Here are words dealing with the subject of TIME. See how many you are familiar with. Match word with meaning that could be used. The first one is done for you. Use any source materials you need.

Words	*Meanings*	*Could be used in or by*
15b epoch	1. occurring in daytime	a. Minister preaching
____annual	2. yearly	b. history lesson
____era	3. ten years	c. a poet's writing
____biennial	4. meantime, interval	d. a math lesson
____centennial	5. certain definite limits	e. music class
____century	6. accounts of daily occurrences	f. session in Congress
____decade	7. 14 days, 2 weeks	g. a writer of newspaper articles
____millenium	8. everlasting, continual	h. farmer talking of seeds
____fortnight	9. measure of time, chronological system from specific date	i. city celebrating
____eternal	10. 1000 years	j. old old lady
____interlude	11. celebration of 100 years	k. describing habits of some birds.
____interim	12. nighttime	l. getting immunization shots
____nocturnal	13. without limits	m. dentist
____diurnal	14. once every two years	n. lesson in geology
____infinite	15. period marked by distinctive series of developments	o. Bible
____journal	16. two times a year	
	17. once every 150 years	
	18. half-time	

Groups of Things

Directions: Man has many ways to categorize (group) things. It is sometimes fun to see just how many different ways we say the same things and/or how we let "usage" become accepted language. Study the following examples, then see how many different expressions of *groups of things* you can think of or find in reference books. Share with other members of the class. One class found eighty-five.

Examples: (1) herd of whales   (2) cry of hounds   (3) knot of toads
              school of whales   cry of players
              gam of whales

Other possibilities students might find:

clutch of eggs	stud of mares	gaggle of geese
nest of cottontails	litter of pups	rafter of turkeys
pride of lions	shrewdness of apes	murmuration of starlings
fall of woodcocks	herd of elephants	smack of jellyfish
exaltation of larks	outfit of sails	swarm of bees
drove of cattle	rag of colts	wedge of swans
skulk of foxes	route of wolves	knot of snobs
pod of seals	colony of ants	bevy of roebucks
troupe of dancers	trip of goats	bale of turtles
school of fish	sloth of bears	drift of hogs, etc.

Categorization as Reinforcement for Vocabulary

After you have introduced the meanings of the words dictator, malevolent, benevolent, voluntary servitude and involuntary servitude in varied interesting ways, let students work in teams or groups and categorize words and phrases from their everyday life under these headings. Only in a practical way such as this will the terms really become meaningful. If the classroom atmosphere is one of inquiry and involvement, students will do much arguing over where many of these terms go. This is where the learning takes place.

Directions: Put the following words or phrases in the columns in which they belong. Some may fit under more than one topic.

slave	Willie Mays	Do as I say, no argument.
minister	President Nixon	Love makes the world go round.
teacher	Mahatma Gandhi	Is this solution agreeable?
chief fire fighter	Hitler	Move over, Punkin'.
thief	George Meany	Shove it, Brat.
spy	Hugh Hefner	Calm down, please.
boss	tenant farmer	Shut up!
nurse	Cub Scout leader	I'll fix you!
Philanthropist	soldier	Yes sir!
You listen!	Cool Cat	Dirty Bastard.
May I stop now?	Scrub the floor.	Shoot him.

Date: Name:

Dictator	Malevolent	Voluntary Servitude	Involuntary Servitude	Benevolent

ACTIVITY: Vocabulary Puzzle

PURPOSE: Expansion of or reinforcement of vocabulary being used in class

Practice of following directions

Practice of dictionary skills in an active fun way

PROCEDURE: Choose key words you want students to know. Need manila folder and envelope.

1. List key words in numerical order down left side of sheet of paper.
2. Choose a relationship you or the class is interested in— perhaps you want to teach the concept of antonyms.
3. List an antonym for each key word and list them down the right side of your sheet of paper.
    So far, this is simply matching and too often students can guess a passable number of match items, and they may do so learning very little. To take care of this:
4. Add a third column in the center. I call mine the subject under discussion. What could they be talking about when they use the key word and/or its antonym?
5. Now you have three columns. Type them on a regular 8 x 11 sheet of paper and stick this paper to a piece of tagboard.
6. On the other side of the tagboard paste a colorful relevant picture. I usually get mine from magazines and use sports, entertainment, or animal pictures. Some subject which students can relate to.
7. When you have this neatly completed, laminate or cover the whole thing with contact paper.

8. Now you are ready to cut your puzzle apart, put it into a manila envelope and write directions for the students.
9. Directions to the students:
   a. Read all of these directions before you do anything.
   b. Take everything out of the manila folder and spread out the pieces of puzzles, word side up.
   c. Lay the manila folder open vertically on your desk.
   d. Find all words with numbers on them. These are your key words and your first column. Lay them numerically from 0 to 21 down the left side of the right side of your open manila folder.
   e. Now have fun finding and placing related words in their proper spaces. The first one is done for you. To add more fun and challenge, see how many you can do without help, and when you have found all that you or your group can find, use the dictionary.
   f. When you think you have all the terms matched up correctly, close the left side of the manila folder over the puzzle. Very carefully, using four hands, or put folder in a book and close it, turn the folder over. Open it up.
   g. If you have correctly placed your words, your picture will be perfect. Were there any words out of place? Why? Could any words fit in two places correctly?

Some of you might argue that junior high and secondary students don't need this kind of play. I would suggest that you try it just one time with any level of student. Make your words to fit the students. I can almost promise that even you will enjoy it.

The following is a list of terms I used with my college students. They enjoyed the activity and learned some new words.

KEY WORDS	SUBJECT UNDER DISCUSSION	RELATED WORD
EXAMPLE: HOT	WEATHER	COLD
1. SWEET	LEMONADE	SOUR
2. AVERAGE	MATHEMATICS	PERCENTAGE
3. LOVE	EMOTIONS	HATE
4. DEMOCRACY	GOVERNMENTS	COMMUNISM
5. POLYGAMY	MARRIAGE	MONOGAMY
6. TAIL	FISH OR BIRD	LORE
7. DULCET	MUSIC	MELODIOUS
8. RUDDY	EMBERS	SLUMBERING
9. DIABOLICAL	CHARACTERISTICS OF A FRIEND	SAINTLY
10. SPORTSMANSHIP	CONTESTANTS	FOUL PLAY
11. ENIGMA	LAWS	LUCID
12. CARNIVOROUS	EATING HABITS	HERBIVOROUS

13.	EXPERTISE	LIFE	CLUMSINESS
14.	MALEDICTION	PRONOUNCED ON SOMEONE	BENEDICTION
15.	METROPOLIS	LIVING AREAS	RURAL
16.	AVIAN	BIRDS	AVICULTURE
17.	SESQUIPEDALIAN	A MAN	ILLITERATE
18.	COVERT	GOVERNMENT PAPERS	PUBLIC
19.	ODONTOLOGY	TEETH	ORTHODONTIST
20.	MELLIFLUOUS	CONVERSATION	SARCASTIC
21.	COGNITION	READING	DECODING

SUMMARY

The problem with vocabulary is not that students do not know enough words, but rather, for a number of reasons, they do not *use* them.

No one method of teaching, reinforcing, or expanding vocabulary should be used exclusively. All methods need the constant reinforcement of daily use such as a good teacher should provide in daily teaching. A model speaking vocabulary used by the teacher, enthusiasm about new words and ideas, good rapport and dialogue exchange in the classroom, new words placed in conspicious places about the room, free reading time with students' choices, student involvement in choosing words he wants to learn, and teacher's conscious and habitual referral to the dictionary or thesaurus—these are boons to improving the atmosphere for and the willingness of students to build vocabulary.

The main goal in teaching students to be word conscious is that they become users of words, that they look for them, that they enjoy finding new ways of expressing themselves. If teachers are on the job, students will acquire discipline and habit in learning about and using words and will do so willingly.

Activities for the Teacher

1. Choose five new words from the materials your students are working with. Decide upon the most interesting way to teach and reinforce these terms. Teach them tomorrow and report the results to your peers.
2. Have a committee of your top students find the etymology of some interesting words. They might want to teach one to the class.
3. Plan a series of five lessons on teaching and/or extending vocabulary as concepts for one group of students you're working with. Share them with your peers.
4. Let your students do one of the lessons given at the end of this chapter. What were the results?
5. See if you can come up with other ways of teaching vocabulary not mentioned here. Share them with your peers.
6. Did you see or hear a new word today? What did you do about it?
7. Find four new words in your reading and decide which strategy mentioned in this chapter would be most appropriate for teaching them. Do your peers agree with your choice?

FIVE

Dynamic Ways to Extend Vocabulary into Comprehensive Reading

TO THE TEACHER:

> *Directions:* Read the following paragraph and discuss it with your group. Decide upon the main idea. You have five minutes.

> You may be floccipaucinihilipilificating an exercise such as this one, but it can be compurgation to a premise I wish to comprobate. Many students in our classes are like a cyprinoid lost in a labyrinth of cyprinoids, impeccably capricious and won't adjudicate a transformation without a hegemonical febrifuge applied with cognition.

1. Did you get the point?
2. What are the key words?
3. Are they in your vocabulary? What happens to comprehension when vocabulary is too difficult?
4. Did you have to know all the words to get the main idea?
5. How could you apply the answers to this exercise to your classroom teaching?

The paragraph above is the way much textbook material looks to the students in your classes. Yet without any preteaching, you assign the material, expecting students to comply with instructions which usually amount to nothing. Be able to answer questions tomorrow and these questions usually turn out to be literal and either right or wrong type answers. And all of this on material which is irrelevant, and which they see as a waste of time.

Chip, an intelligent sixteen-year-old boy, ready to drop out of school, began to drink. He usually came to school sleepy, spent much time "smarting off," was apathetic about his work, and, in general, acted as a nuisance to his teachers.

One day I asked him to come by my office for a conference. During the chat I asked if he'd take an I.Q. test for me. He shrugged his shoulders. It mattered little to him one way or another.

"If you want to know can I do the dumb work teachers assign, I can tell you I could."

"Oh, I already know you can. I'm just curious to see how high you'd really score," I told him.

"Why do you care? No one else does."

"Not even Chip?" I asked.

Chip's mother had died a few years earlier. His father, lonely himself, usually had several drinks on his way home from work and had little patience with his children or their problems.

Added to this, Chip and his best girl had just broken up.

During the conversation Chip made this bitter statement. "Miss Mac, when I walk down the street, not a living soul knows or cares. Nobody gives a _____ whether I'm dead or alive."

It was difficult to convince this young man that he was useful. His I.Q. score—135. Yet his grades were D's and F's.

Changes in education! Changes in human nature, in society, in cultures. The past twenty years have seen a revolution in each. Yet, they haven't helped many of the Chips of our school society.

QUESTIONS: 1. What can we do about the Chips in our schools?
2. What are some causes of lack of comprehension?
3. Are causes of comprehension linked to our techniques of teaching?
4. What are some necessary ingredients, some skills, some activities which will lead to more interest and better understanding of materials used in classrooms?

Comprehension: A Skill to Be Taught

By the end of the first week of school, most of you usually find at least one student who baffles you. Suzy is a good reader, but she doesn't know a thing she's read. What is the matter with her?

A good reader? No, a word caller. Here are some of the main causes of lack of comprehension when reading:

1. No books at home.
2. Not enough books at school.
3. Failure to concentrate, not paying attention, too easily distracted.
4. Lack of vocabulary—no experience background, too much technical vocabulary, level of matetrial too high for child, and poor teaching methods of prior teachers.
5. Poor health and poor eyes and eye movements.
6. Failure to connect words into units and units into thoughts.
7. Finger pointing and word-by-word calling.
8. Timidity.
9. Carelessness.

10. Inability to vary speed for different materials, reads too slow or too fast.
11. Inability to spot key words and sentences, can't tell important from unimportant.
12. Too many teachers have required only recall-type information.
13. Attempts to memorize author's words rather than paraphrasing.
14. Boredom—materials uninteresting and irrelevant.
15. Failure to appreciate and interpret.
16. Inability to associate materials to ideas they already have.
17. Lack of maturity and/or low I.Q.
18. Poor self-concept, "I can't."
19. Too many activities, never any time to read.
20. Wrong kind of teaching or reading—skip and guess, no purpose.
21. Doesn't understand how to do thinking involved in certain kinds of reading or questions on the reading (main idea, inference, and so on).
22. Has difficulty responding in mode and method required (oral, kinesthetic, answer sheets, and so on).

What Can Be Done about this Lack of Comprehension?

Books have been and could be written on each of these twenty-two listed causes for lack of comprehension. Obviously, the teacher does not have control over all of them, but many of them you can eliminate. How?

1. First and most important, give students time to read. If it is important enough to do, it is important enough to use school time. A teacher of piano or tennis teaches a half-hour lesson and admonishes the student to practice ten hours before next week. What does the classroom teacher do? Talk or test for ten hours and let them read a half hour.

2. In close second place would come the practice of assigning the next six pages in a given textbook. A student with comprehension problems in the seventh grade probably can't read material in his textbook. The obvious advice is to get rid of it. Find easier interesting materials on the same topic.

3. Have student read short sections, close the book, and tell you what he read. One time won't be sufficient. If he says I don't know, try again. It may require many times. This one-to-one help is the best to use with low-concept, timid students who sit in the background because they are poor readers.

4. Ask leading questions. Have students look for answers in text, then read.

5. Teach vocabulary. This one can't be stressed too much. Telling a student to look up words in the dictionary, words which are explained by other words she doesn't know, is foolish.

6. Use commercially made kits, easy yet interesting materials.

7. Use teacher-made materials. When you find a student with a particular need, structure some exercises just for him. He is unique.

8. Readiness. Everyone recognizes the fact that first graders sometimes need readiness work before certain academic tasks are given them. Why is it so hard to convince people that upper-grade students need it just as badly? A student who doesn't understand the concepts presented in the materials will not understand the materials. Build background with either concrete or vicarious means.

9. Let the student pretend he or she is the author or one of the characters. Would he have written or acted as they did? Why? Why not?

10. Teach students that speed of reading depends upon their general background, knowledge, and purpose for reading. They should read differently for study, fun, to find out a fact, or to prove a point.

11. Have them say the same things in different ways. Show anger, love, fear, disbelief, or happiness.

12. Make use of the library and free reading on their own interests. A student interested in insects will read about them. But give a boy a book on insects when he's seeing jets in his mind, and you'll lose again. Concentration is more apt to be self-controlled if the student is interested.

13. Be sure they know a few basic word attack skills. If not, teach them.

14. Also, give direct help and practice exercises with the comprehension skills, if needed.

15. Give students more time to react, to talk about what they read. They shouldn't be tested on everything they do. Dull book reports may impede progress.

16. Insist upon their paraphrasing or summarizing when answering questions. Many teachers have fostered bad habits and lack of understanding by accepting (sometimes demanding) memorized word-for-word answers from books.

17. One of the most often repeated complaints about school is the monotony (sameness) of teacher assignments. Students are "turned off" before they begin. If the teacher stays in the same school and the same grade for years, parents will tell their children what they'll be doing in her room. You've seen it. So have I.

Approaches to Vary the Reading Assignments

Lesson I.   Jobcards in Centers

Directions: Read the story silently. Do not call words. Try to improve your speed by making your eyes travel over several words at a time. Try to understand what you read. After reading your story silently, use pencil and paper and work on some of the following exercises. You may go back to the story if you need to.

Purpose: a. To help you find out whether or not you know what you read.
  b. To help you extend your thinking about the events in the story.
  c. If you try to do the tasks without looking back at your book, you will be practicing the skill of recall.

1. Make a list of the characters in the story.
2. Beside each character, write one good picture word to describe him.
3. What did the character do in the story?
4. What happened as a result of what each character did?
5. Did any character have a problem? If so, what was it and how did he handle it? Would you have acted as he did?
6. List some words which you did not know. Copy the sentence from the story where you find the words, then redo the sentences using synonyms for the hard words.

7. Do some transformations on these sentences.
8. Pantomime the most exciting paragraph in the story and let the group guess what you are trying to tell them.
9. Write a different ending to the story.
10. Write the story into a play and direct the acting of it.
11. Rewrite the story as a cowboy would tell it.
12. Find pictures from magazines and make a slide presentation of the story to present to the class.
13. Rewrite the story putting it into another time era in history. Would the characters dress, act, and talk any differently? (Use reference books and make it authentic.)
14. Pick out the most exciting paragraph in the story and prepare to read it orally to the group.

Lesson II.   Directed Lesson: Key Words Lead To Ideas

We began this book with the assumption that efficient reading is necessary and that a definition of efficiency in reading is getting the most with the least effort in the shortest amount of time. If this is true, then *how to* becomes very important.

Step 1. Like all learning, reading is developmental. It is sequential in that it builds one step or understanding upon another. Look at this sentence:
"Procrastination is a most formidable enemy."
Is it easy to understand? What are the key words? If a student knows the vocabulary, he's in business. Now, look at the next sentence:
"Of all enemies known to mankind, it has been said by some of our most renowned scholars, those who have not been guilty of the deed, that procrastination is the most formidable."
What is the difference in the two sentences? What do the students have to know and do in the second one that they didn't need to do in the first one? Do these kinds of exercises with them. Show them the processes involved.

Step 2. When they understand one sentence and its parts, give two sentences and do the same kind of thing:
"The butcher looked down the aisle of his open air market. All morning it had been empty. People were intent on cutting inflation."
What are the key words? Do they lead to the main thought? Is there any problem here?

Step 3. Just as a sentence has key words, most paragraphs have a key sentence, sometimes called the topic sentence. It tells what the paragraph is about and other sentences are details of when, where, what kind, and so on. The key thought of a paragraph may be found in most any location in the paragraph. It may be in (1) the first sentence, (2) the last sentence, (3) the middle sentence, (4) first half of a sentence, (5) last half of a sentence, (6) two places in the paragraph, (7) two sentences together, (8) anywhere within the paragraph, or (9) nowhere within the paragraph.

Titles, headlines, and subheadings are often clues to the main thought. Turn them into questions which the paragraphs will answer. This, incidentally, is one of the best ways to teach the skill of summarizing. Always insist that students answer questions in their own words.

There are three clues to finding a key sentence or idea:

1. Look for a general overall thought.
2. Ask: Do other sentences support that thought?
3. Can you categorize the details? They must be alike in some way.

Step 4. If you are dealing with the skill of key words or sentences in the reading session, then carry the skill through each subject all day long. Find key words or main thoughts in social studies, science, civics, and math problems. Only in this way will the skill be transferred from reading class to other areas and become habit.

Example: In literature.

When Denny was fifteen years old, he went to the Far East with his father and mother. While there, they traveled through many little-known parts of the country in the quest for relics of bygone days. Many places they visited were very wild, and Denny had exciting times. Then four years after he returned to the States, he was drafted into the armed services to serve in a war in Vietnam. He was captured and imprisoned for nearly three years. During his youth Denny had many interesting and sometimes dangerous adventures both at home and in foreign lands.

a. What is the topic sentence?
b. What is the main idea?
c. In this paragraph are they the same?
d. Is this always true?

(See chapter 10 for main ideas in other subject matter.)

Lesson III.   Character Building Words for Successful Living

Purpose: To enrich vocabulary into comprehensive reading and writing.
To teach the meaning behind abstract terms by thinking and action.
To implant character building words in students' minds.
To create a chain reaction of good relations among students, at least for a brief time.

Materials Needed: Directions for the activities, newspapers and other patrons who will cooperate, this list of words.

Word List: (The future of the world depends on how well we understand ourselves and how well we get along with other people. These words are the ones which made America great but many of them seem to be in disrepute today.)

1. belief (in God and country)
2. honesty
3. sincerity

14. enthusiasm
15. humility
16. loyalty

4. perseverance	17. justice
5. respect	18. good health habits
6. self-reliance	19. graciousness
7. thrift	20. patience
8. tact	21. thoughtfulness
9. knowledge	22. attentiveness
10. sacrifice	23. ambition
11. congeniality	24. imagination
12. industriousness	25. forgiveness
13. alertness	26. confidence

Procedure: For one week the teacher and students talk about the meaning of one of the above qualities. Then, in class, on Friday the students write an essay of one page or less on the word of the week. The teacher will select three papers to be read to the class and the class votes which of the three is best, thus giving the entire class an opportunity to become better acquainted with the meaning of the virtue.

Additional Activities:
1. A panel of judges pick a school winner and get local newspapers to cooperate by publishing one or two essays per week.
2. Have students look for person in history who portrayed the quality.
3. Present winners to school assembly or P.T.A. Let them read papers.
4. Students, teachers, and other school employees watch for the practice of the quality in others and report it.
5. Invite a public relations person from some company to make a speech to students telling how these qualities lead toward leadership positions.
6. Role-play and let others guess the quality being portrayed.
7. Ask students to honestly practice the week's quality word for one whole day and record the results. This could be very interesting and inspiring.
8. Read a book or story depicting one of these characteristics. Discuss only if students desire to do so.

Lesson IV.   Vocabulary Patterns as an Indication of Usage Level

Objectives:
To study, compare, and contrast vocabulary patterns at the different levels of usage.
To arouse interest and provide enjoyment in the study of vocabulary.
To build the concept that understanding of and communications with those different from us can be accommodated by the study of usage levels.

Activities: These activities could be used to advantage with senior high students. You may have to adapt or change the terms to fit the particular situation or grade level of the students you're working with.

A. *Directions:* Translate these sentences into your own words and decide whether you think they are slang, illiterate, shoptalk, or dialectical expressions. Work alone until you decide what you will do with the exercises, then discuss them with the other members of your group or class.

1. He ain't high; he's straight.
2. This book is hurn; themuns use that'nt.
3. I heered my pa and ma bitching. Pa sed me and John can't play with white chilun no mow. Ma sed we could and no one wuz gonna stop us.
4. They said the jury wuz fixed.

B. *Directions*: Translate the following sentences. Draw a line under words that you would probably classify as formal. Would they be more desirable in another context? Use a dictionary or other source if you need to.

1. People in a hurry cannot cogitate, cannot incrassate, nor can they coarctate. They are preserved in a state of perpetual puerility.
2. The lucubration on antiquated language leads to flexibility and perspicuity in some speech patterns.
3. Fluorosis is a specific type of enamel hypoplasia caused by ingestion of fluorine and occurs endemically in certain areas.
4. An adilepated beetlehead and his specie divaricate with startling prematurity.

C. *Directions*: Label the following words as usually formal, informal, or vulgate (F, I, V), noting words that overlap two categories.

_____you'ans	_____eradicating	_____hillbilly
_____gotta	_____flinch	_____perpetual
_____decades	_____pipsqueak	_____flophouse
_____protocol	_____antiquated	_____befuddled

D. *Directions:* Give a formal term to fit each of the following definitions:

1. a person very intelligent
2. something easily heard
3. extremely generous; poundfoolish
4. to build completely; to erect
5. to jeer at; insulting remark
6. skinniness
7. inclined to doubt; not believing easily
8. to save frugally; to hoard
9. to lose control completely; to be angry
10. something perfect or healthy

E. *Directions*: Use formal and vulgate synonyms for the following:

persons from the mountains   _____   _____
to compromise   _____   _____
doctor for feet   _____   _____
a piece of furniture   _____   _____
unappetizing   _____   _____

F. *Directions:* From the preceding exercises, choose five words which you want to remember. Use them in sentences.

Lesson V.   Bullfighting and Comprehension

Don't always hide the questions from students. Before they read, let them know some things they can look for. This aids comprehension. Here are some questions which could be used with the following story on bullfighting and given to the students before they begin to read.

1. You will be reading to get the meaning for you of this article. As you read, try to see what the author is trying to say as he tells the story.
2. From the tone of the first two paragraphs, whom do you think is talking?
3. How far do you need to read before you really know what the story is about?
4. Does this delay bother you?
5. Does the writer enjoy bullfights?
6. Is the title appropriate? Defend your answer.
7. Is the sport of bullfighting humane? Defend your answer.
8. When watching the sport, are humans rational or irrational?
9. Summarize in one or two statements the meaning of this article.
10. Make a list of the five senses and categorize words and phrases from the story under each.

	Examples:	hearing	— thunder of gigantic engines
		seeing	— waving a red flag
		feeling	— searing hot pain
		touching	— rib-to-rib
		smelling	— wet manure bed

11. Can you think of another sport where animals are used and write a story from the animal's point of view? How might we humans appear to your animal friend? (Cock fights, horse racing, dog sleds.)

CIVILIZATION STRIKES AGAIN *

The day had been miserable. From morning on, nothing had gone right—nothing at all. Sometimes, when a day starts badly, it gets better as it goes along. This one went from bad to worse. And now evening promised to be worst of all.

The barrage of human voices filled the air around me, over me, through me, permeating my whole being with dread. What were they doing to my brothers out there? The atmosphere was one of disaster.

It had begun even before the sun lighted the eastern sky. We were rudely awakened by sharp instruments jabbing at our sides, angry humans swearing at each other, and lashing ropes whistling through the air herding us uncermoniously into an evil-smelling, manure-caked truck bed. When we were packed rib-to-rib, a tailgate was locked in place. There was no escape.

---

* Source: Unpublished article by Virgie M. McIntyre, 1976.

As the moving vans screeched to life, the thunder of the gigantic engines blasted our ears and the smoke from the exhaust stung our eyes. After a series of convulsive spurts and jerks which were enough to rip our bodies from the leg sockets, and the trucks progressed crab-like down the driveway, we began a jolting giddy-paced journey across the hot countryside.

The temperature soared to ninety degrees. Perspiration on our bodies formed droplets, slithered to the floor, and wet the manure bed. Only by being so closely packed were we able to keep standing.

Finally, around midday, we halted. The tailgate lowered with a bang and on trembling legs so weak we could hardly stand, we were goaded to descend into a pen. What a relief! Perhaps now we could have food and water. With no interest in us, animals in an adjoining lot munched on unappetizing dry straw. Since we had had neither food nor water all day, even that looked good to us. We bellowed in a rage.

Some young human cocks strutted around and examined us.

"You bellow, old boy. Paw that ground. Really get angry. You'll give 'em a good show today." Raucous laughter followed these words.

Occasionally some one of them would throw back his head and whoop. "I'll get you on the first thrust," one bragged as he punched me with a sharp implement which sent a shivering pain through my rump. How I hated them! I lay down on the ground to rest. A gnawing thirst and hunger brought discomfort, but from sheer exhaustion I must have slept, for the next thing I knew, one of my neighbors snorted as he was driven from the pen.

Trumpet blasts followed by murderous shrieks rent the air. My empty stomach retched in fear, but nothing came up.

Shadows lengthened until at last I had a shade. What a relief from the Mexican sun! But not for long.

"Your turn, old boy. Get up from there." Before I could stand, he jabbed me with a thorn-like bar. I flung my head in retort.

He laughed and guided me up an incline toward a gate. On each side of the gate were humans who started punching my sides with sharp stinging spurs. I tried to back away from the pain they were inflicting, but the path was obstructed. I could do nothing. Moment by moment I got angrier. What did they want of me?

The reverberations of shouting filled me with fear. My legs trembled and my head pounded furiously. What was happening out there? How could I escape? I rammed my horns against the sides of the enclosure.

"He's ready," they shouted, and I felt a searing hot pain in my shoulder. The gate in front of me opened. Trying to shake off the piercing instrument clinging to my skin, I projected my body through a narrow passageway out into the open arena.

"Olé," the crowd shouted. First on one side and then the other, humans came at me waving flags. I tried to stop them, but they were too fast for me. The roaring in my ears increased and two huge blindfolded horses, ridden by gaily colored picadores, rode into the ring toward me. This was the worst. I took careful aim and, like a bullet, dashed into the side of one of the horses. My horns only skidded on the soft padding. I moved back for a new attack. Just as I thought I had a good chance, with a death-defying force, a long sharp lance penetrated my shoulder and twisted, twisted, twisted. Oh, the torture of it! The powerful thrust stopped me and the horses pranced off leaving me with rich life blood pouring down my sides.

How the humans shouted. Before I had time to catch my breath, two additional humans (banderilleros) entered the ring. They were carrying a pair of darts adorned with bright-colored streamers. One of them stood taunting me. By now, I was so angry,

I didn't use good sense. I lunged at him and the darts landed in my shoulders. Determined to avenge my torture, I sprang at the other menace. My eyes must have been playing tricks on me. Two more missiles pierced into my aching shoulders.

Gasping for air, frothing in exhaustion, shaking in anger and pain, I watched helplessly while to the thunder of applause, my two tormentors strutted off the field. When the hullaballoo subsided, another human, the most cocky of all, came toward me. I considered ignoring him until he started waving a red flag at me. Would this never end?

I made a series of passes, only to be derided by the shouts of "Olé." Just when I thought I'd figured his next move and could take him, the matador plunged a sword into my body, forcing me in my weakened condition to kneel to the ground. The crowd went wild. Was this what they wanted of me? To see me on my knees? Well, not yet. With a super effort, I raised up again to be met by flying objects on both sides of me. With my breath coming in gasps, my heart aching with its lessening supply of blood, and my eyes unseeing, I tried to decide which one to go after. Without making a decision I felt myself going around, and around, and around, then down. Somewhere in my head something snapped. In relief, I closed my eyes.

The last thing I heard was the explosion of human screams. Human?

Our premise is to let school and what happens there enhance the understanding of life as students live it. This means process, not memorization of content. Use essays to get at process rather than content, yet be aware that a student must have enough facts (what) before he or she can think (how).

Process means evaluating the evidence, accepting or rejecting, thinking for self rather than always memorizing a teacher's lecture, integrating new material with what is already known, and knowing what is important and unimportant. Free discussion in group work, experimenting, searching, throwing out: these lead to more comprehensive reading for most students.

THE GLORY OF GREECE[22]

In this activity, students are assigned parts and actually become that character for a week. In the classroom they wear the costume, they wear a card labeled with the Greek name, and other students call them by their Greek name. They find out all they can about the character they portray and attempt to act and react as he would. Culmination of the week is giving the play. This is much more learning and rewarding than memorizing answers for some teacher's literal questions.

Characters:	Actors:
Announcer	Ricky
Pericles	Ronnie
Phidias	Dennissa
Zeus	Ricky
Athena	Susan
Xerxes	Kathy
Spartan	David
Trojan	Kim

Homer	Calvin
Solon	Ricky
Pisistratus	Gary
Cleisthenes	Darris
Socrates	Jan
Plato	Mike
Aristotle	Tim
Epicurus	Suzanna
Zeno	Mark
Alexander	Mark
Herodotus	Ricky
Thucydides	Mike
Hippocrates	Janice
Archimedes	Carroll
Phythagoras	Thea
Euclid	Karen
Aeschylus	Jerry
Sophocles	Kay
Euripides	Marchetta
Aristophanes	Martha
Closing Announcer	Greg

Announcer:	Today we will meet some famous people of Greece whose accomplishments form the basis for many of today's achievements. The setting is the Parthenon, a temple built in honor of the goddess Athena on top of the hill known as the acropolis in the center of the city-state of Athens.
Pericles:	What a marvel, Phidias! You have created a statue truly worthy of the goddess Athena. Now she will forever smile on Athens as she has done in the past.
Phidias:	Yes, this is my greatest creation. May it be worthy of your great building. The Parthenon will always stand as a monument of the greatness of the Greek people. Look at all the people who come to view its splendor.
Zeus:	Good citizens, I, Zeus, king of the Gods wish to express pride in your accomplishments. You have excelled above all men in architecture, sculpture, drama, philosophy, military might and government. The statue of Athena is as beautiful and majestic as the goddess herself. I shall summon her to fill the marble form you have made of her. Athena, awaken and speak!
Athena:	My beloved Athenians, my heart soars like the wings of an eagle with the glory you have bestowed on me. May all men speak of your great deeds for all times.
Xerxes:	Goddess Athena! I am Xerxes, king of the Persians. I have been defeated and driven from Greece by the might of her warriors. Still, I would like to hear of these deeds in other fields of which you and Zeus boast so nobly.
Spartan:	Athena, I am but a soldier and citizen of Sparta, neighbor of Athens. Pray tell why you and Zeus bless Athens and say nothing of the military accomplishments of Sparta?

Trojan:	Athena, I am a Trojan. No nobler race walks the face of the Earth. I, too, wish to see evidence of the superiority of Athens. Show me so that I can share this knowledge with my countrymen.
Athena:	Worthy subjects, you have heard the cries of those who doubt you. Speak before me now that all men may know and remember your great deeds. Homer, lead the procession.
Homer:	I am Homer: Though blind I may be, I have spent my life traveling, recounting the adventures of the Mycenaeans and how they were so cunning in building a wooden horse to carry these early Greeks inside the gates of Troy. Further, I have spoken of the most courageous of Mycenaeans, Ulyssess, and his wonderings after the fall of Troy.
Solon:	I am Solon. Though tyrant I may be called, I created the Council of 400 which involved more people directly in government. I encouraged trade, and offered citizenship to worthy craftsmen who would settle in Athens and enhance the glory of our city.
Pisistratus:	Goddess of knowledge and wisdom, although I seized Solon's power by the blood of the sword, I continued down the path that he had begun. I also stimulated trade. I redistributed the land and property of the nobles among the poor and landless.
Cleisthenes:	Let me speak of the growth of democracy. I, Cleisthenes, enlarged our number of tribes from four to ten and our Council from 400 to 500, thus, insuring more participation in government. More importantly, I introduced ostracism whereby our citizens could banish officials whom they felt to be dangerous to the Athenian state.
Athena:	True, Cleisthenes, you, Pisistratus and Solon have lead us towards a system of pure or direct democracy which heretofore has not been known to the minds of man. Let men of every time be aware of the ability of the Athenians to rule themselves. Continue the report.
Socrates:	Noble Athena, I am Socrates who has devoted my life to a search for truth. In this search nothing is sacred. Practices of all kinds should be questioned. My teaching of this offends the state and it appears I shall be sentenced to death by drinking the poison hemlock. I shall await my fate calmly. All men must obey the laws of the state.
Plato:	I am Plato, student of Socrates. Man should do the work for which he is best fitted. There should be three classes of people: the workers to produce the necessities of life, the soldiers to guard the state, and the philosophers to rule the interests of all. Private property should be abolished and education designed for the benefit of all. My work is the first attempt of man to devise a planned society.
Aristotle:	Now, hear me, oh mighty Athena. I am Aristotle, student of Plato. My work covers the fields of biology, astronomy, physics, ethics, politics and logic. It is desirable for all men to strike a balance between rash action and inactivity; to live between two extremes by following the Doctrine of the Mean. The best way to meet danger is through courageous action, which is the mean between foolhardiness and cowardice.

Epicurus: I am Epicurus of Samos who used the ideas of Aristotle in forming a philosophy. A temperate life is best for reducing pain and increasing pleasure. Mental activity is the way of gaining inner peace.

Zeno: Hear me, Athena, most beautiful of the Gods! I am Zeno of Cyprus who developed the system of Stoicism. True happiness can be achieved by man when he finds his proper place in nature. Because all nature is good, man must accept poverty, disease, or even death as the will of the God. Thus, man must be indifferent toward all kinds of experience whether good or bad.

Alexander: Oh, princess of the Gods, allow me to speak because my time is short. Permit me to talk of days gone by. It was I, the young Macedonian king, who admired Hellenic civilization, whose heart burned to preserve its greatness and who was determined to spread it to the ends of the world. Though my military exploits led me as far as the Indus River, my greatest pride was my concept of "one world." I envisioned a blend of Greek and Persian culture with the Greek language and Greek law as unifying bonds. I wished to form a cohesive world government in which all men were brothers. I hope my attempts will be considered a worthy contribution.

Athena: Yes, Alexander, your cause has indeed been worthy. May all men remember your name alongside the word "great." I shall always remember you as Alexander, the Great.

Herodotus: Athena, I, too, shall long remember the exploits of the Great Alexander. Other parts of our history will be remembered also for I have given my life to writing a narrative of past events. I call my masterpiece the *History of the Persian Wars*. For its creation I have been called the "father of history." May my work be worthy of the glory of Greece.

Thucydides: And dear Athena, hear me now for I followed the footsteps of Herodotus. Though I was driven into exile, I used my banishment to write a *History of the Peloponnesian War*. From my former service as a general in the Athenian Army, I had come to believe that human events could be explained by fate or by the acts of the gods, and I searched for the human causes of the Greek Wars. In my writing I included relevant material to the narrative. I weighed evidence carefully and admitted no facts unless I was sure of their correctness. May it be worthy.

Athena: Your work will long stand, Thucydides, as a record of our past and as a model for historians of all future times.

Hippocrates: Athena, I have had little to do with politics, military victories, the writing of history or works of philosophy and logic. I am one of the first to believe that every disease has a natural cause. I have founded the world's first medical school where diagnosis and treatment is based on observation and healing practices. My work has helped strip away superstitions and belief in magic which has hampered the study of disease. I have drawn up a code of ethical conduct by which all doctors must abide. May my contribution be remembered in the story of our civilization.

Athena: Your work will save untold lives in all future times. As long as there will be doctors, your oath will be spoken on the lips of men and your ideas will live in their minds. Speak to me now, noble Greeks, of your other work in science.

Archimedes: Then hear me speak, mighty Athena, and judge my deeds. I am Archimedes of Syracuse. I have calculated a way for measuring the circumference of a circle. I have discovered the principle whereby if a body is immersed in a liquid, it is buoyed up by a force equal to the weight of the liquid displaced.

Phythagoras: Goddess Athena, I too have formulated a principle in natural science which bears my name. The principle finds the length of a hypotenuse in any right triangle when the base and the height are known. This principle can be used by craftsmen in making wondrous buildings such as the Parthenon.

Euclid: Oh, noble Athena, I also have worked in the natural sciences. I have been called "the father of geometry" for my textbook called *The Elements*. Another Alexanderian scientist, Aristarchus discovered that the earth rotated and revolved around the sun. Erathosthenes has estimated the circumference of the earth and drawn in a series of lines which he calls the "latitude" and "longitude." May our knowledge in science live with and be used by all men.

Athena: The day will come when man will depend on science to unlock the secrets of the universe. You have made a worthy start. The work of the Greeks has now left us time for pleasure. Speak now of what you have done to entertain yourselves.

Aeschylus: Hear me then, Goddess Athena. I am Aeschylus who has excelled in writing tragic drama. This form of entertainment was an outgrowth of religious rites held at the festivals honoring the god of wine, Dionysus. A chorus of men chanted hymns in praise of the god and accompanied the songs with stately dances. In the sixth century B.C., changes were made in the performances which led to the development of the drama.

Sophocles: Goddess Athena, I am Sophocles, another tragic dramatist. Allow me to continue the story. Individual actors were separated from the chorus and given roles to enact, and dialogue was introduced. Of greatest significance was the use of new themes based on heroic legends not related to worship of Dionysus. Continue our tale, Euripides.

Euripides: Poetic language was considered the proper mode of expression; the chorus remained a basic part of play, commenting on the action as it unfolded; and both masculine and feminine roles were played by men. Most important, tragedy dealt with serious matters—man's destiny and the problems of good and evil.

Aristophanes: Athena, you have heard from three tragic dramatists. Allow me to speak of another form which I call "comedy." No libel law protects the Athenians and important citizens can be held up to ridicule in my plays. Let me speak also of the theater of Dionysus. It is located on the open air slopes of the Acropolis and can seat fourteen thousand spectators. Our actors wear thick-soled sandals

	to increase their height and carry painted masks depicting grief, honor and the other strong emotions portrayed.
Athena:	Let all men recognize that the Greeks stand head and shoulders above other men of the world. So much of our civilization will serve as a standard for all future men that it shall forever be known as "classical."
Phidias:	Look. Athena has returned to stone.
Pericles:	Yes, but she shall forever be known as defender of Athens and goddess of knowledge and wisdom.
Closing Announcer:	In the play you have just seen the glory of Greece. You have heard the voices of men who lived 2,500 years ago. We still recognize their contributions today. Indeed, many people today consider the Greek civilization to be the greatest that has ever existed. A college professor once said that everything that has been accomplished since the time of Plato is simply a footnote. An incredible statement, but then the Greeks were incredible people. We hope that you have enjoyed our play.

Study Guide for Building Comprehension in Literature

Our source is *Winter Thunder*, by Mari Sandoz, from *Insights: Themes in Literature* (McGraw-Hill, 1967), p. 357–76. Motivation and Readiness for the reading of the story is up to the individual teacher. Only you know what will work with your group.

You will probably need to preteach some vocabulary. These words will give some students trouble. Preteach about five and simply list and pronounce the others.

precariously	suppurate	segmented
discernible	aggrogance	incomprehensible
obliterated	derision	adversary
discomfiture	ominous	admonitary

Activity I.   Seeing Relationships: Categorizing

Directions: Below are terms used in the story *Winter Thunder*. Choose the ones you think best fit the listed characters. One or more of these characteristics may fit more than one character. If so, list it under both.

crippled	thinks only of self
prim	arrogant
self-centered	unable to face reality
poorly-dressed	probably pampered at home
spoiled	generous
sharp-eyed	thoughtful of others
rebellious	brave beyond her years
withdrawn	physical condition affected personality

too polite	changed from beginning to end of story
skeleton-thin	self-centered

Characters: Chuck   Maggie   Bill   Olive

Activity II.   Skimming for Information

Directions: Find the sentence which contains the following phrases and tell what is being described.

Purpose: Skimming helps to speed reading. Look only for information needed. Skip the other.

1. Page 357: snowy bewildered bug _____
2. Page 359: long snowy winter-logged animal _____
3. Page 367: the color of a wild yellow canary _____
4. Page 375: hovering like a brownish dragonfly _____
5. Page 367: puffed up and dark as jelly beans _____
6. Page 362: snowy visibility _____

(Note: for average or above students, don't list page number)

Activity III.   Sequence: Seeing Patterns in Writing

Directions: Seeing the pattern in a story or article helps to remember it. The following events happened in the story. Put them in the proper sequence (order). Number from one to ten, one being the first action in the story.

_____ A. Bill comforts his little sister.
_____ B. After eight days, planes rescue the group.
_____ C. Chuck's feet slide off into a hole and he pulls the whole queue after him.
_____ D. The group built a shelter in the willows.
_____ E. The teacher remembers her grandfather's advice.
_____ F. On the third night the children were sick. Lecia broke their fever with willow bark tea.
_____ G. Lecia and Chuck tie the group together so they won't get lost.
_____ H. The bus burns.
_____ I. Chuck walks out to leave but returns with good news. He has discovered a frozen animal.
_____ J. The teacher realized that Maggie had insufficient clothing.

Activity IV.   Abstract Terms

Directions: Often times you are unable to express what you mean. Two categories of words come to your rescue if you know them. These two categories are concrete and abstract terms. Concrete terms are easy—something you can touch, see, or feel. Material things.

Abstract terms are more difficult. You can't put your hand on them—things like love, hate, or fear.

Below are some abstract terms which could be used to describe situations in the story. Use the text, a dictionary, or discussion with your partners and find a definition for each one. Illustrate the term with a situation from the story.

loneliness	courage	isolation
frustration	love	bravery
fear	dignity	rebellion
sympathy	hate	
anxiety	impending danger	

After you have found an incident in the story to illustrate each of these abstract terms, think about times in your own life when you have felt each one. In two or three sentences, describe the situation and the way you handled it.

Activity V.   Comprehension Practice (Level I)

Directions: Write *yes* or *no* before the statements which represent what the author said or didn't say. You may use your books.

_____ 1. The bus was traveling on a winding mountain road.
_____ 2. The bus plunged down the mountain hurting two children.
_____ 3. Lecia took a rope and shovel from the bus before it burned.
_____ 4. Olive offered to share her lunch with the others.
_____ 5. Lecia carried one child on her back through the snow storm.
_____ 6. When they finally found a fence, Chuck knew where they were.
_____ 7. Bill shared his sandwich with the teacher because he knew she didn't eat anything.
_____ 8. Stuffing her frozen feet in the snow probably saved Maggie's life.
_____ 9. To pass the time away, the teacher had school in the small shelter.
_____10. Olive was a spoiled brat.
_____11. Chuck, Bill, and Eddie grew up during the storm.
_____12. Through all eight days of the storm, though the children were sick, Lecia didn't get sick.
_____13. Finding the willow grove was pure luck.
_____14. Maggie came from a poor family.
_____15. The fact that Lecia, the teacher, remembered her grandfather's story of a blizzard in 1888 helped her to save their lives.

Activity VI.   Comprehension Practice (Level II)

Directions: Getting the most from reading means that we are able to put into our own words the main thoughts in a paragraph, section, or chapter. The following problems will give you practice. Read the indicated sections and check the items for each problem. Which one best fits the important thought of the material read?

1. Paragraph 1, page 357:   a. the beginning of a storm
                             b. a school bus was out in a storm
                             c. the trails were winding

2. Paragraph 1, page 358:   a. the bus overturned
                             b. the unloading
                             c. the teacher was overloaded

3. Paragraph 2, page 359:   a. the forming of a queue
                             b. Joanie was tied to the teacher
                             c. Chuck was at the back end of the queue

4. Paragraph 3, page 362:   a. Calla saw a snow shelter at the county fair
                             b. The children helped build the snow shelter
                             c. The snow shelter was high enough for a child
                                to stand

5. Paragraph 3, page 363:   a. Lecia tried to take off her ring
                             b. the snow shelter rebuilt
                             c. Bill ate the food

6. Paragraph, beginning   a. Chuck defies the teacher
   "Unable to reply . . ."   b. the teacher is afraid for Chuck
   page 364:   c. Chuck and the teacher battle silently

7. Paragraph, beginning   a. Indian customs
   "They talked about   b. children play school
   food . . ." page 369:   c. girls learn from women

8. Last paragraph,   a. the boys are lost
   page 372:   b. it was 15 degrees below zero
                             c. the teacher realizes she must help
                                the boys

9. Paragraph beginning   a. Maggie's feet were frozen
   "Bill had looked . . ."   b. a boy grows up
   page 374:   c. the teacher tries to help

10. Paragraph 3, page 371,   You decide what the main idea is and
    beginning "One   write it here. Use only four or five
    clump . . .":   words.

Activity VII.   Comprehension Practice (Level III)

Directions: Read each statement. If you think Mari Sandoz would agree with
             the statement as given, place a checkmark in the blank space. Work
             alone at first, then compare and contrast your answers and try to
             come to some consensus of opinion. Look back at the story if you
             need to defend your decision.

_____ 1. Lecia Terry was a brave sensible girl.
_____ 2. Olive was a "loner."
_____ 3. Bill, the "cripple," changed during the process of the story.
_____ 4. Chuck was a rebellious teen-ager who thought only of himself.

_____ 5. An emergency sometimes brings out the best and the worst in people.

_____ 6. Lecia's grandfather was important in the survival of the people in this story.

_____ 7. The people and the storm in the story are adversaries.

_____ 8. The teacher was responsible for Maggie's frozen feet.

_____ 9. There are times in our lives when hardships are good for us.

_____ 10. The theme of this story is that the basic human needs for love and security can best be found in the company of other human beings.

Lesson: The Language of Physics

Textbook: *Matter and Energy, The Foundations of Modern Physics*
              MacLachlan, McNeill, Bell

Class: Heterogeneous group of ninth graders

Introduction: (For teacher) Most boys and girls want to learn. Many teachers fail to tap that "want to" because of dull unenthusiastic day-by-day drill which kills motivation. Students have been told before they enter a physics class that it is hard, that they'll never use it, and that most of it doesn't make sense.

The language of physics is different. It is technical and numerical. Sometimes it is difficult to get across the use of multiple meanings of words. Hence, it is your job to "kill" those preconceived attitudes, to spark the interests of students, and send them out the very first day with a new idea about an ordinary occurrence.

You can't jump right into vocabulary drill and expect to do this: yet the students have to know right away that physics does have a language of its own and they have to understand this concept before they can understand the very first lesson in the textbook.

Here is one approach which you might use.

First, tell them a story about some physicist, astronomer, or explorer who used physics or who defied the superstition of his day to explain with logical physical principles what was once called a mystery.

Next, talk about the five senses. Explain that the senses of sight, hearing, and touch are basis for branches of physics.

Thirdly, explain to them that the study they will do with this text and supplementary materials will teach them to do five things. List these five items on the chalkboard. (a) experiment (b) discover laws (c) solve problems (d) invent concepts (e) create theses. No need to go into these the first day unless someone asks a specific question.

The next step is to have a simple experiment set up. Explain to them that some of the most interesting things they will learn this year are to listen, to watch, to follow directions, and to record accurately what they observe.

Now caution your students to look out for a problem in the experiment you perform. Do the one with the ball suspended on a string. Swing it. Stop it and cut off a length of the string. Swing it again.

Question the Students: Did the magnitude of the ball's path change during those two swings?

Student writes yes or no on a slip of paper. Count answers. Have several defend their answer. Discuss the meaning of the word magnitude if anyone doesn't understand it. Find the word in the text and decide if they know from context what it means. Was the explanation they arrived at the one you had in mind?

Your sixth step in this introductory lesson is to go into multiple meanings of words and how important this concept is in reading. Some words they already know will be used in physics but with a different meaning. Distribute the vocabulary sheet similar to the one following these directions. Have them to find the word *index*. What is their meaning of the word? Find it in their text. Does it have the same meaning?

Ask this question. Would you say that the difference in the meaning of the use of *index* in these two instances is infinitesimally small or immeasureably large?

Write the words *infinitesimally* and *immeasurably* on the board. Give them time to talk among themselves about the meanings. Suggest using structural clues. Some will know the roots. Some will know the affixes and their meanings. Let them figure out meanings and name some things which could be described with these two terms. Next, find the words in context. Are the meanings the same?

Since physics classifies things in numerical quantities or formulas, have yardsticks and meter sticks standing in readiness. Compare these by demonstration. Perhaps the tallest and shortest boy might measure each other using both. After comparison, ask for the meaning of the word meter. Discuss the advantages and disadvantages of measuring by meter. What are some words they know which use meter as a part of them? (barometer, speedometer, thermometer, etc.) Talk about how knowing word parts helps in unlocking their meanings.

Look for a meter word on the vocabulary sheet. Most of them will know it. Ask for its origin. How many meanings can they give? Show a picture of a centurian. You might ask how many centimeters long their friends let their beards grow?

For the remainder of the period, divide them into groups. Size will depend upon the number of students in class. Let them play around with the vocabulary sheet. Right away they'll probably tell you that they know these little old words. Your job is to convince them that words have many meanings and in the realm of physics they will be different from what they know now.

While students work in groups digging for specific meanings in this textbook, you circulate among them. You may need to clarify a point here, spark up interest there, and get the group process working elsewhere. Do not sit behind your desk reading a magazine or correcting papers, doing records, etc. If you care about your students, let them know it. Sitting barricaded behind a desk won't do it.

The next day follow up by asking if anyone had a question about any of the words. Give some practice exercises such as the ones listed elsewhere in this text to be sure they understand the concepts and for reinforcement. Students will comment, (we hope) "Ah, it doesn't seem like it will be so bad, after all!"

Here is a sample vocabulary page to give them.

Meanings of Words in Context

From pages 7-17 in *Matter and Energy*

Directions: Here are some words we will be using all through the course in this class. Some of them are familiar to you. You know a meaning. But many words have different meanings in different subject matter. We want to find out their meanings in physics. Words are listed with both page and column location. (Teacher may choose different list accordings to competency of class.)

Words	*Meaning in Physics Text*
1. physicist (7,1)	
2. physical (7,1)	
3. physical quantity (7,1)	
4. magnitude (7,1)	
5. index (7,2)	
6. positive (7,2)	
7. negative (7,2)	
8. indices (7,2)	
9. relation (10, table)	
10. digits (8,20)	
11. meter (7,1)	
12. centimeter (10, table)	
13. calculate (13,1)	
14. multiples (10,1)	
15. prefixes (10,1)	
16. variable (12,1)	
17. infinitesimally small (7, table)	
18. immeasurably large (7, table)	
19. density (12,2)	
20. algebraic (11, table)	

Practicing Comprehension (Remedial Students)

I. In each sentence the part that is underlined tells where or when or how. Read each sentence. After the sentence you will see three words. Draw a line under the one word that shows what the underlined part of the sentence tells.

1. A golden coach came <u>down the street.</u>   When?   Where?   How?
2. Our dog likes to stay <u>out at night.</u>   When?   Where?   How?
3. Jan ran <u>as fast as</u> she could go.   When?   Where?   How?
4. <u>Last summer</u> I drank some goat's milk.   When?   Where?   How?
5. I went to the <u>store in a hurry.</u>   When?   Where?   How?
6. I will do this work <u>sheet fast</u>.   When?   Where?   How?
7. <u>In our town</u> the bells ring every hour.   When?   Where?   How?

II. Here are some sayings people often use to compare things. Can you finish them? Do you know what each one means? Add five which you know to this list.

1. bold as a _____   6._____
2. tame as a _____   7._____

3. sly as a _____   8._____
4. strong as an _____   9._____
5. sharp as a _____   10._____

III.   Here are some phrases which have a double meaning. Can you tell what someone means when he says them? Write five more which you know.

1. Was his face red!   6._____
2. As old as Methusalah!   7._____
3. Snug as a bug in a rug!   8._____
4. Walking on air!   9._____
5. Splitting hairs!   10._____

Practicing Comprehension (Average Students)

Directions: The following exercises are different ways to practice getting information from materials you read. Without any additional reading, see if you can answer the questions asked after each paragraph. If you are interested, do further reading on the subjects.

I.

Irrigation, a food-growing method, may cause more problems than it solves. Some environmentalists believe that changing the natural waterflow patterns on a large scale through irrigation may create problems we don't even know about today. We know that it increases the amount of salt in the land and that it may lead to waterlogging. Both of these damage land and cut production.

Problem: Your father is irrigating his strawberry field. You tell him that you want to raise strawberries on this same land when you are his age, but you may not be able to. He asks you to explain your reasoning. Can you?

II.

Birds should not be fed extra food in the summer. *Your question:* Why?

III.

Strip mining seems to be an excellent way of getting coal, since it is cheaper and safer than sending miners into tunnels. But it lays waste to land which must be reclaimed at extensive costs which may be added to actual costs of mining the coal.

Problem: Your father is on the school board. They are discussing whether or not to buy the coal the school needs from a strip miner or from a company which sends its miners underground. Your father argues that there will be little difference in the cost of coal to the school. Is he correct or not? Defend your answer.

IV.

The weatherman reports that the temperature outside is 32° C. What would you like to do—swim or ice skate?

V.

Activities that increase the rate of your heartbeat and keep it at a higher rate for a specific length of time are called aerobics. These activities should make you huff and puff and build up your strength.

Isometric exercises strengthen and develop muscles without much apparent movement. Muscles grow stronger as you learn to tense them and you seldom get tired doing this kind of exercise.

Problem: Look at the following list of exercises and decide whether they are aerobics or isometric:

a.	swimming	e.	holding in stomach while driving
b.	dancing	f.	jogging
c.	deep breathing	g.	raising arms above head and holding
d.	jumping rope	h.	push ups

VI.

A.   Persuade people to buy beverages in returnable bottles.
B.   Ride a bicycle, walk, or take the bus instead of using your car.
C.   Pick up papers and cans on the playground or streets.
D.   Do not burn trash or leaves.

Problem: Check the correct answer in the following choices: (Answer: A)

1.   All of these are ways you can help save the environment.
2.   A, B, and C are ways to help save the environment.
3.   A, B, and D are ways to help save the environment.
4.   B, C, and D are ways you can help save the environment.

The Cloze Technique

For years teachers have used the cloze procedure [23] in one form or another, mostly in sentences. In the last few years it has been advocated as a way to test for and/or practice comprehension of materials read. It gives some indication of whether or not students can use context to help in understanding.

Some teachers use this process to test student ability to handle state-adopted textbooks. If a testee does poorly, he or she will probably have trouble with the reading of the text and will need an easier book.

Using your knowledge of the reading process, try your skill with context clues by filling in the following blanks with the appropriate terms. (Answers to this exercise are at the end of the chapter.)

One of the most important word identification skills which you should be dealing with in grades 4–9 is the use of context clues. This means (1)_____ _____words by searching surrounding (2)_____ for meaning. You should (3)_____students that when they (4)_____to a word they (5)_____know, read the rest (6.)_____the sentence. Does this (7)_____them a clue? According (8)_____ syntactic and/or semantic (9)_____, make an intelligent guess. If (10)_____concept is in his (11)_____, chances are he will (12)_____the word.

How to Construct, Administer, and Interpret Cloze Tests to Determine Students' Instructional Reading Levels

1. Select a typical passage of words from the textbook you plan to use.
2. Give the complete first sentence, then count every fifth, seventh, or tenth word (depending upon competency level of students) and circle.
3. Type a master, replacing circled words with a numbered blank, and make a list of those words deleted.
4. Give the test to your class. It is not a power test nor a speed test. Give students time they need to complete it.
5. To save you time and give students some feedback, let them check papers in class. Later you look at quantity and kinds of mistakes made.
6. You may give credit for synonyms if you wish. If you question scores, give an alternate cloze test over the same passage. (Some people say no synonyms.)
7. Study the results.

Below 40%:   Book is on frustration level. Student will have trouble with comprehension.

40–60%:   Text appropriate for instructional level, if you do your job effectively.

Above 60%:   Student can use text for independent study.

Example of the Cloze Test from a Social Studies Textbook*

The tall "chewing-gum tree" grows in the Guatemalan forests. It's real name is the sapodilla, (1)_____chicle tree. Chewing gum is made (2)_____ _____dried chicle sap. With long sharp (3)_____, workers slash criss-cross cuts on the (4)_____trunk. Then the white sticky sap (5)_____ _____slowly down into a heavy bag. (6)_____, this sap is boiled to make (7)_____thick and hard. Then it is (8)_____to factories to be made into (9)_____.

Answers: or, from, knives, tree, flows, later, it, flown, gum

---

* SOURCE: From *Your Country and Mine, New Edition,* of The Tiegs-Adams Series, Copyright 1965, by Ginn and Company (Xerox Corporation). Used with permission.

I pledge alegents to the flag
of the U.S. ab amrica to the
rewplice for which it stands
and are nation under god inoidle
with juster and libelter lver
all

I plane the leegan to the flage of
tre untle States of amercir one
anigen ounder god in iulilel wetn
libter and Justser o for all

tl pelage the agllinginges to the flag
of U.S.f. to the republic on which it
stond One nation under god etc...

I pledge A legion to the flag
of the United States of America,
And unto his nAme, one indivisal
nation ~~under~~ under God, with
liberty And judice foR All.

I pledge a allence to the
flag. Of the U.S, of America
If the rellazation of Richard
stands. Ome nation under
God indeivesible with justie
and forall-

I peldge Alligence to the flag of the
United States of AMERICA, And to the
Republic on which it stands ONE nation
under God invisibility with liberty
And justice for All

The Pledge to the Flag

Though the Pledge to the Flag is in disrepute in some areas of our country, (some students who have been influenced by the radicals in their environments refuse to participate in the Pledge when it is used in school), there are other places where it is still used and where students and teachers believe we have a heritage and a nation to be proud of.

How the activity is practiced, however, may do as much damage as though it were not being used. As has been stated elsewhere in this book, the *how* is more important than the *what*.

In one sixth grade classroom, students were told to memorize the Pledge and to be able to write it accurately, including the correct punctuation. The results are on page 104. They were decoding and memorizing, but how and to what extent? Were they reading? Did they comprehend? Did they even hear? What learning took place? What patriotic fervor was aroused? You know the answers as well as I. Had the teacher worked some on preteaching vocabulary, on concrete experiences with words, on making a creative task (such as with the Preamble in chapter 13), how interesting and enjoyable this task could have been.

SUMMARY

This chapter has offered some activities to build comprehension using approaches which have worked with many classes. One of the things you must remember about ideas, approaches, and materials is that you must be sold on them before you can sell them to students. It takes much work and planning to prepare lessons with both interest and skills practice. Remember the old cliche, "Variety is the spice of life." Variety is also the spice of good teaching.

Answers to Cloze Exercise (p. 102 -03)

identifying, context, teach, come, don't, of, give, to, clues, the, vocabulary, identify

Activities for the Teacher

1. Use the cloze technique as a comprehension check on some material the students are working on. Can they get words from context clues?
2. For one day, listen to the conversations of all the people you come in contact with. Record any interesting language patterns, pronunciations or dialect you hear. Can you identify it?
3. Choose a subject in one of the so-called content areas and plan a lesson to teach a specific comprehension skill.
   a. List the skill.
   b. How will you go about introducing it?
   c. What materials will you use?
   d. What practice and reinforcement exercises will you use?
   e. How will you decide whether learning has occurred?

SIX

Strategies to Insure Enthusiasm for Reading

Think about these things:

1. Sir Francis Bacon (1590): "Some books are to be tasted, others to be swallowed, and some few to be chewed and digested."
2. Eighty percent of words are learned by reading, not by using a dictionary.
3. There is a positive correlation between children's favorable perception of their teacher's feelings toward them and their academic achievement and classroom behavior.
4. Formal book reports have killed more enthusiasm for reading than anyone will ever know.
5. The teacher's self-concept is important: "I can teach you." Students may not be able to read a book, but they can read you.
6. Let students know there is no stigma attached with having reading problems. Tell them Einstein made the statement that reading is the most complex task that humans ever devised for themselves. Why shouldn't it be hard?
7. Classroom instruction, hence reading, will improve as we connect it to life outside the classroom.

PREMISE VII: Rather than making dropouts of them, the *Middle Years* of students' lives can be the exciting challenge that holds them in school.

If you want to develop lifetime reading habits, use materials, structure, and activities in the classroom which relate to life and make it challenging, pleasant, and success-proof. When you have to teach concepts that are new to students, show how they will help them or relate to their lives outside the classroom. Sarcasm, nagging, comparing with other students, taking away playtime when tasks are incomplete: these are negative characteristics in a classroom.

If Sarah is searching for answers on how to cope with today's free society and free morality, permissiveness she doesn't really want or know how to handle, make the books which deal with the problems available. Let students read what they want to. If they want to discuss problems with you, have the openness to hear them, but don't force the issue.

Or give her and her friends an article similar to the one following and get out of their way. Some of you will say this one is too mature for junior high age students. Have you been to the movies lately? Do you read the books, the magazines, see the dances they do, or watch the television programs they watch? Do you remember the early 70s when some colleges had a minority of their students joining the immature "streaking-freaking" fad? Other students who graduated from those schools and were teachers had their fifth and sixth graders questioning them about this practice. Wake up!

Let them read the article or a similar one and discuss what they think. Whether or not they discuss it with you honestly and openly will depend upon the relationships within your classroom. It may be that they will prefer to discuss it among themselves rather than with you. If so, let them.

ADOLESCENT GIRLS SEEK SECURITY IN RELATIONSHIPS *

In this age of "permissive anything goes," when young people are more and more confused about their personal security, about their relationships with others, about "doing their own thing," and despite the many arguments against it, you need and want guidance in areas that many parents and teachers are afraid to touch.

Adults should still serve as models for teen-agers, they should set limits for behaviors, and they should expect and demand the best from you.

Oftentimes teen-age rebellion is a simple way of begging, "Look at me. I'm someone. Help me."

Just this month in a medium-sized, supposedly conservative high school community, the school newspapers ran a letter from two sophomore girls with these ideas.

"If a girl loves a boy, nothing is taboo. She should show it in any and every way possible. That's what the pill is for."

The fellows, not caring who heard them, laughed and made such comments as these: "Okay. Now we know where to go." "And it's free!" "Blond or brunette?" "With an outlet like this, maybe it won't be so hard on our pocketbooks."

What price, popularity!

And what a sad commentary on the concept of popularity. And love!

The idea of love which you're growing up with—you see it portrayed on TV and movie screens, in popular magazines, and in books—gives you this distorted, narrow, physical view of love which has to be discarded at the first sign of trouble. Before girls reach this sophomore level in high school, someone should give you help and guidance in decision making and facing the consequences of personal decisions regarding sex and other problems you have.

Just as important as your relationship with other people to your total well-being, fulfillment, and well-rounded physical, mental, and spiritual selves (these three can't be

---

* Unpublished essay by Virgie M. McIntyre.

separated) is your relationship and/or faith in something beyond man and his human weaknesses.

One of the basic needs of today's society—adults as well as youth—is a basic belief in the goodness of life. Life is the God in us, and regardless of the expertise of the human brain, no earthling can create a perfect being full of the love, joy, and exurberance of living. Some other creative force greater than man, we call it God, still controls this universe. If you young people want happiness, you must learn that you are not an entity unto yourself or for yourself.

For the Boys: Famous Quotations on Failure [24]

Failure: What is it? Who fails? Can we always recognize it?
  1. They never fail who die
     In a great cause.   *Lord Byron*
  2. Sad soul, take comfort, nor forget
     That sunrise never failed us yet.   *Celia Thaxter*
  3. But screw your courage to the sticking place,
     and we'll not fail.   *Lady Macbeth*
  4. There is not a fiercer hell than the failure in a great object.   *Keats*
  5. We learn wisdom from failure more than from success. We often discover what will do by finding out what will not do, and probably he who never made a mistake never made a discovery.   *Samuel Smiles*
  6. In the lexicon of youth, which fate reserves for a bright manhood, there is no such word as "fail."   *Lytton*
  7. Studious to please, yet not ashamed to fail.   *Samuel Johnson*
  8. Nice guys finish last.   *Leo Durocher*
  9. Don't come home a failure.   *Ty Cobb*
 10. For when the One Great Scorer comes to write against your name, He marks—not that you won or lost—but how you played the game.   *Vince Lombardi*

As the boys read and discuss these comments made by famous people, they are attempting to think through their own idea of the importance of winning. Which ones do they agree with? Some questions you might bring up if they don't:
  a.   What is the meaning of failure?
  b.   Do we all see it the same way?
  c.   Can losers ever be winners or winners losers? How?
  d.   What are the characteristics of a consistent winner? Loser?
  e.   How can we learn to accept failure?
  f.   Can winning and/or failing in sports be compared to winning in other areas?
  g.   Who is a current favorite sports winner? How does he react when he wins or loses?
  h.   Is it always the biggest muscleman who wins?
  i.   Name some current sports figures who are winners despite handicaps, and some who are losers despite their winning.

     j.   There is a quote which ministers often use: "What good does it do if you win the whole world and lose your own soul?" What is your interpretation of this?

Will Books Help?

There are many books which help young adolescents and older teens to find themselves. No two people would choose the same ones and no one can say which exact book will help which kind of student or problem. However, if they are allowed to read freely, they will take from them what they need. This approach is much more conducive to habit forming than a teacher required list on which dull reports are to be made.

For total student involvement, bring to the classroom (or visit the library) a cart of books on the subject of the week and tell them, "Have a ball." Let them browse, discuss, and choose one to read. After reading they can record their opinion of the book and its helpfulness or entertainment on a 3 x 5 index card for their reading peers to check when choosing next time. Peer critics will serve as more effective motivators for reading than most adults.

A teen discussion on the subject of "Sex and God as Portrayed in Fiction" is one of the most intriguing, eye-opening experiences students and teachers will ever enjoy. Compare this technique with a teacher-given lecture! Which will they remember longer?

One of the basic changes needed in elementary and secondary reading is the throwing out of the teacher-required book list on which students make reports. How many students have learned to dislike reading, to cheat, to lie about reading, and have made a mockery of our instructions. If you want them to read, let them have a voice in what they read, then motivate, guide, or lead them into other things. You can do it. Drama, making their own films or filmstrips, debates on issues, placing themselves in the character's shoes—all of these are more appealing activities than that dull report they copy off the book jacket, from a *Library Journal,* or from a friend.

Did you ever see a book report made in this form? The student reads a book and summarizes it in a short paragraph. Or he picks the main idea from the book, then he leaves off the title, leaves out the vowels, and presents it to his friends. How much fun they have trying to figure out which book he read and whether or not it might be interesting enough for them to spend time with. In addition, they see how good they are at recognizing words and the value of consonants in recognizing them.

Study Techniques Which Carry
Over into Lifelong Reading

What is study? What plan of reading best insures learning? What skills, habits, or mechanics are involved in acquiring knowledge? Chapter 12 lists sixty skills students need to know to be efficient readers. Could we just as easily call the skills techniques for study? What plan does the successful student use for retaining what he reads?

In a basic reading class for prospective teachers, out of 160 students thirty-seven had heard of the SQ3R and sixteen had actually used it. After we talked about it, one student who called herself a poor reader began using it in her college study and commented that she wished she had known about it years ago. Another one in the same group tried it and gave a negative reaction. Study techniques like everything else are individual, personal things. You give students these aids and they use them or not as they will.

Almost every book on the teaching of reading today talks about Robinson's SQ3R method,[25] yet many students and teachers have never heard of it. Briefly, it is as follows:

Survey: Glance over headings, subheadings, beginning and ending paragraphs to see the main overall points. This will help you to organize the ideas as you read later on.

Question: Turn these headings and subheadings into questions. This can be done instantly and set up the query for which you read to find the answer.

Read: Read to answer the questions. This is not a passive word-by-word plodding, but an active search for answers.

Recite: Look away from the book and try to recite the answer to your question. Use your own words and try to think of an example. If you can do this, you know what you just read. If you can't do this, glance over the section again and jot down notes for remembering.

Review: When you finish reading the lesson, look over notes to get a quick view of points and their relationships. Now, cover cues, outline, or notes, and try to recall the main points. Expose main points, and try to recall the subpoints (details) listed under them.

Teach your students this method of study. If they use it, they will become faster readers, pick out important points and fix them in memory, and prepare themselves for questions you may later ask.

There are other techniques cropping up occasionally, such as Pauk's EVOKER system, a later variation is OK4R; R.S.V.P. from Scott, Foresman; Norman's OARWET; Charles Winkler and his "One Step Ahead" method; The DRA, and so on. For more on some of these, see chapter 12. The directed reading activity used in primary grades is sometimes used for middle grades when the material is dealing with new concepts, much technical vocabulary, or the students are weak readers.

The use of study guides can sometimes pinpoint important concepts. Questioning before reading is a technique frowned on by some teachers. "They only read to find answers," you complain. If you have made good questions, you have covered the important concepts, so what's wrong with skipping? For many students, much material in our textbooks is not worth reading or remembering.

In my teaching I found that giving students questions surpasses both careful reading without questions and rereading. It saves them time and they have a purpose for reading.

Skimming, outlining, and notetaking are skills of study mentioned elsewhere. Skimming is one of the best techniques of all for insuring future carryover into life situations. Skim until you find what you want, then do the type of reading required to fulfill the purpose for which you're reading.

How do you understand more of what you read? At the beginning of this book we said that efficient reading was getting the most with the least effort in the shortest time. This means adjusting rates to purposes according to task and level of understandings. The purpose must be personal. You should let students help to set purposes for reading, not just the usual "Because the teacher says so," or "Tomorrow we have a test," but because they are looking for something.

J. I. Brown (23) suggests that teachers give students the process for efficient reading. First, when they begin a new reading task, think about the subject matter. What do they already know about it, what do they want to know, and what do they know about the author and his authority to write on the subject? Second, after spending a few seconds in thinking, glance over the material looking for clues. Headings and boldface print will give direction in recognizing important points as they are presented. Third, students can improve concentration and retention of material by concentrating on small portions between headings, with pauses to rest eyes and think about the material, before going on. Last, take a longer time at the end of the reading period to think over what has been read and fix a mental impression of the material. Alternating reading and thinking provides greater comprehension and longer retention. A summary of this paragraph could be: think, read, then react.

Brainstorming

Let's assume you're the teacher with students who read nothing except the funnies, sports, and under-the-counter magazines and who are disinterested in tasks you assign in the classroom. Yet, your job is to build vocabulary, to teach some of the classics, and to build literary appreciation. How can you reach these reluctant readers?

One way which worked for me (even with the most apathetic of students) is brainstorming. How do you go about it? Let's take an example from science. You want to teach the concept of *precipitation*.

Procedure

The weatherman uses the word precipitation every day. Students are familiar with it. Divide them into groups and give them two minutes to write down all the forms of precipitation they can think of. Spelling doesn't count in this task. At the end of two minutes check to see how many each group got. Now, give two more minutes to add to the list. This time they can use any reference book they have.

Why two minutes? Reluctant students lose interest fast, and the two minutes limit also takes care of the procrastinators.

Discuss what they came up with and add a few choices of yours.

A Possible List: (the obvious ones) rain, hail, sleet, snow, fog, frost ice, mist, cloud, steam, water, frost, dew, and others. Fumes, spray, tears, odor, smoke, moisture, sweat, liquid, fluid, tides, rainfall, cloudburst, bath, urine, blood, flood, haze, saliva, hoarfrost, solution, waterfall. Abstract forms such as energy as forms of power, strength.

Continue to expand their thinking and vocabulary by a second session of brainstorming. Ask a question: How many associations can they come up with which go with the idea of precipitation, or one form of it, such as water? Divide them into groups and assign topics for each group, such as:

1. how water feels
2. how water tastes
3. how water looks
4. how water is used
5. how water sounds
6. bodies of water
7. emotions aroused by water
8. how a world without water would be

Some words and phrases which they might come up with are listed here.

1. How water feels: cold, hot, scalding, steaming, flowing, standing, damp wet, moist, with soap in the eyes, velvet on the skin
2. How water tastes: cool, refreshing, tepid, polluted, cholrinated, dank, with medicine, on a burned tongue-hot or cold, sickening
3. How water looks: rippling, surging, clean, clear sparkling, polluted, dank, covered with algae, cascading, bloody, blue, black
4. How water is used: as food, to bathe in, to swim, wade or drown in, gargle, sprinkle, irrigate, soak, drench, deluge, skate on
5. How water sounds: roaring, soothing, bubbling, hissing, spurting, dashing, stimulating, dripping, oozing, percolating, beating on the roof or against the window pane
6. Bodies of water: oceans, rivers, ponds, creeks, swamps, floods, streams, wells, holes, channels, gulfs, swamps
7. Emotions aroused by water: fear—drowning, thunderstorms, lightening
anger—bath and its still two hours before dark, someone used all the hot water, hot weather and no ice, someone splashes muddy water on your new suit, someone spills coffee on your homework
love—summer swimming, lemonade, cooling fountains in parks, beauty of a waterfall, shower, using the same umbrella, ice on a hot day
8. World without water: dry, parched, scorching, brown, shrivelled, unlivable, unimaginable

This type of activity builds concepts, expands vocabulary, motivates for further study of water and its forms, has total class involvement, and leads students toward further reading to find out.

Some Further Activities Built on Brainstorming:

1. Double words with snow as part of them
2. Double words with rain as part of them
3. kinds of clouds
4. kinds of liquid
5. kinds of gases
6. things made from water
7. making weather maps
8. making weather vanes, stations, and so on
9. reading weather maps
10. figurative language: sopping wet, wet blanket, put a damper on, won't hold water
11. stump words: let student find new words about water and teach to the class if they want to learn them
12. collecting statistics to make tables, charts, and graphs to show yearly comparisons of rainfall
13. read newspapers for checking weather predictions

Additional Use of Brainstorming

Choose a subject of interest to students. Let them group themselves into four or five people and choose a secretary. Their task is to see how many related words or phrases they can think of for the secretary to list in three minutes. Let them use reference books if they want to.

At the end of the set time, each student chooses his or her favorite word or phrase from the list and illustrates it for a bulletin board. (See figure 6.1.) It ends up as attractive and creative, with total student involvement, vocabulary reinforcement and expansion, spelling practice, and fun.

The list for the subject "horses" might look something like this:

horse	crop	hay, oats, barley	horse and buggy
cowboy	mare	pasture	work
rodeo	bluegrass	meadow	riding habit
rope	fox hunt	horseshoe	derby
race	pony	lasso	corral
hoof	donkey	lariet	for want of a nail
Pemlico	thoroughbred	wagon	

FIGURE 6.1

Illustration of words

Ten Specific Strategies for Dealing with Remedial Readers

Many young teachers, as well as experienced ones, complain that their college training does not equip them with strategies for dealing with hard-core students who can legitimately be labeled remedial readers and who are found in most classrooms. Those students have the potential but, for some reason, are not performing.

Some of these teachers want magic formulas, sure-fire strategies, and/or expect that what they try will work with all students. When what they try fails to work, those of us in college instruction courses have failed them, they accuse. As stated elsewhere in this book, no one approach, no one set of materials, no one teacher will work for all students. Just as in any business, so in the teaching of reading, we must use common sense. Use whatever methods, materials, and/or grouping practices that seem best for the situation. If one doesn't work, try another. However, be wary of jumping from one fad to another. Give yourself and your students time to know whether or not it works. Remember, one of the reasons for some student problems is the covering of materials at too fast a pace for them.

Here are some specific practices which have worked for some of us. One of them might work for you and your students.

1. The Fernald VAKT method, sometimes called the Tactile-Kinesthetic approach to learning. See chapter 4.
2. The use of *games* and *drills.* Many are given in this book and hundreds of books, kits, series supplements, and so on, are commercially published.
3. The teacher practice of *reading to students.* Don't underestimate the value of this. As a teacher model reading aloud from exciting portions of books, stories, plays, jokes—I've had students who couldn't wait to get the book from my hands.
4. *Programmed materials* are an aid to remedial students *if* they are on the correct level, have a purpose and the student knows this purpose, are motivational, and have teacher follow up. A valid criticism of the use of programmed materials is that too many teachers never know what students are doing in and with them. They may copy answers, use wrong approaches, learn misinformation, and learn to beat the system without the unconcerned teacher ever catching on.
5. *Echoic reading* is the practice of letting a student read with a partner. Either a better reader or the teacher may serve as the model. The remedial student reads at about a second behind the partner who begins loud and confident. As the student reads and begins to show he can go it alone, the partner gradually softens his tone and slows his pace somewhat, letting the problem reader take over. This practice is particularly for those word callers who lack fluency or self-confidence.
6. *Structured comprehension,* example given in this chapter, is a form of imitative questioning which may open up understanding of words or sentences for some students. This can be done on an individual basis or, if well-planned, used with a class. Short frequent exercises are better than

long drawn out ones. Use this approach with students who call words but lack understanding.

7. *Group or team learning* often produces better results with remedial learners than does teacher lecturing. Plan your work around a theme or topic which is of interest to the students. Make study guides, task cards, games, and/or other activities around this theme which will help students understand the concepts you want them to learn and let them work together to find the solutions or perform the tasks. However, this does not mean that you are free to visit the coffee lounge. You should be in the midst of your students, moving from one group to the other, making explanations, correcting misconceptions, guiding them in their struggles to improve. Even when students are working in groups, you must pay attention to their special needs and help each individual to realize that he is an important member of the group. Under the best circumstances in group work, there are times when some guidance from you must be individual.

8. Use the *multi-media*. (See chapter 11.) Especially with remedial readers, audio-visuals of all descriptions—magazines, music, catalogs—should be used. Students can see more sense in reading materials they use every day than in abstract irrelevant textbooks. Make use of these utility type reading instructional aides for your remedial students.

9. *Free reading*. (USSR) Set aside some time each day for free reading. Let students choose anything they wish to and read it for pleasure with no thought of being tested on their efforts. Many teachers are using the uninterrupted sustained silent reading periods today and report excellent results.

10. *Language experiences in the middle grades*. Language experiences can be just as exciting at this age level as in the primary years. One example of what happened in a combination fifth and sixth grade classroom is given here.

The week after Christmas a child, we'll call her Sue, whose family had visited relatives in Florida over the holiday brought an avocado to class. Many in the class had never seen or tasted this fruit. I decided to use the avocado as a language experience for teaching some new vocabulary and reading skills.

While Sue and a friend went to the lunchroom for a knife, some napkins, salt and pepper, other students looked up the word in dictionaries and encyclopedias. They discovered it was also called the alligator pear. The fellows found this interesting and speculated why.

Sue cut the fruit into small pieces and told us how her relatives served it. Each of us got a piece, adding salt and pepper if we desired, and talked about how the fruit tasted. Descriptive terms ranged from blah, to delicious, to terrible.

I suggested that we put as many words as we could think of that might describe the taste of the avocado on the chalkboard. Some of those words: blah, tangy exotic, bitter, delicious, tropical, green and yellow, wormy, scanty, stinky, slick, mushy, and bleeding.

A. From this activity, and while motivation was high, disregarding my preconceived lesson plans, I divided the class into four teams and gave them these tasks with a limit of five minutes to see how many words they could find.

They could use any term they knew or could find in books. Here are some sample words they used.

TEAM I: Name as many fruits as you can. There are over one hundred. Some interesting ones they came up with other than the usual were: cotton, grape, cantaloupe, cranberries, currents, cucumber, tomato, kumquat, acorn, flax, coffee bean, gourd, peas, nuts, grain of barley.

TEAM II: Name as many action words—anything that one can do to fruit—as you can in five minutes. They got over fifty here, including: harvest, produce, damage, ship, spray, shred, grade, devour, savor, treasure, irrigate, salvage, judge, blend, hear.

TEAM III: Name as many compound words using any fruit as a part of the word as you can in five minutes. Grapefruit, watermelon, muskmelon, strawberry, gooseberry, dewberry, dusenberry, pineapple, breadfruit, fruitgrowers.

TEAM IV: Name as many things as you can in five minutes that are made from fruit or with fruit in them. Cake, candy, salad, jelly, pies, cocktail, ketchup, laxatives, drinks of all kinds, butter, jam, sugar, pectin, spice, diet meals, drinking utensil (gourd), paintings, pictures (from seeds, leaves).

B. The next task I devised while they did the above one was a different form of categorizing of words. In five minutes categorize as many fruits as possible that come from trees, vines, bushes, plants, and animals.

Animals! We had fun with that one for a few minutes before they settled down to work. But after all, that was one reason for including it in the list. Try it—an interesting concept.

Fruit of the hen, egg
Fruit of the bee, honey
Fruit of the cow, milk and beef
Fruit of man, more men

C. Task III was more categorizing: fruits which grow in tropical, piedmont, and cold climates.

D. Task IV was phonics practice: review word clusters. Fruits which contain blends, diagraphs, diphthongs and double letters. Only those who need this do it.

E. Task V was an attempt to teach and review figurative language. Some examples dealing with fruit are: fruit of sin, fruit of the loom, fruit of the vine, fruit of labor. Also, what is meant by these old sayings or superstitions?

An apple a day keeps the doctor away.
Carrots make you see well.
Flower reflections on a chin are signs of jealousy.

F. Task VI was the making of an experience story about the avocado.
1. title
2. student words on board
3. arrange sentences in logical sequence for story
4. make duplicates of story for students if they need it
5. students read story

Variation: Let individual students write their own story and read to each other if they want to.

G. Task VII was one almost any age student enjoys working with. Give them some examples, then let them make others.

a. Does the nut crack her?   f. Does the banana peel?
b. Does the vine climb?   g. Does the tomato catch up?
c. Does the grape juice?   h. Does the peach fuzz?
d. Does the apple worm?   i. Does the straw berry?
e. Does the lemon aide?   j. Does the olive oil?

Can you see the possibilities for teaching, extending, and reinforcing vocabulary as concepts with language experiences such as this one? There are over one-hundred kinds of fruits, so this one example could go on and on. The geography, science, and math of fruit growing could be included. Special interest research could be added. Use the seed from the avocado to sprout and grow your own class tree. No basal or teacher's guide is needed here. Teacher's and students' creativity can take you in many directions. Let them. Students need as many stimuli as possible. When you keep in mind that the peak of attendance to a task by these students is about four minutes, it is easier to plan and set up activities which keep them involved and moving.

For *older students* it may become a survival program. Students must realize that the goals are self-motivating. Use (1) driver's manuals; (2) road signs; (3) menus; (4) ads in newspapers; (5) income tax forms; (6) employment contracts; (7) checks; (8) essential vocabulary lists; (9) sight words used in occupations or hobbies that students are interested in (see sports, chapter 14); and (10) make use of the job-type reading series, such as the Rochester Occupational.

Brainstorming with Questions: A Form of Imitative Learning

Did your students enjoy brainstorming with words? Now, try it with questions and sentences. Teach them the art of questioning, judging, evaluating, going beyond the words on the page. They do not automatically know what is important. SQ3R and other study techniques have student turn headlines, subheadings, etc., into questions. Will just any kind of question be acceptable? Like all others, this skill should be performed at the capacity level of individuals—not everyone asking the same question in the same way. This is where you come in.

One approach to learning which children use from the time they're born is imitation. Use it in the classroom to teach the art of questioning.

A structured, teacher-directed activity which students of all ages enjoy, once they understand it, is brainstorming with questions. How many questions and in how many different directions can one statement take them? Who will run out of questions first? It's a game of "beat the teacher."

Try this with your students. Begin with a simple sentence and move to more difficult ones, all the way to complex concepts in their textbooks, as they are ready. One simple sentence and one direction it might take is given here.

a. Teacher gives a sentence: The Western Cats won the ballgame.
   Teacher asks a question: Who won the ballgame?
b. Student answers question: The Western Cats won the game.
   Student asks the question: What did the Cats win?
c. Teacher answers: The Cats won the ballgame.
   Teacher questions: For what school do the Cats play?
d. Student answers: The Cats play for Western Carolina University.
   Student questions: Where is WCU located?
e. Teacher answers: WCU is located in Cullowhee, North Carolina.
   Teacher questions: Were the Cats a better team than their opponent?
f. Student answers: Yes, they were. Or, No, they were just lucky.
   Student questions: How many games have the Cats won?
g. Teacher answers: The Cats have won five out of ten conference games.
   Teacher questions: What does it take to win a ball game?

Teacher gradually leads from the literal to thinking types of questions, and this can go on and on until they tire of it or run out of questions. Or, the questions may veer off on a tangent and end up with a whole new topic of discussion.

When you do exercises such as this one with your students, insist upon full sentences as answers. Remember, in this way you're building good sentence sense at the same time you're teaching the art of questioning and thinking.

Another way to build sentence sense and to help students do a better job on some achievement tests sections (Iowa Basic Skills Test, for one) is to give them practice with *yes* and *no* sentences as a timed activity. Under pressure, students often do poorly on tasks in tests, not because they don't know, but because of the pressure of the timed situation and the fact that test scores so often judge them. If this skill is worth testing for, then it should be worth teaching. Make up a set of sentences, some questions, and have them in one of your centers for individual practice. I like to put mine on regular manila file folders and laminate for longer wear. You might begin something like this.

Activity: Yes and No Sentences

Directions: Read the following sentences and decide whether or not the meaning is clear. Write yes or no on the space provided, or use student answer sheets. After you catch on how to do the task, time yourself. Can you do this page in five minutes? Tomorrow, try one in four minutes. The next day, three.

Purpose: Sentence sense practice, improving speed and comprehension. Check your answers with the list on the back of the folder.

_____ 1. Do all mean people have plenty of money?
_____ 2. In the North, the winter is colder than the fall.
_____ 3. Do fish swim on the wall?
_____ 4. The digital clock showed 1300.
_____ 5. When Sam shaved his beard, his exposed chin got sunburned.
_____ 6. After every ballgame, Sam dresses out in his gym suit.
_____ 7. It usually snows when the temperature is 42° F.

_____ 8. Does a high voltage wire carry electricity?
_____ 9. When people dream, do they remember all the incidents of the dream?
_____10. If Jean is your friend, what will she do if she sees you cheating?

This activity is not as simple as it first appears. The student must read and follow the directions to match the answer check. Take Sentence 3, for an example. The literal answer to the question, of course, is *no*. But the answer on the check list will read *yes*. The directions didn't ask for the answer to the question, only if the question or sentence meaning is clear, and the meaning of Number 3 is very clear.

Creativity and Reading

At no time in the school program is it better to teach creatively and for creativity in students than in the grades we are dealing with. Students in this 4–9 group are no longer babies and are beginning to think for themselves. Also, they are not old enough to be inhibited. However, by junior high age, depending upon how the home, school, and society have dealt with them, some are already conditioned.

While all students can to some extent handle creative tasks in school, every teacher should be capable of and accountable for developing creativity in the top students (labeled gifted, superior, or creative). Books have been written, studies have been made, and controversies rage about a definition for, identification of, and recommendations for handling gifted students. It is not the purpose here to go into all that. Interested readers can study the writings of such men as Torrence, Taylor, Guilford, Witty, Termen, and others. Suffice it to say that these students do exist in most classrooms. One student may show a talent for music and art. Another may have a mechanical aptitude or be a whiz in arithmetic. General intellectual ability, leadership qualities, creative thinking, and psychomotor skills are other areas of giftedness. In many instances, clothing, background, past school failures, dialect, and I.Q. scores disguise the various amounts and divergent directions of special talents in students who are truly gifted.

There was a time when school personnel were accused of discriminating against the slow learners, the disadvantaged, the mental retardates, and teaching only to the good students. With the advent of federal funds, a humanistic teaching philosophy, and the accountability concept, most schools have done an about face and these students are getting the attention of teachers, aides, and counselors, while the gifted who can do most tasks with little help are being denied the stimulation they need and deserve. In the traditional classroom, creative students often get the poorest grades. Because their ideas are advanced and their attention span longer, they possess individuality and originality and reject conformity; they often do not fit into situations with others of their own age. They question what they read, the things they are asked to do, and create problems for a lazy teacher.

If you expect gifted creative students to be content to accept passively the slow pace of other students, to do the same types of worksheets, to be motivated with sitting in seats answering literal level questions day-by-day, you need to do some professional study on meeting the needs of superior students. They have diverse natures, talents, and inclinations. Reading can and should play a vital role in providing for and meeting their needs. Your role as teacher is to guide, facilitate, and encourage creative students to be creative readers and to accept their questions. Motivate before they read, give them a chance to work with the material at the time or after they read. Study guides, independent research, creative activities, a chance to work on their own at tasks they are interested in, and any other ideas you can come up with should be used to promote a creative reaction to reading for these students. Many such tasks are given throughout this material.

One Dozen Practical Suggestions for Teaching Creative Reading to the Gifted

1. Use varied approaches when teaching the skills, and teach these only when needed rather than when they appear in some textbook.
2. Emphasize reading as a thinking and communicative process.
3. Provide an atmosphere conducive to free explorative reading on their interests.
4. Provide books, kits, and other materials on many subjects, and cooperate with the librarian to get more.
5. Cooperate with and advise parents, especially those who ask, as many do, about magazines, books, and other ways of enhancing reading at home.
6. As suggested in chapter 2, use interest inventories and make available materials on those interests.
7. Encourage students to go beyond what is given in their textbooks.
8. Let students see your interest in reading and look for books which will be especially appropriate for a specific student and his or her problems.
9. Guide students into creative activities in language arts and other curriculum areas as a means of using the knowledge they get from reading. (Writing, drama, research, and taping.)
10. Encourage divergent thinking by eliminating the practice of requiring convergent (right) answers to everything. Ask open-ended questions and accept divergent answers. See the samples which follow this list.
11. Create, and let students create, tasks where they interpret, process, and use knowledge picked up from reading rather than usual collect and recall.
12. Give students free reading time. If reading is worthwhile, and if school is the place to learn to enjoy reading so that it becomes a lifetime habit, then why not give time for practice?

One fifth grader told me: "Heck! Why all the fuss 'bout learning to read? Nobody does it anymore. I ain't seen a grownup read in three years. All you gotta do is watch TV like my pop does. He can tell you anything you want to know about most any subject."

If reading isn't important to adults, why should it be important to children and young people?

CONVERGENT QUESTIONS

1. What is the author's main theme in this story?
2. Does this author believe in abortion?
3. What was the argument cited as an example which created controversy about the subject?
4. What did the author mean by "Abortion is not an ethical decision?" Cite his arguments.

DIVERGENT QUESTIONS

1. What are some current arguments you've read or heard discussed by the news media?
2. Do you feel that abortion is ethical or not?
3. If the author had let Mary live, how do you think the outcome of the story would have changed?
4. Is the author trying to convert you to his point of view, or is he giving you the facts and letting you draw your own conclusions?

Creative Tasks to Make History and Geography Relevant to the World as Students Live and See It Today [97]

Directions: Research, discuss and defend your answers to the following questions:
1. Are there slaves anywhere in the world today?
2. Are there any pioneer expeditions left to explore? (space, ocean depths)
3. Are there any new routes being laid today? (pipeline to Canada)
4. Is every book printed worth the paper it is printed on? List some books which have been printed which you know of or can find which we would be just as well off had they never been written.
5. Write a letter to his mother as Washington might have written it on the night before Fredericksburg.
6. Write a diary of an expedition whose plane is down in the jungles of Africa, the Sahara, or Siberia.
7. Make a list of supplies needed, routes to take, languages you should be able to interpret, and most efficient mode of travel for a trip around the world.
8. Recreate the event of Carrie Nation in the bars of Chicago and compare her with today's Women Libber, Gloria Stein.
9. Write a news broadcast script as today's commentators might report Napoleon's defeat at Waterloo.
10. Following the directions for making slides given in Chapter 12, let students choose some historical event to research and make his own slide-tape show on that event. Have him present it to his peers.
11. Write a dialogue on some current political controversy as Winston Churchill and Mahatma Gandhi might have discussed it.

12. Use the unit material being worked on in class today. Have students group into threes or fours and create some lists of vocabulary from the unit. One group might take action words. Another group take names of characters. Another possibility is technical terms. Descriptive words, sense words, setting and tone words, abstract terms, etc. are suggestions for categories. After they have the lists, let them decide upon some tasks they want to use as a follow up using these lists. Creative stories, puzzles, games, poetry, analogies, humorous questions and answers, according to interests of specific groups could be chosen. Junior high students whom I have worked with thoroughly enjoyed this activity and came up with some great ideas.

Learning Centers

Some schools have large learning centers set up with machines, commercial kits, books, special interest booths, teacher-made materials, and reading corners, to make learning interesting and challenging. Students are free to leave regular classrooms to go to these centers to work on their special needs and/or interests and to receive help from the personnel in them. While this is ideal, the majority of schools are not so equipped, and regular classrooms must be set up for the purpose of individualizing instruction. For our purposes we are speaking of learning centers in the classroom where students, when not in groups for direct instruction, work on tasks for special skills and/or interests.

What Is a Learning Center?

A learning center is an instructional program with content, skills, and proficiencies built into it where students practice and reinforce skills which have been introduced by the teacher, where activities are set up for students to use the discovery approach of solving problems, and/or where students are free to work at their own rate and proficiency. These are some of the *major considerations for centers:*

1. The content, skills, and proficiencies to be practiced must change with the subject matter (unit) on which pupils are working and with the rate of progress made by students.
2. As mentioned in other areas of this book, facts filed away for retrieval represent a very limited view of learning. Actual involvement with manipulative exercises, experiments, and equipment is to be desired.
3. Activities in any special area must be related to instruction in the classroom.

There are several words of advice before you attempt to change your organizational set-up toward individualization by means of centers, lest you and your students end up in a classroom catastrophe. ("It was awful," one little second grader told me, "I didn't even have a place to keep my pencil and paper.")

1. Read, read, read. Visit other classrooms. Know what you're doing.
2. Proceed slowly.
3. Make materials.
4. Collect books and equipment, and plan a classroom way of keeping track of them.
5. Be sure you have parents and administration in on the "know."
6. Know your own noise level. How much frustration can you bear?
7. Can you tolerate failure?
8. Do you have to know what every child is doing every minute?
9. Are you able to motivate and guide students into doing what they need to do, or will you have to revert to authority?
10. Do you have a simple system of record keeping?

After you have thought about all ten of these items and still plan to go into centers in your classroom, how will you evaluate effectiveness of these centers and what happens to the students who use them? Here are some questions you must ask:

a. Do your students use the centers on their own?
b. Can the students perform the tasks with little direction from you?
c. Does the material stimulate responses at various levels of activity?
d. Does it stretch thinking of pupils at all levels?
e. Do students feel successful? Do they discuss freely what they're doing?
f. Do tasks require students to be active rather than passive?
g. Can students evaluate themselves—admit they need more work on a skill, ask for it?
h. Can you see progress in student self-direction?
i. Are there groans and moans when you turn them loose for work at centers, or are there smiles?
j. Do students work or socialize? They will need guidance.

Examples of centers and materials to put into them are given in the units on egg-producing animals in chapter 8, in ideas on job cards in chapter 13, and in the unit on cars in chapter 14. In fact, most any of the study guides in this book are examples of materials which could be placed in a learning center. Included here are some job-card activities which could be used in a propaganda center.

By guiding them to develop independent choices and work habits as can be practiced with the aid of learning centers in the classroom, teachers are preparing students for the future when they won't be around to tell them what to do.

Making Tasks Relevant to the Student's Life: Propaganda Techniques

No subject is more exciting to students than what happens in their live-a-day world. What can they believe? What they hear, what they see, and often what they read is confusing, contradictory, and biased. Can you help?

Most middle-grade teachers give a lecture on or have students read a chapter in the English text and fill in some blanks, then wonder why students are so gullible when it comes to advertising. Instead of talking about how we get duped by advertisers who spend millions of dollars yearly to do just that, why not work with the actual materials? Set up a propaganda center.

Somewhere in or near the center should be a poster which tells students what to look for if they want to be intelligent readers. (Critical readers is perhaps a more technical term.) Intelligent readers question, think with the author, argue with him, analyze his words, his purposes, and his inferences. Your poster might list dozens of techniques used to sway the listener or reader. Here is a sample list which they should look out for:

a. bandwagon appeals—everyone is doing it
b. confusing facts and opinions
c. use of emotion words
d. generalities and false analogies
e. use of questionable samples—no reliable sources
f. bias or prejudice—relating only one side of the question
g. quoting authorities or famous persons
h. attacking person, organization, or group rather than the argument

In your center set up tasks from easy to difficult, to more difficult, and let students work at their level, rate, and interest. Five samples of activities which could be used in such a learning situation are given here.

Activity I.   Pictures and Words that Sell

Find some colorful pictures in magazines. Put them in a folder or make a poster. Then make job cards similar to these for students to use.

    A.   Directions to student: Look at the pictures and the words on these pictures and answer the following questions about each.
       1. What emotion-packed words are used?
       2. What emotion is being appealed to?
       3. What inference is made?
       4. Is the inference true or false?
    B.   Find three ads in our consumer magazines and describe the propaganda technique they use.
    C.   Listen to three TV programs. Copy down the advertising slogans. See if your classmates can guess what products are being advertised.

Activity II.   Using Propaganda Techniques in Everyday Life

    A.   After review of techniques of propaganda, use the following sentences to practice. Can you figure which method listed on our poster is being used in each sentence.
       1. All hippies should be banished from the United States.
       2. Religious fanatics are idealistic fools.
       3. Everyone who is anyone wears Weegins.
       4. Teen-agers, say social psychologists, are a product of their environment.
       5. The best people in the world live in the United States.
       6. Leslie Uggams, the TV songstress, uses Mayfair Airlines.

7. Politicians can't be trusted.
8. Research from 200 classrooms proves that teaching today is out-moded.
9. Wearing long hair is a sign of a boy's secret desire to be feminine.
10. Thirty million Americans smoke Vantage.

B. Use any magazine or newspaper available to you and find three examples of each of the five propaganda techniques which we've studied.
C. Read an editorial from today's newspaper and list all of the emotion-packed words.

Activity III.   Fact versus Opinion

A. Directions: Here are some sentences dealing with the car racing world. Read each sentence. Decide whether it is fact or opinion. Mark F for fact and O for opinion. (This activity could be used in the unit on cars in chapter 14.)
1. Americans are the fastest drivers in the world.
2. The United States needs a Women's National 500.
3. The loser of the Charlotte 300 was a picture of depression.
4. Sitting at the infield racer's stand is dangerous.
5. The turbo-charged Porsche engines are the best in the world.
6. A track slick with oil can produce a wild melee of spinning ma-chines.
7. Veteran sportsman David Pearson is a humble winner.
8. Carburetor resister plates on race cars triggered a controversy.
9. Some drivers use American freeways like race tracks.
10. The best racing tire is made by Goodyear.

Answers: Numbers 3, 6, 7, 8, and 9 are facts. Number 1, some are, some are not. Number 2 is opinion; 4 can be but may not be; in 5, one company says so; and number 10 is opinion.

B. Choose a news story and compare and contrast how each of your city's newspapers handled the story.
C. Use our history textbook and a supplementary text. Can you find any differences in the way they handle—(you choose the story to add here). Now, go to the encyclopedia. Does it agree with either, neither, or both texts?

Activity IV.   Bias or One-sided Reporting

A. Critique *Time, Newsweek,* or a newspaper story of a recent event. Did the authors use mainly facts, generalizations, or opinions? Defend your answers with examples from the articles.
B. Listen to three nightly editorial comments on a local television station. Can you detect any one-sided reporting? Was the editorial for or against the subject being discussed?

    C.   Listen to two or three national news programs. Could you detect bias, one-sided reporting, emotion arousing words, lifted eyebrows which punctuated a story, or any other propaganda techniques?

    D.   Go to the media center (if you have one) and listen for fifteen minutes to any program which is being shown at the time. Take notes on the ads used in the show. What techniques does each ad use to "hook" the listener? (If television is not available at your school, students could do this as homework.)

Activity V.   Write Your Own

    A.   Make up a new product, a new company to produce the product, and give a name to each.

    B.   Write some ads or slogans for your product for newspaper or TV spots.

    C.   What propaganda techniques did you use to sell your product?

    D.   Decide upon the package shape, size, and color you will use to get your product to market. Why do you choose these?

    E.   Illustrate your new product and its package, and sell it to your peers. Discuss with them why it would sell or not.

Lesson: Basic Reading in /on Music*

Purpose: 1. To teach the basic note values and other musical notations
            2. As a reinforcer for what teacher has already introduced
            3. A form of game evaluation—behavioral learning

Materials Needed: 1. This short lesson material
                    2. Set of cut outs—notes and clef signs
                    3. 24 x 36 sheet of poster tagboard as a gameboard with staff lines drawn on it for placement of notes

Directions to student: Read and study the following material. Ask for help if you need it. Use the game board and notes in the music center to play around with different kinds of notes and measures. If you need to, use it in answering the questions at the end of this lesson.

    Music is notated on what is called the *great* or *grand staff*. The notes are placed on different lines and spaces on the staff. (See illustration) Musical sound embodies both pitch (the high-low characteristic) and rhythm (the long-short characteristic).

    Pitch is denoted by placing different notes on different lines and spaces. Names are given to the lines and spaces which correspond to the different notes or pitch levels. The higher you move up on the staff, the higher the pitch of the note placed thereon. Look at figure 6.2.

---

*Plan by Donny Gibson, Western Carolina University graduate student

FIGURE 6.2

The treble and bass clef

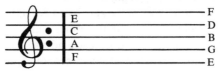

Using the treble clef. Also called the G clef.

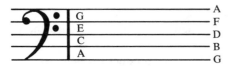

Using the Bass clef. Also called the F clef.

Two numbers placed after the clef sign near the beginning of the staff indicate the meter and rhythm. The upper number gives the number of beats per measure (meter). The lower number indicates the type note that will receive one beat (rhythm). The rhythm and meter determine how fast or how slow a piece of music will be played or sung. See figure 6.3. A line drawn vertically across the staff is used to separate the measures.

FIGURE 6.3

Time signature

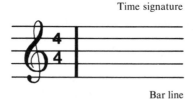

Bar line

FIGURE 6.4

Time signature chart

Time Signature	$\frac{4}{4}$	$\frac{8}{8}$	$\frac{2}{2}$	$\frac{16}{16}$
Whole Note ○	4 beats	8 beats	2 beats	16 beats
Half Note	2 beats	4 beats	1 beat	8 beats
Quarter Note	1 beat	2 beats	½ beat	4 beats
Eighth Note	½ beat	1 beat	¼ of one beat	2 beats

When you think you understand the information given in this lesson, see if you can answer these questions. This will help you understand the material you have just studied. If you don't know the answer, go back to the material and study it again. Answer your group of questions, or you may answer all the groups if you want to.

Group I. 1. What is the purpose of this lesson?
          2. What does the treble clef look like?
          3. What does the bass clef look like?
          4. Where is the time signature located?
          5. Which number in the time signature gives the number of beats per measure?

Group II. 1. How many beats would be in a measure of 3/4 time?
          2. How many beats would be in a measure of 6/8 time?
          3. Look at the example of the treble clef. Which note is pitched higher—G or D?
          4. Draw a staff on your paper. Now, place the following notes on it.
             a. half note on F
             b. whole note on high E
             c. eighth note on A
             d. two quarter notes on C
             e. quarter note on low B
             f. whole note on high D

Group III. 1. Use quarter notes and eighth notes for the correct number of beats in a measure of 4/4 time.
           2. How could a measure of 2/4 time be written to give a feeling of 6/4 time?
           3. Write four measures of any combination of notes in 6/8 time.
           4. Change the four measures in number 3 to 3/4 time.

SUMMARY

Evaluation of learning activities has always been a problem. Using learning centers for individualization is no different. In two hours of working in open classes, I saw four little fellows learning over and over nothing except how to beat the system. In math they got the answer keys and filled in answer sheets. One little fellow pulled six worksheets from various centers and, one-by-one, copied the key. When, as a visitor, I questioned him about his work and if I could help, he said, "Oh, I have to get my work finished. When I do six worksheets, I can play with the blocks." He was a first grader who hadn't learned to read, yet he had worksheets from third-grade kits. For the time I was there, not one teacher or aide spoke to this child. He was keeping busy working independently on his own, they would have said. Yes. Busy, wasting time and paper. Well, perhaps he learned something. The answers were beautifully copied.

Centers are not panaceas. Basic skill teaching must be done. Students must be self-disciplined and motivated enough to actually work when the teacher isn't looking and the material must be on a level that they can handle. If you want them to be lifetime readers you must let your instruction and materials guide toward that goal. By using their interests, problems, and life experiences as avenues, you can show them that reading in school is not a dreaded chore, but a vital pulsating task which leads to new ways of seeing everyday happenings, of visiting foreign exotic places, or meeting and learning exciting, new friends, and of experiencing through print how other people have handled the same problems they may be facing.

Activities for the Teacher

1. Choose some concept you are attempting to develop with your students. Brainstorm with them. How many directions does it take you? Share student reactions with your peers.
2. Try one of the propaganda techniques given in this chapter. If students are interested, plan with them a unit on the subject. Use role playing simulation games, sociodrama, or any other technique you and your students enjoy.
3. Let students pick a concept they're interested in and find sayings of famous people. Discuss some of them.
4. Have a student sit-in on books. Every student reads a favorite book and sees if he can come up with a unique way of reporting it. Challenge each to think of a way no one else has tried. Report the results to your peers. How many different techniques were used?
5. Plan and make materials for one learning center.

SEVEN

Techniques for Effective Middle-Grade Reading for All Students

PREMISE: Given the know-how and the time, teachers will meet the needs of students.

THINK ON THESE:

1. How much can you legitimately expect from students?
2. What are approaches used by some experts in the field of reading which produce results?
3. What is meant by levels of questions and how can this concept help to meet the needs of students?
4. What are some advantages and disadvantages of study guides?
5. How can a teacher better foster creative thinking about any materials students are working with?

By now almost all teachers have read or heard about *Pygmalion in the Classroom,* by Jacobson & Rosenthal, as well as the "Revisit," study done by Elashoff and Snow. This bit of research simply proves what good teachers have known for years—that *expectations* is the name of the game we're in. You get from students, indeed, from most everyone, what you expect to get. In fact, in many instances student attitudes are reflections of teacher and administration attitudes. Adults inadvertently damage young people by expecting too little or too much. How do you decide? From your initial diagnosis. Compare the potential with achievement. Expect, demand, guide. Find, create, and try new approaches. Be willing to *ask* for and *accept* help. New books, professional magazines, commercial programs, systems, and kits are being produced daily. Take from them what you need.

Individualized instruction is a term often verbalized, more often misunderstood, and too seldom actually used. It does not mean that every student is taught every skill separately and individually. This would be tutoring and is humanly and physically impossible in the classroom. It does mean that attempts are made to find student needs and assignments are structured to accommodate those needs.

In classes there will be five or six who need help with the same skill. These can be grouped together for instruction and still meet individual needs. The amount of reinforcement needed to learn the skill will depend upon the individual's different interests in, need for, and intelligence to deal with the tasks.

A Review of Some Current Approaches to Beginning Reading

In an ever expanding effort to find answers to the problems which we face daily in our classes, many hours are spent in trying to come up with "the answer." No one has.

Here is a very brief review of some approaches to beginning reading. The purpose for listing them here is as background for the thesis which says that reading is a thinking process and no one method will suffice in all cases. What is done by the middle-grade teacher will depend to some extent on methods used in the primary grades. This also upholds the argument that teachers should know what is going on in the classrooms around them, and should work as teams to cooperate on the what, when, and why of skills teaching. If you don't there will be overlapping, repetition, and gaps in the sequence. How many times have you heard students complain, "Oh, it's the same old stuff! We've had it all before." Look at these approaches. How many have your students been exposed to?

1. DISTAR	Structured step-by-step approach. Stimulus-Response. Teacher centered concept of learning. Developed for disadvantaged children.
2. ORGANIC TEACHING	No structured basic materials. Relies on the language of the child. Personalized vocabulary.
3. MONTESSORI	Freedom in a prepared environment. No unnecessary interference. Child's intellect is sufficient. Spontaneous activity in carefully graded materials and sequence of experiences.
4. REBUS	Pictures for unknown words.
5. BASAL READERS	Using basal textbooks following a skills sequence and controlled vocabulary patterns.
6. LINGUISTIC PROGRAMS	Little or no story content to begin with. Words and word patterns with few or no pictures. Later materials have more story and pictures.
7. I.T.A.	Initial Teaching Alphabet. A symbol for each sound. Reading for meaning.

8. UNIFON	New alphabet with sound-letter relationship. One letter per speech sound. Printed in block letters.
9. WORDS IN COLOR	Linguistic-phonic system. Each vowel has its own color for different sounds.
10. PHONOVISUAL METHODS	Matching symbols to sounds. Taking what he already knows and building on that.
11. PROGRAMMED READING	Machines, filmstrips, instant reinforcement. Production line if child is ready.
12. LANGUAGE-EXPERIENCE	Based upon experiences children have, in their own words.
13. INDIVIDUALIZED READING	Child reading on his own level in a self-selected book. Individual conferences with teacher. Much record keeping.
14. ALPHA I	Phonics. Letters have characteristics of humans. Combination of characteristics of many types of approaches to teaching.
15. DISCOVERY/INQUIRY	Begin with known elements. Compare likes and differences. Discover how these apply to the unknown they're trying to learn. Student comes up with generalization. In opposition to rote memorization and/or spoonfeeding.
16. ECLECTIC	Teacher makes program what she wants it to be, using what she needs from all the other types of programs.

The eclectic approach is the one advocated by this writer. All programs have good points and most of them have some disadvantages. If an idea works, use it. If not, throw it out and try something else. However as stated elsewhere in this book, one caution: give anything you try time to work. Jumping from one system or one method to another may add confusion to already confused students.

In fact, this is one of the drawbacks of having special reading teachers and rooms. They usually have a profusion of materials and machines. They also have short, interesting activities planned for students. And the student succeeds in the reading room. But what happens when he goes back into his regular class? He's put right back into that basal textbook that he can't handle, and the classroom teacher wonders why he isn't learning to read. After all, he's missing something in her room to go to the reading room.

Throughout this book there are materials devised to help you and the students in handling the tasks in the school program—questions, activities, tasks for centers, all which involve total student participation and interchange. There are also guides to give structure to the reading which students do and hopefully to be instrumental in teaching and reinforcing skills and concepts from curriculum materials they're working with.

Levels of Questions

Olive Stafford Niles[26] picked out study skills that she felt were absolutely basic to the understanding of reading. It is a list which any teacher can handle in the classroom:

a. Understanding thought relationships in sentences, in paragraphs, and in selections of varying length. Students should be able to see that paragraphs, chapters, and/or units have organizational patterns which aid in understanding and in remembering. The four main ones are time, simple listing, comparison-contrast, and cause-effect.
b. Reading with a purpose. In a study done by Harvard, 13 students out of 1,500 got the point in an article they were asked to read. They were reading without purpose. Teachers must give purpose, or let students set purpose for themselves.
c. Comprehension is not spongelike absorption of what is read; it is forceful reaction in the light of definite purpose.
d. Drawing on previous learning. We call it reading readiness at the first-grade level. Students should learn to do associational reading—to draw on past experiences to give more meaning to present reading. How to get them to do this is the big question. Her suggestions are: (1) give questions that teach rather than test; (2) give questions at right time—before is better than after reading; and (3) teach directed reading lessons in the content areas.

Herber [27] agrees with Niles. His three levels of questions and exercises based on levels of thinking can be applied to most curricular materials. Take a look at these examples of questions. Can you see the difference in the thinking ability required to function successfully with the material? Do you understand how this concept could work for you in meeting the needs of all students in your classes?

I. The *literal or recall questions*. What does the material say? This is the lowest level of thinking—in fact, little thinking is involved. Our weakest students can function successfully at this level. The sad thing about classroom practices is that too many teachers never go beyond it in teaching or testing. Examples:

a. What is an elephant, Sarah?
b. What is the fundamental law of jet propulsion?
c. Name the three levels of thinking, Miss Doe.

II. The *interpretative level*. What does the material mean? Or what does the author mean by what he says? Here the student must understand what is meant, implied, or left unsaid. Average students can handle this level adequately. Examples:

a. Why is the elephant called a beast of burden?
b. Does the law of jet propulsion operate in a computer?
c. Why are the three levels of thinking used in making questions for study guides, Miss Doe?

III. The *applicative level*. How can I use this information? This is the highest level of thinking. A student must assimilate, integrate, apply what he is reading to what he already knows. The strong students need these kinds of questions to challenge them. Examples:

   a. Down through history, of what use has the elephant been to man?
   b. In your project "Aerial Trajectory" for the science fair, will you use jet propulsion, Terry?
   c. How are the levels of thinking applied to a science lesson, Miss Doe?

Study Guides: Tools for Learning

All material is not worth mastering. Much of it is repetition of what many students already know. Your job as guide, challenger, and director of the learning process is to help students realize that they should distinguish the important from the unimportant. Give them a purpose for everything you ask of them. Knowing purpose can be motivating, can aid comprehension, and can change the attitude of students. You know that comprehension depends upon their purpose for reading, their interests, and their background knowledge of the subject matter, so let them in on the secret.

One way to guide students work is through the use of study guides. Most of you have used them all your life in one form—the literal level questions you give them to study by. Herber, Burmeister, Robinson, and others suggest taking this idea and building around and upon it to create a tool for active learning for all students according to their various levels of understanding. What does it do, or how does it help?

   1. Gives student some direction and structure for learning.
   2. Provides for individual rate and level of work.
   3. Enables every student to participate, total involvement.
   4. Releases teacher to work with small skills groups.
   5. Can be made during summer and/or at workshops or classes.
   6. Can be traded back and forth by teachers.
   7. Gives student social activity, peer learning, and practice of group process.
   8. There are few absolute answers, therefore it leads to exploration and discussion.

Some things which need to be remembered concerning the use of study guides:

   a. Same one may not work for all students.
   b. They are not tests, so no grades.
   c. Should not be used every day or they become busy work.
   d. Usually used as a reinforcing device after preliminary teaching.
   e. Study guides are not a panacea. One method of providing for individual needs and helping students grow toward independent learning.
   f. In making them, attempt to lead students from simple to more complex. To use effectively, students must be able to succeed.
   g. All material does not lend itself to effective treatment in this manner.

h. The student must feel that you are interested enough to check on his or her work, no matter what the structure.

What are some purposes for reading?

You've heard the story of the effects of pursuing the wrong purpose at the wrong time: Students were assigned the poem, "The Blind Men and the Elephant," to read silently and be able to answer questions later. The teacher pronounced any difficult words for them.

After they had read the poem, the teacher said, "Close your books." For twenty minutes she stood there and asked questions. "What was the name of the poem? Who wrote it? What was it about? How many men were involved in the poem? What animal was talked about? How did the first man describe the elephant? How about the second one? What was the main idea of the poem?" One student answered, "Blind men can't see, and everybody knows that already." The class laughed. Some of the time she answered her own questions and scolded the students for not remembering details. Once she said, "And the poem ended up with the stupid men quarrelling just like you kids do the biggest part of the time."

Not once during this observation did the teacher let them open up the book to defend an answer, to feel the rhythm, or to reread to get the moral. It was easy to see why most of her students dislike poetry and fail to understand it.

What are some legitimate reasons for reading which children and older students can understand? Depending upon the thinking levels of the students, develop purposes with them. They should not have to read everything, nor read for the same reason other students read.

Look at the following sets of questions. There are hundreds of reasons for reading an assignment other than the teacher said to or it's the next chapter in the textbook.

Set I.   Weaker students can handle this type with success.
1. Read story to find facts about snakes.
2. Read selection to find things a beaver uses in making his home.
3. Read to learn about the former life of one of the minority groups in America: where they came from, what they ate, how they prepared their food, what they wore, what language they spoke.
4. Read to find the uses the spacemen made of plastic.
5. Read to find ways we heated our homes before electricity.
6. Find and read sentences to prove or disprove these statements:
   a. A big sea lion weighs about 600 pounds.
   b. A baby kangaroo sleeps in its mother's pouch.
   c. Television has changed the life of American families.

Set II.   These questions are somewhat more difficult than those in Set I. They require some thinking to interpret the material, to organize it.
1. Read about animals to make a summary chart showing where they live, what they eat, how to recognize them, how they get ready for winter, how they protect themselves, and so on.

2. Read to find what police officers do in making a print of your hand.
3. Read to find out how a boy in Alaska is different from you.
4. Read, discuss, and form conclusions about how the space age has changed America.

Set III. More difficult and creative than those in Sets I and II.
1. Read in preparation for doing a newspaper story.
2. Read to make a filmstrip.
3. Read to compare one author's opinion with that of another.
4. Read to plan a radio or television presentation of a story, to obtain the visual background needed to represent it on a stage or mural.

The remainder of this chapter deals with activities and tasks to insure total class participation at levels on which students can succeed. They include many more varieties than the usual questions.

Stories such as "The Legend of Sleepy Hollow" are so entertaining as a whole, I question mutilating them to teach reading skills. Yet, it is one which students thoroughly enjoy working with either before or after initial reading. I've used it more than once. One criterion on which to base one's decision of what to do is what successfully works with students. And the exercises presented in this chapter do work.

While many writers advocate the DRA, including five to eight steps as preparation for reading, others argue that all of these steps are not necessary. R. G. Stauffer (135) questions the practice of always preteaching vocabulary. He says there are times when it destroys some of the initiative, the inquiry, the surprise, and the success a student needs in using his/her own skills in figuring out new words in the story or article.

Reading is a developmental cognitive process which matures as the student matures. These projects are a refutation of the practice and belief that the teaching of reading begins and ends in primary school.

STUDY GUIDE: LITERATURE

Washington Irving, "The Legend of Sleepy Hollow," from *Adventures Ahead*. Harcourt, Brace & World, Inc. N.Y.
Preparation for Reading:

Introduce the word *legend,* a story passed down from older times. Compare and contrast with fantasy, history, and folk tales.

Discuss the idea of superstitions. Can they be proven or disproven? Where do they spring from? Should they influence our actions in the twentieth century? Do they influence us? What part does education play in destroying the influence of superstitions?

Talk about the ideas the students and people in general have about teachers. Are they just? Are teachers any different today than fifty years ago? Are students any different? Why or why not and in what ways?

Introduce the story. Inform the students that this story involves all the ideas you've been discussing. Many people have found the tale of Ichabod Crane amusing and intriguing. Tell them they might compare the characters in this story with the people they know in real life.

Prereading Study of Vocabulary

The words and figurative language used in this tale will necessitate some study of them for some students. There are too many to be used any one day. You, the teacher, will use sound judgment in selection.

Place the words you plan to use on the chalkboard, or better still, use flash cards.

lank	burly	loiterer
sallied	spacious	solitude
conscientious	frolic	burnished
pedagogue	pommel	resume
spindle	viciousness	dismal

Have students examine the words individually. Ask them to pronounce each word and to divide each into familiar clusters which they know. Encourage suggestions of definitions. If they know the word, don't spend time on it. For those unfamiliar, consider the meanings in contextual situations. Use names of students in the classroom if the situation allows. They like the recognition and it helps with recall of meanings. (association) Using names also can be an aid in building self-concept for those who need this type of recognition.

Some sample sentences:

1. Carl hangs around the water fountain as long as he can between bells. He could be called a *loiterer*.
2. Because he always gets his work in on time, Michael could be called a *conscientious* fellow.
3. In all the days you've spent in school, you've found some interesting names for teachers. You might add the word *pedagogue* to your list.
4. The gang attacked the winning baseball team with *viciousness*.
5. On the day I get my report card, I'm usually in a *dismal* mood.
6. After the fire drill, we will *resume* our work on Ichabod.

Word Relationships

Many students are unable to see relationships when they read. Short drills on some kind of exercise like word analogies might be helpful. The better students will do this and enjoy it. Others will need help. Words relating to a particular story or season of the year could lend flavor. Team or group work is fun here. So many of the high school and college board tests have this type exercise on them, teachers should use often so that students are proficient in the process involved.

Directions: Study the two words given. See if you can figure out their relationship to each other. Then think of words which would show the same relationship to those listed here and fill in the blanks. Two examples are given for you.

Brom Bones:	Ichabod	_____	Daredevil:	Gunpowder
Tarry Town:	New York	_____	Chicago:	Illinois
teacher:	student	_____	mother:	_____
food:	hunger	_____	study:	_____
specter:	Halloween	_____	_____:	Christmas
_____:	feeling	_____	fact:	proof

night:	_____	_____	love:	hate	
apple pie:	feast	_____	dancing:	_____	
Katrina:	girl	_____	Paul:	_____	
hurt:	_____	_____	success:	pleasure	

Directions: Listed here are some words. Give three other words which come to your mind when you say these. You may use a dictionary if you need or want to. Several examples are done for you.

ghost:	scary
horse:	one-eyed, headless
noise:	whine of the dog, tables banged against the wall
color:	
pumpkin:	
goblin:	
dark:	
party:	
bridge:	
teacher:	
rattling:	
doughnut:	
vocal:	
dance:	

Directions: The following words are all mixed up. Some of them describe Ichabod Crane, some Brom Bones, and some Katrina. Categorize (put under the correct heading) these descriptive words as you remember them in the story. (You may use your book if necessary.)

	Ichabod	Brom Bones	Katrina
a pedagogue			
lank			
small headed			
glassy eyes			
blooming			
broad-shouldered			
talented in mischief making			
plump as a partridge			
huge ears			
loved a fight			
soft and foolish heart			
narrow shoulders			
rather handsome			
little of a flirt			
noisy fellow			
skilled horseman			
long snipe nose			
famed for beauty			
short curly black hair			
skinny neck			

good dancer
jealous
conscientious
rich
burly

Organizational Patterns

It would be helpful to discuss time order as one of the organizational patterns of writing which helps students in their study and recall of material. An exercise such as the following will give practice.

Directions: The following events happened in "The Legend of Sleepy Hollow." Read them and rearrange them in the proper sequence (order of happening). Number them from 1 to 10 in the blanks provided with Number 1 being first and Number 10 being last.

_____A. Sleepy Hollow is described.
_____B. Brom Bones marries Katrina.
_____C. Ichabod is so scared he can't sing.
_____D. Katrina Van Tassel is introduced into the story.
_____E. Gunpowder has a race with a black steed in the middle of the night.
_____F. Ichabod's schoolhouse is described.
_____G. Brom Bones sits brooding in a corner because of jealousy.
_____H. Ichabod's hat is found by the river.
_____I. Brom Bones teaches his dog to sing and disturb Ichabod's music lessons.
_____J. Ichabod gets an invitation to Katrina's house and is excited.

Reading Is Communication

Reading is a personal thing. Teachers should help students to understand this fact. It means more when we get involved. Honest emotion is a communion between the writer and reader. Too many students are passive word callers, even in fiction. The following exercise might help to get them involved. Page and paragraph numbers will depend upon publication being used.

Directions: The following exercise is one to help you understand that the author wanted you to feel something when you read his story. On the pages given, see if you can find and write a phrase that makes you
1. hear something. _____First paragraph, page 102
2. feel something. _____Last paragraph, page 105
3. see something. _____Last paragraph, first column, page 106
4. taste something. _____Third paragraph, column 2, page 103
5. smell something. _____First paragraph, page 101

A Comprehension Study Guide—Group I—Section I

Directions: The section on pages 98-102 might be called the introduction to the story. Read this section and then read these statements. Place *yes* or *no* before the statements which represent what the author said or didn't say.

1. _____ Tarry Town is one of the quietest places in the world.
2. _____ The chief spirit which haunts this region is a headless horseman.
3. _____ Ichabod's schoolhouse stood on a windy hill.
4. _____ Ichabod lived week by week in homes of the children he taught.
5. _____ Katrina took singing lessons from Ichabod.
6. _____ Brom Bones was a juvenile delinquent.
7. _____ Ichabod had a lively imagination.
8. _____ Ichabod thought that the world turned around.

Directions: Can you anticipate (think ahead) what the writer is going to say or what he means by the cues he gives you? The following exercise will give you practice. If you need help in completing these sentences, read beginning the middle of page 103 . . . Ichabod . . . to the bottom of page 104.

1. Ichabod's horse was old, shagged and had a glaring eye. Yet he was vicious. This means that the horse was _____.
2. As well as being a singer, Ichabod was a good _____.
3. Brom Bones sat in a corner and sulked because he was_____of Ichabod.
4. After the dance, the farmer told _____.
5. According to the author, Ichabod stayed at the party after the others had gone so that he could _____.

Directions: Read beginning bottom of page 104 to the middle of second column on page 106, then read these statements. Put true or false beside them.
_____1. Ichabod remembered all the ghost stories he had heard and was afraid before he saw or heard anything.
_____2. Gunpowder was an obedient horse.
_____3. The ghostly rider carried his head behind him on his saddle.
_____4. The Headless Rider hit Ichabod on the head and Ichabod fell to the ground.
_____5. The goblin rider rode a black steed.

Directions: Do you understand what the author is saying? He doesn't always speak in the style we're accustomed to. Complete the reading of the story and see if you think these statements are true or false.
_____1. Ichabod was drowned.
_____2. The horse with his saddle was found the next morning.
_____3. Brom Bones married Katrina.
_____4. The ladies of the Church believed that Ichabod was carried away by spirits.
_____5. The ghost of Ichabod haunts the decayed old schoolhouse today.
_____6. Early Dutch ladies liked to gossip.

A Comprehension Study Guide—Group II—Read the Directions

The story is divided into six sections thusly:

Introduction: pages 98 to end of column 2, paragraph, page 102.

The Invitation: two paragraphs, last one page 102 and the following one.

The Party: middle page 103, first column to bottom 104.

The Midnight Ride: beginning bottom 104 to last paragraph, second column page 106.

The Search: last paragraph page 106 and following one on page 107.

Ending of story: remainder of story page 107.

Directions: Information on these questions will be found in the first section. Put a check in front of those statements you can support from your reading.

————1. A ghost of a headless trooper haunts Sleepy Hollow.

————2. Ichabod Crane went to Sleepy Hollow to investigate ghost stories.

————3. School in Sleepy Hollow was similar to ours.

————4. Katrina's beauty alone won Ichabod's heart.

————5. Ichabod believed that the witches were responsible for his troubles.

Directions: Read section two. Look for the main idea there. Check the statement below which you think most nearly fits these two paragraphs.

————1. Ichabod was a stern teacher.

————2. Boys could outsmart their teacher.

————3. Ichabod was excited about the party invitation.

Directions: Read these four statements. Then read section three of the story. Check the statements with which you agree.

————1. Though Brom Bones was the best looking fellow on the dance floor, he was no rival for Ichabod.

————2. Ichabod must have known the twist.

————3. Katrina told Ichabod he had no chance with her.

————4. Gunpowder and Ichabod were two animals, well-matched.

Directions: Read these statements. Then read the fourth section of the story. Do you agree with the statements? Check yes or no and underneath each write the statement from the story to defend your answer.

————1. At the beginning of section four, the night was made for ghosts.

————2. Gunpowder cooperated with his master.

————3. Ichabod believed in ghosts. His actions prove this.

————4. Music frightened the specter.

————5. Loss of his saddle caused Ichabod to lose the race with the pursuer.

Directions: Are you able to pick out facts from narrative reading? This exercise will give you practice. Read the next section and find out what three things caused the church people to predict that Ichabod had been "done in" by the spirits. Write them here.

1.

2.

3.

Directions: According to Washington Irving's story ending, check the statement which you think most likely happened.

————1. Ichabod moved away because of his fear of ghosts.

————2. Ichabod moved away because Katrina married Brom Bones.

————3. Ichabod was spirited away by ghosts.

————4. A headless horseman frightened away his rival.

A Comprehension Study Guide—Group III—Strongest Students

Directions: When you have finished reading the story of "The Legend of Sleepy Hollow," by Washington Irving, study this page. Work alone at first, then as a group compare and contrast your ideas. See if you can, as a group, arrive at some agreement.

Read each statement. If you think Washington Irving would agree, place a check in the blank. At the bottom of the page, give the statement or statements from the story to support your decisions.

_____1. Washington Irving believed in ghosts.
_____2. It pays to be rich.
_____3. Men with different characteristics have different values.
_____4. In fiction, as in real life, man's actions are influenced by his emotions.
_____5. Brom Bones was a model young man.
_____6. Men like Ichabod Crane shouldn't be school teachers.
_____7. In good creative writing, authors lead your thinking by foreshadowing events.

Supplementary activities: If you have time while the other groups are working on this story, check in the library for other ghost stories. Read some. If you find one which you think particularly exciting and which you would like to share with the group, you may do so.

If you like, some of you might want to try writing a ghost story of your own.

You might do research on some particular haunted house or other property which you know about in your community.

How Is Cognition Measured?

The Barrett Taxonomy: Cognitive and Affective Dimensions of Reading Comprehension
    How this taxonomy relates to a specific story read by most seventh graders, "The Legend of Sleepy Hollow" by Washington Irving

1.0 Literal Comprehension

Literal comprehension focuses on ideas and information which are explicitly stated in the selection.

1.1 Recognition tasks require the student to locate or identify ideas or information stated in material. These tasks are
    1.11 Recognition of details. What is the setting of the story?
    1.12 Recognition of main idea. What sentence states the theme or main ideas of "The Legend of Sleepy Hollow?" (This question would not apply to this story, because the theme is not explicitly stated.)
    1.13 Recognition of sequence.
        Directions: The following events happened in "The Legend of Sleepy Hollow." Put them in the proper sequence (order). Number them from 1 to 10, with Number 1 being first and Number 10 last.
        _____A. Sleepy Hollow is described.
        _____B. Brom Bones marries Katrina.
        _____C. Ichabod is so scared he can't sing.
        _____D. Katrina Van Tassel is introduced into the story.
        _____E. Gunpowder has a race with a black steed in the middle of the night.
        _____F. Ichabod's schoolhouse is burned.

————G. Brom Bones sits brooding in a corner because of jealousy.

————H. Ichabod's hat is found by the river.

———— I. Brom Bones teaches his dog to sing and disturb Ichabod's music lessons.

———— J. Ichabod gets an invitation to Katrina's house and is excited.

1.14 Recognition of comparison. In what way is Brom Bones different from Ichabod Crane?

1.15 Recognition of cause and effect. At the dance, why did Brom Bones sit over in a corner and brood?

1.16 Recognition of character traits. Locate the sentence which points out the fact that Ichabod was superstitious.

1.2 Recall tasks require that students recall from memory ideas and information explicitly stated in the material.

1.21 to 1.26 could use the same types of questions as 1.11-1.16 and this time answer from memory.

2.0 Reorganization

Reorganization of materials requires student to analyze, synthesize, and/or organize ideas or information explicitly stated in materials in author's words or by paraphrasing.

2.1 Classifying.

Directions: The following words describe Ichabod Crane, Brom Bones, and Katrina. Categorize (put under the correct headings) these descriptive terms as you remember them from the story. List under correct character.

lank	rather handsome
small head	little of a flirt
glassy eyes	noisy fellow
blooming	skilled horseman
broad-shouldered	long snipe nose
talented in mischief making	famed for beauty
plump as a partridge	short curly black hair
huge ears	skinny neck
loved a fight	good dancer
soft and foolish heart	jealous
narrow shoulders	conscientious

Ichabod   *Brom Bones*   *Katrina*

2.2 Outlining. Using the direct statements or paraphrased statements which give the main points of the story, make an outline of "The Legend of Sleepy Hollow" as you think the author might have had in mind when he wrote the story.

2.3 Summarizing. In your own words, using no more than one page, write the summary of the story.

2.4 Synthesizing. Is there a similarity in this story to any of the ghost stories which we read last month?

3.0 Inferential Comprehension

Inferential comprehension demands using the ideas and information explicitly stated, intuition, and personal experiences as a basis for conjectures and hypotheses.

Usually stimulated by purposes for reading and teacher's questions which demand thinking and imagination that go beyond the printed page.

3.1 Inferring supporting details. If you had been the author of "The Legend of Sleepy Hollow," would you have given additional information about what happened to Ichabod and Gunpowder?

3.2 Inferring main idea. What is the basic theme or main idea of this story?

3.3 Inferring sequence. Suppose Katrina had really cared for Ichabod and gone searching for him? Do you think she would have found him? What might have happened?

3.4 Inferring comparisons. Compare Katrina's fickleness to a present day teen-ager you know.

3.5 Inferring cause and effect. If they lived today, would Brom Bones get by with treating Ichabod in the fashion he treated him in this story? Discuss your answer.

3.6 Inferring character traits. Would you conclude Ichabod was a stupid man? Why or why not?

3.7 Predicting outcomes. Read the first two sections. Before reading the third section, write your own ending to the story. Then compare it with the author's ending.

3.8 Interpreting figurative language. What do you think the author meant by each of these expressions?
    a. Katrina was as plump as a partridge.
    b. Ichabod had a soft and foolish heart.
    c. Brom Bones was talented in mischief-making.
    d. Katrina was a little of a flirt.

4.0 Evaluation

Evaluation deals with making judgments. Purpose for reading and teacher's questions require responses by students which indicate that they have made evaluative judgments. Must be accurate, probable, acceptable and worthy.

4.1 Judgments of reality or fantasy. Since there really is a Tarrytown in New York, do you think the story might really have happened?

4.2 Facts or opinions. Is the author attempting to inform you, sway your opinion about ghosts or to entertain you? Discuss your answer.

4.3 Adequacy and validity. What other materials have you read which delve into the idea of teen-age competition in love, in sports, or of pranks played on rivals which play on the imagination of the reader such as this one does?

4.4 Appropriateness. What part of the story best sums up the character of Ichabod Crane?

4.5 Worth, desirability and acceptability. In comparison to today's standards of morality, should Katrina be scolded for flirting with Ichabod?

5.0 Appreciation

How did the story affect the reader? Emotional and aesthetic sensitivity to the work as a whole.

5.1 Emotional response to the content. Would you recommend this story to a friend?

5.2 Identification with character or incidents. Brom Bones taught his dog to sing, to disturb Ichabod every time he taught music lessons to Katrina. If you had been Ichabod, what would you have done about this situation?

5.3 Reactions to use of language (connotations, denotations)
    List five examples of connotative language used in this story.
    Examples: plump as a partridge, goblin rider

5.4 Imagery. Find two phrases each of word pictures which appeal to the five senses. noisy fellow, skinny neck

The Reading of Science as a Cognitive Process

Introduction

Because of technical vocabulary, much of it new, and difficult concept value loads, the discipline called *science* presents many reading problems for students.

Most educators and parents agree that kindergarten and first graders need readiness training for reading with understanding. Why is it so difficult to understand that junior high students, or any others for that matter, also need readiness for some of the learning they are supposed to do? If they could perform the tasks teachers require of them, without help, there would be little need for their wasting time sitting in classrooms.

What is the most favorite assignment made by teachers? As the students leave the classroom for their next activity, he calls, "Read chapter 10 for tomorrow, and be able to answer questions on it." If he's lucky, perhaps a third of them will attempt it. The next day less than the third will be able to answer his too often literal level questions or to discuss its implications. The remainder of the class sit apathetically waiting for the bell to ring or creating their own diversions.

Until teachers see the job of teaching as a cooperative adventure, until teachers of all subject areas can see the need for helping students with the skills they need to perform the tasks demanded of them in specific materials, we will still have situations like the preceding one, with frustrated students passing from one class to the other lacking the skills required by most of their so-called teachers—teachers who expect someone else to be responsible.

One of the problems is that specific subject area teachers are not trained to deal with the processes required for reading with understanding of their content. In college courses they dealt with learning the concepts, not the reading, not the techniques for helping future students understand it, and they are especially lacking in the "how" to teach diagnostically. College and university content area specialists also expect someone else to be responsible for the teaching of reading of their materials.

The following portions of this chapter offer some ways of handling working with content materials in such a way that students are involved in the process of learning concepts at the same time they learn skills of reading the material. These activities are used to create appeal to students, to involve the total classroom, to reinforce science and math concepts that mere memorization of technical terms will not accomplish. Thinking, understanding of relationships, attention to the following of directions, and many other reading study skills are used in the process of using these study guides.

Science Lesson

"Changes in the Earth's Surface" is the title of a chapter included in most junior high science series. The ideas used can be changed to adapt to the series you are using or used with reference books.

A VOCABULARY LIST:

*hypothesis	moraine
*sediment	flood plain
*sedimentary rock	geologist
*glacier	deposits
*fault	deposition
delta	fossils
boulder	*sand blasting
filter	molten
erosion	volcano
windbreaks	earthquake

Pre-teach the words with * beside them. Some of these may not meet all the criteria for selection of what vocabulary should be taught, but they are related to key concepts and will lend themselves to interest getting techniques.

1. *Hypothesis:* this term can be taught by structural analysis. The prefix *hyp,* meaning under, down, or less than, could be related to the meaning they already have for hypo in medicine. It puts one under. Thesis, the act of laying down, a position, or a proposition. Put them together and you have something less than the fact; hasn't been proven yet.
2. Sand blasting can be demonstrated by using an electric fan, rock, and pile of sand. Rocks and sand are examples of sediment.
3. Some child will probably have a sedimentary rock in a collection, or a team of fellows could go to the playground, a field nearby, or other source to find one. The class could go rock hunting.
4. Bring to class ice from around the freezing compartment of a refrigerator in the lunchroom. Demonstrate glacier formation.
5. Use the word fault. Talk about the meaning they already have. Discuss the meaning as used in the science context. Find it in the material, both word and picture. Review of multiple word meanings.
6. Some of the other terms are not familiar to the students, but they are well explained and illustrated in most texts.

Using the Vocabulary: Level I.   Categorization.

TASK I

Directions: Below is a list of words connected with the chapter "Changes in the Earth's Surface." Also listed are three big topics. Categorize. List the words from the long lists under the correct topic. A word may fit under more than one topic. When you finish the exercise, working alone, check with your teammates to see if you all agree.

volcano	glaciers	delta
fault	coal	erosion
swamp land	lava	sand dune
lakes	force	decay
canyon	sea shells	earthquake
calcium	folding	chemical change
molten rock	oil	sedimentary rock
flood plain	freezing	limestone
deposits	salt	pollution

Big Topics: Mountain Formation   Minerals   Wind, Water & Ice

TASK II

Directions: In each of the following groups of terms, three are related in some way and one is not. Select the unrelated terms and give reasons.

1. lava	quartz	volcano	weak spot in earth's surface
2. erosion	vegetation	water	iron
3. sand dunes	deposits	harbors	wind
4. glaciation	swamp forests	condensation	temperature
5. landforms	oceans	plains	plateaus
6. sedimentary	minerals	compounds	hypothesis
7. contraction	heat	sold	expansion
8. earthquake	fault	shifting	evaporation
9. ocean	salt	water	decay

TASK III

Directions: The answers to the following questions use some of the same principles which we will study about in this chapter. How many of these questions can you answer? If you can't answer them, do you know where to find the information?

1. What happens when you put your coke in the freezing compartment of the refrigerator?
2. What makes coffee perk?
3. Why do farmers pay such exorbitant prices for a piece of property which they call "bottom" land?
4. What may happen if pressure builds too fast or is released too swiftly in your mother's pressure cooker?

5. Did you ever see the old-fashioned method of preserving food by canning in the water bath? Filled glass containers are placed in water. Fire is built under the water pot or tub, and the water boils. When the food is cooked enough, what do you think might happen if the hot containers were taken out and a breeze of cold air hit them?

6. Tomatoes and pears are two foods which contain acid. Do you have any idea what could happen during processing if the food was packed too closely in the containers before cooking?

Level II.   Word Association

Directions: In each set of words given below, you will find the following: two words that have a definite relationship, as geology and earth. Following these two words is a single word followed by a blank. Below the blank are three words. You are to choose the word that is related to the word preceding the blank in the same way as the first two words are related. Write your choice in the blank.

Example: geology: earth, arithmetic: <u>numbers</u>
erosion, numbers, girls

1. erosion: change, fault: _____
   earthquake, volcano, folding
2. boulder: large, sand: _____
   freeze, fossil, small
3. volcano: lava, limestone: _____
   contraction, sea shells, pressure
4. slope: steep, water: _____
   speed, fault, delta
5. crops: soil, windbreaks: _____
   ice, wind, sediment
6. sediment deposits: water, sand dunes: _____
   boulders, expansion, wind
7. coal: decaying plants & pressure, petroleum: _____
   minerals, oil, decaying plants, animals and pressure
8. sand blasting: building, wind erosion: _____
   water, lava, canyon

Level III.   Review of Concepts

Directions: Do you understand the ideas (concepts) presented in the unit? Match the process or processes in column B which are responsible for the actions in column A. List their numbers in the space provided. An example is given for you.

Column A	Column B
4, 3 1. sedimentary rock formed	1. expansion
____ 2. broken pepsi bottle in freezer	2. contraction
____ 3. hot glass tubing cooled quickly breaks	3. pressure and/or heat
____ 4. volcano erupts	4. deposition
____ 5. ice spewing out of ground on river banks in winter	
____ 6. sand dunes formed	
____ 7. mineral deposits formed	
____ 8. coal is formed	
____ 9. glaciers	
____10. mountains	
____11. rock breakage	
____12. petroleum	
____13. delta	
____14. Paracutin	

Levels II and III.   Relationships

Directions: Read each section of the chapter "How Has the Earth's Surface Changed?" Decide what word or group of words in the three columns are more closely related to each other and make those combinations as shown in the example. When you have finished the work alone, discuss your choices with the other members of your group and see if you all can agree.

SECTION A.

1, 7, 11 1. fault	5. flows between rocks	9. escapes through weak spot in surface—blows, cools, and forms mountains
____ 2. folding	6. hot pressure	10. pushes earth up to change earth's surface
____ 3. volcano	7. crack in earth's surface	11. earthquakes—shifting rock forming mountains
____ 4. molten rock	8. wrinkles and bulges	12. layers of rock pushed up into air, bend & fold to form mountains

Example: 1, 7, 11. A fault is a crack in the earth's surface. When the earth moves or shifts at the faults, earthquakes occur.

SECTION B.

_____ 1. sediment and water 2. pressure on sea shells 3. coal

_____ 4. mud, sediment, and sand 5. greater pressure from bending and wrinkling 6. hard coal

_____ 7. Appalachian Mountains 8. pressure, heat and decaying plant life 9. petroleum

_____ 10. dead plants and animals 11. heat and pressure from sediment cause chemical change 12. limestone

SECTION C.

_____ 1. moving water 6. carries sand and soil 11. slows wind

_____ 2. slow-moving water 7. trees in rows 12. builds mountains and/or cuts canyons

_____ 3. blowing wind 8. carries sediment 13. cleans buildings

_____ 4. sand blasting 9. drops sediment 14. dust storms and sand dunes

_____ 5. windbreaks 10. carries sand and soil 15. forms delta at the mouth of river

Level I. Comprehension Check

Directions: The chapter you are to read is divided into sections. The sections are listed below, each followed by some statements. First read the section and then the statements below that relate to that section. Place a check before those statements which you think represent *what the author said*. Also list the page number where you find the information. Work alone or in teams of two, then with your whole group to find a common answer.

Section A. (This would depend upon the textbook you are using for page numbers and specific questions. These are general samples.)

1. _____ Geology as a science is as old as the earth.
2. _____ The surface of the earth is constantly changing.
3. _____ Pressure is a two-way force. It can break rocks into sand and gravel, and also it can make fine material into rock.
4. _____ A movement of the earth at a fault can cause an earthquake.
5. _____ Volcanoes are caused by pressure of hot rock underground seeking a release.

Levels II and III

Directions: Read the chapter, "Changes in the Earth's Surface," and decide which of the following generalizations you can support from your understanding of the material. Place checkmarks beside those with which you agree.

1. _____ Limestone, coal, and oil are proofs that the land was once covered by water.
2. _____ The term *Ice Age* would not apply to the United States.
3. _____ Once a mountain is formed, it retains its shape.
4. _____ Sand dunes are the results of wind storms and there is nothing man can do about them.
5. _____ More erosion occurs on the outside curve of a river than on the inside.

Reading and Math

How many of you have students who are fast thinkers, good with number manipulations, yet when they have written problems, fail? To do the best jobs, math teachers must look at the reading achievement test scores of students. The subscores are more important than a total score. Study how they perform on vocabulary, comprehension, and/or rate. Will they be able to handle the vocabulary of the math textbook?

Thomas and Robinson (139) suggest that the very first tasks of a math teacher should be to find out how students can use the textbook. Assign a passage for them to study. Tell them to use scratch pads to make notes as they study. Also, tell them that you will ask some questions later. After a reasonable time, you ask the questions. If they did not finish in the allotted time, ask them to make note of that fact on their paper. They answer questions and turn in everything. This approach gives you help on how well students can (1) handle text, (2) master technical terms and concepts independently, (3) take notes and study efficiently, and (4) who is extremely slow.

Just as some vocabulary should be pretaught in other content, so it should be in arithmetic. With the students, survey the chapter or unit. How much do they already know about the topic? Can they get a total picture of the knowledge to be learned and used? Can they see applications of math concepts to everyday situations?

Some of the things being taught in math today are irrelevant as far as students can see. They'll never use it, they argue. Let's face it; immediate needs have priority. Probably they are correct in their assumptions. So, for these students, many for which junior high school years are terminal, make their arithmetic the utility type. Use the newspapers, mail order catalogues, opinion polls, stock market reports; statistics which deal with their daily life; how much money they need for a Saturday night date. Gas, food, tickets to game or movie? How many hours will they have to work at what wages to get it? How to balance a bankbook, figure interest on debts or savings, how to figure income tax, and so forth.

Teachers can challenge, guide, and encourage them to look at long-range goals. How much difference in the amount of money to be paid for some wanted article if bought now, plus interest which will have to be paid on the debt, versus saving over a period of time and paying cash? How do loan sharks operate? Are things sold at so-called bargain rates, on sale, at advertised liquidation or going-out-of-business extravaganzas always on the level? How can one tell?

One of the most interesting math lessons a teacher can structure for her students is to bring in newspapers and let them actually go shopping via these ads in the classroom. (See lessons in chapter 11 for practice.) Utility math? Yes. They'll get it on their own? No. Go downtown on any day when textile workers get paid, when welfare checks are cashed, or when food stamps are used. I've seen young mothers buy the snack foods (potato chips, pepsis, candy), nothing which could be called basic foods which growing children need. What is a wise buy? They'll get this in another class? Don't bet on it.

Like all the other content materials dealt with in classrooms, proficiency in math means dealing with vocabulary as concepts, abstract symbols—communication through language. As a math teacher do you help or could they get it as well without you? Activities may motivate students toward math when the traditional textbook doesn't. You can find or make up others to fit the interests of your students.

1. Make a visit to the bank. Let the guide explain the value of checking and savings accounts versus cash stored and kept at home. Most banks will give each student a deposit slip and check to practice with as they talk, or for reinforcement back in the classroom.
2. Let students collect unused clothing, utensils, furniture, etc., from the community. They can clean it up, repair, and manage the resale of it.
3. Teach graph making, measurement, comparisons, and/or ratio by beginning with motivational tasks such as enlarging pictures or making their own universe.
4. Around the holidays, turn art projects into financial experiences. Make toys or articles for sale, or collect and remodel toys for sale.
5. Make and market a newspaper. Solicit ads, do the interviewing, decide costs, and so on.
6. Plan a trip to the city or country of their choice. Compare the cost of travel by plane, car, train, or bus. Get actual costs from travel agencies.
7. Study the biographies of famous mathematicians. What forces were at work in their early years to influence them toward a career in math? Are the same forces in operation today? In your community?
8. Research and compare the cost of busing students to school in your county today with that of 1950. Discuss the advantages and disadvantages. Which seems more efficient moneywise? What other factors must be taken into consideration?
9. Find some trick math problems in an encyclopedia, math gamebook, or other source and try them on a friend.
10. Make a 24 x 36 poster illustrating an everyday school-life situation where the theory we're working on currently could be operating.

   Examples: a. football scores graphed
   b. positive and negative number directions to draw a favorite animal
   c. car bought on the installment plan: (1) down payment, (2) monthly payment, (3) interest charged, (4) total

number of months to pay, and (5) final cost versus original cost
   d. geometrically shaped figures which fool the eye
   e. a comparison table of metric measurement and traditional unit measures of inches, feet, yards
   f. a probability chart on a subject of their choice
11. Use music to teach fractions. "Three Blind Mice," or "Row Your Boat" were favorites of my middle-grade students. They can clap, use feet, use rhythm sticks, or drums. Orally, first. Then when musical and numerical symbols are written down, they can understand them.
12. Depending upon the competency level of students, use some of the study guides given here.

Work Sheet for Math Center (For Weak Students)

TASK I.   WAYS WE MEASURE

Look at each of the ways we measure. In figure 7.1, beside each measuring tool, write five things we could measure with it. Draw a circle around the words that name some measuring tool found in this room.

FIGURE 7.1

Ways we measure

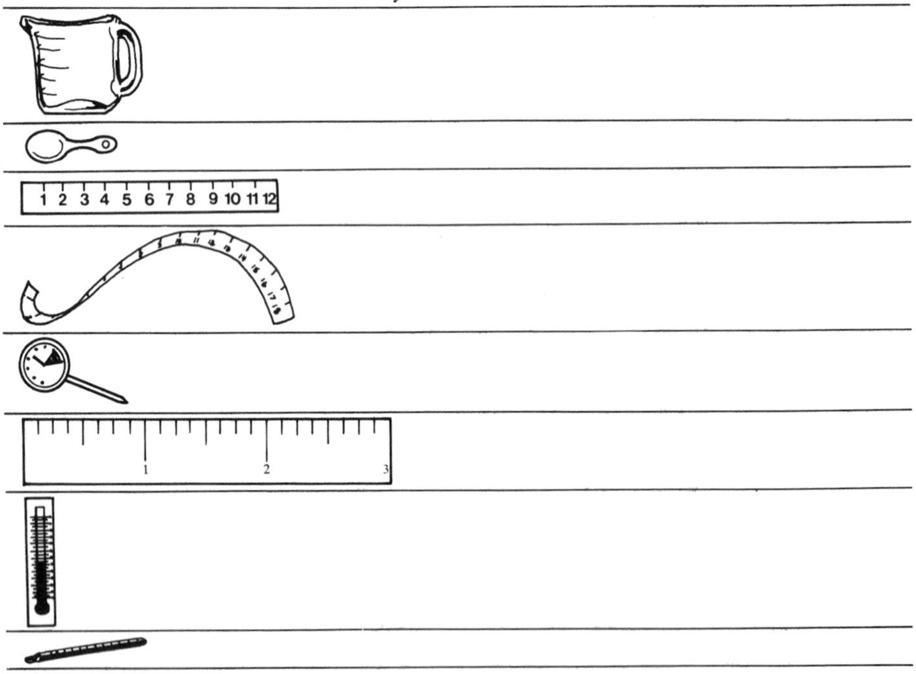

TASK II.   LIQUID MEASUREMENT

Equipment needed: measuring cups, measuring spoons, several different sized containers with numbers on them, sand

Directions: Read the problem. Use the containers in the center to figure the answer.

1. How much sand will container 1 hold?
2. Is container 3 greater than, less than, or equal to one cup?
3. Is container 2 greater than, less than, or equal to one cup?
4. What is container 4 equal to? How many cups of sand does it hold? How many pints?
5. Is container 5 equal to container 4? How much sand will 5 hold?
6. How many containers the size of 6 would it take to fill a cup? What size is 6?
7. How many containers the size of 7 would equal one cup?
8. How large is container 8? How many cups will it hold? How many pints? How many quarts?

Experiment with some of the other containers to see what size they are. You may have to use measuring spoons with some of the smaller containers.

TASK III.   ACTIVITIES USING MEASUREMENTS
(UNIT ON HAWAII AND ALASKA)

Equipment needed: Lei, ukulele, paper fish, igloo and harpoon, tape for measuring string

A lei is a wreath or necklace of flowers used by Hawaiians to show affection to one another. Figure 7.2 is a picture of a lei. Find the lei in the center that looks something like this picture, then find the answers to these questions:

FIGURE 7.2

The lei

a. What is the circumference of the lei? _____
b. What is the distance or diameter across the lei in inches? _____

A ukulele is sometimes called the Hawaiian guitar. Find the ukulele in the center. Strum (play) it. Does it sound like the American guitar? Use the tape measure and find how many inches long the ukulele is. _____ inches

FIGURE 7.3

The ukulele

A harpoon is a weapon used in hunting large fish in Alaska. Below is a picture of a harpoon. Find the harpoon that looks like the picture. How long is the harpoon? _____ inches

FIGURE 7.4

The harpoon

An igloo is an Eskimo hut or house. It is usually made of blocks of packed snow. Figure 7.5 is how it looks. Find the igloo in the center. Measure to find out how tall the igloo is. _____ inches. How wide is it? _____

FIGURE 7.5

The igloo

Look at the cardboard fish in the center. Measure them as you need to answer the following questions.
a. How long is fish Z? _____ fish X? _____ fish Y? _____
b. Which fish is shorter, fish Z or fish X? _____ fish Z or fish Y? _____
c. What is the combined length of fish Z and fish X? _____ fish X and fish Y? _____

TASK IV.   METRIC SYSTEM: LENGTH

Job Cards for Center on Metric System

Objectives: At the end of this experience you should be able to:
1. Estimate metric distances up to 10 meters in terms of millimeters, centimeters, decimeters, and meters, and use proper abbreviations.
2. State your height, the distance you can jump, the length of the room, and various other distances by using the metric system.
Materials needed: Premeasured and cut lengths of cardboards to use for experiment

Procedure: Discovery
1. Take a sample of each length of cardboard and several small cubes.
2. Find the shortest length and measure it in terms of cubes.

shortest = _____ cubes

3. Using either or both of these (cubes and short stick) measure the next size.

next larger = smaller & _____ cubes

4. Continue to compare bigger lengths in terms of smaller units. Use this space to make whatever drawings or comparisons you wish.
5. In order, how long is each of the six lengths in terms of the *number of cubes?*

1 cube _____   _____   _____   _____   _____   _____

Naming
1. Find the stick that is about 100 cubes long. Name it *METER* (abbreviate as **m**)
2. a. How many years in a *cent*ury? _____
   b. How many *cent*s in a dollar? _____
   c. What number does *cent* mean? _____
3. If the meter is equivalent to 100 cubes, what name should we logically call the length of each cube? _____
4. a. How many years in a decade? _____
   b. If you move a *deci*mal one place you are changing its value by how much? _____
   c. What number does *deci* mean? _____
   d. Find the piece you think should be called a *deci*meter.
   e. How would you abbreviate it? _____
   f. How many decimeters make a meter? _____
   g. How many centimeters make a decimeter? _____

Practice
1. *Guess* the length of these lines in *cm*

2. *Guess* the length of the following in *cm:*
   a. your fingers _____
   b. your foot _____
   c. elbow to finger _____

    d. your height _____
    e. length and width of a table _____ _____
    f. floor to ceiling _____
    g. a yard stick _____
3. Repeat estimations in terms of *dm*
    a. _____
    b. _____
    c. _____
    d. _____
    e. _____ _____
    f. _____
    g. _____
4. Repeat in terms of *m*
    a. _____
    b. _____
    c. _____
    d. _____
    e. _____ _____
    f. _____
    g. _____
5. Certain units are more convenient for certain lengths. Cm are convenient for your hand but meters for the floor to ceiling.

Metric System Is Decimal

Metric conversions are based on the decimal system, just like our money.

10 cents = 1 dime	10 cm = 1 dm
10 dimes = 1 dollar	10 dm = 1 m

1. At either end there are bigger and smaller units.
    a. One cm contains 10 millimeters (mm)
       How many mm in a m? _____
    b. There are 1,000 m in a kilometer (km)
       How many dm? _____
       How many cm? _____
       How many mm? _____
2. Measure the following in the most convenient unit of metric length:
    a. radiator _____
    b. teacher's desk _____
    c. length and width of room _____ _____
    d. your shoe _____
    e. height of a chair _____
    f. height and width of blackboard _____ _____
    g. cubby hole _____

TASK V. METRIC SYSTEM: WEIGHT

The basic unit of weight in the metric system is the gram. One gram equals the weight of 1 cubic centimeter of water (about the weight of a paper clip).

If you have learned your meter prefixes thoroughly you will have no trouble with grams.

Note: milligram . . if you have an object which weighs one gram and you divide it into 1,000 equal parts, each part weighs one milligram.

centigram . . if you have an object which weighs one gram and you divide it into 100 equal parts, each part weighs one centigram.

decigram . . if you have an object which weighs one gram and you divide it into 10 equal parts, each part weighs one decigram.

gram   = the weight of one cubic centimeter of water.

decagram = 10 grams

hectogram = 100 grams

kilogram   = 1,000 grams

Procedure

In the metric center you will find a set of scales and several weights (in grams).
I. Find the weight of the following objects:
   1. your pencil _____
   2. a shoelace _____
   3. a dozen paper clips _____
   4. a ring _____
   5. a compass _____
   6. a crumpled sheet of paper _____
II. 1. How many paperclips do you need to have a weight of 7 grams? _____
       2 grams _____? 5 grams _____? 14 grams _____?
   2. Estimate the weight in grams of the following:
       a shoe _____ a trashcan _____ a pound of sugar _____

TASK VI.   METRIC SYSTEM: VOLUME

So far in our study of the metric system we have worked with meters (length) and grams (weight). The next area we will examine will be that of volume. Let's consider volume to be the amount of space (room) we have within a container. In dealing with volume in the metric system the basic unit is the *liter*. There is only a small amount of difference between a liter and a quart. We will use the word liter as we have used the words meter and gram in the past.

Observe

milliliter . . if you had a container which would hold a liter of water and you divided this container into 1,000 containers of equal size each container would hold a milliliter of water.

centiliter . . if you had a container which would hold a liter of water and you divided this container into 100 containers of equal size, each container would hold a centiliter of water.

deciliter . . if you had a container which would hold a liter of water and you divided this container into 10 containers of equal size, each container would hold a deciliter of water.

liter ......a container will hold a liter of water if its length is 1 decimeter (10 centimeters), its width is 1 decimeter and its height is 1 decimeter.

decaliter .. a container which will hold 10 liters of water is known as a decaliter.

hectoliter .. a container which will hold 100 liters of water is known as a hectoliter.

kiloliter ... a container which will hold 1,000 liters of water is known as a kiloliter.

Procedure

In the metric center you will find a quart container, a liter container, and a graduated cylinder.

Step 1. Fill the quart container with water. Next, pour the water into the liter container. Is there much difference? _____

Step 2. Measure the inside length of the liter container. It is _____ long.

Step 3. Measure the inside width of the liter container. It is _____ width.

Step 4. Measure inside height of the liter container. It is _____ high.

Therefore, figure out how much water can be put into the liter container.

Now, let's check our answer. The graduated cylinder will hold 100 milliliters of water. Estimate how many times we must fill the graduated cylinder before we can fill the liter container. _____

FINAL STEP: Check your estimate. In order to fill the liter container, one must fill the graduated cylinder _____ times.

TASK VII.   MY SCHOOL AND MEASUREMENT

1. Measure the length and width of this room. Record your measurements.
2. Go outside and measure the length and width of this building and record your findings.
3. Using the formula on the wall above this math center, figure the area of both Numbers 1 and 2 above.
4. How many rooms this size could be built in this building?
5. Make a map of the building showing the location of this room. (Read page (   ) in your textbook and draw this building to scale. Ask the teacher for help if you need it.

TASK VIII.   GO METRIC

1. Using the same objects and questions in TASKS III and IV at this center, do the measurements in the metric system. Record them.
2. When you finish the tasks in Number one, write a succinct paragraph of comparison. Which measurement system do you prefer. Why?

TASK IX.   A TEST STUDENTS LIKE

(submitted by Alice C. Pfirmann, teacher, Buncombe County, N.C.)

Each student is given the measurements for the recipe of one cupcake. He must measure accurately all ingredients. Different food colors and flavors should be available. The oven is a #10 tin can with gravel in the bottom. A coat hanger triangle holds an evaporating dish which acts as a container for a cupcake paper. Aluminum foil is used as a cover. A bunsen burner is used for heating.

Evaluation is based on teacher observation during the preparation stage and on the final product.

Students, including fellows, like this test. They may even be rewarded by getting to eat their own creation.

SUMMARY

This chapter has talked about one way to attempt to meet the individual needs of students in a heterogenously grouped school. Examples of study guides with questions and activities based on different levels of capacity were given. Study guides should not be used every day or you produce students who depend upon you to always tell them what is important in their reading. They must feel that there is value in the tasks they are asked to perform, that learning will occur, and that the lazy teacher is not simply giving them activities to do on their own to get out of teaching them.

Activities for the Teacher

1. If you have not done so, read *Pygmalian in the Classroom.* Are you guilty of the attitude shown in this book?
2. Make a study guide using the different levels of understanding as advocated and modeled in this chapter. For further study see Herber's *Reading in the Content Area* (73).
3. Create some task cards for one of your learning centers. Make them on different levels of difficulty to suit the needs of your students. If you are working on a unit, your tasks might reinforce the skills and/or concepts of the unit.
4. Share with your peers how your students react to these approaches. Remember these are vehicles for learning, not tests.
5. Find a new idea on teaching in one of the current professional periodicals. Try this idea in your class and share the results with your peers. What are the results? Will you use it again?
6. If you are not presently working with students, choose a chapter or story from any textbook and make ten different activities you could use for teaching and/or reinforcing the vocabulary and concepts of that material. Share it with your peers.

EIGHT

Motivation and Involvement

In selecting any activity for a class project, you should have in mind your purposes and also what purposes will make sense and be acceptable to students. The failure to show relevancy to real life situations has resulted in school as a separate world for many young people. It becomes a duel between what the teacher demands and how little they can get by with and still make passing grades.

Effective teaching based on successful, tested approaches will eliminate such problems and add zest to learning. What is effective teaching? Does anyone really know? Why does a method work for one and not for another? Each of us who answer these questions would do so in our own unique fashion. I'm not sure anyone can tell anyone else how to do anything. I prefer to attempt to show you.

In this chapter you will find many directions for successful, intriguing classroom activities. As you look over this unit, think about these ideas:

1. Motivation is more than saying, "Let's do it."
2. When you have thirty-five students whose reading levels range from the third grade to the thirteenth year level, is it possible to have total class involvement and interest in anything?
3. Are you glued to a textbook, manual, and/or classroom?
4. What kinds of learning centers are possible and practical?
5. What is required in setting up work on a unit basis?

On a final examination day, I told one of my classes, "During your school life each of you should have at least one teacher that you can remember because of his or her creativity. Some call it by other names—nuts, crazy, unbelievable. I choose to be that one for you. So here is your examination." Whereupon, I handed them the following sets of directions.

READING 4343. Reading in the Middle Grades   FINAL EXAMINATION
July, 1775   Mrs. McIntyre

SET I.

Your examination will be in three parts. Read carefully through this first set of directions.

PART A.

1. We will go outside for an activity—an egg throwing contest.
2. Number off in ones and twos.
3. All ones will line up in a straight line on the lawn between Killian and Forsyth Building.
4. All twos will line up in a straight line facing the ones and about ten feet away.
5. Each person in line one will be given a raw egg which he will pitch to his partner in line two.
6. Always wait for the signal to pitch.
7. When you hear the signal, "Toss," toss your egg and both lines move back one step.
8. Line two then pitches to partner in line one, and again each line moves back one step. The object is to see how far apart you can move back and throw without breaking your egg.
9. Continue moving back, pitching to your partner on signal, and moving back again until only one couple is left with an unbroken egg. The couple keeping the egg without breaking the longest time becomes the egg-throwing champions.

ANY QUESTIONS?

There were none, so they numbered off and made two lines. Line Number One picked up eggs from the desk and we moved outside to the lawn.

PART B.   Play the game.

SET II.

Read and follow these directions:

1. Pretend you are a teacher of any grade four through nine. You have taken your thirty students outside where they enjoyed the egg-throwing contest as we did.
2. Plan how you could use this activity as background for reading and/or study skills lessons.
3. Use any outline or plan you like, but actually make some exercises, activities, study guides, etc., to show you would use it. Be sure to remember that reading is used in all areas of the curriculum. Any subject can be utilized.
4. No one is to leave before one hour is up. It will probably take longer.

My purpose for this activity was two-fold; to teach by demonstration and to show students that they could be creative.

This activity gave them a good chance to show what they knew about the teaching of reading, the theories of psychology and motivation, and how to set up structure for classroom activities. No formal examination with memorized answers from a page in the textbook, with little knowledge of how to put that memorized material into classroom practice, could have shown as much.

Student reaction progressed from laughter to disbelief, to "She means it, the eggs are on the desk," to "Hey, this is a keen way to have an examination." Concensus of opinion was favorable. Some of my more sophisticated, soft-droning lecturer friends thought that I had gone crazy. (Crazier, I should say.)

The most interesting part of the experiment was the thinking about teaching which those students did as they attempted to use their knowledge to make plans. Some of the ideas in the following unit came from those papers.

Unit: Eggs and Egg-Producing Animals

Motivation: An Egg Throwing Contest

Directions: See student examination on preceding pages and individual directions for activities.

Skills to be practiced:

Following directions:	to play the game;
	to set up experiments;
	to do lesson guides in centers
Locational skills:	reading of index, table of contents,
	library references, maps, tables,
	the dictionary, etc.
Science skills:	discovery techniques and
	concepts
Math skills:	measurement, graphs, concepts,
	problem-solving techniques
Social skills:	cooperation, involvement, recreation,
	enjoyment
Language skills:	dialogue,
	improvement of vocabulary,
	skimming and scanning,
	transfer of reading skills to other areas,
	main ideas, details, summarizing, etc.,
	creativity.
	In fact, most of the reading and study skills will be involved before the work on the unit is completed.

Objectives:
1. Students will work on projects in centers without complaints.
2. Students will produce more work than is required because they are motivated.
3. Students will know more facts about eggs and the trades surrounding production, marketing, supply and demand, etc., than before the unit began.
4. Students will use the discovery technique to solve problems.
5. Students will be able to use reference books to find answers to specific questions.
6. Students will demonstrate scientific principles with concrete objects.
7. Students will practice reading and study skills in content curriculum.

Procedure:
Read the directions for the game.
Play the game.
Discuss the game.

Look at the list of questions.
Students will choose ten from the list to work on.

Discuss centers and what students are to do there.
Set up special interest groups.

Look at vocabulary to be used. (This will be conspiciously listed somewhere in the
    room and can be added to as students find more interesting words.)
Difficulty of word list will depend upon levels, ages and competencies of students.

Possible Vocabulary List for Grades 4–9

poultry	motion	plumage
embryo	gravity	aviary
roe	caviar	mandible
ovum	supply and demand	vertebrate
fertilize	feathers	lore
incubator	buoyancy	turkeys
contests	oviduct	mammals
olympics	capon	private
competition	fowl	nutrition
germ	velocity	commercial
mosaics	mayonnaise	mechanization
electrified feeding	domestic	marketing
meringue	ovipara	inflation
pesticides	pigeons	supermarkets
metric	squab	migrating
ovi-	fledgling	gallinaceous
gestation	nestling	paleontologists
membrane	roosters	
daily log	conservation	
sex-linked		

Questions for Motivation

1. In the game what did you do to keep your egg from breaking? Did it work?
2. Why did some people's egg break on the second throw?
3. As distance increased, why was it harder to keep eggs from breaking?
4. What principle or properties were involved while eggs were in motion?
5. Why didn't eggs break in midair?
6. How many different uses for eggs can you think of?
7. Who was the first person to work with the theory of motion?

8. Who invented the present systems of weights and measure?
9. What other countries use this system of measure?
10. What are eggs shells made of and what other things are made of the same material?
11. Which comes first, the chicken or the egg?
12. What animal may lay 60,000,000 eggs in one year?
13. What animal lays only one egg a year?
14. What one word describes the overall features of an egg? (fragile)
15. What other things in our daily lives are fragile? (mirrors, picture frames, glasses, lamps, appliances, microscope, baby brother or sister)
16. Which will hatch in the shortest period of time, a turtle's or a duck's egg? Why? What temperature is required for each?
17. Which nation in the world produces the most eggs for food?
18. How are eggs related to heart disease?
19. Can a human eat too many eggs?
20. Suppose that no animal in the whole world should produce eggs for the period of two years. What effects might this have on life as we know it?
21. Can you trace the journey of an egg from the time it is laid in a nest until it reaches the breakfast table of your cousin who lives in New York City?
22. How were eggs used in the early Roman and Greek history?
23. What is the record for the number of eggs eaten by one person at one time?
24. What makes water run off a duck's back?
25. What enables a bird to fly?

Learning Centers to Be Set Up for This Unit

1. Research Center. Study guides, fact sheets, puzzles and pictures general books and references
2. Tactile-Kinesthetic Display Center: Materials and jobcards for activities and experiments
3. Language Arts Center: Materials of all kinds, study guides, jobcards on etymology, sentences, descriptive words, homonyms, words with many meanings, puzzles for vocabulary expansion, etc.
4. Writing Centers: Both creative and factual activities
5. Math Center: Problems, graphs, tables, measurement instruments
6. Art Center: Twenty activities to do using material on hand
7. Games and Puzzles Center: Directions and materials for playing such games as old maid, word shuffleboard, white magic, treasure hunt. Puzzles on different levels of difficulty.

Materials for These Learning Centers

In another chapter we discussed the use of learning centers in a classroom. They are as effective as a teacher or group of students make them. Like any other classroom organization, they can be abused. However, used properly, and with good materials in them, learning centers such as the ones set up for this unit and with these materials in them can produce more learning in a week than many more traditional type organizational set-ups with teacher doing all the work and talking can produce in double or triple the time.

As you look over these exercises, keep in mind that the students are motivated to do the work. If they aren't, centers won't work.

The Research Center

Materials Needed: Encyclopedias, filmstrips, books, study guides X, Y, and Z, projector, job cards
Study Guide for General Information—X

Purpose: 1. To find answers to questions of general information.
2. To read for details to answer questions on different levels of understanding.

Directions: Use any materials we have available to find the answers to questions.
Don't forget! When you're reading for specific facts, you can skip, hop and jump over the materials. No need to read word-by-word.
Answer the level of questions which applies to you.

Level I

1. The average hen lays _____ eggs per week.
2. _____, _____ are tools used by any poultry farmer.
3. A farmer can buy supplies he needs at _____ in North Carolina (any state).
4. When floods come, chicken feed may be _____ expensive.
                            (more or less)
5. A balanced diet is important for poultry if the egg _____ is to be strong.
                            (what)
6. It takes _____ days for an egg to hatch into a chicken.
7. It takes _____ days for an egg to hatch into a turtle.
8. Eggs in an incubator must be kept at _____ degrees.
9. What state in the United States produces the most poultry? _____
10. Did Julius Caesar eat eggs? _____
11. What is the largest recorded egg ever produced? _____
12. An electric belt may be used to take _____ into the chicken house and also to bring _____ out of the nests.

Level II

1. Discuss the concept of "giving" as talked about in the science book. Does it relate to what happened when we threw eggs to our partners? How?
2. Describe the differences between a dairy belt and a farm belt.
3. _____, _____, and _____ are states in the "bread basket." Why might they be called this term?
4. Explain how a bird is able to fly?
5. Describe the differences in size and color of eggs. How do you account for these?
6. Your science books state that an object travels according to the amount of force applied. How do you explain this? Give an example.
7. How are the strains of egg-producing animals improved?
8. Once most of our work on farms was done by hand, but today machines do it. Name as many machines and their jobs as you can find which are used in the production, distribution and consumption of poultry products. Did you realize there were so many?
9. Make a chart showing the comparison of the metric system of measurement and our system of inches, feet and yards. Why are we gradually changing from one to the other? Do you think we will be completely changed to the metric system by the time you are in the first year of college?
10. What is the difference in friction, centrifugal force and gravity?

Level III

1. "What goes up must come down." In your words summarize this theory.
2. What is the relationship of force and speed as demonstrated in our egg-throwing contest? How is this related to what happens in an automobile collision?
3. Two students collide in the hall. One drops his books. The other doesn't. How can you explain this?
4. Using the material we have or that you can get, set up a demonstration of one of the forces mentioned in this unit.
5. Make some transparencies showing the stages from egg to baby in the reproduction of some animal.
6. Discuss the concept of trajectory in flight.
7. Trace the shipping of eggs to market.
8. Describe the likes and differences in a farm belt and other belts we have studied.
9. Look up the sculptor, Jean Arp. What connection is there between this man and eggs?
10. In our egg-throwing contest we used competition. Look up the period we are now studying in history and find two instances where history was influenced for either good or bad by competition. Share your findings with the class.

11. Keep a daily log of what happens in our incubator. Discuss it with a friend.

Bird Research—Study Guide Y

Directions: Here are some research questions about birds which are just for fun. See how fast you can find the answers. (answers given at end of chapter)

1. Which is the largest bird in the world? the smallest?
2. Which wild North American bird is the largest? the smallest?
3. Which bird flies the fastest?
4. How high do birds fly?
5. Can birds fly backwards? If so, which ones?
6. Do all birds build their own nest?
7. Are bluebirds really blue?
8. Do all birds have nests?
9. Are all birds' eggs the same color?
10. How are birds named?

PLAY CONCENTRATION WITH BIRD FACTS

Materials needed: 1. forty cards, or less, depending on students competency level. On one side, number from one to forty in numerals. On the other side, add one fact per card from the list below.

2. *Concentration* board. Place cards, number side up, on board.

3. Play game like regular T.V. *Concentration* game, trying to match corresponding information. No pencils, please.

1.	United States national emblem	bald eagle
2.	feathers change to match season	willow ptarmigan
3.	belong to the game bird family	grouse and geese
4.	carry messages when trained	pigeons
5.	do tricks when trained	parakeets
6.	song bird	canary
7.	sanitary corps	vultures
8.	called street cleaners in South America	marabou
9.	live on nectar	hummingbird
10.	fish eaters	herons
11.	known for their outstanding beauty	Bird of Paradise
12.	can run 50 MPH for short distances	ostrich
13.	most intelligent bird	crow
14.	one collided with airplane at 20,000 ft.	condor
15.	sew leaves together to form their nests	tailorbird
16.	island bird now extinct	dodo
17.	has a statue honoring it built in Utah	sea gull
18.	famous ballet inspired by it	swan

19. Noah sent it to see if flood had receded   dove
20. John J. Audubon   ornithologist

Study Guide—Z—Information on Birds—Level I
(Made by Mary McKenzie, WCU graduate student)

Directions: Answer the following questions. Use any bird book you will find in the room, check the library or get the information through lectures, discussions or films.

I. 1. What do birds have that no other animals have?
    2. A scientist who studies birds is called a _____.
    3. How is the female cardinal different from the male cardinal?
    4. What kind of feathers serve as a bird's "underwear?" List two places where you can find these feathers in your home.
    5. The largest bird is the _____ and the smallest is the _____.
    6. A "cradle" in which a bird lays her eggs and raises her young is called her _____.
    7. What is a bird's most important nest building tool?
    8. Give two uses of a bird's tail.
    9. Describe three birds you see in your backyard at home.
  10. List the 14 parts of the bird we have studied. Label them on figure 8.1.

FIGURE 8.1

Label the parts of the bird

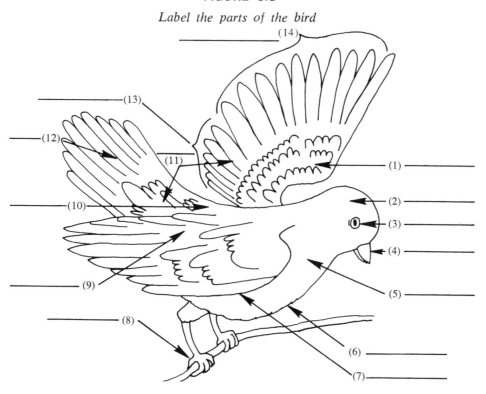

IV. List these colors on a piece of paper: red, black, blue, brown, yellow, white, gray. For one week be observant. Wherever you go and whatever you do, look for birds of these colors. After you see one that is mostly brown, put a check after brown. After you see one that is mostly red, put a check after red, and so on. Of course, you may not see birds of all these colors. After you see a bird, find how many you can identify by checking the references on birds we have around the room. Did you see one which no other student saw? What kind was it? Where did you see it? What was it doing?

V. Check true or false beside these statements about birds.
1. All birds are animals.
2. All birds have feathers.
3. All birds can fly.
4. All birds lay eggs.
5. Birds can see better than people.
6. Hummingbirds fly backwards.
7. All birds have feet.
8. All birds have teeth.
9. Most female birds don't sing.
10. Crows have 884 different calls.
11. Robins belong to the thrush family.

FIGURE 8.2

Label the parts of the feather

LEVEL II

I. Directions: Answer the following questions. Use any bird book you will find in the room, check the library, or get the information through lectures, discussions, or films.
1. How is a female cardinal different from the male cardinal in color? Why do you think this is necessary?

2. All birds have wings. Most of them can fly well; however, such birds as the ostrich and the penguin cannot. Yet they use their wings! How and for what reason?

3. How does a precocial bird differ from an altrical bird?

4. Why is it better to have no feeder than to have one which is not cared for regularly?

5. How does a woodpecker climb a tree?

6. Where do birds look for food?

7. What is suet? How could you build a simple bird feeder using suet?

8. The canary and parrot make good pets. Find the average life span of each. Can you explain the great difference?

II. If you can, watch some chickens. By watching them, find the answers to these questions.
   1. Can chickens fly?
   2. Can chickens fly very far?
   3. How can you tell that chickens are birds?
   4. How does a chicken use his bill? For what reason?
   5. How does a chicken use his feet? For what reason?
   6. How do chickens court?
   7. How do chickens sleep?

LEVEL III

Directions: Answer the following questions. Use any book you will find around the room, check the library, or get the information from lectures, discussions, observation or films.

1. Each type of bird has its own special way to build its nest. The kind of nest he builds depends on how it is going to be used. Observe four birds and their nests. Describe their appearance and the purpose for their being built the way they are.
2. What can you do to attract birds to your home in the winter?
3. How do feathers keep a bird dry? Describe the types of feathers birds have.
4. Why may you see different birds around your home in the winter than you see in the summer? Make a list of birds you see in the winter that you do not see in the summer.
5. Open up a hen's egg. Notice the yoke and the white. All birds' eggs are built in much the same way but some, as you know, are much bigger than others. Draw the stages of a babybird's growth inside the egg.
6. In a small group, observe the bird feeder we placed outside. Keep a daily record of the birds that visit it and what they are eating. Make a report to the class.

Tactile-Kinesthetic Display Center

Materials needed: microscope, egg-beater, bones, eggs, hot plate, containers, plastic models of birds, poultry or other egg-producing animals, job cards which contain tasks such as these:
1. Break an egg and examine its parts. Describe them.
2. Look at parts of an egg under the microscope.
3. Compare skeleton of chicken foot with that of a man. Describe the differences.
4. Weigh a raw egg and hard boiled one. Compare the results. Can you explain this?
5. Use an egg beater to find out what happens when a machine works on a whole egg. Now, separate the parts and beat first the yellow and then the white. What happens?
6. Draw and label the parts of an egg, bird, skeleton. Your choice.
7. Use hot plate to boil some eggs. Alone or with friends, spin a raw egg and a boiled one. Watch what happens. What scientific principles are demonstrated?

Language Arts Center

Materials needed: List of words connected with the unit, dictionaries, study guides, books with stories connected with the unit, job cards.
Examples of job cards to be used in language arts center on birds:
1. Look up the etymology of these words: *mandible, embryo, caviar, omulette.*
2. Read the story, "Tom and His Friends Raid the Chicken Coop," or any stories available to your particular center.
3. Use old magazines as a source and make a collage of either pictures or words dealing with the unit. Display for class.
4. List the words you can think of to describe the way a raw or cooked egg (1) feels, (2) tastes, (3) smells and (4) looks.

5. Name as many movement words as you can think of which could be used to describe the game we played at the beginning of this unit. Examples: catch, cooperate, smash, yell.
6. Name as many different kinds of birds as you can think of. Examples: ducks, chickens, small birds such as the canary, hummingbird, robin.
7. Just for fun unscramble and write these sentences then make some of your own.
   (a) I elki ym gsge drief, hiwt saott nda nocab. (I like my eggs fried, with toast and bacon.)
   (b) na geg si skilc nda darh no eht sediuto.
8. Think of all the words you can which rhyme with egg. (Any word in the unit.)
9. Using the vocabulary and concepts we're learning about, make up a crossword puzzle.
10. Work the cross-word puzzle provided for you. If necessary, use dictionary.
11. Describe some famous inventors of farm machines. Put them in the wrong era. Let other students find the errors.
12. Collect an assortment of illustrations presenting scenes which your friends will find comic, extravagant, or fanciful. (Old movies, tableaus of Victorian age, etc.)
13. Make a time line of events in the history of the changes in farming from the early stick plow to the present big machinery.
14. Make a list of descriptive words concerning a chicken house, snake den, monkey cage, etc.
15. A turkey tells what it's like to be fattened for Thanksgiving feast of humans. Use as many sense words as possible.
16. A city bird and country bird discuss life as they see it in their respective environments.
17. Do some of the exercises under the title "Words Have Many Meanings."

Words Have Many Meanings

One of the major legitimate complaints about the ways we assume to teach vocabulary is the "look up a meaning and write a sentence," technique. This is as outmoded and impractical as the candle in a neon lit room.

Utility is the key. When students use words, they reinforce and remember them longer. If a word can be used in a way unusual to the regular meaning, it becomes more interesting. The following five activities are examples.

Different meanings for common words.

Here are some words which many of us use every day. But they have other interesting meanings, some used as slang, which we may not realize and might even think wrong if we heard a friend use them.

See how many you can match without a dictionary. How many did you recognize? Now, with the help of a dictionary or thesaurus find the others.

Check the terms in Column II. Match them to their counterpart in Column I.

Column I.	Column II.
1. roe	a. fist
2. lore	b. fowl

3. hen
4. roost
5. bird
6. ovum
7. fledgling
8. squab
9. nestling
10. nest egg

c. to rest
d. a young child
e. dress
f. home
g. money in the bank
h. pigeon
i. young bird
j. a sofa
k. short fat person
l. egg
m. egg-shaped ornament
n. artificial egg left in nest to induce hens to lay
o. delicious feast
p. inexperienced person
q. woman
r. a shuttlecock
s. remarkable person
t. part of a bird or fish
u. attire
v. temporary resting place

Different meanings for phrases. The following phrases are often used to express something quite different from the literal meaning. How many have you heard? What do they mean? See if you can discover what the other meaning is. Use friends, reference books, or any other source at your disposal.

1. the gravity of a judge
2. birds of a feather
3. in fine feather
4. caviar to the general
5. germ of an idea
6. to show the white feather
7. a fertile talent
8. a plan in the gestation stage
9. no young chick
10. a feather in one's cap
11. birds on the wing
12. to feather one's nest

Homonyms. We have studied the meaning of homonyms and the confusion some of them can give us in use and in spelling.

Using the words which might be associated with this unit find as many pairs of homonyms as possible.

Here are some examples:

fowl	—	foul
roe	—	row
blue	—	blew
tail	—	tale
red	—	read
yolk	—	yoke

Double Play with Words

What's a chicken yard?	A hen pen.	A jitterbug fowl
What's a proud bird?	Cocky locky.	Jerky turkey
What's a chicken retailer?	A fryer buyer	A sly hen—
What's a crippled chicken?	A lame game	Trickin' chicken
What's burning feathers fragrance?	Plume fume	Stupid sea bird
		Dull gull

Now you make some:

Creative Thinking Activities

 I. What Might Have Happened?

a. Birds chatter noisily and flutter their wings wildly.
    What might have happened?

b. The duck hopped on one leg and its wing drooped. What might have happened?

c. The birds huddle closely against the chimney top. What might be the season?

d. When the storm was over, Jane could not find her pet chickens. What might have happened?

e. The eggs had been in the incubator for five weeks but hadn't hatched. What might have happened?

f. Buzzards fly overhead. What may be near by? What might have happened?

 II. Who Would Like to Live Here? (One way to build vocabulary in remedial readers)

1. A chicken would like to live here _____   tropics
2. A pet parrot would like to live here _____   barnyard
3. A duck would like to live here _____   pond
4. A penguin would like to live here _____   treetop
5. A bat would like to live here _____   snow island
6. A baby chick would like to live here _____   mud puddle
7. A heron would like to live here _____   house, zoo
8. A buzzard would like to live here _____   cage, cave
9. A chimney sweep would like to live here _____ seed house
10. A peacock would like to live here _____   automobile
11. An ostrich would like to live here _____   incubator
12. A flamingo would like to live here _____   highway intersection
        tropical lake
        fish reservoir

III. What Can You Do?

1. Cowbirds are driving all other birds from their nests. What can you do?

2. Snow has covered the ground for one month. The birds are dying. What can you do?

3. The incubator switch burned out. What can you do to keep the eggs warm?

4. Fellows with BB guns are frightening all the birds away. What can you do?

5. Swallows nest in the rafters of your house. Mites are getting into your home and biting you. What can you do?

Connotative language adds to vocabulary growth. In a unit such as this one, vocabulary expansion can be practiced with the connotative uses students make of the language every day. They don't know that is what they are doing, but you can call it to their attention as a way of teaching the meaning of connotation. Remember, our task is to impress upon students that as they progress through school, they learn many meanings for words, not just *a* meaning. One way to do this is to ask students to list as many ways as they can think of in which they have heard the following words, words connected to whatever unit you're working with, used. Some possible answers for this unit are given.

chicken	fowl, coward, yellow, glamorous (cute chick)
bird	birdbrain, What a bird! eats like a bird, pecks at food
egg	good egg, bad egg, egghead, all his eggs in one basket, to egg on
yellow	coward, shy, jealous, color
peacock	vain, over dressed, pretentious, dandy; He's a peacock!
crow	old crow (name for some teachers), to boast, as the crow flies
duck	ducky (cute), waddles like a duck (clumsy), duck breeches, duck a blow
goose	silly, fearful, goosebumps, cackles like a goose, to cook one's goose, to poke one in the backside
canary	yellow color, petite, fragile, chatters like a canary

Vocabulary Practice Continued

A teacher can not teach all of the new words in a unit. She shouldn't try to. Three or four words a day could be well taught and the others left to the attention of the students.

Working with the words is the only way to insure permanent learning—practice or reinforcement in all kinds of situations. Simple matching exercises can be nothing more than a matter of guessing. Add a third dimension and more learning occurs. Look at this exercise.

Matching for vocabulary growth.

Directions: Here are words dealing with our unit. See how many you are familiar with. Match them with their meanings and with a situation or person where they probably could be used. The first one is done for you.

Words	*Meanings*	*Could be used in or by*
A. _6, d_ epoch	1. bird beak	a. banquet guests
B. ____ annual	2. gourmet dish	b. hungry capon
C. ____ nocturnal	3. bird cage	c. building new words
D. ____ reproduction	4. a ground pigeon	d. history lesson
E. ____ caviar	5. prefix meaning of or	e. speech about over
F. ____ aviary	pertaining to eggs	population
G. ____ squab	6. period marked by	f. baker

H. _____ ovi

I. _____ meringue

J. _____ mandible

distinctive series of
developments

7. night time

8. beaten whites of eggs
combined with sugar

9. to make more

10. yearly

g. farmer talking about
planting seeds

h. bird soup

i. describing birds which
fly at night.

j. person who raises
birds for pets.

Answers: A. 6d B. 10g C. 7i D. 9e E. 2a F. 3j G. 4h H. 5e I. 8f J. 1b

Writing Centers

CREATIVE WRITING

Choose one of the following subjects and write on it.

1. Explain an egg to someone who has never seen one.
2. Put a softboiled egg in a "feely box" and describe it.
3. Write a beginning story of the report of our egg-throwing contest. Give it a different or twist ending from what actually happened.
4. Use a suppose type situation:
   a. Suppose you were the eggs. Describe how you felt in the air midway between the two partners in our game.
   b. How did you feel as you hit the hands of Partner Number Two and smashed or not?
   c. You are an egg in an incubator waiting to develop into a bird, a snake, a turtle, a chicken, etc. What are your observations?
5. Write a Donald Duck Cartoon.
6. Write some nonsense poems, jingles, riddles, or lyrics.
7. Write a story on this title: "If I were an egg for one day."
8. Choose any egg-producing animal you wish and pretend you are that animal for an hour, day or week. Write a diary of that length of time.
9. Look at the mounted pictures. Read comments and questions on back. Work with one of them.
10. Pretend you are the fellow or girl who gathered eggs and you have a conversation with a skunk in a chicken house.
11. Pretend you are the fellow or girl who collects feathers. Write a conversation you might have with a wild turkey whose feather you find.
12. Compose a tall tale similar to Paul Bunyan letting some egg-laying animal be the hero.

FACTUAL WRITING

1. Special reports on individual interests of any subject on or connected with this unit. Use unique methods of reporting.
   Drama, demonstration, charades, contest similar to TV games, drawings and/or sketches, bulletin boards, freize, etc.
2. Write article for local school or community paper.
3. Write script for TV or radio announcer about the crazy game we played today. Give the who, what, where, why, how many, and who won facts.

4. Make up a set of directions for doing something and let peer attempt to follow them.

5. Recall—What exclamations did you hear during the time we played the game? Examples:

> Oh, my egg broke!
> What a mess!
> Yeah, We won!
> You threw too hard!

6. Interview poultry farmer and write it up for paper. What are some of his views on these subjects?

Labor problems

Ecology

Trade

Farmer and big business

Curtailing productions

Prices charged in stores in comparison to what he gets

Any other subject either you or he is interested in

7. Visit a poultry farm. Make a booklet of the experience.
   1. Sounds you heard
   2. Things you saw
   3. Smells you encountered
   4. New facts you learned
   5. Drawing of farm scene
   6. A collage of farm pictures or words

8. Write an essay on the *evil* versus the *value* of mechanized farming.

9. Write letters to governor and legislators giving your view on current farm problems.

10. Write the biography of a turtle (or any animal).

11. Trace the history of the art of writing from the quill to present day mechanized reproduction.

12. Do you believe that people's character is revealed in their penmanship? Do some research on the subject.

What is your opinion now?

Math Center

Materials needed: Math books, newspapers, measuring tapes and rulers, string, small scales, study guides or job cards, graph paper, and statistics recorded when egg-throwing contest was in progress.

ACTIVITIES

I. Problems.
   a. In the egg-throwing contest, what was the difference in the beginning ten feet and the winning team's distance apart?
   b. If each partner of the winning team reversed one foot each time the caller signalled, how many times did they move?
   c. We began with fifteen eggs. Five couples broke their eggs on the first throw. What fraction of the couples remained?

    d. The teacher bought one egg for every two people in class. She paid 69¢ per dozen. How much did she spend?

    e. David's mother is a cook at the hospital. There are 300 rooms in the building and all are full of patients. 150 rooms hold four people each. Fifty rooms are private. One hundred rooms have beds for two people. Sixty people wanted scrambled eggs for breakfast. One hundred forty people didn't want eggs. Fifty people, one hard-boiled, twenty wanted one sunny-side up, and 60 asked for bacon and eggs, well done. How many eggs did David's mother need to cook? How many people didn't order eggs?   (190, 660)

II. Graphs and Tables

    a. Use the statistics recorded from the contest and plot a graph to show trials and couples left in game at each throw. Don't forget the title.

    b. Make a graph to show comparison of distances apart with number of trials.

    c. Suppose you own and operate a chicken farm and your electric feeder and egg conveyor belts stop working. Use the telephone directory and list numbers you might call to get help.

III. Measurement.

    a. Measure the dimensions of our incubator. See if you can figure out how many incubators this size could be placed on the teacher's desk.

    b. Measure the dimensions of this room. Could we have had our egg-throwing contest in here? Explain your answer.

    c. Measure the size of three eggs. Weigh the same three eggs and compare weight with size. What did you discover?

    d. Measure your desk with a tape measure. Now measure one of the plastic eggs. Figure how many eggs you could lay side-by-side on your desk.

    e. Use yard stick or tape to measure the floor of this room. Now measure it with a metric stick. Write the dimensions on a card and put in your folder.

    f. A farmer says he needs three square feet for every chicken he has in his poultry house. He has a house which is 125 x 33 feet. Approximately how many chickens could he put in this house?   (458)

IV. Math Alphabet

Make an alphabetical list of math words. Here is a beginning example.

          a — addition   c — cumulative
          b — barometer   d — divide etc.

V. Get today's newspaper. Make out a grocery list and compare prices from Bi-Lo, A & P, Cash and Carry and Community Cash. Where would you save most on your grocery shopping today?

Art Center With Some Activities

    I. Demonstrate (using materials available) how you felt when someone's egg smashed during the contest.

    II. Make a mosaic from egg shells.

    III. Do feather sculpture.

    IV. Blow eggs and make an egg tree.

V. Dye some hard boiled eggs. Experiment with colors.

VI. Make egg words architecture. Use any vocabulary from our unit. Figure 8.3 is one illustration.

VII. See what you can do with the membrane in the boiled eggs.

VIII. Use polaroid camera to catch action shots of students at work in their centers.

IX. Make a freize of the book *Flossie and Bossie* or some other good book you've enjoyed during this unit.

X. Compose cartoons and let your friends write the captions.

XI. Do concrete poetry. Use any word and form. Figure 8.4 is one illustration.

XII. A. Make a bulletin board or other kind of display showing the kinds of nests you know or can find out about.

B. Make a bulletin board or some other display with a collection of feathers.

XIII. Make a chart showing the kinds of animals in the poultry and/or bird kingdom found in this vicinity.

XIV. Make a model of a chicken farm. Use class and other materials available or that you can bring in.

XV. Construct a bird house.

XVI. Construct a bird feeder.

XVII. Using clay and wire or pipe cleaners, sculpture your favorite bird character.

XVIII. Make a mobile of words, pictures or concepts used in this unit.

XIX. Feather word sculpture. Find F words to fill a feather. Begin with F plus one letter, F plus two letters, F plus three letters, etc. Figure 8.5 is an illustration of feather word sculpture.

Games and Puzzles

Many games have been dreamed up to help children with learning. Textbooks on reading, current magazines, pamphlets, commercially made kits and game books are available to the teacher.

However, the creative teacher will adapt commercial games, will devise original games to meet special needs of special students and which do not cost money which may not be available. It takes time, willpower and creative thinking. Another alternative is to encourage strong students to create games to be used with weaker students.

Only a few games will be listed here to be used in this unit. There are many others.

I. Go Fishing (Adaptation)

Teacher or students collect pictures from old magazines or books. The pictures deal with any of the concepts of the unit. Each set of three cards will have the same word but different pictures. Figure 8.6 is an example. Words such as *pesticide, poultry, meringue, incubator* may be used. Twelve sets is a good number for this game.

Rules:

1. Several cards are dealt to each student and others laid facedown on table.

2. Move from left to right, asking for the card student wants. Player must

FIGURE 8.3

Word architecture

```
R   O   E
        M           P
        B           O   W   L
        R           U       E
E   T   Y   M   O   L   O   G   Y
G       O           T           O
G                   R           K
S   A   L   E       Y   O   K   E
```

FIGURE 8.4

Concrete poetry

pronounce and spell the word he asks for. (Skills of word recognition, left to right orientation, spelling sequence of letters and concentration all practiced during the mechanics of this game.)

3. If second player has card, first player gets it and moves on, asking next player in game for a card. If next player doesn't have card asked for, he gets his turn to ask for a card.

4. Object of game is to get as many sets of cards as possible from other players and win the game. When one person loses all his cards, game can begin again, or game can continue until others players are out of cards.

5. If student forgets to pronounce or to spell his word, he loses his turn.

II. Throw to Catch (Action with words)

Two students, two teams or whatever organization needed or wanted. One student throws out a word and catcher must give any one of the following, chosen before the game begins, related word: synonym, antonym, verb, noun, adjective, adverb, definition, use it in sentence, first word which comes to mind, answer a question from story, etc.

If the catcher is unable to do the task, he gets no points for himself or his team. The object of the game is to get as many points as possible in playing time.

FIGURE 8.5

Feather word sculpture

FIGURE 8.6

Set of "go fishing" spelling cards

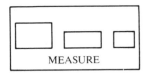  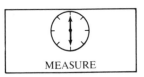

III. White Magic

Students sit in a circle. Music begins and two eggs, one raw, one boiled, and students don't know which is which, are passed around the circle. The holder of the eggs must choose a task from a bag and perform for the group.

The raw egg is used to add adventure and suspense. If it breaks, game stops until another time.

IV. Treasure Egg Hunt (For remedial students)

Directions for playing the game are written out and hidden in plastic eggs. The students are divided into teams. They must read, interpret, follow directions and move on to find the next hidden egg in their search for the prize at the end of the game. Surprise can be anything from bubble gum, a new comic book they've been wanting or an extra play period.

V. Word Shuffleboard (Adaptation of the commercial sport)

    Materials needed: Shuffle Board Court drawn with chalk or tape on floor, table, brown wrapping paper, or bed sheet. Words and number value drawn in boxes.

    Directions: Student player sits at end of board. See Figure 8.7.

Student chooses Task I (one point), Task 2 (2 points), or Task 3 (3 points) and slides wooden disc or beanbag into numbered areas.

        Task 1   Pronounce word

        Task 2   Give meaning

        Task 3   Tell in what situation he would use word

If performer correctly performs his task, he gets the designated number of points, plus points listed in the square on which he lands. If he misses, it becomes the next student's turn. The winner is the student who has most points at the end of a specified playing time. A student who needs no practice may keep score if he wants to.

    Variation: Any type skill teacher wants to use. Other possibilities are number combinations or questions on cards whose number matches number in game boxes.

VI. Synonym Golf (Adaptation of the commercial sport)

    Use words from the unit to put out in the field at each hole. Then teams of students work to find the smallest synonym for the words at each hole. The person or team finishing first with the smallest amount of strikes, letters, wins. Dictionaries or thesaurus should be handy. Let them use them.

FIGURE 8.7

Word shuffleboard court

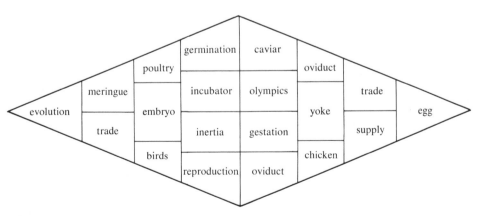

VII. Practice with Naming, Action and Describing Words

Directions: 1. Set up three groups of students

            2. Child from first group calls name of object from or used on farm.

FIGURE 8.8

Synonym golf field

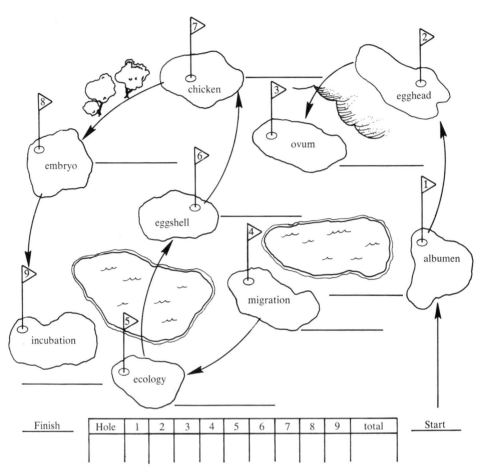

Hole	1	2	3	4	5	6	7	8	9	total

Finish   Start

3. Second student gives an action word related to first word.
4. Third child gives describing words and/or phrases of when, where, how things.

Objectives: Practice, enriching experience, dialogue and fun with sentence sense.

Examples: The wheelbarrow rolls   down hill.
A duck   wobbles   grotesquely.
Boys   ride   fast bicycles.
                                 tractors.
                                 through fields.

Variation: Type and cut up sentences such as these. Put in separate envelopes with directions on the outside. Students follow directions.

VIII. Reconstruct a Skeleton

After you have chicken, duck or squab for dinner, save as many of the bones as you can. Clean them carefully and let them dry. Now paint them with shellac.

Reconstruct the skeleton as nearly as you can. Use tape or straight pins. You may use cardboard to make it stronger.

IX. Gourmet

Prepare different dishes of meat from the bird family, add several other kinds to the variety and have a gourmet contest. Who can correctly identify what is duck, chicken, pheasant, snake, rabbit, opossum or whatever you can get your hands on to prepare. I would add one such as snake, without students prior knowledge, for interest, variety and motivation for later study on types of birds and other animals good for food.

You may have to get your lunchroom to handle this for you. Of if you have good relationships with mothers of the communities, they might do it for you. Another possibility would be a restaurant owner who is interested in what goes on at school.

Our Feathered Friends Puzzle

(To teacher: Adapt difficulty of your materials, even games and puzzles, to levels which your students can handle. Look at figures 8.9 and 8.10. The first one is much easier.)

Level I

Directions: Use any of the books we have available to find information which will help you solve this puzzle. Clues will help.

Down:
1. sometimes called "red breast"
2. white breasted; helps man
3. family pet; mimics people
4. large blue, black and white has bad habits
5. drab color; good eating meat
7. small songbird
9. small, brown, eats weed seeds, many varieties
11. has black cap; named for its song
12. has red cap; named for his habits

Across:
4. blue with red and white breast
6. makes cooing sound
8. red with black wings
9. small brown European songster
10. changes color with the seasons
13. has awkward looking horny bill; loud, harsh roar
14. night bird; said to be wise
15. famous for soft down on its breast; prefers to live near sea water

ANSWERS:

1. robin
2. nuthatch
3. parrot
4. blue jay
5. grouse

7. warbler
9. sparrow
11. chicadee
12. woodpecker
4. bluebird

6. dove
8. tanager
10. ptarmigan
13. hornbill
14. owl
15. eider duck

Levels II and III

PUZZLE

Across

1. many years lived
2. sign of the Zodiac
4. Subject of our unit
8. syllable sound like *ly*
9. many people sell their souls for it
10. Synonyn for **I**
11. center of egg
12. Male and female treaties which produces eggs
16. Denotes relationship of circumference of circle to its diameter
17. short for Albert
18. opposite of little
19. Name of French tribes in New Orleans
20. What working this puzzle should do

Down

1. contest of skill
3. 4th note of musical scale
5. egg shaped
6. used in most homes to beautify floors
7. opposite of no
9. dress of poultry and birds
10. makes a salad tasty
13. ashy flesh color
14. chicken before it hatches from egg
15. abbreviation of *for example*
17. mountains in Europe
19. cocks
21. archaic for *enough*
24. warm weather—the pipes
27. Birds make nests in them
28. Reason for doing

FIGURE 8.9

Our feathered friends puzzle

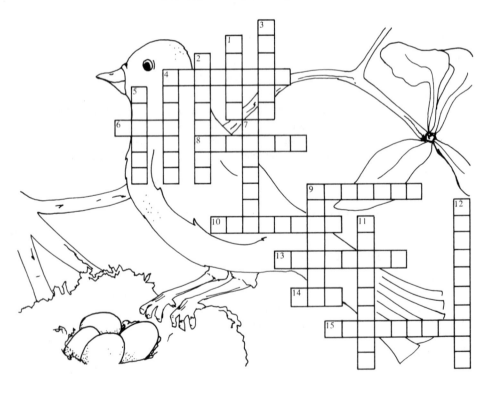

22. What the car did when it hit the ditch.
23. The little chickens that get pushed away from food will be ——————.
25. Suffix meaning one who does
26. Antonym for rough
28. Decoration made by small pieces of things
29. Girls' nickname
30. Place to keep things safe
32. Just born
33. One of something
35. Measures of weight
37. Vowel digraph
39. Fly which causes sleeping sickness
41. female germ cells
43. to send out
44. reproductive organs
47. plants
48. small joints on stem
49. synonym for spoil
51. burns
52. to take the part of one person in an argument
53. female reproductive organ
54. range of hearing

29. 3rd note of musical scale
31. Ride in it
32. Abbreviation for a state
34. One of something
35. fish eating mammals with webbed and clawed feet
36. Born
38. To make a critical estimate
40. Soft hairy covering of young birds
41. State in U.S.
42. ——————major. The big dipper
45. Chicken needs it for digestion
46. all powerful being
50. made from left-overs

ANSWERS

Across:
1. old
2. Leo
4. poultry
8. le
9. fame
10. me
11. yoke
12. alliance
16. Pi
17. Al
18. big
19. creole
20. teach
22. careened
23. puny
25. er
26. smooth
28. mosaic
29. Mol
30. shed
32. new
33. item

Down:
1. olympics
3. fa
5. ovid
6. linoleum
7. yes
9. feathers
10. mayonnaise
13. livid
14. embryo
15. eg
17. alps
19. chanticleers
21. enow
24. thaws
27. trees
28. motive
29. mi
31. bus
32. N.C.
34. member
35. otters
36. nee

35. ounces		38. assay	
37. ea		40. eider	
39. tsetse		41. Ohio	
41. ovums		42. Ersa	
43. emit		45. grit	
44. ovary		46. God	
47. herbs		50. bed	
48. nodes			
49. rob			
51. sears			
52. side			
53. ovary			
54. earshot			

Questions for the Reader

1. Before you read any further in the text, flip back through the exercises of this unit. We'll probably agree that students in grade 4–6 would enjoy and learn from these activities. But suppose you teach grades 7, 8 or 9.
   Will students in upper grades be too sophisticated for such activities as here suggested?

2. If you answered no to the above questions, no problems. But if you answered yes, using the same subject matter, list five ways you could change, adapt or create for your sophisticates.

3. There's no doubt about it. Students in rural areas respond to these activities, but how about urban students? What will motivate them?

   It will depend upon the maturity of the students, their years of retardedness or acceleration, and how the teacher handles the tasks. Some of the activities would be adaptable for older students; some would not. Many of them could be worked up into a more challenging form so that students could use the information they get from research. Of course, remedial readers in upper grades would need much of this material just as it is.

   We have controversy after controversy raging in our economic, political, and ethical arenas: economic inflation, strikes creating a situation for more inflation, gasoline and gasoline products making cars very expensive to operate, and Federal give-a-away programs including campaign millions. Of course, urban students are interested. For the few who might not be, look at a mini-list of topics which could be used to create interest.

Careers	Raise and sell squabs
Hobbies	Management, marketing, etc.
Prices	Big Business versus small business
Conservation	Poultry and products used as "come-on" by
Feed and food	supermarkets
Labor	Education required for any of these fields
Mechanization	Where can one find information about these
Supply and Demand	subjects
The Bird Watchers	Advantages and disadvantages of being one's
Zoo Keeping	own boss
The Audubon Society	Game laws

Puzzle to Use in Unit on Poultry and Eggs

FIGURE 8.10

Poultry and eggs puzzle

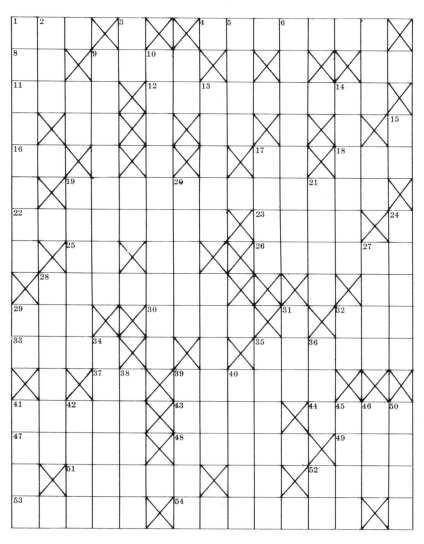

At the beginning of this unit, we listed questions which could be used to create interest with younger students. The same kind of thing will work with older students. Questions which could be used to motivate and on which they would have choices of working will cover a number of interesting things. Some of them are listed here. You could think of others.

1. What are the state laws concerning animals as pets in your state?
2. What are the migratory habits of birds? Do they really fly South in winter?
3. What are some superstitions surrounding bats? Are these founded?
4. One of the funniest pets is the goose. Tell the life story of a goose.

5. How does one teach a Myna bird, a parrot or a crow to talk?
6. Why is a pigeon called a pouter?
7. Which bird is the greatest acrobat? pest? most mischievous? valuable?
8. Some birds have soft bills and some have hard bills. What are the differences in the habits, food, treatment, etc., of these two groups?
9. What must poultry have in the diet to make hardshelled rather than thinshelled eggs?
10. Where does one find a bird to tame and what are the procedures for taming?
11. Describe the songbirds from the Harz Mountain, Germany, the Myna Birds from the Far East, the birds of Japan and China, etc. (Your choice).
12. DDT can no longer be used to control flies around commercial chicken houses? Why not? And what will the chicken farmer have to do to control pests?
13. How do birds help in the balance of nature?
14. How do poultry and poultry products help the economy? (supermarkets often deliberately lose money on these products—used as drawing cards for shoppers)

Some Activities for Older Students

1. Write the Department of Agriculture, Washington, D.C., for directions on how to (1) help conserve our wild life, (2) get into the forest rangers, (3) set up a pigeon business, (4) trap wild birds, or (5) any other subject of interest.
2. Check the literature for interesting stories of how birds have played a role in history making events.
3. If you are interested in becoming a dietician in a hospital, hotel or other business where you deal with food, find out about the nutrition value of poultry products. Also, how to preserve, cook and use the meat in other foods.
5. Make a list of some of the sonnets, odes, songs, plays, etc., which have used birds as inspiration.
6. Compose a present day parody on the poem, "The Raven."
7. Cook squab, chicken, duck, turkey, eggs or any other poultry product and serve it to your classmates. One remedial reading group did this in a high school home economics class and served it to the visiting Evaluation Committee, of which I was a member, and it was one of the best meals I have ever eaten.
8. Build bird houses, feeders, water troughs. (carpentry class)
9. Write original stories, poems, riddles poems, etc. (language arts)
10. Visit a reservation, zoo, or museum.
11. Check newspapers, grocery counters, sidewalk markets. Compare the prices, advertising, and people's reactions you observe.
12. Organize a bird-watcher's club for the interested few and report observations to the class. What birds live in your neighborhood? What are their

habits? Are they afraid of people? What do they eat? What are their songs?

13. Write an original play using nothing but characters from the bird family. Produce it. Make sets, costumes, etc.

14. Visit commercial growers, processors, egg producers, or other businesses connected with our unit. Choose one of these activities and set up a model which might be more productive than the one you saw.

Culminating Activities

Up to now our problem has not been too difficult. Our students were motivated, they worked, they set up all kinds of displays, they built things, they used varied books, pamphlets, magazines, and other supplementary material. One even invited the president of the local Bird-Watcher's Club to class and she made a funny informative speech, illustrated it with slides, and did bird calls. My, she was interesting!

Now: What have they learned? How do you grade them? Remember that nothing they've done up to now (at least nothing in my unit) has been a test. They were not working for grades, only to learn. What you do now will depend upon you, your security, and what you must have to back up grades which you assign. What did you stress in that preplanning period? What concepts did you or your students label as important during sharing periods? What particular learnings occurred?

If one is to be honest, and I always try to be, I don't believe any person can tell another how to test or grade a group of students and their learning. We're not there, we don't know the students, we don't know you nor what you stress, we don't know what went on during the time the work of this unit has been going on.

Suffice it to say that out of all the techniques you know for evaluating learning, you choose what you think most appropriate for *you* and your *students*. Also, remember that any evaluation of student learning is an evaluation of teacher teaching or teacher structure for learning. There are those in the field of education today who disagree with that statement, but let's face it. Why are we there? If we are afraid to be evaluated, we have no business in the profession. Other than the regular memorized pencil-and-paper tests, here are some possibilities for evaluating a unit such as this one.

For *remedial* students: Girls: plan a menu using products discussed
shop for groceries
cook according to directions
serve a meal

                                   Boys: follow directions and without help build something
work some practical problems
check and compare grocery shelf lists

For *regular* classes: students write their own summary
students make a list of questions which they think would be good to cover the material of unit

oral reports in some creative fashion

use cloze technique in a summary teacher has written

For *enrichment* classes: write essay on modern market practices

dress the part of poultry products and dramatize their importance to economy

make some analogy exercises, puzzles, or other exercises for next group to use when they study the unit

write essay on how business men manipulate prices

give them a chance and they'll come up with their own evaluations

How Does One Go About Setting Up A Unit?

Let's consider how you would go about setting up a unit for your class. There are any number of ways, and most of us would do it a little differently. However, here is one way to approach preparation for unit work with a class:

Ask: Who are my students? What do they want to learn about? What are their current interests? Can I incorporate the basic concepts our curriculum guides say we must cover into some plan of action compatible with student interests?

We know about the curriculum guides, school requirements, and principal's dogmatic rules laid down that first day, plans you're supposed to have ready to display if the supervisor comes around, or parents who complain that Miss Doe's class is fifty pages ahead of you in the textbook! The important question still remains; are your students happily achieving?

Some Basic Steps You Must Think of

I. MOTIVATION

A. Create an interest in the topic on the part of the class. Better still, plan a unit around their natural interests.

B. Give the class some idea of things involved.

C. Discuss some possible activities, some skills to learn or reinforce, some concepts to be understood.

II. STUDENT-TEACHER PLANNING

A. Don't do it all yourself. Remember it's their learning. Ask what they would like to learn about the topic.

B. Put these things down in writing.

C. Depending upon the atmosphere of classroom any number of questions, experiments, or relating activities will emerge from students' thinking.

D. Any important ones left out, you should supply.

III. WORK PERIOD

A. Gathering information:

1. Reading and collecting data

2. Watching films

3. Doing experiments
4. Using learning centers
5. Finding supplementary activities

B. In lower grades, shorter work periods and frequent questioning and sharing. In upper grades classes may work for several days in a variety of ways before sharing. Teacher watches for any opportunities to help. Sometimes students like to be left alone to work. We may disturb them. Watch for this.

IV. SHARING OF LEARNING

Sharing periods enable students to share information from different sources so that all members do not have to do all things. This sharing is important also to answer unsolved questions or correct mistaken ideas which some may have picked up. It can also stimulate further questions.

V. CULMINATING ACTIVITIES

How many teachers spoil the fun and learning of creative school with the threat of tests and grades! Does it always have to be so?

Yes and no. Yes, you have to have something to go on when students, parents, and/or administration want to know: What kind of grades is he making? No, you don't have to spoil the fun. Think of intriguing ways to evaluate. Let them think of things they can do to show how much they know. Try some of the following: (1) TV quiz games, (2) debates, (3) class movies or slide presentations, (4) notebooks compiled on basic activities and ideas, (5) newspaper writeups, (6) original puzzles which incorporate vocabulary and concepts, (7) discussions of most interesting things each student learned, (8) original plays, dress-up parades, and creative reports to other classes.

VI. PROBLEMS ENCOUNTERED

A. *Students can't work in groups.*

The inability of students to work in groups is a big problem. For fifteen years I wrestled with it. In fact, I'm still wrestling. College students do not always know how to function as groups. Why should they? Most of them seldom have a chance to try it.

Give help. The social interaction skills needed are just as important as the subject matter. After all, we're thinking about teaching for life situations. Isn't the group basic? They may forget the facts they memorize from a text-book, but there will always be people.

One way to handle this is to decide with the group what each will be responsible for. What is their task? Which questions do they answer? What study guides, job sheets, textbooks, exercises are they responsible for? You may have to sit down with them and help. After all they came to you from that "you can hear a pin drop" classroom next door. Use differentiated materials.

B. *Differentiated materials can be a problem.*

Using different materials for different students is a must in today's class-rooms. With the emphasis upon individualized instruction, open classes, and centers for learning, the teacher is not expected to follow one textbook, one plan, or one procedure as some formerly thought they had to do. With the abundance of materials, such as multiple adoptions, multi-level texts, commercial kits, in-service courses, and all the other modern helps, there is no excuse for putting thirty-five students on the same page in the same book unless they need it. Even if you get little in the way of added materials, read current professional magazines. Most of them have sections of ideas for the busy teacher.

You may use differentiated materials and still have problems. The materials will need to suit the students' needs. Knowing both these gives the teacher a basis to work from. He must look at several things before he decides what to do.

1. Word recognition: Students may need special help with new words before silent reading. Do they need word recognition exercises, puzzles, or programmed materials on word building? Borrow, beg, make your own, but help those who need it.

2. Word meanings: Are the concepts in the context difficult or beyond their experiences? They may need help before or during silent reading. Are they proficient with the dictionary or do they need help? Do they need some vocabulary exercises before silent reading? The answers to these questions will decide, to some extent, which centers and which tasks in the centers they work on.

3. Study guides: Study guides will need to take different forms on the same information. Are they to teach skills, to reinforce already learned skills, to present new information? Are they for the weak or the strong reader?

4. Experiences may be needed: If concepts in materials are beyond students' experiences, vicarious or firsthand experiences may be required before they can understand the silent reading. Trips, films, pictures—maybe the text needs to be written on a more simple level.

C. *Study Guides—you aren't familiar with making them.*

Forget the terminology of study guides, you've probably used them all your life. You simply make questions, exercises, and set up activities to guide the students in their reading and working with the materials. What do you want them to learn? Why keep it hidden from them? Some things to remember in making your guides:

1. Questions should be on two, three, or four levels of difficulty and used in different ways depending upon your students' needs.

2. Questions should concentrate primarily upon the thought processes, understanding of material, relating reading to life, showing relationships of words and ideas, and summarizing ideas to insure retention.

3. Some questions should be easy enough to let every child succeed and some hard enough to challenge the best of thinkers.

D. *Problem: time to do all these things.*

Making plans, study guides, letting students help decide upon what they learn, attempting group work: these things do require time, patience, and perserverence. But, you do what you want to do. Just make a few, see the excitement in learning which takes place in your class and you'll find time for the next ones. Make them and save them. You can use them again.

SUMMARY

This chapter has emphasized the importance of using creative, yet realistic, ways of incorporating real life situations and problems into everyday school learning. If students are busily occupied on tasks which have meaning for them, they'll work and not complain. I've actually seen students, who were formerly "hard to get to," groan when the bell summoned them to other places.

First, by example of one, then by giving you the steps, you have been shown how a class can be set up and lessons planned around one theme so that the schoolroom activities become a living thriving society with all students involved in tasks they can handle. Only by going through all the agonies and fun of planning for and making guides, will you ever know the satisfaction of having students sigh, "Hey man, that was fun. I learned something, too."

You can hold that 8 o'clock umph through the 2 o'clock slump. But don't let anyone tell you it is easy. It is not. It takes professional techniques of know-how, time and overtime, barrels of loving care, and often times families who'll put up with sandwiches for dinner and dinner and dinner. However, if you survive, and you will, the Bridge Clubs, the Sewing Circles, the political activists, and any other groups which find so many things to criticize in our school systems, may not have the facts to complain that you are not worth your paycheck.

Activities for the Teacher

With the cooperation of your peers, plan a teaching unit on some subject which is of interest to all of you. (A unit here refers to gearing all the curriculum areas— science, spelling, math, music, social studies—around one theme.) You might assign tasks on the basis of each teacher's strong points.

Include: a. objectives—what behaviors you want students to have after they work through the unit
b. motivational techniques and activities
c. skills to be utilized—do students have them or must you teach them?
d. materials to be read and activities to be carried out
e. reinforcement activities, if needed
f. evaluation procedures.

Answers to Bird Research, Study Guide Y, page 170:
1. Ostrich, Cuban hummingbird
2. Trumpeter swan, Heloise's hummingbird
3. Mesopotamian swifts—200 mph
4. Vulture—25,000 feet
5. Yes, hummingbird
6. No, example, cowbirds
7. No, no known blue pigment
8. Yes
9. No
10. Common and scientific names

Use Basic Student Interest as a Clue to Instruction in Reading Maps, Graphs, and Tables

1. What are some basic understandings students should have about the use of visual forms of information?
2. What are some skills needed in order to read and interpret visual information?
3. What behaviors will be promoted?
4. What are some procedures to follow in making these skills interesting to the students?
5. What special problems are encountered in the reading and visual materials?
6. What basic types of information are usually found in visual forms?

The reading of graphic materials is a basic skill often ignored by content teachers. You assume that students will automatically know how to read and use them, or you assume that some other teacher has or should teach them, or you ignore them all together. None of you should do assumptive teaching.

Learning to read visual aids poses some of the same problems as learning to read print. They present additional problems. Let's face the fact. Who can get excited about reading tables, charts, or graphs? Can you? Yet, if you want to, you can make the task interesting and meaningful.

Reading pictorial materials, especially maps, is not an intelligence but a perceptual task. If you are aware of this, much confusion may be cleared up. Color, legends, strange words, complex grids, differences in shapes, areas, distance, directions, space, planes trying to imitate spheres, and so on. What a number of additional meanings added to the print!

Pictures often look deceivingly simple, and students are apt to skip over them unless they're taught the techniques of reading them. Remind them to look at maps, tables, charts, and graphs critically. All graphic materials must be studied because each one is distinctive and unique. The captions and legends are helpful, extremes can be easily spotted, and comparisons are easy to make because most

199

of them are numerical, vivid, and easy to read. However, seeing in three dimensional figures is difficult because we are so accustomed to only two.

An Informal Inventory on Using the Textbook, talked about in chapter 2, will give you the information you need to know about students and their reading of graphic materials. If they show a weakness in any area, make a more analytical diagnosis to find specific skills you need to stress and get on with the teaching of them.

And how does the most efficient teaching and learning take place? By active student involvement, either alone or in groups. They learn better and faster working with materials than by listening to someone tell about them.

What can the teacher do? (1) Call attention to illustrations. They take material from the abstract to the concrete. (2) Demonstrate on the chalkboard. Use the five-step process for teaching skills. (3) If difficulty appears, have students reread the print and look at the picture. (4) Read orally, if necessary. Often they'll read something silently several times, then read aloud and say, "Oh, now I see."

One simple way to show that that flat map projection is a "take-off" on a sphere is to cut the peeling from an apple or orange, or place the cover of a soft rubber ball onto a flat surface. Talk about the differences in the round and flat ball. Explain that usually we see flat, not three-dimensional. When studying maps, space, or the ocean depths, we must think in 3-D.

Another way to approach the skill of graphic understandings is to present them as something analogous to a chapter or story in print. The map, table, or graph has a title similar to the title of a story. The title gives the main idea or general subject topic. Subtitles make more specific points. Headings, pictures, numbers, and symbols give specific information (details) which may be used to make generalizations and comparisons, draw conclusions or infer trends, all of which may, or may not, be covered in print.

Some Basic Understandings Which Should Be Developed in the Middle Grades

1. There are many means of presenting information in visual form.
2. Each type of visual has advantages and limitations.
3. Each type uses special techniques or devices.
4. Information presented in visual form must be interpreted in the light of purposes for which the form is intended.

Basic skills of reading and interpretation which should be developed:

1. To identify the type of graphic and to read with understanding the titles, subtitles and captions.
2. To understand the language of graphics.
3. To locate specific information or details from visual forms.
4. To make comparisons using data or details.

5. To evaluate the data so as to draw conclusions, make inferences, and form generalizations.
6. Ability to use examples of graphics studies as means of presenting information.

Behavioral objectives for a unit of study on graphic materials

1. Student will be able to obtain information from visuals, both in and out of school.
2. Student will be able to use visuals in presenting research projects and data in his or her daily routines.
3. Student will be able to transfer skill of reading graphics from one content area to another.

Types of Charts

One of the most useful of all teaching devices is a well-prepared chart. A chart is visual; it can be used repeatedly; it may be a preservation of time-consuming research. It can be used to set standards, to record achievements, to create motivation and interest, and to record creative expression.

Achievement Charts

Many teachers use charts to record progress in classroom activities: library readings, spelling, achievement test scores, timed tasks, and so on.

Creative Expression Charts

Creative expression charts are made to record or display creative work by an individual or a group. Songs, poems, stories, and so forth can be charted.

Games That Are Charts

Many educational concepts can be taught through the fun and method of games. Many of these utilize tables and charts.

Manipulative Charts

The most useful charts are those requiring some manipulation by the students. These bring kinesthetic and visual senses into operation and can be used with individual children for remedial work or with classes for review. Many charts can be used as curriculum games.

Reference Charts

Reference charts are usually made to record facts which require considerable research. By recording research on charts, the facts found are preserved and, therefore, available for repeated using.

Standards Charts

Standards indicated on a chart eliminate the necessity for rewriting such on the chalkboard each time students check a problem, give a report, or take an excursion.

Hints for Making A Good Chart

1. Decide on topic, message, and type.
2. Collect all materials.
3. Plan arrangement and color—tone is set by color, one line can change it.
4. Plan lettering size and style. Don't crowd.
5. Draw guide lines. Sloppy charts are losers.
6. Letter lightly in pencil.
7. Mount pictures and other illustrations.
8. Check for balance. Is everything easy to see? Is there a central point of interest?
9. Ink in.
10. Look at the caption. Is it short, simple, easy to read, eye-catching, interesting?
11. Add rings if wanted and available.

Reading Tables, Graphs, and Maps

TABLE 4

Some approximate tire sizes

Kind of Tire	Width of Tire	Circumference of Rim
Airplane	6.00 in.	6 in.
Bicycle	1½	16-27
Boat Trailer	4 – 6.00	4 – 12
Camper	3 – 12	16
Car	6	12 – 15
Cycle or Scooter	2 – 4	8 – 23
Tractor	10 – 13	24 – 33
Truck	6 – 7.5	15 – 17

Questions

From the information given in table 4 , answer the following questions:
1. What is the title of the table?
2. What type vehicle uses the smallest width tire?
3. If you were building a go-cart, what size tire would you probably need?
4. What tire has the widest range of possible circumferences?
5. If you are looking at both width and circumference, which tire is largest?

The radius of a circle is half the diameter. The distance around a circle, its circumference, is equal to 3.14 times the diameter. Using this formula, d $\times$ 3.14, figure these dimensions:

1. What is the diameter of an airplane tire?
2. The diameter of a tire is 4 inches. What is the circumference? From table 4 , what kind of tire might this be?
3. The diameter of a tire is 8 inches. What is the circumference and what kind of tire might it be according to approximate figures in this table?
4. If a car tire has a diameter of 30 inches, what is its circumference? How many revolutions would this tire make on a 200-mile trip?
5. Find a newspaper which has a sale on tires. What was the original price and what is the sale price? What percentage off will you get if you buy four new car tires on sale? How much money would you save if you buy now?

Use Charts and Tables for Spelling Fun

One way to motivate for and reinforce practice of reading charts and tables is to create them to use in conjunction with other subject areas. Below is an example of one which any teacher could adapt to his/her own needs.

PURPOSE: a. To motivate for spelling fun
           b. To increase vocabulary
           c. To practice reading a chart or table
           d. To practice the skill of following directions

TABLE 5

You can't spell too well . . . how about some hints? ? ?

R	I	G	I	D
O	T	R	E	I
T	A	P	S	T

HINTS: 1. Begin—bottom row, middle letter
          2. Middle row, middle letter
          3. Middle row, second from right
          4. Now use the letter which makes a hissing sound
          5. Bottom row, right-hand corner
          6. Now use a letter which appears three times
          7. Top row, right-hand corner
          8. Top row, fourth from left
          9. Middle row, top letter
         10. Letter which appears the most times
         11. Middle row, second from left
         12. First letter of the alphabet
         13. Letter which appears two times on bottom row
         14. Left-hand row, vowel
         15. A sound you hear in this blend: gr

BONUS: Put your pencil on the first letter—and trace the path of the letters as you found them from items one to fifteen. Now write the new word on this line: _____

Activity: Completing a Projection Chart

Purpose: To become acquainted with problems of population growth and demands.
To practice reading charts and tables with understanding.
To practice math and reference skills.
To work with materials and ideas which are real life problems.

Directions: Read the introductory information.
Then study the items listed on the chart.
Use the information given in the first block to figure out the missing numbers in the other blanks.
Work alone or with a friend.
Compare and discuss your findings.
Go to any reference materials for further information.

Introductory Information

Statistics say that a new baby is born in America every eight seconds. This means a population growth and heavier demands upon natural resources, food supplies, and living space. We have learned that all living things are interdependent and that we must keep a balance in nature if we are to survive.

Some people are predicting that if present trends continue by the year 2000 we will have 300 million people in the United States. With more technical information, more preventive medicines, as well as more cures for diseases, the life expectancy throughout the United States and the world is increasing. What will happen when there are more people than there are trees, space, and/or other supplies on earth? What will this mean to our communities, schools, and businesses?

During the past few years, there has been serious debate regarding the number of children people should have and the use of energy, water, air, pesticides, space, and food. Only ten countries in the world grow more food than they eat, and only four countries produce enough wheat to help poorer countries.

Work on table 6 . Can you figure out and fill in the information asked for? Are you interested in a particular subject mentioned? If so, do some reading on the problem and, if you like, share it with the class. Do you think we will have an oversupply, an undersupply, or an adequate supply of these commodities by the year 2000?

If needed information is not given on table 6 , use reference books to find what you need to complete the work.

TABLE 6

Projection chart for the year 2000

1. a baby born every 8 seconds	____ (number) of babies born in an hour	____ babies born in a day	____ babies born in a year	at this rate ____ new people will be added to population by year 2000
2. 4 lb. meat eaten by each person per day	____ lbs. meat eaten by person in one week	____ meat eaten in a month	____ lbs. of meat eaten by one person in one year	____ eaten by one person during life time of 70 years
3. .36 lb wheat used each person daily	____ lbs. of wheat needed per person in one week	____ lbs. of wheat needed in a month	____ lbs. of wheat needed in a year	____ lbs. of wheat needed during lifetime of 70 years
4. average of 91 gal. of water per hour per person	____ gal. of water used by person per week	____ gal. of water used in one month	____ gals. of water needed in a year	____ gal. of water used during a lifetime of 70 years
5. milk and cream 1.1 lb. needed per person daily	____ lbs. milk and cream used per person weekly	____ lbs. of milk and cream for a month	____ lbs. of milk and cream used per year	____ lbs. of milk and cream for average life of 70 years
6. average person inhales 625 qts. of air per hour	____ qts of air inhaled per day	____ qts. of air inhaled per person per week	____ qts. of air inhaled per month	____ qts. of air inhaled during lifetime of 70 years
7. 1640 lbs. of energy used daily by each person	____ lbs. of energy used by each person weekly	____ lbs. of energy used monthly	____ lbs. of energy used yearly	____ lbs. of energy used during lifetime of 70 years
8. approx. .82 gal. of gas used daily by each individual	____ gal. of gas used weekly	____ gal. of gasoline used monthly	____ gal. of gas-oline, on average used yearly by one person	____ gal. of gasoline used during span of 70 years
9. 133 new homes built on open land every day	____ new houses built on open land every day	____ new houses built monthly	____ new houses built yearly	____ new houses to be built by year 2000
10. ____ deaths occur every minute	____ deaths occur every hour	____ number of deaths which occur every day if this average holds up	____ deaths yearly	____ deaths will occur by year 2000 if this number holds up

Cognitive Activity Based on a Projection Chart

DIRECTIONS: Look at the Projection Chart figures you worked out in table 6 and answer these questions.

1. How many people are in your family? _____
2. If your family eats the average supply of meat, how many pounds of meat will they eat in one week? _____
3. If meat is $1.99 per lb., how much will it cost your family for a week? _____ a year? _____
4. How many students are in your class? _____
5. According to estimates of inhaled air per person, per hour, how much air has this class inhaled during the past hour? _____
6. Can you find the figure for the approximate amount of carbon dioxide exhaled during the same period and add it as number 11 on the chart?
7. Does the clean air balance the carbon dioxide?
8. What kinds of energy are being discussed in number 7 on the chart?
9. Can you find the amount of human energy expended during an hour and add it as number 12 to the chart?
10. At present day prices, figure the cost of a month's supply of milk products for a family of five people.
11. How much does one loaf of bread weigh? What percentage of the loaf is wheat? How many slices would you have to eat to get the daily average of wheat given on the chart?
12. If the approximate cost of building an average house today is $35,000, and if your project chart figures are accurate, how much money will be spent during the coming year for building?
13. Can you find the rate of yearly depreciation usually accepted by realtors?
14. If houses depreciate when an owner sells, why can he demand more than it cost him to build?
15. Compare the number of babies born to the number of deaths as your chart figures project them. What does this say to you?
16. Look at the supply of food, water, and energy supplies needed during the span of an average lifetime of seventy years. Compare this with the number of houses using up the space. What problems do you foresee here? Discuss these findings with a friend.

Holding Hands Leads to the Skill of Making Graphs

Make the teaching of reading graphs relevant and interesting. It can be done. Before class, draw a grid on the chalkboard. When students arrive, have them seat themselves in a circle. Announce to the class that they're going to do some action research. For this they have to hold hands. Reaction will depend upon levels of maturity in class. You will get some groans, some "Oh, boy's" and some disinterest. Surprise them. Make it exciting.

Appoint one person in the circle to be the leader who holds a stop watch and begins the activity. The person next to the leader will be the last one in line and will stop the activity by yelling stop when the time comes. You stand at the chalkboard to record.

Everyone joins hands and the leader gets ready to set the stop watch and start the hand squeeze. The object is to find out how many seconds it takes for the hand squeeze to get around the circle. No one must squeeze his neighbor's hand until his right hand has been activated, after which he passes it on quickly. When everyone understands and is ready, the leader begins the action. When the last person in the circle feels the squeeze, he yells stop. Time is recorded on the chalkboard. "Now we can beat that," you tell them. "Let's go again." Five trials is a good number to use.

When the five trials are over, use the students to work out the graph on the grid. Where do you label the grid to record the time, the trial number; how do you chart them? Make it a class project, but you are directing it.

After the information is plotted, ask questions about it. Erase the information you recorded earlier. Can they now read the graph?

Since 1945 I've been using this activity to introduce the skill of reading and making graphs, and no group has failed to understand. The added bonus is the fun of the activity. They find they can cut their trial times speedily downward. You can make another point here. I always do. The more you work at something, the more proficient you become, even hand squeezing. They get the point.

Students' heights, weights, colors of hair, eyes or skin, pulse-beat rate, temperatures of the weather, and so on, are other relevant subjects which can be measured and graphed. You've told them, shown them, guided them through the process, now put them on their own.

Activity Project 1: Circle Graphs

The pupils in grade six chose a class heroine. All of the pupils in the class voted. Here are the votes.

Susan Mayberry	49 votes
Terri Jones	24 votes
Ima Flunkie	98 votes
Sarah Watson	27 votes
Mary Brown	202 votes

Fill in the following circle graph. Each part of the graph shows one girl's share of the votes. Write each girl's name on the part that stands for her votes.

Write a good title for your graph here.

FIGURE 9.1

Circle graph, project 1

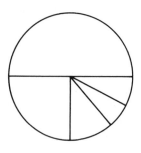

Now fill in the blanks below:
1. Who was elected class heroine? _____
2. The purpose of the graph is to show _____
3. How many girls got more votes than Terri Jones?
4. _____ got about one-fourth of all the votes.
5. Susan Mayberry got about _____ times as many votes as Terri Jones.
6. Ima Flunkie received about four times as many votes as Terri Jones.
7. _____ of the girls each got more than one-eighth of all votes.
8. _____ and _____ got about the same number of votes.
9. _____ got about one-eighth of all the votes.
10. Mary Brown got about as many votes as _____ got together.

Activity Project 2: Circle Graphs

Camp Lab School has a carnival every year. Last year the children spent $200 for refreshments. They spent $100 for ice cream, $50 for soda pop, $25 for candy.

This year they also plan to spend $200. *You* decide where they should spend their money this year.

Divide the circles below to show these facts. Label each part of the graph. Each part should show a share of the refreshments. Write a good title and good subtitles for your graphs.

FIGURE 9.2

Circle graph, project 2

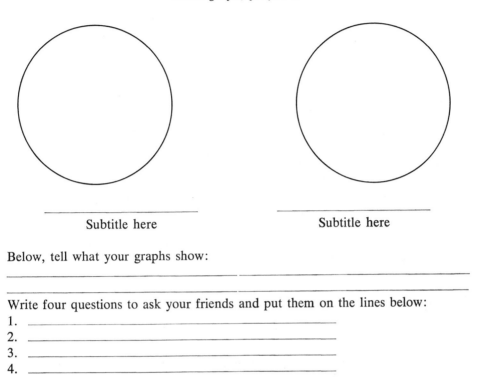

Subtitle here   Subtitle here

Below, tell what your graphs show:

_____

_____

Write four questions to ask your friends and put them on the lines below:

1. _____

2. _____

3. _____

4. _____

Activity Project: Picture Graphs

Farmers in (name your county) grew fewer and fewer bushels of tomatoes after 1966. The following figures show how many bushels the farmers grew each year:

1966	10,000 bushels
1967	8,000 bushels
1968	6,000 bushels
1970	5,000 bushels
1972	4,000 bushels
1974	3,000 bushels

Make a picture graph in the following space to show these facts. You can use the symbol shown in the legend. Draw all of the symbols about the same size. Try to keep the symbols in a straight line.

_____

Write a title for your graph here

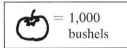

LEGEND

= 1,000 bushels

Now fill in the blanks below:

1. How many bushels of tomatoes were grown in 1967? _____
2. Five thousand bushels of tomatoes were grown in _____.
3. In 1970 the farmers grew half as many bushels as they grew in _____.
4. Fewer bushels of tomatoes were grown in _____ than in any other year.
5. The farmers grew the most bushels of tomatoes in _____.
6. How many bushels of tomatoes were grown in 1968? _____
7. The total number of bushels for the entire six years was _____.
8. Fewer bushels of tomatoes were grown in 1967 than in _____.
9. How many bushels of tomatoes were grown in 1974? _____
10. The farmers grew more than _____ times as many bushels of tomatoes in 1966 as they did in 1974.

Activity Project: Bar Graphs

During March the (name your school) Ecology Club tried to get new members. Each club member was asked to bring in as many new members as he could. By April Bob had brought in 5 new members. Bill got 2. Fred brought in 6. Ted got 8, and Ed recruited 7.

Make a bar graph on the grid below. Show how many new members each boy got. The lines for each bar are started on the graph. Fill in the other parts of the graph.

Write a good title for your graph here.

FIGURE 9.3

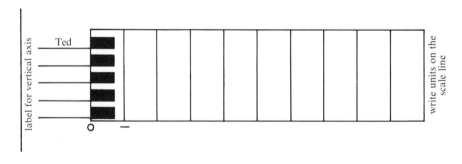

Label for horizontal axis

Now fill in the blanks below:

1. Each vertical line on the graph stands for _____
2. The longest bar shows _____
3. The scale line on the graph is divided into units of _____
4. The purpose of this graph is to show _____
5. The shortest bar shows _____
6. The only boy to get more new members than Ed was _____
7. How many boys got more new members than Bill? _____
8. All the boys except _____ got at least five new members.
9. Only _____ got more than six new members.
10. _____ got four times as many members as Bill did.

Using the Telephone Directory

A Study Guide for Utility Reading

Purpose: To motivate, to reinforce, to teach alphabetizing and reading of tables.

Materials: Study guide, copy of telephone directory, pencil, and paper.

Directions: Read the following questions and find the answers in the telephone directory.

1. If fire broke out at your house, what number would you call for quick help?
2. Suppose you do not get the number you call in the first question. Whom should you then call for help?
3. If your telephone breaks down on a holiday, on Sunday, or at night, whom should you call? (From someone else's house, of course.)
4. If you have a question regarding your monthly telephone bill, what should you do?
5. You've been told that Belk's Department Store is having a going-out-of-business sale. What number would you call to verify this rumor?
6. The thermostat on the heater of your Chevrolet isn't working. Your father tells you to call and find out whether Chevrolet Sales and Service has one. What would you look for in the directory? What is the number to call?
7. It's Sunday noon. You have 15 pounds of meat in your refrigerator. You hear a loud click and the refrigerator stops running. Where can you get help?
8. You want a fishing license. Will your telephone directory help? If so, how? If not, why not?
9. Which flower shop in town gives S & H Greenstamps?
10. What are the office hours of Dr. Doe? (anyone in your town)
11. For fast service and high quality heating oil, call _____.
12. Unexpected out-of-town guests (15 in number) show for Sunday afternoon and stay for supper. You do not have groceries you need. You seldom shop on Sunday. Is there a grocery store open?
13. Your mother's wig needs reconditioning. You can't get the beauty shop. What number would you call for information in reaching this number?

14. List the following names in the order they would be listed in your directory, then list their telephone numbers. How many have both office and resident phones?

Dr. John Smith	Pineville School	Sears Catalog Store
Lucy Choo	Preston's Dress Shop	Byron's Auto Supply
Pierce Singleton	Dorthy Peercy	Lucille Daniels
Craig Chase	Jeannette Greene	Jane's Florist Shop
Al Cline	Sandra Holcomb	Western Union

The Instruction of Map Skills

Maps and globes, which are representations of the earth on a small scale, are important tools for almost everyone. Boys and girls begin to use them early in their lives and continue to do so as long as they live. Therefore, they should learn to use them efficiently which is no easy process and involves a wide variety of skills.

Since students learn to read graphic materials at varying ages, just as they learn reading at different age levels, no special reference is made here to grade level. However, because of the curriculum materials and concepts used and developed at the middle-grade level, if students do not have map and globe skills, this certainly seems the logical place to teach them.

Teachers should be aware of some of the important aspects of instruction in map and globe reading. The following information might help.

A. Some of the skills which need to be developed:
1. The reading of keys and legends which are man-made symbols.
2. Land and bodies of water on maps and globes are distorted representations. The real world is three-dimensional. Maps and globes are two-dimensional, therefore distorted. This sometimes confuses students.
3. Directions. North and South do not mean up and down. Begin with directions to general and nearby places in relation to where you are. Eventually more specific directions and abstract concepts: northeast, southwest, and so on.
4. Location of cities, starting with one's own city—latitude and longitude.
5. Climate, starting with general and gradually developing ability to interpret weather maps, indicating rainfall, wind currents, and earth and sun relation to climate.
6. Time zones.
7. Determining distances by using the scale of miles.
8. Various bodies of water: lakes, oceans, rivers.
9. Political features: countries, regions, capitols, continents.
10. Comparing maps of different sizes of the same area.
11. Beginning the use of the grid system for locating places on the earth.
12. Transportation, elevations, human factors, cultural factors.

B. Some reasons for the study of maps and globes:
1. They are used in day-to-day living and will continue throughout life.

2. They help students to observe more closely.
3. They help students to understand many relationships which they will not acquire otherwise.
4. They enhance their understandings of their homes, their neighborhoods, their country, and other parts of the world.
5. They help students to understand television programs and newspaper articles relating to current events.
6. They can lead to vocations for a few pupils.
7. They provide involvement and enjoyment.

C. Teachers can arouse student interests in maps:
1. Begin with places close to their daily experiences and let them be successful with the tasks you set up for them.
2. Display all kinds of maps and globes around the room and give time for perusal. Let them browse.
3. Display cartographer and architectural tools and invite a resource person to the class to demonstrate some of them.
4. Let students make maps to show some facts they are interested in. Economic, social, historical, or weather maps.

D. Kinds of maps that students can make:
1. Damp sand maps to show topography.
2. Papier-maché maps. Tear newspapers into fine strips. Soak for twenty-four hours. Squeeze the water out and mix with salt and flour. Three parts paper to one part flour and one-third salt.
3. Maps enlarged by squares. (See chapter 12.)
4. Salt and cornstarch maps. Four cups of coarse salt to one cup cornstarch. Heat salt until it is very hot. Mix the cornstarch with water to the consistency of thick cream. Pour into the hot salt. Form the map.
5. Maps drawn freehand or traced with pencils or crayons will probably be most popular.
6. Clay maps on glass, on cardboard, or in trays. Use aluminum foil on the bottom to get the clay out easily.
7. Enlarged maps. Use opaque projector and let each student trace size he wants.
8. Overlay maps made with special overhead projector sheets and pencils or from a drycleaner pliofilm and magic markers.
9. Jigsaw puzzle maps. Paste map on cardboard or glue on plywood. Cut into puzzle pieces.
10. Electric maps with batteries.

Lesson: Map Skills

Purpose: To foster positive attitudes toward maps and to teach students how to use them.

Objectives:
1. To give in-depth meaning to the kinds and aspects of maps.
2. To reinforce concepts of direction and scaling.
3. To introduce new vocabulary.

4. To make maps seem more important by showing their frequency of use in day-to-day living.

5. To emphasize that maps are pictorial representations of real or imagined situations.

Materials needed: Maps of all kinds, shallow box with damp sand, rulers, construction paper, glue, graph paper, index cards, scissors, tooth picks, drawing instruments, activity sheets

Procedure:

Before class: Write the word "cartographer" on chalkboard.

Cover walls and bulletin boards with different types of maps.

Set up tables with architectural drawing equipment.

During class: Discuss the word "cartographer."

Let students browse from table to table and wall to wall.

Let discussion flow spontaneously and answer questions as they arise.

Have students work on activity sheets as needed. A few given here.

Evaluation: Can they do the tasks you want them to do? Observation, dialogue, was any interest created?

Reinforcement: Have students move on to a larger project, such as making a papier-maché topographical map of the school, a relief map of the community, a population map of the school, a puzzle map for special education class, etc. Here all the skills taught will be incorporated.

TASK SHEET A: MAP MAKING

Materials needed: large piece of wrapping paper, magic markers, felt pens, crayons, yardsticks, scale of student's choice.

Directions: Today you will make an imaginary park. Select a convenient scale and use the materials provided to make a model of your park on the floor or use the heavy wrapping paper on the table. Read and follow one item at a time in the following instructions.

1. Your park is 12 miles long and 6 miles wide. Outline the perimeter using the scale you have decided upon.
2. The entrance to the park is on the south side, two miles from the eastern edge.
3. A river runs north and south through the park two miles west of the entrance.
4. There is a camping area three miles from the southern and western boundaries.
5. Lover's Lane begins at the northwest corner of the park. Take it any direction you choose.
6. There is a hotdog stand to the east of the entrance.
7. A bridge crosses the river three miles from the northern boundary.
8. A convenience house is located at the camping area.
9. A United States mailbox is located at the northeast side of the bridge.
10. A flagpole stands right in the center of the park.
11. Now, devise a legend for your park.
12. Compare your park with the ones made by your friends. Did you agree?

TASK SHEET B: TOPOGRAPHIC MODEL

Materials needed: Work sheet, construction paper, tooth picks, damp sand, rulers, index card

Directions: Look at the simple topographic map on the work sheet. Contour intervals have been marked. Using the contour intervals as an index to the terrain, build a model of this map in the sand. Mark contour intervals by cutting different colored construction paper strips, each color signifying a designated elevation, and mount them in the sand with tooth picks. Show a key to your model indicating which colors stand for which elevations and a scale. Use the index card provided.

FIGURE 9.4

Contour map

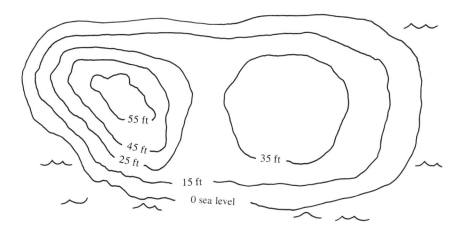

TASK SHEET III: SCALING

Scaling is a term used by cartographers, architects, artists, mathematicians, etc., to show relative dimensions, without any difference in proportion of parts. For instance, on a map the legend might state that one inch represents 100 miles. This process is used to show representations of things larger or smaller than they actually are.

Lesson: Reading of Maps, Charts, and Tables

Purpose: To practice reading of graphic materials, to review some interesting facts about our state, to learn to follow directions and to enjoy the activity.

Materials needed: Travelers' Guide Map of North Carolina (or your state), teacher-made study guide, time.

FIGURE 9.5

An architect's scale (approximate)

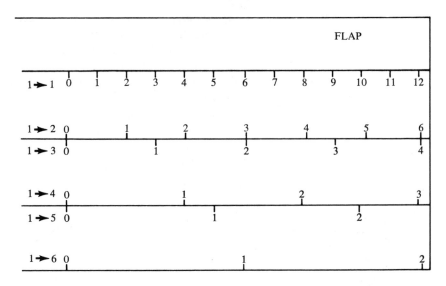

FIGURE 9.6   **FIGURE 9.7**

Scaling down

Directions: Study both sides of the map carefully and answer these questions. You may work alone or with a partner.

Picture Side

1. Who is the present governor of North Carolina?
2. Where could you order a supply of this map? How much will it cost?

3. On this picture side, Joyce Kilmer Memorial Forest is pictured? What is noteworthy about it?
4. Linville Caverns is North Carolina's only underground attraction. If you were on a vacation and passed through Linville at night, would you be able to see the Caverns? Why or why not?
5. Why is North Carolina called a golfer's paradise?
6. North Carolina is ranked number one in state supported highways. How many miles of highway do we have?
7. If you had a good idea for improving the highway travel, to whom could you write and offer your suggestion?
8. Suppose you wanted to see the outdoor drama "Horn in the West." Toward what city would you travel?
9. List three areas where you might camp out.
10. Craggy Gardens is famous for what native flower?
11. What wild animals still exist in North Carolina?
12. List three places one could visit in North Carolina to get a touch of pioneer days.
13. Name the three regions in the state.
14. How many state parks and forests are listed on this map?

Map Side

Directions: Turn the map over so that you are looking at the map side. Study the legend at the lower right hand corner. Study the mileage table. Look at the index to cities and towns. Do you know how to read these aids? Read the map to find answers to these questions.

1. Ten of North Carolina's largest cities are shown in insets at the top of the map. List them, then rearrange them in alphabetical order.
2. Which of these cities is nearest the seacoast?
3. Trace the Blue Ridge Parkway with your finger. Is it completed? From where to where?
4. Use the index of cities and towns to find Southern Pines. What famous military reservation lies just south of this city?
5. Look at the mileage chart at the bottom of the map. How many miles from Raleigh to Asheville?
6. According to the legend, what does this sign ———mean?
7. How many miles from Manteo to Wilmington?
8. What river runs just east of Fayetteville?
9. A man from Alabama travels up I-85 to Charlotte, N.C. He stops at your filling station for directions to a little town you've never heard of, Manson. His question: "Can I stay on I-85 and reach Manson?" From studying this map, what is your answer?
10. The ferry across the Hatteras Inlet costs how much?

True—False

1. Chinquapin has a population less than 2,000.
2. The city of Hendersonville is located in Henderson County.
3. Cullowhee is the setting for Western Carolina University.

4. Wilkes, Caldwell, Surry, and Mecklenburg Counties all claim to be part of the Blue Ridge Mountains.
5. The population of Wadesboro is approximately one-half that of Laurinburg.
6. This map is two years old.
7. North Carolina is bounded by five states.
8. Elizabeth City is in the southeastern part of North Carolina.

Map Skills for M.R. or Remedial Readers

Part I

Directions: Look on page _____ of your textbook, or on the individual map available. Find the answers to these questions and complete the missing letters.

1. The capital city of Georgia is -tl-n-a.
2. There is a long river that flows through St. Louis, Memphis, Baton Rouge, and New Orleans. The river's name is the M---iss-ppi River.
3. Florida is a state in the Southeast Un-t-d S--tes.
4. Alabama is bounded on the East by Ge-r-ia, the South by F-or--a, the West by Mis-i--i--i, and the North by Te--e--ee.
5. The large city located in southwest Tennessee is M--ph-s.
6. The large body of water along the East Coast of the United States is the A--a--ic O--an.
7. The large body of water on the southern border of the United States is the G--f of M--i-o.
8. The state to the east of Georgia is S--th C--ol--a.
9. Cincinnati is a city located in O--o.
10. Washington, D.C., is the c-pi-ol of the United States.

Part II

Directions: Look at your maps to answer these questions.

1. Which state is larger—Texas or Maryland?
2. Which state is further south—Alabama or Utah?
3. Name the states that have a part of the Rocky Mountains running through them.
4. If you were traveling from New York to Kansas, what large body/bodies of water would you cross.
5. Find Charlotte, North Carolina, on the map. In what county is it located?
6. Find the Grand Canyon. What part of the U.S. is this—East, North, South, West?
7. How many states of the U.S. touch the border of Canada?

Following Directions and Maps

The following activity is an exercise in following directions and map making which may be used as a listening task or as a reading task. You may put it on tape and use it in a listening center. There are eleven steps and many variations. You make your own, easier or more complicated, to fit the needs of your students. Perhaps both are needed. All levels of student proficiency enjoy this one.

DIRECTIONS TO STUDENT: This is an exercise in following directions. There are 11 steps you must follow. Listen carefully to the directions for they will not be repeated. You will need a sheet of paper and a pencil.

Draw a circle on your paper. This circle represents a city for which you are going to draw a map. Are you ready to begin?

1. Main Street runs from North to South through the middle of the city. Draw this street on your map and label it. (If directions are on tape, you must wait long enough for them to carry out the direction before giving the second item. Or they could stop the tape.)
2. First Street runs east and west through the north edge of the city. Draw and label it on your map.
3. Third Street runs east and west through the south edge of the city. Draw and label it on your map.
4. Draw Second Street where you would expect to find it. Label it.
5. East Avenue runs parallel to Main Street and is east of Main Street. It runs from First Street to Third Street. Draw and label it on your map.
6. West Avenue is parallel to Main Street and is west of Main Street. It runs from Second Street to Third Street. Draw and label it on your map.
7. Be careful now!!! In the northeast corner of the intersection of First Street and Main Street, there is a small lake. Draw and label it.
8. A river runs from the lake, crosses under three streets, and runs out the southeast edge of the city. Draw the river, and make symbols for bridges where they are needed.
9. A railroad runs in the northwest edge of the city, crosses two streets and runs out the south edge of the city. Draw a railroad symbol where it should be on your map.
10. Every town should include buildings of some sort. Draw symbols for the types of buildings and landscaping you wish this city to have, placing these buildings and landscaping where you would expect to find them.
11. Make a legend in the lower right hand corner showing and explaining all symbols you used on your map.

    This is your city. Give it any name you like.

    (There are many versions of this one, and you should make your own.)

Lesson: Working with the Globe

Directions: Here are questions, problems, and manipulations to do with your plastic globes. Use any textbook, map, or reference material you need as you work.

Purpose: (1) To review old sight and spelling vocabulary and become familiar with some new terms, (2) to practice following directions, and (3) to work as a group and enjoy learning.

1. Use your grease pencil and label the continent we are studying. Also, label the surrounding continents.
2. Label the bodies of water, if any, adjacent to our continent of the day.
3. With your plastic ruler, measure the vertical and horizontal distances of this continent.
4. On a map, what are these lines of measurements called?
5. On what line of longitude and latitude does the capital city of the largest country of this continent lie?
6. How many degrees of longitude is this capital city from Washington, D.C.?
7. When it is noon in our country, what is the approximate time in this capital city?
8. Fifteen degrees on your protractor measures one hour on a map. How many time zones are represented on this continent?
9. Measure the distance around the globe at the equator. What fraction of the earth's equator distance is covered by the continent we're studying?
10. On your globe, find the approximate location of New York City. Label it. According to your textbook, what is the largest city on this continent (the one you are studying)? Use any source you have and find five natural barriers you would have to cross in traveling between these two cities.
11. According to the materials you're reading, what is the most famous city on this continent? Find the approximate degree of latitude of it and follow it around the globe to North America. What city in North America is approximately nearest the same latitude?
12. What is the shortest distance from New York City to Tokyo, Japan? Is it possible to take this route? Why or why not?
13. Using the mileage legend, estimate the shortest distance by boat, plane, and a combination of the two from the city where you live to Sydney, Australia.

One Dozen Activities Which Are Sure Interest Getters [28]

1. Construct a model planetarium. Read charts, follow directions, use creativity, use dimensional thinking and socialize.
2. Plan a vacation tour for the years 1600, 1776, 1847, and 1976. Show some contrast and comparison.
3. Trace the life of a criminal from the time he is born until he lands in jail. Are there circumstances which he could or could not have changed?
4. Plan, prepare for, and carry out a formal party in the native style of the country being studied. Use costumes, decorations, foods, and so forth, of that country.
5. Have a schoolwide election for some political office. Let students role play candidates with campaign speeches and everything.
6. Plan a safari to hunt animals. Make tables, charts, and schedules. Consider days, time, food, costs, travel how and what, how long, precautions to take for the habitat, etc.

7. Which United States presidents have visited the *wonders of the world?* Have students make a timeline to show events in the country (one being studied at the time) from the time one of the wonders (student choice) was built until the present.
8. Make an etymology chart for some of the interesting terms found in reading.
9. Change the course of the Blue Ridge Mountain Range to run from the state of Georgia to the state of Wisconsin, rather than the present course. How might this have influenced settlement, industry, climate, and resources?
10. Trace the making of a law. Could students get a law passed?
11. Some teen-agers are unhappy in the country they live in. They refuse to participate in the Pledge to the Flag, they won't salute. They say, "It isn't my flag."
    a. Have them choose a country of the world in which they think they would like to live. Have them list the advantages of that country over the United States. Also, what are the disadvantages?
    b. Have them plan a dream country—utopia—of their own. They must locate it somewhere and it must be accurate in climate, time, weather, and industry that would be possible. Think of all the charts, maps, graphs, and tables of comparisons they could make.
    c. Let them rewrite the Constitution as they think it should be stated today.
    d. Let them list the things that they think are wrong with our country. For every item listed, have them give at least two ways to change or improve it.
12. Bring to class an odometer, pedometer, sextant, compass, speedometer, or any other instruments you think your students might respond to, and have students experiment with them. Have them construct an astrolabe.

Activities for the Teacher

1. Go through the process of how to take a survey—types of questions to be asked, how to tally answers, what population you want to reach. Then, with students, select a topic which they are interested in. Set up committees to do the various chores. Try to include every student in the class. Take the survey.
2. After the questionnaires are back in, use the findings to teach the skills of table and graph making.
3. Make a study guide on a map of the country you are currently studying. Let students use the guide. What are their reactions?
4. Using the graph made in number one, show students how to transpose the information onto other types of graphs—bar, circle, line, or picture.
5. Let each student find a graph in a textbook, reference book, magazine, or newspaper. Can they interpret the information? How many different kinds did they come up with?
6. If you are not working with students this quarter, choose a country which is usually studied in the middle grades and make up a kit of activities to teach, motivate for, and/or reinforce a skill (skills) to be used in a center on that country.

TEN

The Five-Step Process for Teaching Any Skill in Any Subject

PREMISE V. Teachers can meet the needs of students.
1. Are principles of learning involved in reading as a cognitive process?
2. What are some strategies teachers can use to insure learning?
3. What is this five-step process a teacher needs to use?
4. How can a teacher insure transfer of skills from one subject area to another?
5. Are basal textbooks the answer? What is the place of the basal texts?
6. Upon what does comprehension depend?

You are paid to teach and to do so successfully. How many times do you fail? How do you know what to teach, to whom, and when? That is what the first section of this book was about. Find out where the students are now, where you want them to go and build for success on a level they can manage. The public, who pays for our schools, will no longer tolerate some of our failures. Assessment, merit, competency, and accountability are terms we must deal with.

Students in grades 4–9 should develop the ability to recognize new words, to use topic sentences, to pick out main ideas, to distinguish main ideas from details, to understand inferences and cause and effect patterns, and so on. Your responsibilities include training of these skills. H. D. Herber, in class lectures at Syracuse University, has suggested five steps in teaching any skill.

Step I. *Tell them about the skill*, how it can help in understanding and organizing for remembering, how much of what they read does or does not need to be remembered by rote.

Step   II. *Show them how it works*. Have examples of materials which lend themselves to a particular skill and its use. Work through the materials with the students, showing, explaining, and encouraging.

Step III. *Guide them through the process*. Use two or three examples from the materials you're working with. Have students use the skill while you are guiding them to answer any questions and correct any misconceptions.

Step IV. *Put them on their own*. Can they perform? This is where seatwork or homework can be utilized and make sense to your students. It is practice on skills after the teacher has taught them in class.

Step   V. *Reteach if necessary*. When you check their work and realize some didn't get it, then to be an efficient teacher you must reteach the skill to those few.

Most of you are proficient in Steps I, II, and IV. But the most important step, III, too many times is neglected. This is the time you move about among students checking on what they're doing. You can clear up any points they don't understand before they do that twenty problems, all incorrect, and learn the wrong way. A student is much more apt to ask for help if you are available and willing than if you sit immovable and stoic-like behind your desk.

Reteaching, likewise, is neglected. Many of you will argue you don't have the time. You have so many units or books to cover. You can't waste time repeating. Think on these questions: Which is more efficient teaching—covering 400 pages with frustrated students who understand little or covering 275 pages with student success? What good does it do you to finish that textbook if your students don't?

Transfer of Skills Is Very Important

If you're a reading teacher who has a student for two or three sessions per week, you have a big responsibility. Your peers may expect miracles, but it isn't that easy. How often you hear students say, "Sure, it's fun, but I'll never use it." Apparently a weakness of many of you is this lack of explaining to your students the *why* of assignments. Therefore, they return to their regular classrooms and there is no relation to what they did in your reading class to what is going on here. The classroom teacher is guilty of the same neglect.

Psychologists have given us some hints in making instruction or knowledge transferable from task to task and outside the classroom.

A. Wise teachers know the power of telling a student what he will be able to do when a particular learning situation is completed. For instance, he will be able to read the "funnies" better by himself, to understand the pattern used in his science reading, or to take a driver's test.

B. If the learner finds rewards for her work and can see improvement in it, it is not unreasonable to suppose that she may learn to enjoy learning which is one hurdle many of you have not succeeded with, yet.

C. Students must be weaned from dependence on the teacher or other external agents to themselves. As they progress they need less verbal communication from the teacher.

D. The teacher (1) must provide a stimulus situation for motivation, (2) give verbal communication to direct and guide learner's attention, and (3) allow for feedback. Allowing for feedback seems to be one of the major generalizations that educators agree on. Let the student have time to think about what he/she is learning and to know whether or not he is thinking logically.

E. Some students find it easy to transfer what they learn from task to task, while others need much more guidance. Your job is to manage the learning situation so that transfer can be learned and applied. A prerequisite is mastery. Be sure they understand what they are to do, how to go about doing it, and are allowed to practice. Once mastery is complete, generalizations can be expected and transfer attempted.

F. If you are the manager of the conditions of learning, there are certain decisions which you must make. Decisions are the springboards for action. Robert Gagne says (61, p. 263) that these decisions must be given priority if the most proficient learning in the individual student is to take place. Decisions about:

1. Motivation:	If you don't produce this in your students, the others won't make much difference.
2. Transferability of knowledge:	Be sure of mastery of skills before trying to build upon them.
3. Assessment:	You should know more than anyone else what questions to ask to determine whether or not the student has learned what you wanted him or her to learn. There is a great need for better question askers.
4. Conditions for learning:	While you are responsible to set up classroom structure, you may need help from psychologists and other guidance people. Preplanning on your part is also required for most efficient teaching and learning.
5. Structure of knowledge:	Much of this is done by specialized people such as writers and scholars. Yet you must adapt it to your situation.
6. Specific learning objectives:	Society, parents, the school, and students all have a hand in setting up objectives for a school program, but you still have to decide exactly what specific objectives you have for a lesson. Should the student know where to put a period as terminal punctuation at the end of this lesson? Tell him exactly what he should be able to do and how it will help him.

The psychology of learning doesn't have all the answers, but it can help us to understand some of the issues involved. Let's look more closely at some of them which affect learning to read as a cognitive process.

Some Principles of Learning and Reading as a Cognitive Process

Principle I

Behavior which represents achievement of an educational objective should be *reinforced*. The problem is how? Methods which many of you have used for years are today being questioned. Isn't practice and reinforcement needed?

Studies suggest that although praise may be a reinforcer, blame is better in some cases. A student knows when he's playing around, not living up to his potential. You'd better let him know that you know it, too. The efficiency of each type can be predicted with some accuracy even with a fairly crude questionnaire measurement of student personality. Certain kinds of information may serve as reinforcers under some conditions. Knowledge of results sometimes will function as a reinforcer. There are times when a student wants to share what he or she reads. Other times it becomes a burden and if forced can engender hatred for reading.

Principle II

Introduction of cues which arouse *motivation* toward achievement of educational objectives will increase the effectiveness with which that objective is obtained. Is this always true?

Some students will learn with no cues, and no method exists for determining which cues will produce what behavior. A lecture may succeed with some students but not with others. Activity will work with most. Many different motivational variables from which the teacher may choose to motivate her students lends flexibility to teaching. The most efficient motivation comes from within.

Principle III

Practice in applying a principle to a solution or problem will increase the probability of transfer to new problems which require the use of the same principle. This idea has led to the theory of "sets" in learning and to programmed materials.

Principle IV

Learners differ in their capacity to make the responses to be acquired. Learning will be most efficient if it is planned so that each learner embarks on a program suited to his or her capacity. Therefore, the teacher must guarantee that every classroom situation will have in it tasks which are interesting in terms of intrinsic content and which cover a range of difficulty as great as the variability in students. What a job! Structured lessons planned by the teacher would seem to be necessary. It also seems that materials on different levels are required.

Principle V

If a pupil has had training in *imitation,* he is capable of learning by observing demonstrations. Explain a problem as you work it on the chalkboard and the child should be able to work it. We do learn by imitation, but research in the last few years indicates that learning is more effective when the learner is involved.

What does this say about the habit of continuously feeding students new words without any effort on their parts to figure them out? What does it say to the lecture-spoonfeeding of high school and college professors who expect students to regurgitate on a specified day?

Principle VI

Experiential background is the basis of learnings and also the basis for learning to read. An understanding of words and concepts begins with what the child knows. If he doesn't know, *build* background. During the last decade this attitude has led to literally thousands of dollars and countless hours of preparation for field trips. The payoff? Only time will tell. Research is scanty. What there is seems to indicate that trips with a resultant language-experience approach to reading is a good method.

Principle VII

Attitudes and emotions affect learning of and subsequent joy in reading. How would you feel if you had failed for eight years? If you couldn't please the "Old Bag" or the "Wise Guy" up front? They call us much worse. This winter I overheard a tenth grader tell his buddies at the beginning of a physical education period, "Fer six months I've been trying. Today, I finally did something that pleased the old gal." There must have been something wrong in this classroom.

Self-confidence is the memory of past success. Every child has the right to leave school every afternoon with a feeling of "I did at least one thing well today." He/she is more apt to be willing to return tomorrow.

Some educational goals may be achieved with equal efficiency by any number of teaching methods. If efficiency is measured by child response and learner time, the danger of adhering too strictly to one principle is that of excluding the other methods. Much research is needed on how children learn most efficiently.

These seven principles are only a few of the things you must think about. It seems, however, that most theories could be covered under three categories: the stimulus-response with reinforcement, the "Gestalt" or cognitive learning, and the motivation-personality theories. They should be integrated and used as the need arises in the classroom situation, and one should not be favored over another in all cases.

Teaching Strategies and Reading as a Thought Process

Many teachers have one method of teaching. Your minds are set—this is the way to do it—and if students fail, it isn't your fault. Many of you fail to take into consideration the goals or objectives of a reading program, what methods would best achieve these goals, and particular student needs. Even though most people (nonprofessionals included) recognize individual difference in humans, they still see them as "peas in a pod" in the classroom situation. There are many teaching strategies known and/or talked about by educators. Some are more successful than others. Most of you have your favorites.

Your choice of strategy will depend upon your definition of reading and your understanding of the role of the teacher in a classroom. With all the recent publicity about our reading failures and the money poured into supposedly innovative programs, there is in reality little new. True, many schoolrooms have more gadgets, more materials to work with, and a few walls have been knocked out. What really happens in some of these huge open spaces of organized disorganization is unbelievable.

One little first-grader told his mother, "It's so noisy, I can't hear myself think." Another one complained that he didn't know which Miss Teacher to go to when he needed something. "I don't have anywhere to call my own. My books get scattered all over the room," cried a bright little girl who was frustrated with too much, too fast. What strategy will best work for a particular child, teacher, and skills? If reading is to be taught as a thinking act, which of the following methods of teaching strategies will best accomplish the job?

Directive	versus	Nondirective
Basal texts		Many books
Rewards		Punishments
Lecture		Group process
Thinking		Recall
Inductive		Deductive
Memorization		Problem solving
Testing continuously		Guidance through study guides
DRA		DRTA
Dependence on teacher		Self-direction
Teacher as conveyer of information		Books and machines as conveyers of information

There is overlapping in these concepts. No one teacher is equally good in all. Yet, if you're interested in being a professional, you'll know and use different approaches to find out which one fulfills your needs and the needs of the students at a particular time in a particular situation.

The social climate of the classroom, the content of subject matter being taught, the objectives of instruction, and the ability and behavior patterns of students are all important in decisions about what strategies to use. Even in remedial reading situations, some teachers give more of the same—"mere repetition" of what the students already failed in. It seems trite to say it, but needs should determine methods.

For teaching to be effective, you must plan, structure, and select materials which contain different ways of activating children, different ways of presenting sequences of skills, and different opportunities for some children to skip parts which others may work step-by-step. Just as many roads lead to any city, so many tracks lead to the general goal of education—learning.

It is impossible to predict which strategy will work with which child, but those which allow the students to go toward self-direction, toward problem solving, toward total involvement in the learning process (away from the traditional row-by-row Round Robin, every child on the same page at the same time), hold more promise for the purpose of guiding reading as a thought process. Study guides which require students to actively seek answers, solve problems, think about concepts being worked with, and open-ended questions—these will lead to more productive learning than the rote memorization of facts to answer your literal level questions, which require nothing more than lifting answers directly from the textbooks with no learning involved.

It is impossible and not the aim of this writer to elaborate on these strategies nor on how a consultant, supervisor, or reading teacher can go about developing flexibility with them. However, experimentation is encouraged, and elimination of "fixed" attitudes is imperative. You must also be secure enough to let students question what you are doing.

The final decision on which strategy to use is what will work most efficiently to lead students toward success in the tasks you set for them.

Materials for Teaching Skills

In an effort to capitalize on and to fulfill a need in the classrooms, thousands of books, workbooks, games, and kits have been developed and published. Super salespeople can make each of them sound like a panacea. Then you with your limited sums of money to spend question which should you buy? There are at least four criteria to judge from:

1. Flexibility. Will they fit the diverse needs of your diverse students, enhance learning, and create interests?

2. Durability. When students begin to work, materials get rough treatment. Will they hold up? (This is something you have to think about when you make your own materials.)

3. Practicability. Are costs prohibitive? Would something else less expensive do the job just as well? Will they have to be replaced each year?

4. Suitability. What materials, textbooks, workbooks, and related tests are supplied by the state or local boards of education?

Most states adopt basal textbooks, and some have multiple adoptions. Which is used in your school? What are some advantages and disadvantages of each?

Single Text Versus Multilevel Texts Versus Multiple Texts

SINGLE TEXT

Arguments for:
1. State adopted for curriculum.
2. Less expensive.
3. Saves teacher time. Guides.
4. Other materials, maps, charts, etc., selected to accompany texts.

Arguments against:
1. All students not capable of reading material. Frustration results.
2. One text gives students one-sided view of information. May be biased.
3. Our goal: growth in understanding

5. All students exposed to same concepts, can discuss or be familiar with what is being discussed.
6. Some students learn only slightly better from simplified materials.
7. Must guide students through whatever materials you use.
8. Possible to use one text with all students succeeding at different levels.

and development of skills and attitudes. Is this possible with a text which students can neither read nor understand?
4. Teacher is limited to lecture (some say) because of students' inabilities to read.
5. Teachers don't know how to make materials on different levels to meet needs of students, or if they do, it takes too much time.

MULTILEVEL TEXT

1. Gives student material he/she can read.
2. "Peer" texts let students study the same concepts, be able to discuss and not feel left out.
3. Permits teacher to cover curriculum content with all students.
4. Much available material other than text which can be used as a time saver and meet individual differences. Commercial and teachermade games, study guides, kits, etc.

1. Stupendous problem of providing enough varied and interesting materials. If it be true that the range is two-thirds of student age, a tenth-grade history class, average age 15, would have 10 levels of reading. Think of the materials needed.
2. "Peer" texts are not greatly different.
3. Regardless of level, student must still be given guidance.
4. Problem reader is so designated because of problems with textbooks. Analogous materials not likely to offer much of a solution.
5. Teacher could spend all her/his time making materials.

MULTIPLE TEXT

1. More depth in teaching of certain units or areas of curriculum.
2. More views presented to students.
3. Can compare and contrast and make up their own minds.
4. Students learn to listen as they must gather information from each other.
5. Differentiated assignments with student responsible for his/her share.

1. If student can't read the basic text, he can't read others.
2. Still has to learn to use materials. This makes more of them.
3. Teacher must be familiar with content of many books.
4. Doesn't provide for individual differences.

While there are advocates of all these patterns, it seems safe to say that the utilization made of the materials, showing the students how to do what you want them to do with the materials, and providing the time for doing it is more significant than the organization or the materials. No organization and no text eliminates difficulties and/or levels of ability. The job of the teacher is to change attitude and strategy so that you utilize materials to the best advantage for the learners.

Basals are just that—a basic source to be used as a guide for inexperienced and experienced teachers. They give sequence to skill and knowledge building (so they claim) and act as a take-off point for teaching and learning. The wise teacher pulls from a basal the things she needs to use with a particular class and utilizes scores of other materials. Newspapers, magazines, audio-visuals, skills kits, resource personnel from the community, libraries, and the streets: some students would read more and see more sense to it if a teacher took them on a walk downtown, reading all the signs along the way.

The idea of language-experience activities, so stressed in primary grades, could and should be used in the middle grades, especially with reluctant or disabled readers. Making individual books on subjects of interest (books to be printed and bound for others to read) creates more motivation than any basal ever written. Making a school newspaper with all the learning activities involved—interviewing (oral language); reporting (writing, spelling, and grammar); editing (reading, language, grammar); managing and marketing (arithmetic)—is a beehive of learning in action. Of course, they would have to study, read, and understand the regular newspapers to make a good one. This is purposeful reading.

Many students and teachers (you and I included) criticize textbooks for being dull, too difficult for students, and poorly written. In many instances this is true. Yet, our adopted books are still one of the good sources to use for sequences in learning. It's up to us to make the best use of them. You can use the materials in a too difficult textbook to meet the skills and knowledge needs of all students in your classes, and you can do so in a manner students will enjoy. It takes time, preplanning, creativity, and downright hard work. This text is full of ideas and materials which have been adopted from textbooks, encyclopedias, and other references too difficult for some students to read.

Perhaps you don't have Titles I and III to buy all those expensive commercial kits you see at conventions. Don't despair. Many times I've worn out-of-fashion styles and gone without steaks to put money into duplicating and construction paper for my students.

Yes. Use the textbooks assigned to your class to teach skills. Remember reading is a process of getting meaning from printed symbols. The remainder of this chapter gives example of using textbook material to practice the skills of getting that meaning.

The Skill of Getting Main Ideas

Begin with easy familiar materials for skill teaching. If students have to struggle with decoding, they get bogged down with this task rather than working on the skills.

Divide your class into three groups and give them a definite timed task to do to show that they have the main idea of a selection. (Timed so that they get to the task rather than playing around.)

An in-service group was given ten minutes and the story, "Three Little Pigs." One group had to write a poem, one group had to write a song and sing it, and the third group had to dramatize the story. Here is the song and poem they came up with. Your students could do the same thing.

POEM: Based on "Three Little Pigs"

The three little pigs
Were sent out by their mother
To build their own houses
Separate from each other.

One built with straw,
One built with sticks.
One made a wise choice,
He built with bricks.

Before long a wolf came round
A wolf well-known for eating pigs—
He huffed and puffed two houses down
Because he was not bothered by straw or twigs.

Being greedy and on the prowl,
The wolf soon discovered the house made of bricks.
He huffed and puffed and let out a howl
He'd have to get this one with tricks.

An apple, a fair, then down the chimney he came.
But the third little pig, wise, it is said,
With fire and water built his fame.
He outwitted his enemy by scalding him dead.

SONG: To the tune of "Row, Row, Row your Boat"

All: Three, three, three little pigs
               Happy as can be.
               One day left home, singing a song
               Deedle, deedle, dee!

1st Pig: I will build my house of straw,
               The wolf won't bother me.
               I'll work and work and work all day,
               Deedle, deedle, dee!

2nd Pig: I will build my house of sticks,
               The wolf won't bother me.
               I'll work and work and work all day—
               Deedle, deedle, dee!

3rd Pig: I will build my house of bricks,
               The wolf won't bother me.
               I'll work and work and work all day—
               Deedle, deedle, dee.

WOLF: Huff, huff, huff
(spoken)   Let me in.

PIGS: Not by the hair on our chinny, chin, chins.
(spoken)

ALL: Three, three, three little pigs
Happy as can be.
They scared the wolf
And away he ran,
Deedle, deedle, dee!

Have students try this with one of their favorite stories then ask how they knew how to put the story into different art forms. Discuss how knowing what the story means, its sequence, the details, and so on, are all skills of comprehension of reading which help them in all areas of their school work. Then go into other materials to practice doing the same things except with different processes.

Step I.   Transformation and Expansion of Sentences

One of the basic sensible ways to show students that keys words lead to key ideas is to begin with the simpliest sentence—the kernel sentence and lead them through the process of transforming and expanding this sentence. This process should follow the pattern for teaching any skill discussed on pages 223-24.

Basic sentences or kernel sentences are positive statements made by putting certain kinds of key words in a certain order. They can be used to make new sentences. (124)

Example of a Basic Sentence: This is a bird.
                                  The car is beautiful.

Transforms are sentences that can be made from the basic sentences by following rules that make new sentences.

1. Basic Sentence: This is a bird.
   Transform into *negative* sentence: This isn't a bird.
   Basic Sentence: The car is beautiful.
   Transform into negative sentence:
2. Basic Sentence: This is a bird.
   Transform into a question: Is this a bird?
   Basic Sentence: The car is beautiful.
   Transform into a question:
3. Basic Sentence: A bird is on the perch.
   Transform into There-transform sentence: There is a bird on the perch.
   Basic Sentence: A car is in the yard.
   Transform into There-transform sentence:

You have just taken basic sentences and transformed them into three kinds of transforms: a negative sentence, a question, and a there-transform sentence.

Basic sentences can be expanded into more colorful and meaningful sentences when we add certain descriptive words to them.

Examples: Basic Sentence: The coat is warm.
                    Expanded: The white fur coat is warm.
                               The coat is extremely soft and warm.
                               Mother's white fur coat is extremely soft and warm.

Basic Sentence: The dog is black.
Expanded:
You have just taken a *basic sentence*, and by adding descriptive words, *expanded* it.

Through the use of expanding and transforming basic sentences, writers make our reading more interesting.

Practice: (on your own)

1. Transform the basic sentence into a negative sentence:

                Basic   *Negative*

The movie was exciting.
The motorcycle was stolen.
Groceries are expensive.

2. Transform the basic sentence into a question:

                            Question

John is sixteen years old.
Sue is high.
The dinner was lousy.

3. Transform the basic sentences into There-transforms:

                         There-transform

A police officer is at the door.
The plane took off in a storm.
A door is creaking.

4. Expand the basic sentences by adding descriptive words.

                            Expanded

My dog has disappeared.
Betty is shy.
This school is different.

It takes skill to spot the main thought or key words. It is difficult for many students to see meaning in long sentences. They get lost and give up. It is your job to give them practice. What is the simple thought in the longer passage? What are the key words?

Try these examples with your students

1. Poised within two feet of the sleeping enemy soldier, Byron, intent on his instinctive dislike for violence, prepared to fire.
    a. What are the key words?
    b. Is poised a key word or part of a detail?
    c. Intent on his dislike—key or detail?
    d. Is the sentence about the enemy soldier or Byron?
    e. What about Byron?
        Who? Byron   What? prepared to fire.
2. Proving to be a knowledgeable conversationalist, humorous, and with a flair for putting me at ease, Terry had been delightful company.
    a. What are the key words?
    b. Is conversationalist a key word?
    c. How about humorous?

    d. Is the sentence about conversation or about Terry?

             Who? Terry   What? had been company

Details to add meaning?   What kind of company?   delightful

           How delightful?   knowledgeable, humorous

                       put me at ease

3. Throwing the gears into high, grimly pushing the foot-feed, and praying under his breath, Tom expertly maneuvered his long slick sedan through the traffic pileup.

    The key words are _____Who?   Did what?

Step II.   Practice with More Than One Sentence

1. All day long we hiked up and down the hills. We certainly enjoyed our vacation in the _____.

    a. What word belongs in the blank space?

    b. How do you know?

    c. What are the key words?

Step III.   Main Ideas in Expository Types of Writing

A vast field of snow which moves is called a glacier. One might visit a glacier year after year without seeing any sign that it moves, movement is so slow. Scientists can measure this movement by use of metal containers on poles which record the slightest change. They have found that glaciers advance slowly, only a foot or two a year, or perhaps even inches, but they do move.

    a. What is the key idea? What is the paragraph all about?

    b. Is there a key sentence?

    c. Are all the other details relating to this key sentence?

An interesting place is a book store around Christmas time, or any time when parents and children are looking at books before purchase. A child will pick up one book, pull his parent's coattail, "I want this one," he'll beg. The parent will glance at it and if it is one he doesn't remember from childhood, he will put it back on the rack and pull one he does remember. "Now, here's a good one," he'll tell the child. Almost invariably, he will buy the one he wants, not the one the child picked. Then he will wonder why the child doesn't read it.

            Main Idea _____

    a. Is the main idea stated? Is there a topic sentence?

    b. What are the key words?

    c. Here, you are doing what is called inferring. You take what is given in the form of details and decide what the main message is.

Vipers, milk aphids, and foxfire was the subject of Dr. Spiker's speech last night. The audience trembled in fear, laughed in excitement, and applauded for more as in his natural dialect Dr. Spiker unraveled the folktales of half-suspicion, half-truths handed down by generation to generation of woods-loving mountaineers. Every person there will remember one of the tales and pass it on to his posterity. Only in this way can the true beauty of folklore be preserved.

            Main Idea: _____

This paragraph has only four sentences. Could any detail be deleted and produce the same effect? What is the main idea? Is there a topic sentence? Are they the same? How do you know?

Step IV.   Try Longer Sentences, Stories, or Essays

Doors stood open, lights blazed in every room, and the aroma of burning strawberry preserves permeated the area.* As though it had been carelessly discarded, a shotgun lay halfway under the table in the middle of the room.

With fear and dread in their hearts, neighbors stood panting on the threshold of a house they'd never visited.

Reluctantly, Sam Price entered. He glanced furtively through the rooms, turned off the burner under the preserves, and rejoined his compatriot outside.

"Ye think he shot her?" Mary Brown, holding her heaving chest, asked.

Sam Price scratched his half-shaved beard and shook his head. "No blood any place I can see."

"More likely she shot him, the brute."

"Now Mary, they've been married only a few months. The honeymoon's still on," Sam argued.

"Honeymoon, my foot! That's been over since the day they moved here. You should hear them fight. I been expecting something like this." Mary Brown flopped down on the edge of the porch.

Sam joined her. "We've known Bruce since he was a kid. He would do nothing to hurt anyone. But that woman! Why do our boys have to go galavanting all over the country marrying foreign girls they know nothing about?"

"Good grief, Sam. Jan ain't no foreigner. She comes from just across the county line like me and you."

"Not like me, Mary Brown. She's too all-fired stuck on herself."

"You jealous, old boy? Won't she flirt with you? 'Ull I can say one thing. She sure don't look like me nor your Molly." Mary Brown's laughter echoed in the quietness of the summer night.

At that moment a car careened around the corner and skidded into the driveway. Sam and Mary watched Bruce jump out, move to the other side and solicitously help the young girl.

"Hi, Sam. What you folks doing here?" Bruce, tall and lanky, towered over his neighbor.

"Well, son, we heard a shot and . . ."

"We thought she'd let you have it," Mary interrupted. She wobbled over, put her arms protectively around Jan's shoulder and continued, "Did the brute hurt you, Honey?"

The two young people looked at each other and their laughter was music in the night. "Darn those mosquitoes." Bruce slapped the side of his neck. "Let's go in, folks." Moving up the steps, he motioned to them. "Come on."

"Just for a minute, honey," Mary Brown answered. "Your preserves burned. Sam cut off the stove."

---

* SOURCE: Virgie M. McIntyre. Unpublished story. 1976

"Oh dear, my beautiful berries! My very first ones. I'd forgotten them." Clasping her hands to her chest, the beautiful blond sighed.

Putting his arm around her trim, firm waist, the young man comforted her. "We'll get more, honey."

Bruce picked up the gun, squinted down the barrel, and propped it in a corner. "And what's more, next time I'll get the jars. Okay?"

"Okay. Have a seat, Mary. Sam. Darling, I'm burning up. Would you get us some lemonade with ice?" Jan appealed to her young husband.

Mary Brown tugged at her falling gray locks, plummeted her 200 pounds onto the couch and gazed about the room. Just like a doll's house, she thought. When is she going to tell us what really happened?

Disregarding their curious stares, Jan moved to the Hi Fi set and twisted a button. Soft chamber music floated through the room.

Kicking off her scuffs, petite young Jan flung her hair back from her face, and propped her curvacious leg on an ottoman. A stinging sensation caused by the poison which had entered the bloodstream before they could reach the doctor's knife, ricocheted from toe to hip, making her want to jump up and run. She sipped the lemonade. "Um, that's good."

Bruce gazed at the delicate beauty of his lovely wife and tortured himself. If I hadn't been so pig-headed! Poor kid, bed-ridden for two weeks all because of my stubborness. The worst thing about the whole affair, he thought, is that the fight was so trivial, I don't even remember why we quarrelled. He shook his head. But here, I'm forgetting my manners.

"Honestly, Sam. You should've seen that devil. When I sighted my gun on it, from the middle of a barrel-like coil, it swayed its head, cast supercilious eyes toward me and warned me with rattlers that it was ready to give me a lethal jet of poison, too."

"But you killed him, didn't you, dear?"

"You mean you shot a stupid snake? We thought . . ." Mary Brown failed to mask her disquietude.

"I'm sorry to disappoint you, Mary." They all laughed, except Mary.

"It's no laughing matter, young man. The earsplitting explosion of that gun thundered death."

"It sure did. I killed that brute on the first try."

"But what happened?" Mary exploded. "Why did you go tearing out of here like . . ."

Jan interrupted her. "I needed jars from the barn for my strawberry preserves. Barefooted, as usual, I sprinted after them, and bingo. When I felt the sting, I beamed the light toward the ground. Beady eyes stared at me and a forked tongue projected in and out ready to strike again." The girl shivered.

"Jan flew back in here and told me what had happened. By the time I grabbed my gun and got back out there, he had crawled into the barn and was resting on top of a pile of shucked corn. He sure won't crawl any more though."

"Then what?" Mary asked.

"When Bruce got back in the house, my leg was already hurting. I could feel a stinging sensation traveling upward. Bruce wrapped a towel tightly around the ankle and one at the knee, and though I don't see how, we made it to the doctor's office without an accident."

"What did the doctor do?"

"He cut the skin with a razor and attempted to draw out the poison."

"Gosh! I've heard that rattlesnakes are dangerous. Will you die?"

"Mary!" Sam reprimanded.

"No, hopefully not. The leg will probably swell to twice its size, turn green and ache some. Dr. Hugo said to stay off it for about two weeks."

"Look, dear. You do what he says, you hear?" Mary heaved her voluptuous body from the couch. "I'll come over in the mornings and do your chores. I'm glad it wasn't what we expected."

"Good night, you two." Sam guided Mary toward the door. "I'd stuff that creature and keep him if I were you."

"Good idea," Bruce agreed as he fastened the screen door.

Several days later, from her position on the couch, Jan watched as her young husband clumsily experimented. "Hon, are you really going to drape that six feet of mud-brown leather on our newly decorated walls?"

"Uh-huh. Just in case I ever need reminding of my childish stubborness, it'll be there." He leaned over and gently touched her cheek. "I'd be no good without you. I love you. You know that, don't you?"

She nodded. "Yes. And you know something, too! This incident has probably saved our shaky marriage. We both were just too darned stubborn. I wouldn't have asked you to get those jars for a million dollars. In fact, I was arguing with myself about leaving you when it happened."

"I'm sorry, honey. You shouldn't have had to ask. If I'd been the mature kind of guy I want to be, I'd have been in there ready to help."

In their newly acquired wisdom, the young couple smiled at each other.

Occasionally, now, Bruce takes down his souvenir, dusts it, and treats it with a special oil. "I gotta take care of this baby. Someday, he'll belong to you."

And it's my turn to smile. You see, I owe my very existence to that stuffed monstrosity. Bruce and Jan are my parents.

Thinking About the Story

1. What would be a good title for this story?
2. Did you expect it to end the way it did? Why or why not?
3. Do you know anyone like Mary Brown? What was her main characteristic?
4. Would a doctor treat a snakebite as this story suggests he did?
5. This snakebite didn't kill. Some do. What kinds of snakebite will kill?
6. What kind of neighbors had Sam and Mary been up to this time? Will they be any different tomorrow?
7. Summarize the story in your own words in no more than one-half page.
8. Make a puzzle using some of these vocabulary words from the story: *threshold, careened, supercilious, reprimanded, discarded, disquietude, lethal, plummeted, voluptuous, ricocheted, monstrosity, compatriot, sprinted.*

Some Creative Tasks for Practicing Main Ideas

Students become tired of working, doing practice sheets, independent study, and tired of centers. They need to be with the teacher for a little while, or they simply need a break in routine. Try these:

1. Let them talk for one minute on any subject they want to. Stay on the subject.
2. Let them write for three minutes on any topic they're concerned with.
3. Have an impromptu panel discussion on a current topic of interest or unrest. Follow the rules of discussion, one at a time, and so forth. How many got off the topic?
4. Listen to television or radio for ten minutes. Anything that's on at the moment. Did the program have a story line, stay on the subject, give more than one side? If it is a game, what is the purpose?
5. Listen to a currently popular record. What is the point to the song?
6. When students get proficient at these tasks, make them longer. Write for twenty minutes, talk for three minutes. Watch for improvement in the number of words, ease of thoughts, spontaneity of involvement. Can they stay on the subject?

Main Idea in Art

All learning is classified. Students take from experiences that which their level of thinking can master. As there are different levels of concepts with words, so also with pictures. Just because all of your students aren't talented artists is no cause to deprive them of the beauty which can be found in other people's work.

Occasionally use a painting or a photographed print to add variety to your class work. Your reading lesson today dealt with the skill of finding main ideas. All day long you've been reinforcing this skill by showing how it can be used in all areas of the curriculum. Add the art class to the list.

What would be a good title for this picture? What is the artist trying to say? Write a story about the picture.

Though not directly stated, these questions deal with the skill of finding the main idea. Of course, there would be nothing wrong with direct questioning: What is the idea the author is portraying by this treatment of the subject?

Further study can use questions which progress from the easy (literal) to more difficult (interpretative and creative), so that all students can succeed with some of them. The literal questions would deal with title, who, what, colors, shape, and so on. The interpretative level could go into mood, how it changes, the part color plays, what the artist is attempting to say, and how background helps. The creative or applicative level could have students show their understanding by creating with words what the painter or photographer did with pictures.

Take any given picture which you or your students might be interested in and use it in the art center, talk about it as a class, let the regular art teacher handle it, or use whatever approach works best for you. Let's take a make-believe picture of a cat in a desert setting with a cactus plant in the background. Here are some sample questions.

Literal:
1. Make a title for this picture.
2. How many basic shapes are used in this picture?
3. Why is the white more prominent on the legs, mouth, and right side than on the remainder of the cat?
4. Use the encyclopedia and find the name of the cactus plant showing on the left side and the plant on the right side.
5. From the environment which is visible, what area of the United States could be the setting for this print?
6. Name the colors in the pictures. Which one is predominant?

Interpretative:
1. Why did the artist choose black as a background for this shot?
2. How is shadow used?
3. What does the expression in the cat's eyes do for the mood of the rest of the picture?
4. Suppose the details of quills on the cactus and sticks on the mound were removed. Would this affect the realism?

Creative:
1. Use the encyclopedia and find out what you can about the articles in this picture and write a story about one of them.
2. Make up your own story about this picture.
3. Find other pictures by this artist and compare the moods.
4. Do your own art work on the subject matter of this picture.

At no place is the name of the animal given, only the category. This is deliberate. Many students will know, but for those who don't, learning is more fun and more lasting when some work is involved. As stated elsewhere in these pages, we tell too much.

Workbooks: Boon or Bust?

The use of workbooks has been and to some extent still is, especially when you ask administration for money to purchase them, a controversy. Though originally set up for additional practice on pretaught skills, too many teachers have misused them.

A boon or bust? You don't like slang in a textbook? Even when it's the language of the boys and girls you teach? There are times when their words express more eloquently than all the formal correct grammar of theoreticians. Failure to capitalize on student language to produce learning is your failure. Putting them down for their language is one way to tell them you neither know nor care about them as persons. There are other ways.

One young failure remarked, "Just look at these pages! All red marks, the last one no better than the first. What good is there in doing all this junk? If he'd help me just once in a while to see why the answers are wrong, but all he does is (mimicary), 'Next time, read the directions before you start.' We get zero if we don't do the five pages a day and D or F if we do. Heck, I'm a poor reader and these workbooks are a (profanity) bust if you ask me. Just like him. He's too lazy to teach, so uses this way to keep us busy. Just wait 'til I'm sixteen."

Workbooks are of two kinds. Those which accompany basals and independents, which follow no prescribed texts. Both are expensive and you should practice creativity in using them.

Resource teachers and aides in Haywood County, North Carolina, have torn up various workbooks, pasted them on tag boards, laminated, and filed the pages under categorized skills. When a student needs help he goes to the file and pulls just the pages he needs. Teachers in this county are attempting to practice individualized instruction on students' levels.

For the successful use of workbooks, consider the following items:

1. Preteach the skills.
2. Be sure the student knows purpose for a skill and how it can help him or her.
3. Directions for use must be clear and brief.
4. Material must be on the comprehension level of student. If he can't read and understand the assignment, he can't do the work.
5. The student must know you'll help her evaluate her work.
6. Do not assign workbook materials unless a student needs practice in them.
7. Skills should be relevant to on-going projects in the classroom.
8. If one practice is not sufficient, reteach and assign more, not the same page again.
9. Immediate checking and evaluation is better than delayed.
10. Most work should be self-checking, with the teacher helping only when needed.

Workbooks are like all the other materials available to the teacher and student. If used judiciously, they can be a valuable tool for learning or reinforcement. Unwise use leads to waste of time, talent, and money.

The Skill of Sequence

Sequence, say some teachers, is one of the hardest skills to teach. Is this the result of poor memory, poor concentration, poor perception, lack of interest on the students parts or simply a lack of teacher know-how?

Most children in the normal learning range can tell you a story they've read or heard. (My three-year-olds could tell me when I left out a word in one of their favorite bedtime stories.) Most students can report almost verbatim television shows they see. So what's so difficult about sequence in the classroom? Is it the atmosphere? How many classrooms make learning an exciting challenge, a joy, a rewarding experience? How many relate the skills to the actual life as students live it daily? If you, teacher, will use the following sequence in teaching this skill, students will improve.

Begin with the comics. "Peanuts", or "Charlie Brown." Cut them apart and let students reassemble into sensible stories. Next step, take the words off the pictures and let the students fill the balloon spaces with words of their choice. Thirdly, let them write and draw their own comics.

Do a science experiment in class and have students record, orally at first, steps in sequence as they were performed.

Perform three, five, or seven (according to maturity level of students) operations and have students repeat them in the exact order, each student adding one until someone forgets. One second grade group got up to twelve activities in the list before a child forgot what to do in what sequence. Even college students like this one. Examples of things to do: close the door, switch the light off and on, pat a friend on the cheek, write a name on the chalkboard, repeat "Mary had a little lamb," etc. Whatever comes naturally in your classroom will suffice.

Next, move into context. After students have read material, give them exercises such as the following two from social studies. Can they rearrange the mixed-up order in the sequence the author used. This activity also summarizes or organizes the concepts you want students to learn. Some activities in science are also given in this chapter.

Paragraph Comprehension—Sequence and Sentence Relationships*

Directions: Read the following groups of sentences. Find the topic sentence and write a number one (1) beside it. The other sentences will be details about the topic sentence. Make them into a sensible paragraph by putting them in the proper sequence (order).

Such words as so, therefore, neither, then, later and whenever help to bridge thoughts and ideas. They are called transition words and will help you decide the order.

PARAGRAPH I.

_____ a. So people pitched tents or built rough shacks for shelter.
_____ b. The gold hunters found many hardships in California.
_____ c. Neither was there enough reasonably priced food to go around.
_____ d. A loaf of bread cost a dollar and eggs sold for $3.00 each. Sugar cost three dollars a pound, and a chicken might bring as much as $10.00.
_____ e. In the gold fields, there were no comfortable houses.

PARAGRAPH II.

_____ a. The tall "chewing gum tree" grows in the Guatemalan forests.
_____ b. Then the white sticky sap flows slowly down into a heavy bag.

---

* SOURCE: From *Your Country and Mine, New Edition,* of *The Tiegs-Adams Series,* © copyright 1965, by Ginn and Company (Xerox Corporation). Used with permission.

_____ c. Its real name is the sapodilla, or chicle tree.
_____ d. Later, this sap is boiled to make it thick and hard.
_____ e. Chewing gum is made from dried chicle sap.
_____ f. With long knives, workers slash crisscross cuts on the tree trunk.
_____ g. Then it is flown to factories to be made into gum.

Seeing Relationships—More than one paragraph*

Directions: Below are sentences on four different subjects which we have studied in Social Studies. They are all mixed up. As we've already talked about, each sentence in a paragraph is related to every other sentence, and they follow a sensible order. Read the sentences and decide under which heading each belongs.

Inland Valley Farmer   Food to Market   Ocean Waters   Along the Coast

1. Mr. Ryan is a dairy farmer.
2. He catches fishes to sell.
3. Because of the tide, his fishing shack is built on poles.
4. Fresh food can be taken quickly to market.
5. Bill Smith is a fisherman.
6. So people living inland are affected by the ocean currents and travel.
7. In winter when tourists are gone, he sells his fishes to nearby cities.
8. Fishermen store their boats in the harbors.
9. Truck farmers provide food for roadside markets, for the city open-air markets and sometimes large trucks haul it away.
10. Some of these harbors are deep and large.
11. Mr. Ryan feeds corn and hay to his cows in winter.
12. Every state in the Northeast region except Vermont can be reached by ship.
13. He provides fresh milk for people in the surrounding areas.
14. In winter, he can spend some time in front of the fire, but he still must milk his cows.

Further Directions:
a. After you have decided under which heading each sentence goes, re-read them. Now organize them into a sensible paragraph. Find the sentence which you think gives the most logical beginning and which other sentences (details) should be listed. Write the paragraph.
b. When you have finished, check with the answer key. How well did you do?
c. If you enjoyed this activity, try another one. The next one is somewhat more difficult and is taken from the field of science. The categories are

Seed   Fish   Insects   Platypus

1. The platypus is a member of the mammal family and is about 12 to 18 inches long.
2. Many people speak of any small flying or crawling animal as a "Bug."

---

*Sources: *The New Book of Knowledge.* Grolier Inc., New York., 1973.
The World Book Encyclopedia. Field Enterprises Educational Corporation., 1964.
Young People's Science Encyclopedia. Children's Press, Inc., 1962.

3. The fish's most acute sense is that of smell.
4. We define a seed as a matured ovule and as the final product of plant reproduction.
5. Scientists have conducted extensive experiments to discover the reaction of fishes to odor in the water.
6. Then she hugs them to herself and rolls into a ball to incubate them.
7. Second, what some people call a bug may actually be a spider or a centipede.
8. The part in which food is stored will vary with different seeds.
9. To speak thusly is wrong on two counts.
10. The platypus usually lays two or three eggs.
11. Scientists believe that odors direct fishes to feeding areas among water plants.
12. A very interesting fact about the baby platypus is that after hatching, it feeds on milk from sweat glands that are similar to mammary glands.
13. These are not insects at all because insects have three body regions; (1) head, (2) thorax, (3) abdomen.
14. A seed is made up of a tiny living plant, the embryo, stored food and the seed coat.
15. It has waterproof fur, feet modified as paddles and a horny ducklike bill.
16. It has been found that fishes can tell the difference in odors of many water plants.
17. Its home is a burrow, dug several feet into a bank, with a grass-filled nest at the end.
18. First, a true bug is a member of only one order of insects.
19. Eggs are kept in the body of the female for some time before they are laid in a nest.
20. Similarly, they can detect the odor of hands washed in a stream and odors of many animals.
21. In some seeds food is stored in thick seed leaves called cotyledons.
22. It is possible, too, that salmon find the mouths of rivers and streams during the spawning season by the odors of plants living in fresh-water bodies.
23. Another name for the platypus is the duckbill.
24. The stored food nourishes the young plant from the time it starts to grow until it can produce its own food by photosynthesis.

Can you organize these categories into paragraphs? Its fun to try. See how near you can come to the teacher's order. Write your paragraph then check with the key.

Cause and Effect

What is meant by cause and effect? How does one teach this skill? Will the five-step process work? Cause and effect is a technique used in writing to show relationship between what something does (cause) and what happens as a result (effect). Middle grade teachers complain that their students don't use this pattern to help themselves understand and recall material. How can they use what they haven't learned?

Here is one possible teaching strategy. List one-word and/or phrase cause and effect items which have the 3-F characteristics: functional, familiar and fun.

Cut the list apart and put segments in an envelope with directions written on the outside.

Let student groups compete to get them matched. We did this in one sixth grade. The lowest level student group took them at face value and completed the task ahead of the top group who saw subtle and creative ideas and argued. Imagine the self-concept value for the low group.

Directions: Here are some words and phrases. Some are things which happen or could happen and others are the results. Make two columns headed

Causes   Effects

and place the words and/or phrases under the correct category. Here are some examples of things you might use to begin with.

1.	didn't study	failed test
2.	sharp tongue	few friends
3.	pepsi	burp
4.	faulty brakes	accident
5.	won ball game	had a party
6.	electric storm	no lights
7.	snow	no school
8.	played with matches	fire
9.	overate	stomach ache
10.	slept late	missed school bus

Do the same thing with the content area concepts you are attempting to teach. Science and social studies use this pattern of writing and students need to be able to recognize it when they see it.

The following exercise is one made for a review of the materials a sixth grade class had studied. Remember, always give the students purpose for what you ask them to do. I like to put it right on the task sheet as part of the directions.

LESSON: CAUSE AND EFFECT IN SOCIAL STUDIES

Directions: Most material which you study is written in patterns. If you learn to recognize these patterns, it makes understanding and recall much easier.

One pattern of material, especially in science and history, is the cause and effect. Here is an exercise for practice in relating cause and effect from material we've studied on the country of Greece.

Study the cause column. Then look at the results or effects column. Place the letter beside its corresponding number. The first one is done for you. (More items in one column than in the other will add the cognitive dimension which otherwise might be guessing at matching.)

Cause	Effect
F___ 1. Olympics became unfair	A. Parthenon destroyed
___ 2. Solom's wise rule, freeing of salves and poor people in the assembly	B. Socrates had to die
	C. Stadium buried underground
	D. Little travel in early Greek history
___ 3. War with the Turks	E. The Athenian League was formed
___ 4. City-states separated by mountains or other natural barriers	F. Olympics discontinued by Roman conquerers
	G. The beginning of democracy
___ 5. Earthquakes	H. Jurymen voted
___ 6. Taught men to seek the truth	I. Peninsula named Balkan Peninsula
___ 7. Union for protection needed by the small city-states	J. We cannot read Crete writing
	L. Europe's people have had hard time getting along
___ 8. Many countries and many languages	K. Greeks sacrificed to gods and goddesses
___ 9. Balkan mountains located there	
___10. Hippocrates introduced scientific methods to medicine	M. United States helped the Greeks rebuild their country

_____11. Greeks thought they gave super-
       natural protection
_____12. Little fertile land in Greece

N. Farmers must move about, and
others must look to sea or some
other occupation for a living
O. Hippocratic oath upholding the best
in medical practices still practiced
today in some schools

When you think most of the students understand what you're talking about,
give them sentences and paragraphs and let them work on the skill.

Analogies can also be worked up using this pattern, thereby giving students
practice in cause and effect pattern along with analogous thinking tasks. Here are
some examples:

wound:	blood	storm:	flood
heat:	fire	accident:	damage
turkey:	dinner	gasoline:	car
pollen:	allergy	germ:	cold
onion:	tears	garlic:	bad breath
pepsi:	burp	alcohol:	drunk
gun:	death	fire:	destruction
drought:	famine	snowstorm:	avalanche
sunshine:	cheerful	rain:	gloomy
egg:	chicken	bulb:	flower
salt water:	thirsty	picnic:	satiated
ruler:	straight lines	mixmaster:	smooth batter

Exact words need not be the same. Accept any word that shows cause and
effect relationship.

Let students make up some of these.

Some Follow-up Exercises

a. Let students make study notes using the two columns listing cause and
effect items from materials they're reading if these materials are conducive to this
type exercise.

b. Games and other exercises, both teacher-made and commercial, may be
placed in the centers for further practice on this skill.

c. Have students go to reference books and find an event in which they have
an interest. Study this event. What led up to its occurrence? What might have
happened if one thing had been different? Was timing important?

d. What controversy is currently raging in politics. What are the causes of the
controversy? What may be some of the effects? Could it have been prevented?

SUMMARY

Comprehension is a complex part of the reading process. If we are to get
away from the word callers produced by the Round Robin, still prevelant in too
many reading classes, teachers must understand the part comprehension plays
in the process. You must also understand your part in helping students see how
this process operates for them. Give them these understandings about the process
of reading:

1. They must know words. You will help them with words, vocabulary expansion, and they must help themselves. If they don't know words, reading becomes a frustrating chore. Teachers can't do the reading for them.

2. School is for learning. The educational experiences and environment gives them ideas, understandings, and practical knowledge. Through personal contact with each other and experiences in building concepts before abstract symbols are given them, they'll be more likely to profit from teaching—to understand.

3. Students must learn to concentrate. You must set up an atmosphere where this is possible. Remember the child in the open space school who said, "It's so noisy I can't think." Some students need quiet. Some teachers need it. Students must learn to stick with something until they master it. How many of them fail to get concepts, do not ask, and go from one failure to another, simply because a teacher didn't know they needed more help! Why don't you know they need help?

4. Students must know the reasons why they are learning something. It gives them incentive, focus, and goals toward which to work. Comprehension is a structured, deliberate mental manipulation. Both you and your students must understand that while we want learning to be interesting and fun, it is also difficult.

5. Interests in reading or any other task can be cultivated. Success is the key. Once they find out they can do something successfully, it is no longer a chore. You must see to it, with their help, that they learn the skills with which to succeed.

6. Another understanding, which this author believes is the most important one of all, which both you and your students need, is that the best way to learn to do anything well is by doing it. Let them read. Easy materials, materials they're interested in, time every day for free reading, no dumb questions to be answered, challenging and current materials attractively displayed, currently popular controversies discussed in class—all of these will improve comprehension more efficiently than ditto sheets from workbooks on skills which too often they see as busy work so that the lazy teacher doesn't have to do anything.

Activities for the Teacher

1. Review the lessons you taught in your classes today and answer these questions.
   a. What kind of teaching strategies did you use? Would a different approach have been more successful?
   b. Did you use one basal text on the subject, or did you use multiple sources?
   c. What skills did students need to be proficient in to succeed with the tasks you assigned? Were they? Or did you need to help?
2. Choose one skill which most students in your class need help with and plan how you can use it in three different subject matter lessons which you plan to teach in the near future.
3. With a particular objective in mind, plan a field trip with your students.
4. If you're an undergraduate and didn't work with students, choose one of the classes you attended this week and answer questions number one above in relation to what your professor in that class did.

5. Select an easy story, such as the "Three Little Pigs," and plan creative activities for students to perform which will show mastery or comprehension.

6. Use one of your favorite classics and write it in the vocabulary which students are using today. Read it to your students, or if not teaching, to your peers. What are their reactions? Have students rewrite one of their favorites in their individual choices of style.

ELEVEN

Capitalize on Real-Life Reading Situations: The Multimedia Approach

A student who can legitimately be labeled *remedial* is one who is mentally capable of learning but for some reason is not living up to his or her potential. You should not confuse him with the slow learner who may also be behind some of his classmates, but who is working up to capacity. Neither of these should be confused with the mentally deficient child who lacks the intelligence to work up to the level of his more fortunate peers. A good developmental reading program will take care of all of these students.

An Organizational Plan for a Developmental Program

A. Developmental Readers

Classes for all students working at capacity level, whatever that level may be, and can be handled by the regular classroom teacher.

Three types:
1. Average group of readers
2. Slow learners, moving at their own slow pace
3. Gifted or top thinkers moving at a fast pace

B. Retarded Readers

Readers not working up to capacity. These may also come in three categories.

1. Corrective: have one or two weaknesses and can be handled by classroom teacher.
2. Remedial: capable but behind what is expected for students of their age and capability. Can be handled in regular class, in special reading classes, or in a clinic situation if available.
3. Remedial: High I.Q.'s doing passable work but may need help as badly as other remedial readers if not living up to their potential. Can be handled in regular classroom.

C. Special Education Classes

For physically or mentally handicapped or the emotionally disturbed who cannot function properly in the normal classroom and who need special help. These students need special classes and/or clinical help.

How do you decide which label fits which student? By doing a careful assessment as suggested in chapter 2. From test scores, informal reading periods, and observation, do your initial planning. As time progresses you may find students who have been misplaced. If so, move them.

But you've converted to open classes, team teaching, learning centers—individualized learning stations. What does this do to that beautifully planned developmental reading program?

It's time someone said it. There is no such thing as completely individualized teaching or learning—unless you convert to a tutorial system. Even in the so-called open classes, there is need for group work, full class instruction, and/or committees for unit chores. Students who have the same needs can be instructed in a group and at the same time meet individual needs. The amount of skills practice needed later, also, individualizes. While one teacher takes eight students to the library for reference skills practice, another may have fifty in a group to watch a film, for music, or for physical education.

While a teacher works with a special group of ten on sounding out words, the other students are doing silent reading, working in centers practicing skills they need, and they know what they need because together student and teacher have planned ahead, and one student may be doing an individual project which meets his needs and inclinations.

In this set-up, do we need remedial classes? Some students will need more help, guidance, and/or attention than others. The help should be given in the classroom using the materials they're working with. Sending students off to a special reading teacher, to the dumb room, just hasn't paid off. If reading teachers and regular classroom teachers would get together and plan the work so there could be a carry-over into regular classroom work, the special room for help might work. But it hasn't worked out that way, and, much of the time, effort and money has been wasted. The big problems of handling the remedial student in the classroom are the amount of materials available, the levels of these materials, whether they are easily accessible and self-checking, and whether or not students can handle self-direction.

Remember what first year studies told you. The teacher is still more important than method or material. How you structure; how you create an atmosphere of inquiry, learning, and dialogue; how you diagnose, evaluate, and prescribe —these lead toward relevancy in the classroom. If you want students to believe that your program is worth their time and effort, then it must relate to life as they live and know it. Once you get them interested in learning, then you can branch out into the areas which you think are necessary for their full educational diet.

Suppose your principal set up in-service meetings which you had to attend, you're a captive audience as students in our public schools are, and at the first session he announces these topics:

1. The philosophy of Jacobinism
2. How to conserve the tiger beetle
3. How to assemble a Jaguar engine
4. Why the powder horn is obsolete

How would you feel? Are these the subjects you have been longing to find out about, they'll help you in your fifth year teaching material, they'll improve your personality, make you more money?

On the other hand, give you a newspaper, a magazine, a film to view that you've been longing to see to compare with its book version, a television tape to find the inconsistencies, the propaganda, or the quick-sell techniques and watch you cogitate.

Do the same thing with your students:

1. Does Dick Tracy use standard detection procedures? Defend your answer.
2. Do you know any businessmen like Dagwood and Mr. Dithers?
3. If you were Blondie would you put up with Dagwood?
4. Is Roscoe Sweeny a dope or a genius?
5. Would Little Orphan Annie survive in New York City? (your city)
6. Peanuts is a good teacher. Do you agree or disagree? Why?

Questions similar to these can lead students from the comics into other materials. What are the standard procedures used by detectives? Where can you find out? What books will help? Invite a detective or police officer in to talk to the class.

What characteristics make a successful boss? Interview some leading business people. What do hygiene books list as personal attributes which lead toward success?

There are hundreds of ways to use the newspaper in the classroom. Following is a short list of tasks which you could put on job cards to be used in the multi-media center in your classroom. Students should work on the tasks which utilize skills on which they need practice.

Thirty-four Ways to Use the Newspaper

1. Choose a story from the newspaper. Draw a red line under each noun. Draw a blue line under each verb. Draw a green line under each adjective, etc.
2. Choose a story from the newspaper. Circle the transitional words or phrases. Words like *therefore, while, but, however,* and phrases such as *on the other hand, in the meantime,* etc.
3. Choose a sports story. Rewrite the story using formal English for all the unique sports terms. What does this do to the story?
4. Categorize one week's headline news stories into subject areas. What area furnished the most excitement this week? (Science, music, space, accidents, politics, war)

5. Separate headlines from stories and ask students to test their skill at matching titles to stories. Check the answer key to see how well they did.

6. Separate headlines from stories and ask students to write headlines, then match their attempts with the original ones.

7. Separate pictures from captions and attempt to match. Check with key.

8. Using the articles on the front page, write a television news broadcast script. Using the ads, write commercials to sponsor your news program.

9. Check all advertisements of cars in this issue. Which company offers the most benefits on a trade-in? Do these benefits sound reasonable or an advertisement come-on? Explain your answer.

10. Study the stock market reports to answer these questions:
   a. Jerry had 20 shares of T & T stock. Susan had 20 shares of Bell Telephone. Tom owned 20 shares of Radio Corporation of America. All three stocks advanced this week and our owners sold. If they all had the same original investment, which made more money this week?
   b. According to the television news report, stocks fell 2.98 today. What three stocks bore the main thrust of this loss?
   c. For the last three weeks, American Mobile Home Corporation stock has advanced ½ to 1 percent. If this trend continues, what will be the price of this stock at the end of a ten-day period?

11. Choose an editorial and rewrite it as it might have been written in pioneer days, during World War I, or during any period you're studying in history class this week.

12. Choose your favorite comic strip. Paste it to a tagboard and cover with contact paper. Separate it into the segments and make an answer key. Put all of this into an envelope on which you write directions for the task of sequencing and add it to your sequence file. Practice on some of the story comics already in the file.

13. Select five new words from the latest issue of the paper. Find out all you can about these new terms and rewrite the sentences where you find them using synonyms. Put the new words into your card file. If they are interesting, you might want to share with a friend or prepare to teach one to the class.

14. Make a newspaper using modern day features of what it might be like in a world with no electricity and/or no gasoline. All features and articles must follow a format as though we had neither.

15. Analyze advertisement appeal. Go through your favorite ads and circle words which would help sell the merchandise. Then place these words under categories which determine to whom and for what emotions the advertisers are reaching.

16. Speed reading: Study the front page for three minutes. Then see how many facts you can remember. Daily practice for six weeks will amaze you.

17. Choose some controversial issue of the day and write a letter to the editor of your local newspaper.

18. Recall game: Class divides into two teams. All students study the paper for a designated time. Then one team acts as experts—they ask the questions. For

each question they can think of, they get one point for their team. For each question team II can answer, they get a point. If team II fails to answer, the question reverts back to team I, who must answer or lose the point. Skills practiced in this game are relevant to most reading tasks, and students thoroughly enjoy the challenge. They can also see their own progress.

19. Rewrite four want ads using synonyms for all nouns.
20. Rewrite four want ads as a creative story.
21. Rewrite four want ads as they might have been written in 1820, 1920, or 1930.
22. Study the want ads—both buying and selling. Write an ad for something you want to buy and one for something you want to sell.
23. For Girls: Using the available papers, choose, plan for, and figure the cost of the furniture to set up housekeeping, a beauty shop, or any other adventure you're interested in.
     Then attempt to locate an old newspaper of 20, 30, or 50 years ago and compare the prices for the same amount of equipment.
24. For boys: Using the available papers, choose, plan for, and figure the cost of setting up a garage, a bowling alley, or any other business adventure you're interested in.
     Then attempt to locate an old newspaper or catalogue and compare the prices for the same amount of equipment.
25. Stage a dramatic incident which students view. Have them use the format of who, what, where, and when and write their version of what happened as they might do it for a newspaper. Let them compare stories. They'll be amazed at the differences in what they saw.
26. Use the inquiry technique. The teacher gives the class a headline. Students interview her to get the information for their news story. To write the article they can use only the information they get from direct questioning. The first time they won't get much, but they'll learn.
     Examples of headlines: a. Three Teenagers Find Car Submerged in Lake
                                      b. Highway Commission Says School Building Must Go
27. Give students a problem situation and ask them to skim rapidly for the solution as offered in some newspaper.
     Example: You need a hearing test but do not have money to pay for it. Is there any help in your community?
28. Choose one article from the editorial section of the paper and pick the five most important words in the selection. Explain your choice.
29. Make who, when, where, and what columns and fill in from five stories of the day. This practices note-taking skills and finding details.
30. Work the daily crossword puzzles, or if you prefer, work up an original puzzle and submit it to the editors of your local paper.
31. Visit a newspaper plant. Interview people at work on different tasks, if permissible. Write up the interviews as you would for publication.
32. Read the weather forecast. Record it on a chart. Read the actual weather

outside. Record this on a chart. Keep these charts and records for one month. Figure the percentage of correct forecasts. If you are interested in finding out more about how weather forecasts are made, use the *Science Encyclopedia*.

33. Find articles and cartoons on the current controversy in the news and make a bulletin board. Include any devices you choose to show comparisons and contrasts, prejudicial treatment, or propaganda techniques. You may need more space than the bulletin board. If so, use one side of the wall in the classroom or get permission to use a part of the wall in the hallway.

34. Pull a study guide from the newspaper file and work on one you haven't done before.

Add Films, Records, Tapes, and Other Machines to Media Centers

Will film improve the learning situation? Are costs prohibitive? Will audio-visual materials lend themselves to definite lessons?

There are teachers and parents who argue that film is a waste of school time and money. They use many reasons, some of them valid.

a. Students already spend too much time watching junk.
b. Films show stereotypes of life.
c. They over-simplify.
d. Machines won't work when scheduled.
e. Cost is prohibitive to most school budgets.
f. Films are filled with violence and clichés.
g. They're passive—demand nothing from students but sitting and being entertained.
h. Too many films are not suitable and simply repeat what students already know.

Regardless of one's attitude toward film in the classroom, because of television, movies, radio, and records, you have to accept the fact that youth are media-oriented. Just as they enjoy a book from free reading and take from it what they want or need, so a film gives them a chance to relate personally to characters, emotions, and actions portrayed. They learn to interpret, to live vicariously, and to get a new insight.

Books have been and are being written on the use of film in the classroom. It is a tool—an effective interesting tool—of learning in today's world. When we consider the impact of filmed materials as propaganda to the masses, it becomes important that we allow, even teach, students to be critical, analytical, and choosey; to recognize how words, phrases, actions, even choices of shots—all can influence emotions and attitudes of viewers. The mere lifting of an eyebrow by a newscaster can change the entire thrust of his words. Students need to be skilled in the critical aspects of film watching.

While there are disadvantages, as with everything, teaching by and with film also has merits. Consider these:

a. Vocabulary is expanded and concepts built.

b. Interest in reading is created.

c. History can be made more palatable. Costumes, manners, furniture, and dialect lend atmosphere to period pieces.

d. Literature of an era is more understandable when seen on film.

e. Ethnic differences are accepted and likenesses understood.

f. Standard speaking patterns, not particularly to be stressed, can be imitated.

g. Glamour and variety are added to an otherwise dull, routine classroom.

h. Enrichment—the camera can roam the earth and beyond.

i. Take-off point for class discussion leading to depth of thinking and oral communication.

j. Probably most important and inclusive of all the others: special assignments can be given in correlation with all other study:
   1. background research, interest beyond textbook
   2. comparison with books
   3. character study
   4. evaluation—discriminating between superior and inferior
   5. teacher not an "answer" person—students' ideas and insights are developed
   6. interest in film study and making of student film

Just as with books, charts, field trips, and/or other teaching resources, with film you are responsible to motivate interest, anticipate vocabulary problems, establish good classroom viewing conditions, set up practical follow-up activities, and evaluate learning. Here is one approach for using film.

A. BEFORE SHOWING:

1. Review previously learned concepts to be explored in the film.
2. Ask leading questions:
   What do we want to find out about the subject?
   Is there any difference in today's climate?
   If the people had lived or the incident had happened today, how would it be different?
   What are some things we want to know in order to understand why it happened?
   What act in present day politics can be compared to the film presentation?
   (Mutual student-teacher planning produces better results than either alone.)

B. AFTER SHOWING

1. Class discussions: plot, theme, bias, stereotypes, agreement or not, comparison with films on a similar theme, and so forth.
2. Paper and pencil procedures: fact and opinion, multiple choice items, main ideas, recall of facts.
3. Problem-solving creative activities—reflective thinking:
   a. What if they were alive today?
   b. Dramatizations by students

    c. Radio talk shows, interviews, etc.
    d. If I had to make a choice . . .
    e. Write newspaper articles or reviews
    f. Debate pros and cons
    g. Judge character of the person: What constituted courage? fool-hardiness?
    h. How does a career in politics make or break people? What hazards, rewards?
    i. Compare with the book. How much was left out or added? Why?

A Study Guide for the Newspaper and What It Tells Us

Objectives:
1. To familiarize students with the sections, make-up, and information in papers. They are more than sports and comics.
2. To get across the concept that the paper is functional.
3. To teach the skills needed in understanding a paper.
4. To practice using the information in the paper.
5. To motivate for reading of material in reading text.

Materials:
Newspapers from several different cities or several papers from the same city. Study Guides on these papers.

Procedure:
A. Before class. Cover the boards and walls with papers for which you have made questions.
B. During class. Discuss the purpose for the lessons. Ask what they read and how. Tell them that later you'll go into how to cover the contents of a paper in five minutes, but today it's going to take much longer. In fact, we won't be able to finish the work in one day. We're going to have our social studies, math, reading, English and spelling right from the newspapers.
C. Talk about free speech, advertising, entertainment, libel—any subjects which come up in connection with their questions or comments.
D. Give them study guides or task cards to work with. Also, give them the privilege of working alone, in groups, or coming to you for help if they need to.

Your study plans for them could be something similar to this one which I used in the unit I did with my class when we studied "The Legend of Sleepy Hollow" by Irving and talked about in Chapter 7. You would need copies of recent hometown papers before making your guides.

Working with a newspaper as part of a bigger project would call for special pre-planning on your part. In case you use it with a particular story as I did, you would need to write the Chamber of Commerce of the town setting from which your story is written. For the "Legend of Sleepy Hollow" it was Tarrytown, New York.

Some morning when the students enter, the chalkboards and/or side walls are covered with newspapers. One side with the Tarrytown papers, the other side with Sylva, Waynesville, Asheville (whatever towns you live in or near) papers. Immediately you have their interests. "What's going on?" they want to know. There are possibilities as to the way you might introduce the activity. It will depend upon goals you have and sophistication of the group you're working with. However, this is especially good for slower students because of the built-in motivation.

On the work sheets there should be varied kinds of activities, and students certainly should have more than one day on it. I used a week with my group of sixth graders I talked about earlier in this chapter. One star indicates the easy literal questions needed by weakest students. Two stars indicate somewhat harder questions or problems and three stars are for your top students. The first time you use this activity, you may prefer that all student do all questions. I did.

One other caution to those of you who must have quiet. This is not for you. Students get excited, argue, ask questions, make some noise. But it is good noise, and learning is going on. That, to me, is the important thing.

*	1.	List the name, date, and editor of the papers. Be sure to use capital letters, punctuation, abbreviations, etc. correctly.
*	2.	What is one main headline of each paper?
*	3.	What was the temperature for the day of (date of newspaper) January 4 in Tarrytown? in Asheville? in Waynesville? Which place was colder? How much?
*	4.	Look in the want ad section of the Tarrytown paper. What is the highest salary listed for secretaries?
*	5.	Check the Spartanburg paper. What is the highest salary offered there?
* **	6.	How much more per month would a secretary make (according to these ads) if she chose to work in New York?
** ***	7.	Look on page 13, section 2, of the Asheville January 4 issue. Read the cartoon. What is the meaning of this one?
** ***	8.	Look on page 7 of the Tarrytown January 6 paper. Read this cartoon. What is the meaning here?
***	9.	Which cartoon is more sophisticated? (Let them struggle with this for awhile. It is a learning situation. You may have to help if they've never done this kind of activity before.)
* **	10.	Look on the Sports pages of the *Asheville Citizen*. Who was Al Smith? Why was Al Smith barred from participating in the Tryon Open Golf Tourney?
* **	11.	Tarrytown had a town election on December 1. What office was vacant and who won the job?
All	12.	Dear Abby has an advice column for teen-agers in each copy of these papers. What main idea is she stressing the January 4, Tarrytown column? the January 5, Asheville Citizen?
** ***	13.	Do you think Ichabod Crane would have agreed with the advice she gave as answer to the questions posed? Why or why not?
Boys:	14.	Sears Roebuck is having sales in both Asheville and Tarrytown papers. You will see that boys' suits are on sale. If you bought your suit

in Tarrytown rather than in Asheville, how much money would you save? Now check the Waynesville paper where no sale is advertised. What interesting fact did you discover?

Girls: 15. Both the Big M stores and the A & P stores have sheets of advertisements in the *Greenville News*. Here is your grocery list for this week. At which store would you buy today to save you some money? How much money would you save? (Make out a grocery list from the papers you use.)

All   16. Choose one news story in either one of the papers and answer these questions about it. (Teacher may have to explain this one a bit—that every good news story uses a format which answers most of these.)
Who?   Where?   When?   What happened?   Why? (if given)

All   17. Find the editorial page. Read one editorial from it. Is the material presented in your editorial fact or opinion? Upon what do you base your answer?

All   18. Write a news story for your own local school paper.

***   19. Make up and show how to solve three problems dealing with purchases you could make using the advertisements listed in any of these papers.

These are samples of activities you could make up using any set of newspapers. Why bother to go to all the trouble and time it will take you to get set up for this kind of activity when you have many books and commercial kits, programmed workbooks, etc.? Because of the built-in motivation. It is practical. Some of your students will leave school before they should and they need to know how to use a paper. You're teaching reading, English, math, spelling, citizenship by practice, and creating an interest (we hope) in the newspaper. Group and team work, so badly needed in our world today, is practiced. They can succeed, something they haven't done in other materials, perhaps. It also makes Tarrytown, or whatever setting you're dealing with, come alive. It's a real place. They might go there someday.

Working with the Newspaper

1. What number should one call to get reservations at Cabana Terrace for a vacation?
2. What college student has enough integrity to give up a beauty title to someone else because she can't go along with some of the things they require of her?
3. What do you think the cartoonist means by the picture on page 12, upper left?
4. Two friends were discussing what they did last night.
   Friend A. "Last night I saw the 9:00 movie "Wild Weekend" on Channel 3."
   Friend B. "You did not. There was a ballgame on Channel 3 at that time."
   Which boy, according to the program listings in the paper, was right?

5. Is Neil Armstrong interested in another trip to the moon? Why or why not?

6. Centerville High School has a science program going strong this summer. What will the students be studying?

7. Find the July 17 comic section. What bad news did Peanuts have for Snoopy?

8. On the front page of Monday's (your date) paper, what country is causing the United States a deep concern at this time and why?

9. What group of people in (your town) are trying to give help to drug addicts?

10. Five girls called aquanauts have just spent two weeks under the sea. They came up Monday. Find the story and the reason the authors give for the importance of slow decompression of their bodies. What would happen if this process of returning to sea-level pressure were speeded?

11. Airman First Class John Doe of Centerville has been serving in the U.S. Armed forces in many places of the world. What is his opinion of the actions of many citizens who refuse to stand up for their country? What does he say these dissatisfied loafers need to do? Do you agree with him? Why or why not?

12. The Dodgers are very happy about something which happened in the game with Philadelphia? What reason does the headline give?

13. Dr. Crane is a psychologist who writes a daily column for our paper. What advice does he give to those of us who would like to be good at public speaking?

14. _____ is advertising a sale on household appliances this week. Go to our files, find the paper for one month ago and check these items for price. What did you find? What does this say to young people about learning to read papers critically?

Numbers in Newspaperville

Vocabulary we will learn during this newspaper experience.

marked down	clearance sale	deposit
third off	dollar down	50% off
½ price	anniversary sale	advertisements
specials	estimating	temperature
grocery specials	going out of business sale	schedules
computation	circulars	ads
down payment	accidents	graph

ACTIVITIES which you are to do in connection with our unit on these newspapers.

1. Each boy and girl is to make up ten problems from the newspapers. Use the samples we make up in class. You may use the newspapers on the walls or use your own personal more recent copy.

2. Make a list of groceries your mother might need when she goes to the store on this week end. Total the cost from the figures given in the town paper.

3. Imagine you are buying a new home. You want new furniture for it. Choose which room in your house you want to furnish first. List the furniture, its cost, and the total money needed to finish your project.

4. Using one of the television listings of programs, write down in a column the times given for all the news broadcasts on one station. Name that station.

5. Figure out how many people had accidents as reported in the papers on the boards and walls. Also, list the types of accidents they were.

6. Count the deaths listed in Newspaperville.

7. List the names and editors of the different papers displayed.

8. Pretend that you are buying your winter clothes for school. Make a list of the items, what they cost, and figure how much money you will need.

9. Make a sign that might be displayed in a window where some kind of sale is coming.

10. Do you like this type of assignment? Why or why not?

A Study Guide for Making Reading Relevant to Students' Lives: Television

Many students spend more time during a week watching television than they spend in the classroom. Use this medium as an incentive toward practicing reading skills. Make a study sheet similar to the one given below and watch them become involved in reading for enjoyment. After they have fun with the one you've made, make an assignment for them to listen to one hour's television and copy down every advertising slogan they hear. Bring it to class and see if they can stump the class.

Purpose: Practice in listening, reading, concentration, writing, and spelling. To give an assignment relevant to students' lives. Motivation for reading.

Directions: The news media control your lives, your speech, your dress, and your entertainment. You question the validity of that statement? Consider the propaganda of the following slogans. You know them. Read each slogan and identify what product is being sold.

1. Kills germs by the millions on contact.   Listerine
2. Call and share a smile today.   telephone
3. The big fresh flavor.   spearmint
4. Building a better way to see the U.S.A.   Chevrolet
5. It's the _____ generation.   Pepsi
6. The man handlers.   Campbell's
7. Toughest four-letter word on wheels.   Jeep
8. It doesn't write words, but feelings.   flair
9. To get a good job, get a good _____.   education
10. Today's _____ wants to join you.   Army

DIRECTIONS: Look at these song titles. Pretend you're a high school English teacher or a college professor. Change these catchy titles into formal grammar as the teacher would use it. What does it do to the song title?

1. Me and You and My Dog Boo
2. The Times They are A'Changing
3. It's Whatcha Do With Whatcha Got
4. Gotta Have Tenderness
5. Ain't No Way
6. Ain't That a Lotta Love?
7. A Change is Gonna Come
8. Joshua Fit the Battle of Jericho

Activities for the Teacher

1. Take your students on a trip to the nearest newspaper printing office.
2. Do a unit on the newspaper and let your students make their own.
3. Using current copies of newspapers, make a study guide for your students and watch their reactions. Do they know how to use a newspaper?
4. Let students choose a story, write a script, and make their own film. (Of course much preplanning and reading for information must be carried out before the actual activities. This is the reason for this activity.)
5. Let students plan a TV watch party and discuss the program in class the next day. What were the propaganda techniques used, dialogue patterns, use of action to get interest or carry the story along, transpositions, quick-sell devices? If they watched a movie, how different was it from the book?
6. Using the vocabulary or facts from the materials you are working with, make up a game similar to the ones students watch regularly on television. Play the game with them. As a follow up ask students to adapt their favorite game show into an educational activity which they could play in class. Here is one example as used by Dr. George Maginnis, a Western Carolina University Reading Professor.

BEAT-THE-CLOCK VOCABULARY
A member from each team is called upon to perform some crazy timed task in competition with a member from each other team. The tasks involve a vocabulary word taken from an assignment or vocabulary list. Examples of activities might be:
a. Write on the chalkboard as many complete sentences as you can in one minute. Each sentence must contain the word. Most sentences win.
b. Arrange these letters to make a word found in the assignment. First one to finish a correct writing of a word wins.
c. List as many nouns as you can think of that were in the assignment. You have one minute. Most nouns win.
d. Here are five words from our assignment. The first one to write them backwards wins.
e. Write as many different forms of this word as you can. You have thirty seconds. Most forms win.

TWELVE

Reading Skills and the Thought Process

Apparently there is more known about the kinds of reading skills and the teaching of these skills than has been put into practice in the classroom. Or perhaps each of you expects someone else to have done the job. Or is it the curriculum planners who are at fault? In any case, more emphasis is being placed on study skills than formerly, and this is as it should be. The abilities of how to find information, how to evaluate it, and how to use it are more important than memorizing much of it, which may be obsolete by the time it is needed. The big questions are where, what, when, and how?

Different authorities place emphasis on different sequences and different lists. Some say these skills can be categorized according to content areas while others contend that there is overlapping. Nila B. Smith (125) lists the following as common study skills, and in this order because, she says, all others depend upon the first one.

1. Selecting and evaluating content, or recognizing what is important in reading.
2. Organization or putting ideas that belong together, together.
3. Recall.
4. Locating information in textbooks, reference books, and periodicals.
5. Following directions.

Ruth Strang (138) begins with vocabulary building, then goes to sentences and paragraphs, locating, SQ3R, interpretation and appreciation, critical reading, free reading, and communication skills.

Can specialized skills be categorized into separate areas for separate content materials and grade levels? Different writers make different claims and different lists. Research says there is positive low correlation between reading abilities in different areas. The same abilities are common to most reading situations. However, this is not clear, especially in the elementary school. G. L. Bond (20) found differences in reading abilities in areas of history, science, and social studies. One can understand literature without reading every word, but in math every word counts. However, problem solving ability in math showed little relation to comprehending at a particular rate, getting a central thought, or interpreting content. Yet some skills needed in math may be related to some subject areas but not to others.

There are those who argue that science can be taught by observation and experimentation, and reading is unimportant. Others argue that, while all kinds of reading may not be used in this area, it is important to be able to read science material to build up a background of information, to develop attitudes, and to prepare for experiments. In science, of course, one might read for different purposes from those in literature or social studies.

In answer to the question—Can skills be separate?—any study situation is a complex of related skills and abilities. Can there be a sharp delineation in grade or subject? My answer is *no*. Skills are an integral part of the entire learning process and should be taught where suited to a particular purpose, cause, or need. It should be obvious, however, to anyone in the teaching situation, that some skills must be mastered before others are attempted. Alan Robinson suggests that teaching skills in clusters worked for him. Basal textbooks sometimes follow sequences of skills. If you use basal texts and their suggestions, it will depend upon which one you use as to the skills you teach, and when.

Suggested Skills Which Develop
Reading with Understanding

Anyone who is satisfied with the practice of "Round Robin," the "Reading Round," or any other "Round" type of teaching reading should study this list. Is there any question why we have so much publicity about the poor reading abilities of school graduates?

The majority of these skills require cognitive thinking. Some writers may quibble about the particular terms used; for instance, study skills versus reading skills. Some would delineate. How can one function without the other? And how can a student perform these tasks without using the thinking processes?

This list is not exhaustive, but it covers a wide field.

I. Study Skills

    A. Locational skills
        1. Using the table of contents
        2. Using the index
        3. Using the glossary
        4. Using the dictionary
        5. Using cross references
        6. Using a telephone directory
        7. Using headings or other typographical aids
        8. Using encyclopedias

    9. Using the *Reader's Guide*
    10. Using the card catalogue
    11. Using a time table
    12. Using an atlas
    13. Using maps, graphs, charts, and pictures
    14. Using skimming
    15. Using tapes, films, magazines, and newspapers
B. Using information found in these references
    1. Following directions (organizational skills)
    2. Outlining (critical reading)
    3. Taking notes (organization)
    4. Classifying information (critical reading)
    5. Paraphrasing (critical reading)
C. Selection and evaluation of information
    1. Selecting suitable sources for information desired
    2. Using several sources to find information and solve problems
    3. Distinguishing between important and unimportant information
    4. Recognizing differences between fact and opinion
    5. Judging the adequacy of one's information
    6. Judging the validity of one's information
    7. Recognition of relationships of concepts
    8. Relating skills in one area of material to those in another area
D. Familiarity with at least one study method

SQ3R (Robinson)	PQRST (Spache)	SQRQCQ (Fay)	RSVP (Scott Foresman)
1. Survey	1. Preview	1. Survey	1. Review
2. Question	2. Question	2. Question	2. Study
3. Read	3. Read	3. Read	3. Verbalize
4. Recite	4. Summarize	4. Question	4. Preview
5. Review	5. Test	5. Compute	
		6. Question	

OARWET (Norman)	"One Step Ahead" (Winkler)
1. Overview	1. Survey—to get general idea of material
2. Ask	2. Outline—using titles and subtitles
3. Read	3. Add details—from further study to outline
4. Write	4. Blank space—leave blank space for further
5. Evaluate	notes from lecture
6. Test	

II.   Remembering What Is Read

A. Recognizing key words
B. Reading for main idea
C. Reading for minor ideas
D. Reading for details

E. Selecting details to remember
F. Immediate recall
G. Delayed recall
H. Discovering sequence of ideas
I. Discovering cause and effect patterns

III. Speed of Reading

A. Scanning
B. Skimming
C. Adjusting rate to content and purpose
D. Maintaining a high accuracy level

IV. Higher Reading Skills

A. Organizational Skills
  1. Reading to take notes
  2. Reading to outline
  3. Reading for main idea
  4. Reading to see relationship of details to main idea
  5. Reading to follow steps in directions
  6. Reading to follow a time sequence
  7. Reading to recognize different patterns of organization
  8. Reading to recall in same pattern used by author
  9. Recognizing inductive and deductive patterns of organization
B. Critical Reading Skills
  1. Recognizing author's purpose
  2. Detecting bias and prejudice of author
  3. Detecting propaganda devices
  4. Interpreting
  5. Recognizing assumptions
  6. Reading to examine basic assumptions
  7. Reading to note inconsistencies
  8. Judging validity of information
  9. Judging adequacy of information
  10. Evaluating material according to criteria
  11. Classifying information into categories
  12. Distinguishing between fact and opinion
  13. Distinguishing between relevant and irrelevant information
  14. Distinguishing between important and unimportant information
  15. Summarizing
  16. Understanding implied meanings
      a. Connotations of words
      b. Figures of speech
  17. Drawing inferences; recognizing implications
  18. Making deductions, or drawing conclusions
  19. Comparing or contrasting

20. Determining cause and effect
21. Predicting results
22. Reading to discover illustrations of an idea
23. Reading to compare with known information (elaborative reading)
24. Reading to verify conclusions
25. Reading to judge character

C. Elaborate Reading
   1. Reading to form sensory impressions
   2. Reading to visualize
   3. Relating new information to previous knowledge and experience
   4. Reading figurative language
   5. Reading to generalize
   6. Generalizing from content
   7. Identifying self with characters

V. Vocabulary

A. Word analysis to secure meanings
   1. This involves:
      a. Awareness of unknown words when seen
      b. Awareness of multiple meanings of words
   2. This involves facility in the uses of:
      a. Prefixes
      b. Suffixes
      c. Root words
      d. Syllabication
      e. The Dictionary
      f. Context

B. Development of word meaning
   1. Formal word study
      a. Connotations
      b. Denotations
      c. Etymologies
      d. Synonyms
      e. Antonyms
      f. Homonyms
      g. Associations
   2. Informal Word study
      a. Puzzles and games for reinforcement of B-1 above
      b. Trace classical or legendary words
      c. Avoid overuse of *cool, said,* and so on
      d. Collect meanings for words with multiple meanings
      e. Find words from other languages
      f. List words which suggest sounds
      g. Construct new word combinations or compounds
      i. Substitute for monotonous words

         j. Trace idioms
         k. Study personal names and their meanings
   C. Vocabulary development through the higher mental processes
      1. Figures of speech
      2. Associative thinking
      3. Critical thinking
      4. Organized thinking

    Books have been and could be written on each skill. The purpose here is to emphasize that if you want efficient reading and study, Grades 4–9 is an ideal place and time to teach and use many of them. It can be done in an interesting practical manner which reinforces the skill and works as an avenue for building the students' vocabularies, which after all is the basis for more sophisticated reading.

Lesson: Using the Dictionary

Objectives: 1. Review: about five minutes on syllabication
           2. To introduce to the students all the varied forms of information
           3. To understand and practice using guide words for quick reference
           4. To make the dictionary skill a functional and efficient one
           5. To get across the idea of a meaning rather than the meaning of words

Materials: Overhead projector, study sheets, transparency, filmstrip and film-strip projector, lists of words

Procedure: 1. Review syllabication. You might use words such as these to see how well the students can divide them for pronouncing (Words selected will depend upon students. These are for older ones.):

           stenophagous   collumvium   revivification
           mutability   arboriculture   draconic

           2. Give practice. See how fast they can find these words in their dictionaries. Then they check their divisions.
           3. Discuss guide words. Check for student use of them. If they need help, give it. If not, go on.
           3. Take a general survey of the dictionary. Ask if they know why Webster made the first one. If not, find out.
           5. Show filmstrip on using the dictionary. Discuss, check to find ideas mentioned in the film. Are they present in your copies?
           6. Give students a worksheet with the different kinds of information listed and let them find and use the sections in dictionary as you talk about them.
           7. Summary of the lesson can be made using the guide sheet.

Caution: Any lesson working with reference books and/or skills should be short, quick, and have at least one question or area to create interest, humor, or even disbelief. Frequent, short drills are much more challenging and rewarding than long sessions which bog down and become boring.

TEXT: *Webster's Seventh New Collegiate Dictionary* (Springfield, Mass.: G. & C. Merriam Company, 1966)

INTRODUCTION: Most people do not realize the vast store of knowledge given in the dictionary. Different dictionaries treat knowledge in different ways. Some are more complete than others; some use different keys and symbols; others have different diacritical markings. Let's take a look at this particular dictionary. It has at least twenty kinds of information.

1. Why do we use a dictionary?
2. How do we locate words quickly?
3. Principle and secondary definitions
4. Preferred spelling
5. Pronunciation keys
6. Root words, plus variations
7. Symbols and their meanings
8. Abbreviations
9. Proofreader's marks
10. Biographical names
11. Pronouncing gazeteer
12. Rhymes
13. Pronouncing vocabulary of common English names
14. Colleges and Universities in the U.S.
15. Colleges and Universities in Canada
16. Pictures
17. Vocabulary of abbreviations
18. Forms of address
19. Punctuation and capitalization
20. Italicization

Lesson: What's in the Dictionary?

1. Find the meanings of the following words: *limpid, Romany, gambit, neaptide* (any interesting words you want to use) *denim, horse, hornbeam.*
2. What does your dictionary tell you above the origin or derivation of the following words: *tapioca, pajama, beverage, trampoline, pedigree, mammoth, kibitzer, home, croquet, moccasin, algebra, vulcanize,* and *knapsack?*
3. Look up these words in your dictionary and classify each one according to the part of speech: knot, regular, row, down, shell, low, run, forward. (If the word may be used as three or four parts of speech, say so on your paper.)

4. Write the plurals of these interesting words: *bus, d, mongoose, motto, Iroquois, bais, alloy, tuna, fungus, also, crisis, 9,* and *dictionary.*

5. a. Where would you find a pagoda?
   b. How many strings does a mandolin have?
   c. What did the Stoics teach?
   d. What is unusual about a Manx cat?
   e. What is the outstanding characteristic of Gothic architecture?

6. Use the section at the back of your dictionary to learn.
   a. How long is the Welland Ship Canal?
   b. Who was Hannibal, and when did he live?
   c. Locate Mount Washington and tell how high it is?
   d. What is the population of Charlotte, N.C.
   e. Write what you can find about James Polk, Dylan Thomas and Aaron Copeland.

7. Miscellaneous questions from the dictionary in general:
   a. What is the difference between a dauphin and a dolphin?
   b. In the Roman calendar, what was October?
   c. What is meant by *dramatis personae?* by cat's cradle?
   d. What can you find about a lotus and any legend connected with it?
   e. When it is 12 noon in New York City, what time is it in (1) Perth, Australia, (2) Denver, (3) Halifax, (4) Paris, and (5) Jackson County, North Carolina.

8. What is meant by   a. Davy Jones?   b. Oceanus?   c. dewpoint?
   d. How many meanings does "derby" have?
   e. What are two of them?

9. In what city is the temple Imoversout located?

10. Huron College, Ontario, Canada is a school for boys, or girls or both?

11. Do you think this exercise helped you to learn anything about what is located in or what information can be found in a dictionary? What?

Lesson: Use of Dictionary for Concept and Vocabulary Practice

Purpose: To sharpen your word knowledge and use of words

Directions: This exercise consists of five parts, all of which have to do with words and their uses. Don't hurry; select your words carefully; use your word power to build word-power. If you're not sure of a word, experiment with a number of possibilities and choose the one you think is best.

Part I.   Without using a dictionary or thesaurus, which word in each group below most nearly defines the underlined word?

1. freeze	to dissect	to dry	to congeal	to remove
2. develop	unfold	to revel	admit	mix
3. firmness	ghastly	memory	solidness	horrible
4. malevolent	beaten	bad	noisy	stuffy
5. bizarre	fanciful	ornamental	odd	whimsical
6. tranquil	calm	kindness	mark	grotesque

Part II.   Without using a dictionary or thesaurus, list three other verbs similar in meaning to the following. For example: to obliterate—to erase, to cancel, to destroy.

1. to feel	5. to refuse	9. to speculate
2. to hit	6. to command	10. to try
3. to liberate	7. to hope	11. to jeopardize
4. to yell	8. to rebel	12. to manipulate

Part III.   Now that you have checked the words *without* the use of a reference book, go to your dictionary or thesaurus and select two more *synonyms* for each of the words. This is helpful practice in extending your vocabulary.

Part IV.   You've checked the list and you've looked up synonyms. Now, to show you how to put these words to practical use, write a sentence, a riddle, a funny saying or a poem using each word or its synonym. The best way to enlarge your vocabulary is not to memorize words but to use them in actual writing and speaking.

Part V.   For fun and reinforcement, make a puzzle, a riddle, a reading skill game or some other kind of activity which we could use in the reading center for other students to enjoy working with.

Skimming—What and How?

What is skimming? Skimming is a rapid and versatile form of locating information. It is not a substitute for reading and it is not a superficial task. Skimming enables a skillful user to:

    a. locate specific information quickly
    b. read part he's interested in when no time to read entire book
    c. locate dates, answers to specific questions fast
    d. bypass information he already knows, thereby making more efficient use of time
    e. get a quick overview of article, chapter, or book, a prelude to reading
    f. learn to concentrate because student must focus attention
    g. understand that every word is not sacred and should not be thought so

Skimming varies according to the purpose for which it is done. Some sample purposes which you can practice with students to show that difference are:

    a. to find a telephone number, fast
    b. to find information in an index, a little slower
    c. to skim references for particular subjects of interest, fast to slow
    d. skim contents of similar books to find additional information, contrast or substantiate statements, fast to slow
    e. skim portion of content swiftly until particular sentence, paragraph or section catches attention, then read
    f. skim newspaper for controversies of the day, fast

The middle grades is an ideal time to practice this skill. By senior high, students should be proficient.

How do you teach skimming? There are different techniques of teaching the skill of skimming. You must explain that there are different eye movements, that they should not read every word and that they use all of the previous skills they have learned.

1. Demonstrate with a newspaper. See the lesson in this chapter. During the bicentennial year, most newspapers put out a special issue with front pages of some of the dramatics of past years. I used issues of the *Asheville Citizen* for a fun reading lesson in my college freshmen reading class. I made up some questions on the material, then had students to study one front page at a time for three to five minutes, lay it down and see how many of my ten questions they could answer. It took only about four tries for them to move from three correct answers to seven or eight, and they enjoyed the activity.

2. Make lists of specific questions on classroom materials. They should be simple at first. Something like the index of a textbook is ideal.

   Examples: A. Science—How fast do jets travel?
   What is a vegeburger?
   What is the speed of sound?
   B. Newspaper—What was the high temperature yesterday?
   How much rain did we get in June?
   What film is playing at "City Theater?"
   C. Dictionary—Would you use a lampoor in fishing?
   A grouse is a member of the bird, rock or human family?

3. After learning to quickly locate specific bits of information, give practice in several books to locate information where different speeds are used.

   Why do clouds produce rain? (rapid)
   How is pollution scattered? (rapid to intent)
   Name some animals that are nocturnal. (rapid)
   Describe what happens to a brain that is deprived of air. (rapid to find information, then intensive study type reading)

4. Another technique is to use the timed exercise. Give students two minutes to skim a chapter or book to get author's main points and to find his general conclusion. Students love to try this on light fiction then compare their summary with the critics, the Library Journals or the jacket blurbs.

5. Some follow-up practice, assuming you've taught the skill.

   a. Find a word in the dictionary, fast.
   b. Look for one specific statistic on a table of facts.
   c. Skim table of contents. What page number begins Chapter 10?
   d. Find the sentence that proves a point.
   f. Find sentence that portrays character of person.
   g. Find answer to question given by teacher when page number is given.
   h. Skim to find key words.
   i. Review for a test.
   j. Skim to write a summary of chapter, article or selection.
   k. Skim to find time for TV programs, number of doctor's office in telephone directory, address of electrician, etc.
   l. Preview before any reading assignment.
   m. Skim to make an outline.

Lesson: Skimming and the Dictionary

Purpose: To acquaint students with some encyclopedic aspects of the dictionary
          To practice the skill of quick skimming
          Involvement and fun

Directions: Unabridged dictionaries, duplicated question sheets or leader may read the questions orally

Players: Teams of players or competing pairs

Materials: Divide into teams. Each player compete with a member of another team. Each player is given a question sheet. The player who first finds the answer to the question assigned to him announces it and wins a point for his team. All players write answers on their papers. Team with the most points win.
          Here are some examples of questions and their answers which might be used. When you first introduce the game, underline the key words. After students become proficient, do not underline.

1. What is an <u>okapi</u>?	African animal
2. What is the symbol for the element <u>Krypton</u>?	Kr
3. Who wrote the <u>Star Spangled Banner?</u>	Francis S. Key
4. What does the acronym AWOL mean?	absent without leave
5. In what category is the term *avoir du pos* used?	U.S. & British weights
6. What kind of animal is a ferret?	weasel
7. From what language do we get the word coquette?	French
8. What was wampum?	beads used as money by Indians
9. Who is buried in the Taj Mahal?	Emporer Shah Jehan & wives, Country of India
10. Some religious sects practice excision. What is a synonym for this word?	excommunication
11. What are the dates for World War II?	1939–43
12. Other than its obvious meaning, what is a cat's-paw?	light breeze, or a used person
13. Is there any such thing as a moho? If so, what is it?	yes, a honey-eating bird
14. Why is one line of black storks called the episcopal?	its dress
15. Their students fail to do their best work because of their desultory habits. What kind of habits are these?	sloppy, disorganized

Recall: A Part of Comprehension

Many times a student will say to you, "I read that lesson, but I just can't remember what I read." He or she has a problem. However, it is one that you can help to overcome.

Recall is mostly *literal comprehension*. Children and older students should practice remembering. One way is to memorize—that is if you let them memorize something which they want to know. Some authorities question the value of this—it's an isolated method. Perception of the reading process, knowing why he is reading, his motivation, whether the material is familiar, how he organizes his thoughts and his concentration while reading—all are aids to remembering. Of course, this assumes that he/she can understand the material. A student can't remember if it is too difficult for his thinking power.

Other methods to aid remembering may be psychological. (1) *Association.* Associate what you are reading with what is already known; (2) *Delayed recall.* Practice what you learn. The teacher can ask for or review materials a week or a month later; (3) *Whole versus parts.* Pupils should practice or experiment with this one. Can he learn better by studying section by section, by reading the whole chapter at a time, taking notes, making lists, outlining, or putting things in sequential order.

The teacher can:
1. Alert students beforehand on what to listen or to read for.
2. Give materials on the maturity level of the students.
3. Encourage students, especially younger ones, to make posters.
4. Let students talk and think about what they hear or read. Let them agree or disagree with what they take in.
5. Let each student know that you as a teacher and a person think what he has to say is important.
6. Practice good listening habits.
7. Remember about attention spans, long drawn-out lectures, discussions, and so on.
8. Encourage students to argue with the author of the material they read.
9. Remember that what works for one student may not work for another.

Some Practical Ideas or Suggestions for the Practice of Recall

A. In math: short, frequent practice drills in listening. No pencils:
   9 plus 3 minus 6 divided by 3 times 5 plus 2 times 10 equals _____
   100 divided by 4 times 8 plus 35 divided by 5 minus 2 equals _____
   Split dates: Expose a number like this one for a few seconds: 19177688
       Or use a multiplication pattern: 61218243645
B. In art: show pictures or symbols all mixed up, then in order. Which is easier to remember? The same works in reading.
C. In science: Read and attempt to remember the steps in doing an experiment.
D. In spelling: use nonsense words, expose them shortly and have students write what they saw. They soon catch on to organization (syllables) as a great aid in remembering. Add a letter as you go: *il, hol, stok, tabuh, lokwa, dayhol, antpel, stolkaup, tapokwady*
E. In music: Play a series of notes, clap a rhythm, and let them imitate.
F. In writing: Authors give clues to help students understand, organize, and remember the information in their materials. If students can learn to recognize the pattern of organization of the material it will be

easier to understand and remember. Here are some comprehension skills which teachers and students must recognize and work on:

1. Does the author use questions and vocabulary aids at the beginning or the end or within the chapter?
2. Does he use key words in italics?
3. Where are the topic sentences in the paragraphs?
4. Does he use boldface subtopics?
5. What is the structure of the material? Look at the following list. Being able to recognize these patterns is not automatic. The teacher must help.
   a. numerical order
   b. sequence
   c. comparison and contrast
   d. description
   e. presenting principles with explanation
   f. presenting evidence followed by interpretation
   g. presenting a problem following by a solution
   h. illustrating a process
   i. giving directions
   j. begins with generalization and explains with details
   k. begins with details and leads up to climax

Remembering depends upon (1) the student's understanding of what is read; (2) having a purpose for reading the material, other than, "The teacher said so": (3) seeing the organization of ideas; and (4) the training of memory.

G. Practice remembering with fun activities:

1. Have three students stand in front of the room, then leave the room and exchange some articles of clothing, jewelry, etc. When they return, can the students who were left in the room tell what was changed?
2. Lay eight to ten articles in a row on a desk. Have students close eyes. Move one or more articles. Can they remember the order? What was moved to where?
3. Play a record of noises which you have taped. Can they recognize them?
4. Depending upon students you're working with, flash five to ten scenes on a screen. Can students remember the scenes and in the correct order?
5. Take a field trip and listen for sounds. How many can they remember when they get back to the classroom? Another time you may look and try to remember all the things you see, feel, or smell.
6. Listen to a taped speech. When it is over, see how many questions they can answer from the speech.

Practice Sheet: Learning to Use Reference Books

To the teacher: One of the tasks my students enjoy most is the one they do on how to teach the use of reference books. We have class in the children's library of our main library. I give them a study guide and a list of the main references similar to this one and say "Go to it." The follow-up assignment is that they make a guide similar to mine which they could later use in actual teaching. I've had many students say they learned things they didn't know by doing this assignment. It is called practicing the skills.

To the student:

Group yourselves into threes.

Here are some questions whose answers can be found in one of the reference books on your list. Study the question, as a group decide which book you think might answer it, then find out if you were correct by attempting to find the answer. If you fail to find it in the first reference you try, use another one.

If you have problems or questions, attempt to solve them in your group. If you can't, ask the teacher.

1. Who is the author of *How to Hide a Hippopotamus?*
2. Francis Bruns was a Negro leader in the 1800s. What was his occupation?
3. Flag Day is a custom celebrated in American cities on certain days. Use the reference *Childcraft* and list six days when we who are patriotic might fly a flag.
4. Who won the 1973 World Series?
5. What was the value of the pound in American dollars in the United Kingdom (Britain) in 1959? Does it give the value for 1976?
6. Check the magazine *Time* for the week of Oct. 21, 1976. What is the main idea of the editorial for that issue?
7. In what book would you find the origin of the word *school?* Does it mean the same today that it once meant? Explain your answer.
8. Use the *Atlas of the World*. Find the airline map of the United States. From the information shown on that map, answer this question: Could you fly direct "non-stop" from the Hendersonville-Asheville airport to Washington, D.C.?
9. Find three reference books which tell something about Australia. List one title and page number from each of the three sources.

For students who need more difficult questions as a challenge, give fewer clues, add more variety and make more problems. Some examples follow.

1. "When in doubt, tell the_____" Finish this quotation and tell who made it and in what selection.
2. What and where is the world's largest hotel?
3. Does the nickname "Churchill Hill Cats" refer to boys, girls or cats?
4. Who wrote the short story "Why the Milkman Shudders When He Perceives the Dawn?"
5. An 8th grade boy wants to be an architect. Someone told him to go to Stephens College in Missouri. Was that good advice?
6. According to Emily Post, when should a flag be hung upside down?
7. I want to make a wheelbarrow doghouse. Where can I find directions?
8. The first president to use a telephone for campaigning was _____. Where did you find this information?
9. Jason Hanley brags about having descended from a famous English professor who rated in *Who's Who* during the period from 1951–1960. Could he be telling the truth?

Practice Sheet: Whales—for Remedial Readers or MR's

To the Teacher: The object of any practice opportunity for students, especially those in trouble or those who can never do the cognitive things our good students can do, is to let them succeed with their assignments. If they are successful they are more willing to try the next tasks which might be a little more difficult. Nothing is more interesting, even to the weak students, than working with world reference books. From these activities, you may help them to develop other interests and motivation for reading.

Remember that at this level and with these students the questions must be the literal ones so that they can get them right from the material. They do not have to be able to read to succeed with a task similar to this one. Yet they are doing a form of reading and practicing the skill of skimming without knowing it.

Directions: Read each statement on your study sheet. Then use the *World Book Encyclopedia* to find the information to fill in the blank spaces. If you do not know all of the words, try to find the sentences in the book and see if you can figure out what goes in the spaces, anyway. The page and column numbers are given for you to work with.*

Page 8728-C.1
- a. The _____ is the largest animal that ever lived.
- b. Whales breathe through _____.

Page 8729-C.1
- a. A thick layer of fat called _____ keeps whales warm even in cold water.
- b. A whale has no sense of _____.

Page 9730-C.1
- a. Whales have two enemies: _____ and _____.

Page 9732-C.1
- a. Some things made from whales are _____, _____, _____ and _____.
- b. Whale catching is called _____.

C.2
- a. Whalers can tell the different species (kinds) of whales at a distance by their _____.

Activity: Practice with Skimming and Reference Books

Materials needed: List of questions, reference books, pencil and paper.

Directions: Read each question. Find the answer by skimming any set of reference books you have available. You may work with a partner if you like.

1. How many presidents have been elected on the first ballot?
2. Name the presidents who have died while serving in office.
3. Which presidents, if any, did not have a college education?
4. If one judged by the hair on a man's face, which presidents would be in style today?

* Source: The World Book Encyclopedia (Chicago: Field Enterprises, Inc., 1957) V. 18

5. Fifteen of the Presidents of the United States have come from two states. What are these two states?
6. List the names of men who have been in office when the United States has been involved in a war. And which war?
7. How many different religious faiths have been represented in the White House? Name them.
8. How many Vice Presidents have later become Presidents and name them?
9. How many presidents have left office before their time was up, other than by death, and for what reasons did they leave?
10. How many presidents have had some degree of scandel surrounding their names while they were in office?
11. Has any man ever been elected to the presidency who did not first serve in some other political office? If so, who?
12. Which president was the first to do each of the following things?

a. remain unmarried	f. use a telephone
b. ride in an airplane	g. have a son to become president
c. campaign on television	h. use electricity
d. talk on a telephone	i. travel all over the world
e. ride in a helicopter	j. tape his speeches

Reference Practice Sheet: Famous Quotations' Recognition

Purpose: To reinforce previously learned facts about history
Motivation for learning new facts
Fun and group involvement

Directions: Work in teams if you like, or work alone. Read each quotation and see if you can recall the world famous personality who made it. How many did you know? Use reference books to find those you didn't know.

1. We have met the enemy and they are ours.
2. Four score, seven years ago.
3. I hit the first home run in Yankee Stadium. God knows who'll hit the last.
4. You may fire when ready, Greeley.
5. Lafayette, we are here.
6. I regret that I have but one life to give for my country.
7. I propose to fight it out on this line, if it should take all summer.
8. Old soldiers never die, they just fade away.
9. With malice toward none; with charity for all.
10. After me the deluge.
11. We are standing like a stone wall.
12. Go West, young man, go West.
13. Mr. Watson, come here! I need you.
14. I never met a man I didn't like.
15. What God hath wrought.
16. Genius is one percent inspiration and 99 percent perspiration.
17. I have always been fond of the West African proverb: walk softly and carry a big stick.
18. Sleep is like a drug, too much of it will make you dopey.

Answers: Perry, Lincoln, Babe Ruth, Adm. Dewey, Stanton, Nathan Hale, U.S. Grant, MacArthur, Lincoln, King Louis XV, Stonewall Jackson, H. Greeley, Alexander G. Bell, Will Rogers, Samuel Morse, William Duncan Vandivar, Teddy Roosevelt, Edison.

Make Use of the Magazines in Your School Library

Your poorest reader will enjoy and perhaps be motivated to try to read magazines which most schools subscribe to if you will introduce him to the many interesting materials to be found in them. Puzzles, mysteries, riddles, hidden pictures, contests which they might enter entice students. Those who have failed in textbooks can be hooked with other materials if you care enough. Here are two examples of how magazines can get students doing cognitive activities.

Riddles. Almost every human being likes a riddle. He likes to think that he is smart enough to figure out anything another human has thought up.

What a pleasant way to practice reading, do creative thinking and use constructively that ten minutes before lunch or that afternoon bell! Many classrooms waste as much as 45 minutes daily waiting for things to happen. The GOOD teacher does not allow this waste of time, human intelligence and tax dollars.

Try these riddles yourself. Then try them on your students.
1. What is the hardest thing about learning to ride a bicycle?
2. How is a girl and a stamp just the opposite?
3. Who earns his living without ever doing a day's work?
4. When were there only three vowels in the alphabet?
5. What is a cat called that drinks lemonade?
6. What did the mother firefly ask the teacher?
7. Why were the Indians the first people in North America?
8. What did the bird say when the cage broke?
9. When does a teacher need dark glasses?
10. Why didn't the baseball player get to meet Cinderella?

Answers: Pavement; girl is a female, stamp is a mail fee; night watchman; before U and I were born; sour puss; will my child be bright?; they had reservations; cheep, cheep; when all her students are bright; he missed the ball.

In addition to figuring out other person's riddles, most students like to create their own. This can lead into a more complicated task—writing. Each student creates one and exchanges it with his neighbor who tries to figure out the answer. Following this you can discuss with them what good writing is, how authors use devices to catch the interest of readers, how they arouse emotions by words and pictures, the ways they use them in advertising propaganda techniques, etc., all examples of critical reading skills. (More on this in chapter 6.)

Current magazines, from *Highlights* to *Reading Teacher,* are invaluable sources for interesting ideas for teaching reading in any grade. How many school library shelves are littered with copies which have never been used? What a waste and what a sad commentary on professionalism!

No matter the grade level you teach, you will have problems. Other teachers have had the same problems, have successfully coped with them and written up their experiences for some magazine. Maybe they can help you and your students.

Back in 1969, *Wee Wisdom* carried an article by a classroom teacher who had used what she called "Write a Picture." I used this with some of the students I was working with. In one tutoring session with a fourteen-year-old fifth grader who was labeled a non-reader, I used this idea. He chose the category horses as his subject. We pulled books about horses and encyclopedias from the library shelves. He went to work. First he listed names of horses and things directly related to them. Of course I was right there giving him help with decoding. Then he lightly shaped a horse about as large as his 8x11 sheet of paper would allow and chose the words from his list to write in his picture. He, as well as his tutor, was proud of his accomplishment. When he returned to his regular classroom his teacher praised his work like this: "Well, I don't believe you did it." His face registered his defeat. How many times he had been treated like this! No wonder he was a non-reader.

Skills involved in an activity such as this: creativity, spelling, art, categorizing, measurement, interest and reading the encyclopedia for fun.

One of the legitimate criticisms of special reading classes is that there is no carry-over into the regular classroom. Why not? Because skills "do not automatically transfer from one subject area to another" (75, p. 18). The transfer is a matter of teaching.

If school administrators planned it so, all teachers in a school would know what every other teacher was doing, they would have planning time, the regular classroom teacher could inform the special reading teacher about needs and tasks of the students, then together they could work out supplementary reinforcement. Ideally, the special reading teacher could teach the skill needed or the technical vocabulary necessary for understanding the science assignment. Since he doesn't know what that assignment is, since the science teacher is often more interested in getting through a textbook or rid of a discipline problem and since there is no released time for team planning, the reading teacher merely does what he thinks may help the student.

Suppose the science teacher told the reading teacher that a group of students couldn't follow directions well enough to participate in experiments. They couldn't write up the experiments done by others and seldom even tried. Suppose he gave the textbook to the reading teacher and asked his help with these skills. What could be done?

Here is one way he might approach the tasks—tasks which students could succeed with because someone is there ready to help, if needed, and they're not overshadowed by the precocious ones. These students need to know that the teacher believes they can do things on their own. So many times they're the ones who sit on the back seats. An activity such as an experiment is functional. Because so many of the important reading skills are needed to understand it, the science content lends itself to the teaching and/or practice of them.

But, before you get into the science material, for motivation and success appeal, do easy fun tasks of following directions and lead progressively into harder, content-oriented materials.

The "trick" exercise listed in the following motivational exercises is one way to get started on the skill of following directions. It dramatizes the importance of reading carefully, yet they enjoy it. Some other activities for following directions are given here. My students have enjoyed all of these.

TASK I. READING TO TEST FOLLOWING DIRECTIONS

Directions to students: Read everything carefully before doing anything. Read as quickly as you can for you have only ten minutes in which to complete the exercise.

1. Take out a clean sheet of paper.
2. Put your name on this paper, right top corner, please.
3. On the top left corner of this paper, draw three circles.
4. Write a Number I and work this problem: $10.30 plus $3.99 plus $0.54.
5. On the back of this paper that you took out, multiply 8 by 92.
6. After you finish number 5, and if you think it is correct, say your name out loud.
7. Write your last name backward on the front of this paper.
8. Count by 5's to 50 out loud, please.
9. Get up out of your chair, walk to the door, and then sit again.
10. Now that you have followed directions and have read everything carefully, just complete numbers one and two.

TASK II. READING TO MAKE A SLIDE

Purpose: To learn how to make slides so you can use them in reporting, for pleasure, and to practice following directions.

Materials needed: colored pictures cut from magazines or other source
piece of clear contact paper, damp paper towel

Directions:
1. Choose a brilliantly colored picture to your liking.
2. Decide what part of your picture you want to preserve on the slide. Shape it.
3. Take backing off contact paper and lay it on the table, sticky side up.
4. Lay your picture facedown on the adhesive surface of contact.
5. With finger tips or other edge, gently press picture onto contact paper until you think it is stuck.
6. Use damp paper towel and gently wipe off paper. Color will remain on contact paper. (Some prefer soaking in warm soapy water.)

TASK III. ENLARGE A PICTURE (following directions)

1. Choose an interesting picture from a magazine, book or newspaper.
2. Use a ruler and divide the picture into equal squares, graph form.
3. Label horizontal and vertical sides with numbers or letters of the alphabet.

FIGURE 12.1

Enlarge a picture

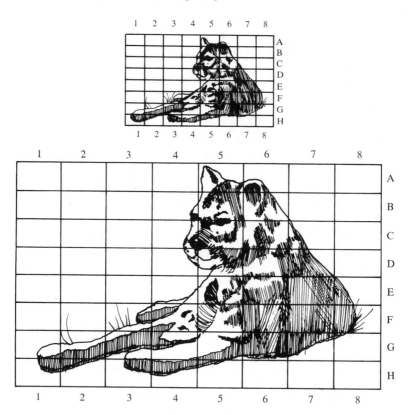

4. Decide on how much larger you want to produce your picture.
5. With ruler draw a larger grid with the same number of squares (the size you decided upon) as the small picture.
6. Copy the pattern, square for square, onto the larger paper.

TASK IV. EVERY LETTER COUNTS (following directions)

Directions: Let's follow these ten directions. Each time rewrite the word in the blank space using deletions, additions and changes called for. Use the new form of the word for the next step. See where the word *migration* takes you.

Our word is *migration.*
1. Write the word on the blank.   _____
2. Drop the first consonant of the blend.   _____
3. Drop the third vowel from the end and in its place add the vowel in the word *pup*.   _____
4. Change the position of the fourth letter so that it becomes the first letter.   _____
5. Drop the last letter and in its position add the letter which follows it by five in the alphabet.   _____

6. If the first two letters make a word, drop the second letter and change the position of two letters to make a two-letter word with the first vowel sound of the word *ulterior*.   _____

7. Reverse the fifth and sixth letter.   _____

8. Add the 12th letter of the alphabet.   _____

9. Change the seventh letter of the word to the first letter of the alphabet and add another one of the same following the eighth letter.   _____

10. Take the fourth letter and place it in a position to form an ending vowel digraph.   _____

     Wouldn't you enjoy such a migration?   _____

TASK V. A STRANGE TEA PARTY
(An exercise in following directions)*

This exercise is like Task IV, except more difficult. You will find out how well you can concentrate and follow directions. If you do so correctly, you will change the name of a skill we have practiced in language arts to the name of a state which held a strange tea party.

Write the word *alphabetizing.*
Double the letter *X* if it appears.
Whenever two or more consonants appear together, drop them all.
Double the middle consonant.
Replace the first and last consonants with a double *S*.
Switch the order of the first, third, and fifth vowels so that the first takes the place of the third, the third takes the place of the fifth, and the fifth takes the place of the first.
Move the last vowel in front of the last double consonant.
Drop both *I*'s
Put an *M* in the middle of the second double consonant and at the beginning of all the letters.
Switch the order of the ninth and tenth letters and place them between the second vowel and the letter that follows it.
Drop the first *M* and put the second in its place.
Write the second syllable of the sound you make when you sneeze (practice the sound if you don't remember) between the second *A* and the third *S*.
Replace the double vowel with a *U*.
Do you know the name of the state where the strange tea party was held?

TASK VI. LESSON: FOLLOWING DIRECTIONS IN SCIENCE

Textbook: *The Physical World,* 2nd ed., Harcourt, Brace & World, 1963. Page 441

Objectives: 1. To stress the importance of reading correctly in following directions.

---

* Made by Katie Lalor, student at Western Carolina University.

2. To show that reading accurately entails understanding vocabulary.
3. To review word attack skills learned earlier.

Materials needed: Textbooks or study sheets with experiment typed on it, four dry cells, copper wire, carbon rods, water, copper chloride, two test tubes, rusty nail and beaker.

Procedure:

1. Set purpose for lesson.
   a. Show cells and ask students where they're used? (cars, radios, flash lights, etc.)
   b. Ask for the purpose of cells—boys will probably know
   c. The word *electric* will surely come up during the discussion. See how many words they know which have this as part of their make-up. (At least 60, some of which they use every day.)
   d. Add electrodes and electrolysis to their vocabulary by means of review of skill of analyzing new words, structure.
2. Look at and discuss the study sheet which contains other words they must know in order to know how to perform the experiment. Discuss the word *plate*. There are 24 meanings given in one dictionary. Which meaning is used in today's context?
3. Read words in context from sentences on sheet. Elicit meanings from context. If they can't do so, use dictionary.
4. Read directions for doing the experiment, silently.
5. Elicit from students step-by-step, in their words, directions and list them on chalkboard.
6. Perform experiment. Teacher or students.
7. Evaluate: (a) review steps on chalkboard, (b) ask about process just demonstrated, do they understand how it would be used in real life, (c) erase steps from board and let students write up their version in their own words, and (d) when they finish, rewrite steps on chalkboard and let them check their own accomplishment.

Assignment:

Twelve people divided into four groups of three each. Assign each group one of the 84 experiments in back of this text or whatever material you're using. They are to study their special assignment and as a group perform the experiment and give explanation to other class members or to the teacher. How you do this will determine upon your purposes and goals for your students.

Cautions:

1. If you work in a rural situation, you may have to collect the materials needed and bring to the reading room because students ride buses and many do not get there in time. It would be ideal if you could take your reading groups to the science lab, but it usually isn't free when you need it.
2. Be sure the students are aware that they are using reading skills which they

Evaluative Reading

will need for the rest of their life, whether it be baking a cake or repairing a TV set.

One of the skills which too many teachers overlook and which leads toward lifetime habits of reading is the skill of critical or evaluative reading. This is about as far away from literal recall as we can get, but one which students (who can do it) thoroughly enjoy. Now, let me digress for a moment to make a statement which many of you will disagree with. Almost any human being, regardless of comprehension level, can do some evaluative reading. Even the MR student knows whether or not he or she likes a story. Some stories will be requested again and again, while students won't sit still to listen to other stories.

In going toward more individualized instruction and attempting to meet the needs of students, evaluative tasks are ideal ways to check comprehension and creativity and to let students produce because of an inherent interest. Look at these tasks which can be used to enhance your reading assignments.

1. Helen Keller judged the character of a person by his handclasp *(Helen Keller Story)*. What rationalization did she give for this practice? Do you agree with her? Why or why not?

2. Read all that you can find on the life and times of Abraham Lincoln and Richard Nixon. Make a chart and show issues involved, public responses, news media coverage, bias and prejudice, likenesses and differences, and any other topics of interest to you.

3. Can you make any prediction of how history will record the Nixon era?

4. Become an expert on the character of one of your favorite political, sports, entertainment, or other famous personalities, past or present, and write a play about his/her life. Develop the staging, background music, costumes, and action for your play. If you can get personnel to help you, produce it.

5. Compare and contrast life as depicted in Frank Bonham's *Durango Street* with that of Daniel Defoe's *Robinson Crusoe*. If you had a chance to take a two-week vacation, which setting would you choose and why?

6. In *The Witch of Blackbird Pond*, by Elizabeth Speare, Kit Tyler was a colorful vivacious girl in a stern Puritan background. Her outgoing spirit and willingness to help others got her labeled as a witch. After you read her story, discuss whether or not you think this could happen to anyone today.

7. What are some similar characteristics of these horse stories: *Smoky, The Black Stallion, King of the Wind,* and *Black Beauty?*

8. Compare the characters of Amos in *Amos Fortune, Free Man,* by Elizabeth Yates and Martin Luther King.

9. Have a modern day Women's Libber write a letter to Madame Curie and have Madame Curie respond.

10. Discuss points of likenesses between:
    (a) A lonely crippled boy in Harlem and his music in *The Jazz Man.*

(b) A lonely Indian girl and her dog in *Island of the Blue Dolphins.*
(c) A lonely boy and his fawn in *The Yearling.*

These ten activities are samples of the kinds of tasks you can create to get students to think about, to evaluate, to compare, and to question what they read. Your job in grades 4–9 is to challenge students to become knowledgeable in the techniques which authors, news media, or any of the forms of communication use to get an audience. Just as there is no one method of doing anything, there is no one person who has all the answers on a problem, nor all the bias. Students need to be able to analyze, to question and to come to some value judgment on what they see, hear, or read. Only by practice with this skill will they get it.

SUMMARY

Reading and/or study skills do not develop nor transfer from content to content automatically. It is the job of a teacher to show students how to use the skills they need to make their acquisition and organization of learning more efficient. However, too many times teachers drill and drill on skills while students learn to hate the reading process.

Spending too much time on the mechanics (how to), instead of reading, accounts for students' lack of forming the lifetime habit of reading for enjoyment. You must remember that skills, or a sequence of skills, are not divinely inspired nor ordered, and attempting to make them so takes the fun out of learning to read.

Activities for the Teacher

1. Make a set of questions for skimming and the dictionary. Be sure your questions fit the maturity and proficiency levels of your students or of the students you hope to work with.
2. Select one skill given in the list in this chapter and, using all subjects you teach, make up a set of materials which will practice this skill.
3. Create five questions for evaluative reading on some subject your class is dealing with. Let the students work through them. What is their reaction?
4. Find an article in one professional magazine and critique it for your peers.
5. Make an original game for teaching a skill with which most of your students need help. Try it out with your peers. Does it work? Does it need revising?

THIRTEEN

A Jackpot of Ideas

Many years ago, before we had our fancy bulletin boards, our pigeon-holed woodcraft or embossed memo pads, we made much use of the versatile wall calendar. It was a shopping list, a reminder that Preacher Jones was coming to dinner, the chickens were due to hatch Monday next, the sauerkraut needs pressing three days hence, and so on.

Birthdays, deaths, weddings: if an argument occurred, just check the old calendar on the wall. Across the top, too, you would usually see a vivid picture accompanied by an ancient, or not so ancient, proverb.

> Idle hands are the devil's workshop.
> A stitch in time saves dimes.
> Out of an empty head cometh empty words.

A teacher's job is similar to that abundantly loaded calendar. You cannot effectively do your tasks unless you are fully loaded with reminders, plans, ideas, methods, materials, and the ingenuity to use them. You must be able to take all of these, sift, adapt, and supplement into practical, workable ideas for all kinds of students learning at different rates and in different ways, and you must do so with inexpensive materials in everyday situations as they arise.

This is no easy task. It calls for constant assessment of student achievement and needs, for creativity in the use of throw-away merchandise and for constant alertness to what is going on around the students in their work-a-day world.

You've heard of the teacher who put on her old boots, drove her husband's old pickup truck to the community dump, and there enlisted three young fellows to help her load it with materials. When they asked what she wanted with this old junk, she responded, "Oh, this bathtub will make a lovely reading center. This oil drum will be an ancient tunnel to a hidden city, the orange crates a universe, and these curtain rods—antennas for our space center."

"You have a space center at your school?" the boys asked.

"No. But we will have if you fellows will help me find a crate which refrigerators are packed in," she answered as she tripped off in search of one.

"Batty as a bed bug," one young fellow said as he shook his head.

"Just like most school teachers," his companions agreed.

They didn't know they were watching an exceptional teacher and human being at work—a teacher who spiced her classroom routine so that even the most reluctant student didn't want to leave when 3 o'clock came.

This chapter takes a look at some ways and means of answering the following four questions.

1. What are ideas to use to break the monotony of everyday routine?
2. How can a teacher use that extra ten minutes when students have finished a chore, that in-between time which often incubates discipline problems?
3. What are some creative tasks which, though fun, create or reinforce learning situations?
4. What are some inexpensive everyday materials which are easily adapted to the needs of a classroom and which add variety to any age or level of maturity?

Choral Reading

How many of you, during junior high years, had to memorize the Preamble to the Constitution? Other than a chore to be done because the teacher required it, what did it mean to you? Yet, at the time this was good history pedagogy, or so your teacher thought. You were learning about democracy, our American heritage! Perhaps some of our history teaching practices contributed to the current lack of respect for the ideals which have made the American Dream. There are other ways.

Choral reading is one good device to use with poetry but should not be limited to it. Some of the more famous literature, documents, or inspirational readings which you want to give students, but also want them to appreciate and enjoy, can be done as choral readings. At the same time you're teaching oral reading, concepts, enjoyment of expression, and are including all students. How many times poor readers complain that they never get to do anything because they can't read well. Choral speech is one avenue where even the poor reader can shine. He or she can learn to read a solo line, and these studnts need this chance.

Vocabulary and concepts can be taught and/or reinforced through the medium of choral reading. Look at the one which follows, adapted by a group of teachers in an in-service class and used by a sixth grade as the basis for a patriotic assembly program.

However, the prelude to beautiful reading in any oral form is that students *understand* what they're saying. Only in this way can they communicate meaning to someone else. They need prestudy, vocabulary practice, and oral reading for a purpose—both academic and pleasurable. For more interest in the following selection, use different tones of voices—high, low, medium. Assign parts, tone sections, and have students study. Any words they need help with, you are there. Always give students a chance to study silently before performing orally.

THE PREAMBLE TO THE CONSTITUTION
Choral Reading

Solo:	The Constitution of the United States of America is our plan of Government. The men who wrote it prepared an introduction which they called the Preamble.
Solo:	Listen to the meaningful words.
Choir:	"We, the people of the United States,"
Voice 1	"In order to form a more perfect union,
Voice 2	"Establish justice,
Voice 3	"Insure domestic tranquillity,
Voice 4	"Provide for the common defense,
Voice 5	"Promote the general welfare,
Voice 6	"And secure the blessings of liberty to ourselves and our posterity,
Choir:	"Do ordain and establish this Constitution for the United States of America."
Choir:	"We, the people of the United States,"
Solo:	"We," That was a big word. No king on a throne three thousand miles away, but "We, the people," were going to make the laws from that time on.
Boys:	For the first time in history, all of the people in a nation had a part in making laws for themselves.
Solo:	The writers of the Constitution thought it especially important to explain at the very beginning that this constitution was an expression of the will of the people.
Solo:	We're told the original document was written by hand. The penman wrote those first words, "We, the people," in large letters.
Choir:	"In order to form a more perfect union."
Solo:	Anytime a new nation emerges and begins to control itself, there are problems. And those early days were troublesome times. The states had been quarreling among themselves, and there were no courts with authority to settle their differences. The Constitution joined them into "A more perfect union."
Choir:	"Establish justice."
Solo:	Before that time, the colonists had little chance for justice in the English courts, so these patriotic men attempted to plan a government which would insure just and fair treatment for every citizen in the new nation.
Girls:	For the first time everyone was granted the right of trial by jury.
Choir:	"Insure domestic tranquillity."
Solo:	Laws were written into the Constitution which would give all the states equal rank. It was hoped that this would promote peace and harmony.
Boys:	The people wanted to be sure of peace at home or "Domestic tranquillity."
Choir:	"Provide for the common defense."
Solo:	Those men of Revolutionary War times knew that they would have to plan for a strong army and navy to protect this new country from attacks by foreign countries.

Solo:	So, when they wrote the Constitution, they gave Congress power to set up armed forces.
Choir:	"Promote the general welfare."
Solo:	This is another way of saying our government which is made up of us must do what needs to be done to make the United States the best place in the world to live for all of our citizens.
Boys:	we want all of our people
Girls:	to have a chance to be prosperous,
Boys:	healthy
Girls:	and happy.
Choir:	"And secure the blessings of liberty to ourselves and our posterity."
Solo:	The Constitution has made it possible for each of us to live our life in the way we choose.
Solo:	These patriotic, brilliant men who wrote the Constitution wanted to build in America a free country, not for themselves alone, but for posterity,
Girls:	which means for those people who come after us. Our children and grandchildren. The generations to come.
Choir:	"Do ordain and establish this Constitution for the United States of America."
Solo:	So that "We, the people," you and I, might enjoy justice,
Girls:	peace,
Boys:	and freedom,
Solo:	the wise men of early America set up a Constitution for the United States of America.

Junkpile Craft

1. Plastic Containers

The classic object made from empty containers of many descriptions is the train. Plastic containers make a lovely one. If you think this too elementary for your group, have them make a health train, a zoo train, a medical train, or a VIP train and donate it to the lower grades. Perhaps even let them teach a lesson to younger students where they use the train as a prop.

2. Old Bathtub

Clean up an old bathtub, paint it or decorate it according to children's taste. Use it as a basic piece of furniture in an interest center and change its function according to needs.

It can be a very appealing reading center. A reluctant student who wants to get away from everyone else may enjoy laying in the bathtub to read. It can become a pirate ship, a submarine, or a spaceship.

And old bathtub could be a container for animals such as a snake or turtle; a hermit's cave; a lost mine. Let the students decide.

3. Doormat or coaster

Have students save bottle caps or ask filling stations or other business establishments for them. Choose a wooden board the size and shape wanted and nail caps to it.

4. Oil Drum

Stand on end, saw down through center. File the sharp edges down, paint, and have two beautiful containers for plants; cover with chicken wire and have a cage bed for animals; or line and make a cradle for the kindergarten. Let students decide on ways to use them.

5. Yarn Ball

There are always days in a classroom, at parties, or sitting around watching a dull television show when you'd like to have something safe, easy, and light to play with. One of the best gadgets to have around is the yarn ball.

Use regular sweater wool. Cut two cardboard discs six inches in diameter. From these, cut centers four inches in diameter. Place the two discs together and wind the wool tightly around them in and out from center. When the center hole is almost filled, cut the outer edge of wool with a razor blade, slip strong cord between discs to the center and tie tightly. Tear away the cardboard, and fluff out the wool. Different colors of yarn add to attractiveness. Older mentally retarded students could make these, and anyone can use them.

6. Make Your Own Universe

Materials needed: four or five orange or apple crates (number will depend upon size of dome you plan to make), chicken wire or house screen, nails, twine, construction paper, paste, strong brown wrapping paper, scissors, and aluminum foil.

Procedure:
1. Decide on size—both floor space and height of dome.
2. Space orange crates on sides on floor in circle facing outward leaving space for door.
3. Nail chicken wire to bottom of crates on one side of the circle.
4. Loop wire up and over as tall as you choose to form the dome.
5. Nail wire to bottom of remaining crates.
6. Line wire with brown wrapping paper. Staples, twine, or any other way you discover to hold paper to wire will work.
7. Next, line this layer of paper with aluminum foil.
8. Calculate, measure distances for sun, moon, and planets using dimensions which fit according to your space.
9. Calculate, measure, and cut out planets from construction paper.

10. In their correct locations and distances apart, according to your space and their actual distances, suspend them from dome with twine.

11. Light bulb can be suspended for the sun and lesser stars added to the sky.

12. For interest, a Milky Way may be added by pasting a profusion of stars in a path across the sky (yellow construction paper). Now, you have your own universe and are ready for observers.

7. Tin Can Animals

Decide upon an animal you want to make. Find cans (plastic bottles or cardboard boxes will serve just as well) in sizes needed for the animal you choose. Use pipe cleaners, coat hangers, or stiff cardboard to give shape. You also need wire and tin cutters, hole puncher, and file. (This can be dangerous; needs supervision.)

8. Foam Rubber

Visit a furniture store and tell them you're a teacher looking for things to use in making games to teach reading to children who are hard to reach by the usual methods. You're looking for throw-away foam rubber used in packing or making furniture.

They'll probably give you scraps or charge a nominal fee, depending upon demand.

Use an electric knife or saw to cut the material into blocks the size you want for the students you're working with. Use magic markers and write words, phrases, or whatever you want on all sides of the blocks of material. Students can use these to build basic sight words, to build comprehension if you use words and phrases which will go together to form sentences, and to reinforce pretaught vocabulary through games.

Throw the block and, using all sides which will work together, make sentences. This activity makes no noise if the material hits the floor and is good to use with students who are retarded.

9. Magazines and Newspapers

Have students, friends, organizations, and anyone who will to save them, donate their old magazines and newspapers to the school. These can be used to make games, to reinforce skills, to make puppets, and so on.

To teach basic sight words: after you've introduced them, let students find and underline or cut them out. They can make a collage of words which will be interesting as well as attractive.

To teach main ideas: make a collage using words under the same category and let students decide what main idea you are trying to convey. Middle-grade students of mine used *love* words and made beautiful, meaningful collages on tagboard to hang on the walls in their rooms at home.

10. Games

Use words and pictures to make games similar to "Go Fishing" or "Old Maid." Make concept cards, matchings, basic sight words, or whatever your group needs.

11. Old Books

Don't throw away or burn those old books or magazines. Cut them apart and make separate smaller booklets—*skinny books,* some people call them. Add manila, construction paper, or cloth backs which students can make when practicing following directions. They may even like to illustrate the story on the front cover.

Some students, especially those who are having problems, dislike the class textbook but will tackle a smaller one. File the skinny books for students use during free reading periods.

12. Leftover Short Candles and Crayons

The clank of knives, the odor of smoke and burning wax, and the sound of boys and girls busily laughing and chatting as they work—all are part of the oldest painting technique in history. Painting with wax.

A design is sketched with a pencil on stiff paper or cardboard. Some students may prefer to work without a design. The knife is heated by a candle flame or hotplate. Old crayons are pressed against the knife until the required amount is melted. Transfer the melted wax to the picture with the knife.

Little preparation is needed. Halloween scenes, winter scenes, Christmas scenes, modern art, animals, or anything your students wish to attempt, can lend themselves to this technique.

Use Personal Things to Hook Them

One way to make materials interesting to students is to use personal experiences connected with them. When a fourteen- or sixteen-year-old has failed in school for several years, it has become habit. He or she doesn't expect anything else. So part of the trouble is his/her attitude.

At the fourth session of working with a group of five over-aged eighth graders who wanted to stay in school to play ball, I handed each fellow a sheet of paper with his name as the title. I told them I knew some things about them they didn't know I knew, and for them to read their stories and see how near the truth I had come. If I was wrong about any one of them, I would redo the story. They were to draw one line under each word they didn't know. Then I would help them with those words as they studied silently. When they were ready they were to read their story orally for me.

I had them. How could I learn so much about them in just three sessions, they wanted to know. Of course, they didn't know how much I had talked to their teachers and studied their records. I didn't have to redo one story. When Ron read to me, he also miscalled the words I have underlined twice. This proves the theory that most poor readers do not recognize when they don't know words.

From that session forward, those five boys worked for me without complaining. The sad thing about it: eighth grade was too late to begin, and twice a week was too few lessons, especially when there was no transfer from reading class into classes with their other three teachers. The big change, according to their homeroom teacher, was in attitude. Four of the five fellows improved.

Look at this sample story about one reluctant reader (fictitious name); it motivated him to try to improve his reading skills during his ninth year in school.

RONALD MACK

A short biography of an adolescent boy

Ronald Mack, a handsome blond with an engaging personality and a quick temper, is a reluctant member of the Mills Town Elementary School's Eighth Grade class. He has come to my reading session for three times—sad to say, not because he wanted to but because it's the lesser of two evils.

This sixteen-year-old lad is interested in raising horses and is approaching a crucial era in his life. He likes to get by on what he could do rather than on what he does do. Let's hope he uses better judgment with his horses. Will he train his thoroughbreds to jump the fence, or will he let them do the way he does—look at the fence but because it takes effort, never learn to make the jump?

Math is a logical science which requires a great deal of straight thinking to master it. Ron doesn't like Math. Does this mean that Ron doesn't like to think?

This young man wants the respect of adults. He wants to be trusted yet deliberately does things to earn suspicion of his actions. Let's hope maturity brings contentment and self-satisfaction for Ron.

Study Plan for Remedial Reader— Black Beauty (Pages 1–14)

(by Anna Sewell)

For this activity, the student works alone at a reading center equipped with a tape recorder, books and study sheets. All of the words written on this page are recorded on the tape. Student listens and reads simultaneously, including the words Direction Number 1.

Direction Number 1.   You will need the book *Black Beauty*, a clean sheet of paper and a pencil. Stop the player and get these. When you get them, start the player again.

Direction Number 2.   Before you go on to Direction Number 3, spend some time looking at the pictures and the title page of this book. Take as long as you need before you start the player for Number 3. Stop the tape.

Direction Number 3. Now follow the directions on this tape, They are the same as the ones written on this page. Read them as you listen and do as you are directed. One day you will know all the words and can read them without the tape. Ready?

This is the story of a horse named Black Beauty. Write the name Black Beauty on your paper beside a number one (1). I will wait for you.

Direction Number 4. Black Beauty lived in a meadow. A meadow is a grassy pasture where horses and other animals like to eat and play. See how many times you can find the word meadow on page 3 of the story, then write the word three times beside a number two (2) on your paper. Turn the tape recorder to the stop position until you finish.

Direction Number 5. Look on page 3 again. The story gives you three things which Black Beauty likes to do. Find them and write them on your paper like this.

(3) Black Beauty likes to (a)
                         (b)
                         (c)

Turn the tape recorder to the stop position until you finish.

Direction Number 6. A baby horse is called a colt. Look on page 5 and find out what colts like to do. Write it on your paper beside the number four (4). Write it on your paper like this.

(4) Baby colts like to ————

Turn the machine to the stop position until you finish.

Direction Number 7. Duchess gives her baby colt, Black Beauty, some good advice. Look on page six (6) to find out what she told him and write it like this.

(5) Duchess told Black Beauty to (a)
                               (b)
                               (c)
                               (d)

Be sure to turn the recorder to the stop position until you finish.

Direction Number 8. Farmer Gray was kind to all of this horses, but on page eight (8) the author tells us that Black Beauty and Duchess were his favorites. What does the word fa/vor/ite mean? Use the dictionary if you need to. Write the meaning on your paper, then make a sentence using the word favorite in it. This is number six (6) on your paper. Turn the machine to the stop position.

Direction Number 9. Read page eight (8) silently. Why did Farmer Gray call Dick a bad boy? Answer the question like this.

(7) Farmer Gray called Dick a bad boy because he ————.

Turn the recorder off until you write your sentence.

Direction Number 10. When you have your paper finished and as neat as you can make it, put it in your folder for your teacher to see later. If

you want to, you may read some more in the book.
Turn the tape recorder off, now.

It doesn't take long to make simple guides such as this and students love to work with them. I used this one with a fifth grader who was called a non-reader. The repetition which slow or remedial students need is used to facilitate recognition of words which are already in their speaking vocabulary. Giving specific directions and models for sentence answers is much better than trying to build sentence sense by English grammar rules which they may memorize but not understand.

Strong students who want extra work to do can occasionally be given the responsibility to make study sheets like this on a story which most of the students want to read. Often times just this much work on a story will motivate the slow or remedial student to want to read the book, especially if his peer says it's a great one.

If you are pressed for time and the student needs more than one practice to get the words on this lesson (machine, direction, recorder, position, etc.), you can use the very same directions with another book by changing key words. The name of the story, the page number, the man's name and sometimes the wording of the direction.

Look at Direction Number 4. Changed for the story of *Flossie and Bossie,* it reads like this.

Direction Number 4.   Flossie and Bossie lived in a barnyard. A barnyard is a grassy spot around a barn where horses, chickens, cows and other animals like to eat and play. See how many times you can find the word barnyard on page _____.

Learn by Doing—Prefixes and Suffixes

Purpose: This exercise illustrates one approach which teachers can use to insure learning. Introductory exercises can deal with one prefix and/or suffix. These can be followed by exercises using all affixes taught so far. Having students make sentence using the base word, then a sentence using the same word plus the affix emphasizes the meaning of the affix.

Procedure:

1. Make a sentence with each of the following words. What happens to the meaning of each word lettered *b?* What can you say about the prefix *un?*

   a. clean
   b. unclean
   a. fair
   b. unfair

   a. load
   b. unload
   a. kind
   b. unkind

2. Make a sentence with each of the following words. What happens to the meaning of each word lettered *b?* What can you say about the prefix *re?*

a. fill	a. visit
b. refill	b. revisit
a. read	a. test
b. reread	b. retest

3. Make a sentence with the following words. Each word lettered *b* has a prefix. Explain what each prefix does to the word meaning.

a. view	a. agree	a. happy
b. preview	b. disagree	b. unhappy
a. ability	a. play	a. clothed
b. inability	b. replay	b. unclothed
		c. reclothed

Suffixes are word endings which give root words different shades of meaning. (*er, or, ist, an, al, ure, ty, ment, ism, age, is, en, el, ive, ful, less,* etc.) Since there are a great number of suffixes and very few have an absolutely fixed meaning, an attempt to teach concrete meanings for the majority would probably produce more confusion than learning and be a waste of time. If students develop the habit of seeing the known root words, the new words are not likely to cause trouble. Composing sentences using the different forms is a better method of teaching than having students tell the precise differences between words like *joyful, joyfully, joyous.*

Older students and bright young ones enjoy activities similar to the categorizing exercise in figure 13.1. Use the words in the unit you're working with or let students find their own words to play around with and let them try their luck with decoding.

Directions for Your Project "Painting on Glass"

You will have to read these directions to me before you begin to paint. This is to be sure that you know exactly what and how to go about your project. It is rather expensive and one which you will be proud of, so let's do it correctly and well.

1. First of all, STUDY this page and READ it to me.
2. SELECT the picture you want to paint from those on display.
3. WASH your glass, and please do not break it. If you do you will not have another one. (A 9 x 14 size window pane will be fine.)
4. DRY the glass thoroughly.
5. LAY your picture on the table on newspaper. We must not get the paint on our tables or floor. Now lay the window pane over the picture.
6. STIR the paint before using it.
7. CHOOSE small DETAILS to paint first. Things like the EYES, small LINES, or other very small areas.

FIGURE 13.1
Structure of words

Structural Analysis to Aid Pronunciation and Understanding

Students can be guided to see that the make-up of words will help in understanding and pronouncing them. Here are two variations on categorizing words.

Directions to Students

Study the words on your vocabulary sheet for this unit. (Whatever unit you're working on.)
List them under the correct category on this chart. (Either one or both.)

A	Compound Words	Words in which you recognize the root. Underline root.		Words in which you see no recognizable root.		Words you are not familiar with and need to work on.

B	Single whole words	Prefix plus root	Compound Words	Root plus suffix	Prefix plus root plus suffix	Root plus suffix plus suffix
	port	report	airport	portable	transporting	porters
	race	rerun	racetrack	racing	rescheduling	resistors

8. Paint ONE color at a time. Let that paint DRY. It will RUN together if it is wet.
9. When one color is DRY, another color can be painted right over it. This lets your work go faster on the last stages of the picture.
10. At all times, be careful of each other, of open paint, of our picture patterns and of other people's work on the table.
11. PLEASE, do not overturn the paint.
12. DO NOT MIX THE PAINTS. Always CLEAN your brush before you stick it into a different color jar.
13. Keep containers tightly closed when not in use.
14. Always clean up your brush and picture when you finish for the hour. Don't leave it for someone else to do.
15. Everyone can not paint at the same time. WE WILL TAKE TURNS.
16. The painting is to be done while others are working at something else. EVERYONE WILL HAVE TO TAKE RESPONSIBILITY.
17. Don't blame someone else for YOUR FAILURE.
18. If you can't follow these directions, the privilege of painting will be TAKEN AWAY from you. In this I will be firm so you had better CONTROL YOURSELF and your working. If you have any questions, please ask. That's what I'm here for.

Activity:	Definition Grab Bag
Purpose:	To motivate for, to reinforce already taught, or to teach new vocabulary you want students to know. Involvement and fun, (69, p. 26).
Directions:	Select 50 to 100 (any number you want) key vocabulary terms from current materials being worked with in classes. Make a copy of the most suitable definition on a small strip of paper. Put the strips of paper in a cigar or any other small suitable box for easy handling and storage. Class sits in circle. Two or more teams. First student draws a strip from the box and reads it aloud. His task is to give the word for the definition he drew. If he can do so, his group gets a point and the next person gets a strip. If he doesn't get the word, play moves to the next team. If they know it, they get a point and play continues.
Materials needed:	Strips of paper with definitions on them. Score sheet. Teams. Here is a list of word definitions you could use. However, it's better to make your own to fit the needs of your curriculum and students. These are for good junior high students.

1. To produce something extemporaneously or from whatever is at hand.
2. A short musical, dramatic or ballet offering given between the acts of a play or opera.

3. Causing death, deadly, fatal.
4. An embankment, especially along the bank of a river, built for protections against floods.
5. A little world, the universe in miniature.
6. A polygon having eight sides and eight angles.
7. Of or belonging to the beginning, origin, or first stage of existence of a thing.
8. A fabric of cotton, rayon or silk with raised cord or welts running lengthwise in the fabric.
9. A high state of attainment in some knowledge, art of skill; expertness.
10. A high collar that fits snugly about the neck, usually rolled or turned over double.
11. One who oversees; superintendent, inspector.
12. The selling for regular publication of a column, series of articles, comic strips, etc., to a number of newspapers or periodicals.
13. A space absolutely devoid of matter.
14. A vessel specially built or fitted for racing or for private pleasure excursions.
15. The science of animals dealing with classification, structure, etc.
16. Belief in, or in the existence of, God; a god or gods.
17. Any of various plants yielding a blue dyestuff.
18. Notably devoid of trimness and smartness in dress; frumpish.
19. A confusion of many voices or languages; tumult.
20. One who keeps drugs for sale and puts up prescriptions; a druggist; pharmacist.
21. That part of a race course farthest from the spectators.
22. A mollusk having a shell of two lateral valves hinged together as the oyster or clam.
23. Accredited diplomatic agent, the highest rank, appointed to represent one government to another.
24. To enthrall by excellence or beauty; fascinate; charm.
25. A signed paper granting its possessor the freedom to write his own conditions; unrestricted authority.

Answers: 1. improvise 2. intermezzo 3. lethal 4. levee 5. microcosm 6. octagon 7. original 8. pique 9. proficiency 10. turtle neck 11. supervisor 12. syndication 13. vacuum 14. yacht 15. zoology 16. theism 17. indigo 18. dowdy 19. babel 20. apothecary 21. backstretch 22. bivalve 23. ambassador 24. captivate 25. carte blanche

Activity: Game—Stump the Panel (adaptation of television game)

Purpose: Book reporting, not the usual copied synopsis, total class involvement, reading for pleasure and appreciation of literature.

Directions: One person reads a book. He then discusses the story with two other members of the class. Three other students will serve as panelists to question the three on the book. The panel tries to discover who is in reality the reader of the book.

The remainder of the class is involved by listening and making individual decisions. Do they agree with the panel?

To have long range interest, an individual chart of guesses might be kept by each student who will figure his percentage of correct decisions at a specified period of time.

Activity: Game—Meet the Press

Purpose: To develop study skills of using references, organizing for reports, recall of information, sensory reaction (identify with characters), fun learning situations, encourage creative activity, group work and appreciation.

Directions: Divide class into groups. Character and/or events in curriculum to be explored, assigned. One person in a group plays role of a character or authority on the event. Other players in group serve as interviewers.

On the day their character "meets the press," they interview him. All persons of the group will have to work together in planning for the interview. Person being interviewed will need to have the questions to be asked before hand.

Groups can flavor presentation with comedy, dress, speech, background scenery, music or whatever they can create.

Activity: Game—Answer with a Blend (Contributed by Janice Burnette, Graduate Student, Western Carolina University)

Purpose: To reinforce consonant blends, to build vocabulary, for challenge and for fun.

Materials needed: Chart or game board with pockets made out of tagboard or strong fabric. Cloth more durable. Cards with questions to be answered in appropriate pockets.

Directions: Choose a who, what, when or where card from pocket and try to answer question on card with a word beginning with the indicated blend. If you answer correctly, you keep the card. Winner is student with most questions cards at end of playing time. If you can't answer, let other students help and replace card in proper pocket for later playing.

Here is a sample board with questions. You use questions to reinforce whatever is going on in your classroom.

TABLE 7

Answer with a blend

Blends	WHO?	WHAT?	WHEN?	WHERE?
CL	The funny man in a circus is called a_____	What is another word for a lump of dirt?	It tells you when to get up each morning.	North Carolina enjoys this type of folk dancing.
TW	Miss Mode's name is_____	The small branch of a tree is call-ed a_____	When it is be-tween sunset and dark, we say it is_____time.	An even num-ber that appears between 18 and 22 is _____.
BL	Who was a famous pirate?	What is the fat of a whale called?	When dynamite explodes, it makes a loud _____.	Up in the sky over Rose Bowl flies the Good Year _____.
TR	The president just before Mr. Eisenhower was _____.	Car, trains, planes and ships are all forms of _____.	When your hair grows too long, you have a _____.	You are in it when you have done something bad.
FR	You call the person you like a _____	One way to cook chicken is to _____it.	When a day comes before Saturday, it is called _____.	We live in America where people are _____

Book-Movie Titles Hide-and-Seek
(for Honor Students)

How well do you know your books and movies? Here is a fun way to find out.[29] Titles of popular and classic literature which have been made into movies are hidden in   table 8 . A title begins at each numbered space. Letters for titles move in all directions, but are always adjacent to each other.

Example: Number 38 begins with a D. Find it. Move down one space, diagonally up one space, down three, diagonally down one, down another one, and forward three.

Did you spell *Dr. Zhivago?* Have you read the book? Did you see the movie? Now, try your luck. Thirty correct titles will be a good score.

Answers for Book-Movie Hide-and-Seek

1. *To Kill a Mockingbird*
2. *The Thread That Runs So True*
3. *Gone With the Wind*
4. *Good-Bye, Mr. Chips*
5. *Jane Eyre*
6. *Shane*
7. *Bridges of Toko-Ri*

TABLE 8

Hide-and-seek book-movie titles

S	O	T	R	U	E	O	T	M	E	A	T	I	O	[4]G	O	O	D
✕	[33]S	H	O	W	B	[30]R	A	O	H	T	N	E	N	S	✕	R	B
[5]J	A	N	E	E	Y	I	S	R	T	C	T	V	E	[35]S	I	[36]S	Y
[12]E	O	D	U	S	L	A	C	N	U	E	E	H	I	B	O	W	E
A	X	✕	S	R	✕	F	I	I	H	P	E	U	G	M	M	E	M
C	[13]V	A	N	I	T	Y	E	N	O	X	H	N	D	U	E	L	R
C	A	N	I	E	O	A	[40]B	G	G	E	I	T	H	S	N	T	C
E	H	F	P	[14]J	E	[15]R	H	V	A	[39]K	T	A	E	R	[9]G	T	H
[7]B	T	R	P	D	Z	H	I	T	C	I	O	N	T	I	N	I	I
[11]R	[10]E	O	O	N	[38]D	R	T	O	D	M	S	R	[27]M	K	I	[24]L	P
I	✕	M	P	Y	R	A	[28]M	E	[31]R	A	E	N	A	I	[25]L	A	S
D	E	E	S	I	N	A	[17]I	[29]V	O	L	E	T	H	[26]O	R	E	S
[8]G	R	N	N	O	L	S	J	A	H	T	[32]C	R	[6]S	L	A	L	I
E	[34]B	M	A	[16]L	O	R	D	N	✕	O	A	M	H	D	E	L	E
S	O	R	I	A	F	Y	T	I	L	D	E	L	O	T	Y	H	A
O	N	K	E	C	T	H	E	W	I	W	D	N	I	W	E	V	R
F	O	E	H	E	G	A	N	D	[18]H	O	Y	T	S	I	R	H	[37]C
[1]T	R	[22]T	[20]T	[21]T	G	[19]T	H	E	[2]G	O	N	E	W	I	[23]T	H	[3]T

8. *Green Mansions*
9. *Great Expectations*
10. *Ethan Frome*
11. *Rebecca*
12. *Exodus*
13. *Vanity Fair*
14. *Joy in the Morning*
15. *Red Pony*
16. *Lord Jim*
17. *Ivanhoe*
18. *How Do I Love Thee*
19. *The Good Earth*
20. *The Egg and I*
21. *The Robe*
22 *The Call of the Wild*
23. *The Yearling*
24. *Little Women*
25. *Lassie*
26. *Old Yeller*
27. *Mrs. Mike*
28. *Mary Poppins*
29. *Vanity Fair*
30. *Rascal*
31. *Ramona*
32. *Camelot*
33. *Showboat*
34. *Born Free*
35. *Seventeenth Summer*
36. *So Big*
37. *Christy*
38. *Dr. Zhivago*
39. *Kon-Tiki*
40. *Ben Hur*

Activity: Where Do You Get Off
Rapping about My Slang?

Purpose: To call attention to the part slang plays in communication.

To let students know you are aware of language they use and are not nagging about it, and there are different ways of saying the same thing.

To bring relevancy to the classroom.

Directions: Read these sentences. Transform them into formal grammar.

1. How to get through college without being a china-chopper is my can of worms.
2. Most every day the general sends around his poop sheet.
3. Imagine! The top banana had a balloon for lunch.

4. So what's wrong with using a keek? Most every business does.
5. A beekie is also a blister.
6. A culture vulture would use a crew-cut approach to the problem.
7. The most entertaining spectacle on Saturday night is a passion pit.
8. The main objection to participation in sports is the skull sessions.
9. Do you ever look at your young man and long for the white sidewall?
10. His wet sock made me doubt his sincerity.
11. He was so stupid he let a cabbage control his joystick.
12. A schnook is constantly losing his grazing ticket.
13. Many college students are satisfied with being a barb.
14. Never think when you can use a cheat stick.
15. A commando performance leaves me cold.
16. He was browned off at so many boodles in office.
17. We paid a fin for a dish of fish eyes.
18. He may be a foozle, but he tried to play footsie and offered me ice.
19. That rip had enough pizzazz to dupe any pigeon.
20. When I'm going to talk turkey, I like to have handy a sinker, a cup of java, and a brain.

Answers:

1. How to get through college without being a dishwasher is my unsolved problem.
2. Most every day the principal sends around the announcements.
3. Imagine! The best comedian had a frankfurter for lunch.
4. So what's wrong with using a peeping Tom or spy? Most every business does.
5. A nosey person is also an annoying one.
6. A devotee to intellectual concerns would use a collegiate approach to the problem.
7. Most entertaining spectacle on Saturday night is a drive-in movie lot.
8. The main objection to participating in sports is the lectures on how, why, and so on.
9. Do you ever look at your young man and long for the short haircuts again?
10. His limp handshake made me doubt his sincerity.
11. He was so stupid he let a young girl steer his hot rod.
12. A dope is constantly losing his meal ticket.
13. Many students see no stigma in not belonging to a fraternity.
14. Never think when you can use a calculator.
15. A rough and obvious courting manner leaves me unaffected.
16. He was angry because there were so many corrupt politicians in office.
17. We paid five dollars for a dish of tapioca pudding.
18. He may be an older person, but he courted me and offered me diamonds.
19. That disreputable guy has enough pep, power, and aggression to trick any naive girl.

20. When I'm going to discuss facts frankly, I like to have handy a doughnut, a cup of coffee, and an intelligent person.

FOLLOW-UP ACTIVITIES:

1. After students work with these examples, let them make up some sentences using present day slang then transform them into formal grammar or let their peers attempt to translate them.
2. Some students may want to do research on period slang and report to class.
3. CB radios and trucker slang is another interesting language phenomenon of the middle 1970s. You might have students who would be interested in finding out more about this subject.
4. Many words, once considered slang, today are accepted as good form. One group could look into this.

Lesson on Famous Black Americans

Purpose:
1. To acquaint students with some interesting black Americans.
2. To have students practice reading skills.
3. To promote creative thinking.
4. To motivate for further research on famous black Americans.

Materials needed:
1. Handout with short biographical information.
2. Study guide with specific tasks indicated.
3. Answer key for parts of the material.
4. Reference works for those who want more.

Procedure:
Give students materials, give them time to read the short biographical sketches, give help with pronunciation, if needed, then let them do the activities they need and/or choose. You may need to assign certain things for specific students.

ACTIVITIES:

I. Make a timeline showing names, dates, and major contributions (one or two words) of twenty black Americans.

II. Choose your favorite of these black Americans and do an in-depth study of his or her life. Make notes to be used in a three minute talk to the rest of the class. These notes will be checked by the teacher. Use any form of note taking which works for you.

III. Scan the information given you to find the following facts. See if you can do this exercise in five minutes.

A. Called "Mr. Civil Rights"
B. Served in World War II

C. Sold newspapers as a boy
D. Gave concerts at the age of ten
E. A voice that comes once in a century, her critics said
F. Received Distinguished Service Medal in 1948
G. Took part in 1770 demonstrations against unjust taxes
H. Earned name of Moses because of freedom journeys from South to North
I. Founder of Tuskegee Institute
J. Taught to read and write by the wife of his master
K. First man to set foot on North Pole
L. Authority on preservation of blood
M. Published two volumes of poetry at age of twenty-one
N. Worked his way through college as a waiter
O. Won Nobel Peace Price in 1950
P. Killed in automobile accident at age of forty-six
Q. Co-discoverer of North Pole
R. Early producer of synthetics

IV. Of the people whose succinct life statistics are listed in your handout, skim to find out the following specific statistics. Try to finish in five minutes.
A. How many had college degrees
B. How many were inventors
C. How many were musicians
D. How many were famous in sports
E. How many were famous in politics
F. How many were famous in medicine
G. How many were famous writers
H. How many were orphans or had only one parent

V. Here are some terms used in your reading. Do you recognize and understand the meaning of each of these? Can you pronounce them?

shrine	revolutionized	periodicals	personnel
eminence	tactics	abolitionist	wharves
boycott	Intolerable Acts	emancipation	improvisations
eloquent	martyrs	shanty	clients
Croix de Guerre	Philharmonic	Brigadier	lieutenant
exhausted	regiments	narrative	

VI. Can you match three columns below? Use a dictionary or encyclopedia if you need to do so. The first one is done for you.

A <u>1, f</u> wharves
B_____ improvisations
C_____ eminence
D_____ abolitionist
E_____ shrine
F_____ Croix de Guerre

1. loading place for vessels
2. clever maneuvers or plans
3. the act of setting free, liberation
4. monument to someone great
5. a hastily built shack

a. Randolph
b. Douglas
   Tubman
   Attucks
c. Dunbar, Carver
d. David

G____Intolerable Acts	6. decoration for bravery	e. Henson
H____periodicals	7. against something	f. Attucks
I____domestic	8. superiority in rank, power	g. Satchmo
J____emancipation	or achievement	Armstrong
K____shanty	9. prelude to a queen	h. Washington
L____tactics	10. a produced change in something	i. Davis
M____revolutionized	11. unjust taxes imposed on the	j. Tubman,
N____Brigadier	American colonies	Douglass
O____eloquent	12. spur of the moment produc-	k. any of them
	tions without previous fore	l. Carver
	thought	m. Jackson
	13. forceful, fluent, convincing	n. Davis
	in writing, speech or emotion	o. Washington,
	14. magazines or some other printed	Marshall,
	published materials	Drew,
	15. high rank in military	Dunbar,
	16. blowing with a roaring sound	Randolph,
		Bunche,
		and others

VII. Would these famous Americans agree or disagree with the statements made by some current Americans? Defend your answer with at least one idea.

1. Thurgood Marshall. Would he agree with the statement, "My initial fee is $5,000 to defend you. The remaining $50,000 is due at the end of the trial."
2. Louis "Satchmo" Armstrong, "The world owes me a living."
3. Harriet Tubman, "I don't have to work. My welfare check and food stamps will keep me going."
4. Booker T. Washington, "The federal government should subsidize the education of college students."
5. Jackie Robinson, "Put your mother in a rest home and get on with your life."
6. Marian Anderson, "The woman's place is in the home."
7. Brigadier General Benjamin O. Davis, "The black man has a chance to get to the top in the world today. He should take it."
8. Dr. Charles R. Drew, "Medicine and physical education won't mix."
9. Ralph Bunche, "The way to world peace is understanding."
10. Frederick Douglass, "The white man is not interested in the black man any- more than the black man is interested in the white man."

VIII. Compare and contrast the life and times of Crispus Attucks and Brigadier General Benjamin O. Davis, Sr.

IX. Write a newspaper story as you think Frederick Douglass might write it using any topic of interest in the news today.

For example: O. J. Simpson—Man of the Day

Senator Edward Brooks—Conservative or Liberal

X. Write the dialogue for a television interview with George Washington Carver, Harriet Tubman, Mohammed Ali, and Barbara Walters. What are some subjects they might discuss. What opinions would each of these have on that subject? Would they agree?

ANSWERS TO NUMBER VI.
    A. 1, f   F. 6, i   K. 5, h
    B. 12, g   G. 11, n   L. 2, n
    C. 8, k   H. 12, a   M. 10, 1
    D. 7, j   I. 9, m   N. 15, d
    E. 4, c   J. 3, b   O. 13, o

The Santa Claus Family

Santa Claus	Robin	Old Rudolph
Mrs. Santa Claus	Pixy	Old Pudolph
Grandpa Claus	Pigwiggin	Sleigh
Grandma Claus	The Twins	Sack
Pucky	Baby Brownie	Workshop

Directions

Name each person in your class as one of the characters in the story. A student can be more than one character if there are not enough people to cover them all. As each name is called in the story, the person rises, shakes one foot and says, "jingle bells," and sits down again. When "Claus Family" is mentioned, everyone gets up and turns around.

The Story

Once upon a time there was a family by the name of Claus.

There was a Santa Claus, Mrs. Santa Claus, Pucky, Robin and Pixy, Pigwiggin and the Twins, and Baby Brownie Claus.

One day right after Christmas when the Claus family had worked so hard to make all the earth children happy, Santa Claus said to Mrs. Santa, "Suppose we hitch up Old Rudolph and Old Pudolph to the sleigh and spend the day at Grandpa Claus's workshop. Mother Claus said, "All right. I will get Pucky and Robin and Pigwiggin and Pixy and the Twins, and Baby Brownie all ready while you, Pa Santa, hitch Old Rudolph and Old Pudolph to the sleigh. Then we can go to Grandpa and Grandma's workshop."

So Santa drove the sleigh with Old Rudolph and Old Pudolph around to the side of the workshop, and Pucky and Robin and Pixy, Pigwiggin and the Twins all skipped out to the sleigh and got in. Then Mrs. Santa Claus came out with Baby Brownie and got into the sleigh. So Santa Claus started up Old Rudolph and Old Pudolph and the sleigh and away they all flew to the workshop of Grandpa and Grandma Claus. But in the rush Mrs. Santa Claus forgot her sack, so Santa Claus stopped Old Rudolph and Old Pudolph turned the sleigh and flew back into the workshop to get Mrs. Santa's sack. He soon found Mrs. Santa's sack and flew out and onto the sleigh.

Santa Claus whistled to Old Rudolph and Old Pudolph and the sleigh started off so fast that the Twins fell out of the sleigh, and Pixy and Pigwiggin screamed and Mrs. Santa yelled and the Baby Brownie cried and Santa Claus stopped Old Rudolph and Old Pudolph and the sleigh and sent Pucky and Robin back to where the Twins were sitting beside the workshop.

Robin and Pucky made the Twins run and get into the sleigh. So once more Mr. Santa Claus started Old Rudolph and Old Pudolph and the sleigh again and all of the Santa Claus family were on their way to Grandpa and Grandma Claus's workshop.

VARIATION: Use vocabulary from the unit you are working with. Where Santa Claus and other Christmas words are used, substitute. For instance, a unit on space might be the Universe family with children like Mars, Uranus, Big Dipper, perigee, apogee, etc; for Easter, Peter Cottontail and his family.

Science, Superstition, and Reading

According to folklore, when the maple turns white, that's a sign of rain the following day. Many people still believe this phenomenon is a reliable indicator of rain. Is this a scientific fact, a superstition based on old sayings or is there some truth in it?

Is there a way you could test the statement to find out if it is fact or fiction, or fiction based on part fact?

Leaves of the silver maple are light green on one side, silvery-white on the other. The leaves are attached to the tree by a very slender and delicate petiole and the slightest breeze causes them to turn and show the underside. One theory is that the tiny "hairs" on the back of the leaf pick up moisture from the humid air, increasing weight on one side, causing it to turn.

North American folklore is filled with other signs of rain. Have you heard these?

Thunder before seven, rain before eleven.
When rain is coming, the bullfrogs sing.
Fuzzy "horns" on the moon foretell rain.
A hog running around with straw in its mouth is a sure sign that bad weather
    is coming.
When clouds move crosswise to the surface wind, rain is not far away.
When earthworms, slugs or snails come to the top of the ground in great
    numbers, rain is on the way.
When bones ache with rheumatism, rain is coming.

Which ones of these sayings seem to be true in part?
Here are some other sayings. Can you find the origin of any of them?

1. Break a mirror and you have seven years bad luck.
2. Walking under a ladder is bad luck.
3. Sweep under your feet and you'll never get married.
4. Hear a hoot-owl cry near by and someone is going to die.
5. If a black cat runs across the road in front of you, it means bad luck.
6. Dream of a muddy river and you're in for bad luck.

Beanbag Reading (Idea created by Charlotte Black, Teacher, Buncombe County, N.C.)

Materials needed: A game board (side of big cardboard box such as the one a refrigerator is stored in will work), a bulletin board may be used, construction paper, contact paper, magic markers, beanbag, reading tasks to suit the levels of your students.

How to make the game board. On different sizes, shapes and colors of pieces of construction paper, write big enough to be seen about 20 feet away tasks which will reinforce and add zest to the learning going on in your room. Paste these tasks haphazardly on the large section of cardboard or other material if you prefer. Cover with contact paper for longer wear. Figure 13.2 is a small area of how it might look.

Purpose: reinforcement, fun, involvement

Directions: Student teams, any number but small group works better, take turns tossing beanbag at the board. They must read and perform the task which their toss touches. If they succeed, they get a point for their team. If not, the other side gets a chance at it. It becomes their turn. The winner is the team with the most points at the end of a specified playing time.

FIGURE 13.2

Beanbag reading game board

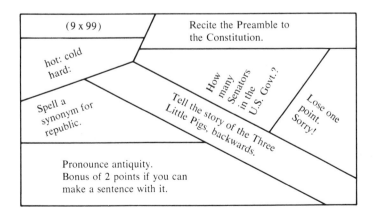

Activities for the Teacher

1. Choose a favorite poem or other selection and adapt it for choral reading.
2. Use one book which you would like for your students to read and make job cards for it.
3. Create an original game (can be a take-off of some commercial one turned educational) to teach or reinforce some material you are currently working with.
4. Make a lesson plan for teaching some skill you usually teach about this time of year. Use the discovery technique.
5. Make a tape or cassette on the material some student needs special help with. Be sure to take into consideration his needs, personality, level of thinking ability, and interests. Let him work with the material. What happens?
6. If you are not working with students right now, choose the grade and thinking levels of your special interests and do the above tasks as you might use them some day.

FOURTEEN

What to Do When Nothing Works: Ask the Students

"Sure. If you have an ideal class, if you are working in an ideal university laboratory situation, or if you have all the fabulous materials to work with, your fancy ideas are fine. Me? I'm no magician. I have $30 per year to spend for supplementary books and $30 per year for supplies. Tell me, how will I put these ideas you advocate to work with my class of apathetic, lazy, good-for-nothing kids? After all, I'm not God. I don't give them the brains or the will."

QUESTIONS: Are you guilty of making such a statement?
Is this a legitimate alibi?
Are there times when we must accept failure?
Can students give us clues for helping them?
What can you do when the state adopts, the superintendent orders and the principal issues textbooks written on an eighth grade level and your class average reading level is fifth grade? Are you limited to issued textbooks?

Ways of approaching school problems are as numerous as the people using them. After doing two to ten weeks of summer school work at a nearby university, you reenter your elementary classroom determined to lick all problems. Your students will not be like those in Miss Doe's room, you vow. She just couldn't see that Sarah could do her work if she got help. And Johnny! All he needs is someone to tell him he can do it. If that poor teacher only knew how bored the students were!

With reborn enthusiasm and faith, you make materials talked about in the summer methods courses, you collect games, you plan TV programs, find records and tapes to use, all beautifully integrated in units. Then come student reactions:

"What a dumb game. That's kid stuff."

"If I wanted to watch television, I'd stay home."

"Say, teach, got any jive records? These things are 1920 stuff."

313

And those beautiful bulletin boards! In fifteen minutes they sprout horns, tails, and obscene words.

Students, with tongue in cheek, anxiously await the first outburst for which teachers are famous. Will you cry, rage, punish everyone, call them dumb brats? Or will you simply cry and give up like Miss Doe did last term? "Oh, this will be good," their downcast eyes shout as they furtively glance at each other when you enter the door.

You see but don't shout. You feel but don't show it. You smile as though nothing is amiss and go about the chores of classwork. If you handle it correctly, it won't be long until someone will lose control and you'll find out who the culprits are. They'll ask if you see what someone did.

With hands on hips, you thoughtfully study the work. "Delbert and Sue are good at art. I like their creativity. Looks much more interesting than the original."

"Sue and Delbert didn't do it. We did, Sam and me," Frank will boast.

"Frank! I didn't know you could draw like that. Gee, am I lucky. Four good artists in one class. How about you four serving as our decoration committee for the first quarter? You plan for, select, and take care of all displays, exhibits, and bulletin boards. Okay?"

Frank sits up a little straighter in his seat, glances around to see how the class is taking all this, and answers, "Yes m'am."

Begin Where the Students Are

"Begin where the students are" becomes a meaningless phrase when teachers still assign every student the same work on the same page and expect them to finish in the same amount of time. Educational psychologists have found that all ages prefer to deal with subjects, materials, and concepts which have personal meaning for them. Meaningful learning comes more easily and is remembered longer.

When you know this fact, why do you constantly bombard them with boring, out-of-date, and often useless trivia to be memorized and parroted back to you? Your major task is to lead the student toward maturity in discriminating and generalizing from the materials and experiences he encounters. As is stated elsewhere in this book, there is no one best method, no clear-cut pattern to follow, and no panacea of materials or plans.

This leaves the teacher and the student. What is to take place? How can you help the learner? "I've tried everything. Nothing works." Do you accept this too often repeated lament? What are some things you can try?

Larry's Story

Larry was a tall, handsome tenth-year student singled out of his class to attend reading classes one hour per day. At the same time Larry attended the center, six young sixth- and seventh-year students, not yet past their "growing spurt" were there. Larry resented this and said so in loud caustic terms.

With very few books and materials, the teacher attempted to give Larry something on which he could succeed. His response: "Who cares about that junk?" He was a discipline problem and the teacher dreaded to see the hour approach.

Some new books from one of our federally funded projects arrived. Knowing of Larry's interest in cars, I hurriedly searched through the box for books related to cars. A beautiful "technical" manual, suitable for a high school library, was among the lot. I suggested to the reading teacher that she give it to Larry.

"That's much too hard. He'd never master it. He won't even try," she argued.

Students often stretch for something they want, so I insisted.

The first day Larry pretended no interest, but the pictures were there, and he did look. The second day he attempted to read some of the captions. He even asked the teacher for help on a few words.

The third day, and subsequently for the rest of his six weeks in the reading center, Larry marched straight to the library shelf, pulled down "his car book," and was a constant agitator at the teacher's elbow. "What's this word? Does this say _____? Hey, Man. I can make a better car than that!"

Larry, a discipline problem? Larry, the fellow who didn't care whether he learned or not? No. Like so many before and since, he was an unreached student who for ten years had failed to succeed with school tasks. How many of you would survive ten years of failure? If just one elementary teacher could have understood and done something about his problems.

What are some ways this teacher helped Larry with reading skills? What directions did she take to help him branch out into other areas of the curriculum? Did they work?

What the Teacher Did

Using some of the words he had asked for help in pronouncing, the teacher launched Larry into a study of words.

"Larry, which words do you want to remember?"

"Oh, any of 'em. None of 'em. All of 'em." He pointed to *trioval.*

"All right. Do you recognize anything familiar about it?"

"Yeah. Let's see. T r y, t r e e—a l. I remember back in some of them dumb reading classes in elementary school there was a rule we had to learn had something to do with—let's see—Oh, I know. When two vowels go walking, the first one is quiet and the second does the talking. No, the first one talks and the second one is quiet. Anyway, I'd say the word is trival, troval, whichever the dumb rule says." He looked at her and beamed. "Right?"

"You're on the right track. You're thinking," she encouraged.

"But I'm wrong," he responded before she could say anything else. "Wrong as usual. Just dumb Larry." He shrugged his shoulders. "Well, what is the fool word? Just tell me. That's easier."

"Sure. I could tell you, but would that help when you see another new word? Wouldn't you like to be able to figure words for yourself?"

"Well, I ain't learned in ten years. Just don't expect me to now, and I'm quitting next year, anyway. Guess there ain't no chance. I don't learn as fast as some guys."

"That may be true, but you didn't answer my question. Don't you want too. . . ?"

"Oh, heck, Miss Brown. Any dumb teacher should know that all kids want to learn to read."

"Well, this dumb teacher ain't seen you act like you wanted to learn anything," she stormed back at him in the same tone he had used.

His eyes gleamed with surprise. "Gosh, I guess you ain't, have you?"

"Now that we have that settled, there are two other things we'd better settle." She looked him right in the eyes.

"What?" There was a glimmer of interest she hadn't seen before.

"First, I can help you. Do you believe that?" He nodded.

"Second, and more important, you've got to help yourself."

"Huh!" he grunted.

"Let's see if we can find out just why you have reading trouble. Do you know? What is there about reading that bothers you?"

"Heck, I just can't read like other guys my age."

"Why?"

"How do I know? Cause nobody ever learned me, I guess," he answered as truthfully as he saw it.

"If you're going to improve, you must stop blaming someone else and get with it. Now, look at this book." She pushed over an open book.

He looked down at the page and back at her.

"You already know in your head what is written there. When you look at this material, why can't you read it?"

"I just don't know the words. I used to memorize what they looked like, but there got to be so many I couldn't remember them all and I got further and further behind. I don't know how to figure how they say what they say." He shook his head. He was tired of talking. "What's this word, Miss Brown?"

She told me later, that inwardly her heart shouted hallelujah. Outwardly she pulled over a pencil and paper and wrote:

tri   oval

Larry's finger covered the o and he said, "That's Val. We gotta girl in class named Valerie. We call her Val. Oh, that Val! She's a card. Do you know Val, Miss Brown?"

(You see, one of the characteristics of students such as Larry is that they have short attention spans. With the slightest provocation, their minds drift off. This practice causes them to miss many salient points in lectures, in discussions, and in reading. One of the teacher's biggest jobs is to hold their attention. How would you pull Larry back to the word?)

"Yes, I know Val. Let me ask you a question. Is there anything about Val that you would call oval?"

"Hey, that's it. I know that." He pointed to the syllable on paper. "Man, yeah. She's oval all over."

"Give me the specific names of parts of the body where you say Val is oval. The exact dictionary name."

"Now, that ain't fair, Miss Brown. You're sneaky. You know I'm no good with words. Let's see. Her face. That's a good dictionary word, right?" He laughed. He'd outwitted his teacher.

She nodded, smiling. "Another one."

"Hey . . . her . . ." he stammers, then motions with his hands to indicate her figure.

"Give me the word."

"Her figure, her hips, her legs, her . . . gosh, her all over."

"Look at this part of the word again. What is it?"

"Oval."

"Good. What does it mean?"

"Round."

"Exactly round, like a ball?"

"I guess. I don't know. Never thought about it till now."

Miss Brown pulled over the dictionary. "Here. Find the word and let's see what it says."

Larry fumbled with the dictionary, in no hurry, because, you see, Larry is never in a hurry. Miss Brown waited patiently thinking of all the other students in her school which need this same kind of help. No wonder teachers let them slip by. With 30 to 35 individuals, how can the classroom teacher put this much time on each child who needs it?

Finally, he finds the word. "Here it is. It says: (1) hav, having a figure or shape of an egg v, vew, ew, viewed-ll-ll, what's this? lengthwise. (2) Re, re, what's this? Yeah, resembling an ell i ps. Wow. What a word! Ell i ps. What's that?"

(You're the teacher. What would you do now?)

Well, to make a long story short, Miss Brown asked Larry if he ate eggs. Then she told him to look at her face and describe its shape. (Luckily, she had the right shape.)

"Hey, I know now where I heard that word. My mother told Sue, that's my baby sister, that she ought to wear her hair style to suit her oval face. She'd look better. That word (he points) means round but not completely. Right?"

"Right. Now, look at the other part. What does it say?"

"Try, tree, I don't know."

"What other words do you know that begin with t-r-i?"

"Trip."

(Isn't that the way it goes! You have the structure all set up, you think, and they blow it. Now, where to?)

"What else?"

"Trial."

"Keep going. Some more."

"Let's see. In math last week, Mr. Queen talked about triangles."

"What's a triangle?"

"A three-sided figure."

Miss Brown sighed. Ah, at last.

"So *tri* on a word has something to do with the meaning, you think?"

"Yeah. Tricycle, triplets. Let's see. There was something else in math. Tri, tri, something to do with circles. What was he talking about? Trisect? Is there any such word as trisect?

Miss Brown nodded. "What was he doing?"

"Cutting up circles and . . ." he paused, frowned, then exclaimed joyously. "Hey, man. This is neat. Now, I know what the dumb word means. Cut the circle three times. I never really understood what he was talking about in class. Well, I'll be dogged."

The beginning of the skill of structural analysis—understood in the tenth year! How sad. How many students, how many teachers?

The discovery technique in operation. No one called it that at the time. But you know the ending of Larry's story. When his six weeks with the reading teacher were up, he asked if he could come back and was heartbroken when she told him no. Someone else needed to come worse than he did. His final comment when he left that last day was, "Thanks, Miss Brown. I just may drop around to this dumb room after school sometimes. Is that all right?"

Everytime Miss Brown tells Larry's story, she cries. Like many other school success stories, it did not carry over into his regular classes. No one else had the time. They had to cover pages of materials.

Despite his success with Miss Brown, Larry dropped out of school the next year. Now, he has little children ready to enter the school system and dreads the day. Can we blame him?

If all teachers in the first six years of school life gave help with the decoding skills, then worked on building concepts, there would be fewer problems. Just a few pointers on how to approach new words, if instead of memorizing rules, rules, rules, you reinforce words and skills by frequent *practice* there might be less criticism channeled your way.

What are some other things Miss Brown might have used to capitalize on Larry's inherent interests and knowledge? We said earlier that he is interested in cars. What reading skills would fit into a study of cars?

Hot Rod It

There are many ways for vocabulary development. For remedial "I-don't-care" students, the teacher may want to find (no, let *students* find) as many words and phrases having to do with the subject as she can—words which can be listed and used in a variety of practice exercises. Vocabulary and phrases used in newspapers, magazines, and other news media which a student who is interested can find, and the list might look like the following.

SPECIAL INTEREST READING VOCABULARIES: CAR RACING

tracks	*tires*
high banked	wheels and axle
2.66 mile trioval	new rubber

circular
long back chute
dirt apron
evasive action
handicap
strategy
freeway
outside pole position
slick as oil
infield racer's stand
wild melee of spinning machines

speed

acceleration
turning laps
posted fastest laps
front straightway collision
flying debris
sand bags
time trials
impact
flaming accidents
jarring grinding impact
disaster
caution
wind velocity
massive pile-up
major upsets
chain reaction
spun sickeningly
speed freaks
record breaking
speed demons

racers

portrait of depression
championship smile
triggered a controversy
contenders
qualification
popularity
businesslike demeanor
all-out assaults on racetracks
notorious-irascible manner
veteran sportsman
point standing

safety features
cord piles
bedded construction
fiberglass belts
traction
maximum mileage
hugs the highway
craftsmen recaps
shock absorbent
budget account
reduce tread "squirm"
efficiency
balance
bearings
evolution

engine

oxidation
chief machanic
pit crews
pistons
horsepower
reliable
mini-motor
hemi-motor
carburetor resister places
economy kick
turbo charged Porche engines
dependability
faulty magneto
exploded into flames
lubricant
cylinder

others

damaged alignment
officials
intercom
spectator sport
chassis
shattering glass
fireproof suits
genocide
dominated the circuit
low sleek styling

Organizational Skills

Many students, including some of the good ones, lack the skills of organization. That's one of their problems. Outlining, note-taking, summarizing, and following directions give them trouble. If they have failed in the "dull grammar" classes, and you want to teach the skill of outlining in a remedial class, don't mention the word outlining. You'll lose them before you begin. Use this approach. You know they are interested in cars.

ASK: What are some things you want to find out about cars? Let them talk.

MAKE: A beginning outline and let them fill it in from their present knowledge and add to it from research.

As they work, you'll hear conversations such as this:

"We've got twenty."

"Okay, smarty pants, we've got 19. Give us that book."

"Hey, did you know that a bulldozer is called a car?"

"No such thing."

"It is too. It says so right here in the encyclopedia."

"What encyclopedia?"

"The Encyclopedia World Book, that's what. And a motorcycle, too."

By now they're all gathered around READING the encyclopedia. A little noisy, yes, but oh what good noise!

(Of course, if you're that traditional deskbound, straight rows, quiet classroom, you'll go right on losing those potentials.)

After they use encyclopedias, encourage them to use magazines, newspapers, travelogues, brochures put out by auto manufacturers and any other material you or the class may have collected.

Let's go back to our basic lesson for teaching the skill of outlining and use it with this subject of cars. Begin with the single topics—the ones the students give you.

Step 1 in teaching the skill of outlining. *Name the big topics of interest.*

kinds of cars
body styles
jobs in the field
types of races
names in racing
associations in racing
facts about racing

Step 2. *Give numbers to the big topics.*

   I.   Kinds of Cars
  II.   Body Styles
 III.   Jobs in the Field
  IV.   Types of Races
   V.   Associations in Racing
  VI.   Facts about Racing

Step 3. *Fill in some sub-topics.*

I.   Kinds of Cars
    A. Ambulance
    B. Bulldozer
    C. Bus
    D. Farm Machinery
    E. Jeep
    F. Motorcycle
    G. Snowmobile
    H. Snowplow
    I. Tanks
       1. Destroyer
       2. Military
    J. Taxicab
    K. Tractor
    L. Truck

II. Body Styles of Cars
    A. Coupe
    B. Two door sedan or coach
    C. Four door sedan
    D. Limousine
    E. Convertible
    F. Hardtop
    G. Station wagon
    H. Sports Car
    I. Touring Car (open)
    J. Hot Rod
    K. Custom-built
    etc.

Step 4. *Fill in the details.*

III. Job Opportunities in the Auto Industry
    A. Unskilled: Factory assemble lines
       1. one operation
       2. good pay
    B. Skilled
       1. expert mechanics
       2. pattern makers
       3. chemists
       4. metallurgists
       5. tool & die makers
       6. physicists
       7. artists
       8. lawyers
       9. economists
       10. engineers
       11. writers for advertisements
       12. teachers and doctors

IV. Types of Races
    A. Speedway
    B. Stock Car
    C. Drag
    D. Road
    E. Midget
    F. Soap Box Derby
    G. Indy-type Cars

V.   Names in Racing
    A. DePalma, Ralph
       1. Races won
       2. Prix money
    B. Oldfield "Barney"
    C. Shaw, Wilbur
    D. Allison, Bobby
    E. Pearson, David
    F. Petty, Richard
    G. Isaac, Bobby
    H. Parsons, Benny
    I. Yarborough, Cale
    etc.

VI. Associations
   A. NASCAR
   B. U.S. Autoclub
   C. Antique Automobile Club
   D. Fisher Body Craftman's Guild
   E. Buckeye Cup Can-Am
   F. Daytona International Races
   G. Grand National
   H. Talladego 500
   I. Automobile Manufacturers Association of America
   J. Permatex 200 National Championship Sportsman Race

After students have their vocabulary and their outlines, put them to work on any number of activities you have set up, or anything they have an interest in learning. Remember, that in any activity both teacher and student should know the skills involved in the activity, how this skill can be used in many areas, and activities should be planned on levels of understanding and competencies of students.

Build, Build, Build Possible Activities for Study and Practice

Make jobcards, study guides, or whatever structure you wish to use, and put the students on their own to work. Give help only when needed. Here is a list of activities which might be used in a unit on cars. Some are simple, some are difficult. Student works where he can succeed on the skills he needs.

   I.   Draw and label the parts of your favorite style and kind of car.

   II. Follow the directions and assemble the model car in the center.

   III. Make a car alphabet. Use these directions to the student:

      (1) Write the alphabet in a vertical column down the left hand side of a sheet of paper.
      (2) Think of words having to do with cars, hot rods, racing or a connected category and make a car alphabet.
      (3) A beginning example: a—accelerator   b—brakes   c—carburetor
                               d—dashboard   e—and on through z.

   IV. Use any references available and see if you can find out the answers to these interesting facts about the car racing world.
      1. The longest world record for a racer is _____.
      2. The fastest record speed for an automobile is _____.
      3. The kind of car with which this speed record was set is _____.
      4. The largest cash prize ever awarded a racer is _____.
      5. The largest race track in the world is _____.
      6. The most expensive car in the world to date is _____.

7. The number of racers killed on the tracks is approximately _____.
8. How does a racer select his pit crew?
9. Who sponsors a specific racer?
10. Who decides the speeds a car can be built for?
11. What safety precautions must the builder of race cars take against fire?
12. What is the most expensive race car on record?
13. When did automobile racing first begin, what city and who drove?
14. Which car is better for racing, a heavy or light weight one?
15. How does the wind help or hinder a driver in a race?
16. What other kinds of races can you find out about? (horse, pigeon, turtle, etc.)
17. What should a driver do if criminals order him to throw a race?
18. What percentage of his prize money must a racer pay in taxes?
19. How did your favorite racer get into the business of racing?
20. Which rubber company makes the most enduring tires?

V. Race Tracks

List the major race tracks in the United States and the prizes they pay to winners.

VI. History of Racing

Make a timeline showing the history of automobile racing in America.

VII. Laws

Who makes the laws which control automobile racing and which one do you think is most fair or unfair?

VIII. Gambling

Is it legal to gamble at races? Explain your answer.

IX. Moonlighting

Many men race. Few men win. What other ventures do racers get into to make money? (advertise for companies, work in garages, let companies use their names on merchandise, etc.)

X. Unions

Do race drivers have a union? If so, is it good or bad?

XI. Insurance

Will all companies sell insurance to race drivers? Why or why not?

XII. Interview

Write a letter of invitation to a race driver to come to your school. Prepare in advance some questions you want to ask him. After the interview, write a thank-you note to him.

XIII. Build a Model Race Track

Build a model race track to specifications. Keep in mind these concepts: elevated tracks, grandstand seats, guard rails, pit space, pit crew signs, etc.

XIV. Art

Make a poster showing the history and development of cars. Expand it into a bulletin board if you like.

XV. Speech, Grammar and Organized Practice

Write a speech about the part of racing which appeals to you. Put it on tape for others to hear. Here are some possible topics you might like to find out about.

a. My new motor design for race cars
b. Racing should be abolished
c. How racing has changed in the past twenty years
d. The history of cars
e. My favorite race car driver
f. Felson and his books about hot rods
g. What to do if your car catches on fire
h. How to get along with your pit crew
i. Sportsmanship on the racetrack
j. What I would do with a million dollars

XVI. Extending Sentences

A. A fun (English) lesson for any type student is that of creative writing. One trick which any student can do, if taught how, is that of taking a kernel sentence and extending it into a longer one by answering these questions about the kernel idea. *Sentence:* The driver won the race. What driver? Where? When? How did he feel? What kind of car? With his championship strategy of purposefully staying a few feet behind the lead racer for 99 of the 100 laps, _____ (name of current champion) triggered a controversy when, like a pistol shot, he slammed that low slick turbo charger past his one contender and in the last two seconds of a grueling, grinding, wild melee of spinning machines won the photo finish in the Talladego 500.

B. *Just suppose type of creative writing*
Suppose for one week everyone in the world agreed to use no type of automotive transportation. Tell what you think might happen during that week.
a. How would we compensate?
b. What would happen to the food industry?
c. What would happen in peoples' homes, offices, schools?
d. What are some alternatives?
e. What would be the emotional tone of the week?

XVII. Old Driver Manuals

Use the old driver manuals and tests in our reading center. Study the Manual first and take some of the sample tests. When you think you know most of the information, make a test for another student to take. Also, make the key for correct answers.

XVIII. Free Reading

Choose one of the books in your bibliography or another one that you know about and read it. When you finish you may, or not as you choose, tell the teacher why you liked or disliked the book.

XIX. Newspaper and Magazines

Pick up your favorite daily newspaper or current magazine and check for racing news. Share it with someone if you like.

XX. Accentuate the Positive

There are many games, commercial and teacher-made, which can be added to your learning centers. They will teach, reinforce and/or initiate other activities which utilize the vocabulary of this unit. A few examples are listed here.

A. Following Directions:

Look at these wheel words. Use them to fill in the blank spaces below to see if you can find the mystery word.

tire   bike   wagon   wheels   round   diameter

1. The third letter in the third word.
2. The fourth letter in the first word.
3. The second letter in the third word.   __ __ __ __ __
4. The first letter in the fifth word.
5. The sixth letter in the fourth word.

B. Practice with Naming, Action and Describing Words

Directions: 1. Student calls name of some object, car or part of car, race, etc., or some concept dealing with the unit.
        2. Second student gives an action word or phrase which will go with the first one.
        3. Third student gives describing words and/or phrases.

Examples:	Hot rods	speed	dangerously.
		shine	beautifully.
		streak	through the night.
	The freeway	allows	ordinary people to race.
	A circular track	calls for	expert mobility of cars.

C. Vocabulary Analogy Game—Motorcycle Anatomy (Adaptation. 87, p. 43)

Purpose: Motivation, especially for fellows. Word recognition. Involvement and fun. To use what they are interested in to get to what you want them to learn.

Materials needed: For retarded readers: two lists of words. One deals with body parts, the other with motorcycle parts.
        For students who only need a nudge, give directions and several examples.

Directions: 1. Make a list of words which name the body parts of a motorcycle. There could be as many as 40. Use references.
2. After you have your list, do the same thing with the parts of the human body. How many can you name?
3. Now the fun begins. See if you can associate the names of the motorcycle with the names of the body. Match them.

Fifteen is a good score. Twenty, very good. Twenty-five, excellent.

SAMPLE LIST	Body words	Motorcycle words
1.	legs	wheels
2.	hips	fenders
3.	nails	chrome
4.	nerves	ignition
5.	skeleton	frame
6.	kidneys	exhaust
7.	nervous system	battery
8.	adrenal glands	accelerator
9.	sweat glands	radiator
10.	vocal cords	horn
11.	muscles	motor
12.	nose	air intake
13.	stomach	carburetor
14.	feet	tires
15.	blood	gasoline
16.	lungs	air filter
17.	heart	fuel pump
18.	liver	oil filter
19.	spinal cord	transmission
20.	pelvis	differential
21.	eyes	lights
22.	heels	brakes
23.	synapse	spark plug
24.	posterior	back bumper
25.	skin	paint

D. Practice with Figurative Language

Use the well-known phrases in students' life to motivate their thinking about how words are used daily by people in all walks of life. What is meant by an individual when he says one of these phrases?

a. a wild goose chase
b. buy a pig in a poke
c. hug the tracks
g. know the ropes
h. chip on one's shoulder
i. face the music

d. break the ice
e. white elephant
f. engine purrs like a kitten

j. eat humble pie
k. track like a sea of glass
l. with a grain of salt

Let students talk about other figurative phrases which they may know or use. Some may want to find other interesting ways which people use to say things in a different pattern from the usual. Use the language of cars and the race tracks. How many unusual expressions can they find? In this way students can see the relevancy of words to their everyday life and are more interested in studying about language and how it is used.

Activity: Build Your Word Power— Practice with Vowel Digraphs

In this unit we have done several exercises. Figure 14.1 will reinforce vocabulary which you may have fun with. Remember a digraph is two letters working together, but only one is used in pronunciation.

Begin with number one and work your way around the wheel. Read the clue and think of a word which might fit. Use only words which have digraphs listed in the center. The answers are given on the last page of this chapter.

Activity: Build a Wooden Car (See figure 14.2)

Purpose: Motivation for reading
Practice in following direction

Materials needed: Old steering wheel with shaft. Can be picked up at most junk yards
2 pieces of 2 x 4 lumber
1 piece of 2 x 8 lumber about 16 inches long
1 piece of plumber's pipe 6 to 8 inches long
2 pieces of lumber 2 x ½, 16 inches long
nails
brace and bit, saw, ruler, pencil

Directions:
1. Measure and saw pieces of 2 x 4 lumber. You need 4 of them 16 inches long. (Can be longer if higher car is desired.)
2. Measure one piece of 2 x 4 lumber 12 inches. Saw it.
3. All pieces in numbers 1 and 2 must be sawed at an angle on one end.
4. Bore a hole the size of the pipe in the 12 inch piece of lumber.
5. Nail legs on to a 2 x 8 piece of lumber at an angle about 6 inches from the end.
6. Nail remaining 12 inch piece at an angle on top at one end of the 2 x 8.
7. Fit pipe into hole in handle.
8. Nail 3 x ½ braces to legs.

9. Insert steering wheel shaft into pipe.
10. Sand just enough to remove splinters.
11. Ready for children to play with. Can be painted but not necessary.

FIGURE 14.1

Vowel digraph wheel

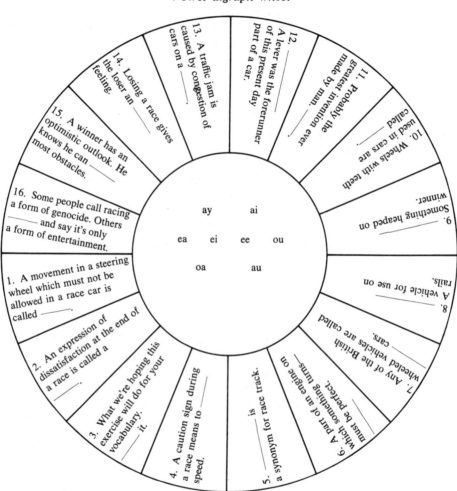

A piece of equipment like this in a K–3 classroom (even higher in some cases) is worth every effort put into making it. Less expensive, more fun, more durable than a shiny new red car from a toy shop, and caters to the imaginative play of children.

When students have failed for seven or eight years in our public schools, no wonder they become discipline problems. They have to succeed at something. A creative teacher will change this. If they make a car like this for the primary children, think of all the help they're getting: reading, arithmetic, spelling, involvement, fun, and the building of self-concept. This last one so needed by most of them!

FIGURE 14.2

Build a wooden car

Answers to the "Build Your Word Power" Wheel:

play, complaint, increase, race course, gears, jaunting, freight car, praise, decrease, gears, wheel, steering wheel, roadway, unpleasant, surmount, disagree.

Activities for the Teacher

1. Ask a group of students what they would like to study about for the next two weeks. Plan some activities around their answer. Take the students through some of the activities. What are their reactions? Share with your peers.
2. If you are not working with a class, choose a topic which you think will be of general interest to students you hope to work with in the future and do a unit of work around that topic. Research to see what materials are already available on the subject, then choose, adapt, and make exercises that will motivate for, teach, and reinforce skills, as well as concepts, you want them to learn.

FIFTEEN

Reading in a Revolutionary Society

What techniques have been used in the previous chapters to help individualize instruction?
What is a learning module?
What is a learning activity package? (LAP)
Should every student be required to cover every chapter, take every test, and do every page in the workbook?
What is the fallacy of behavioral objectives?
Suppose you are in a school which remains traditional, or that you are moved into such a school. What can you do in your self-contained classroom to individualize instruction?

A sixty-year-old principal lambasted today's noisy permissive classroom:
"Nobody cares about learning any more. All they want is to be entertained and to play. Well, they waste enough time at home and on the streets doing nothing. School should teach them discipline. What worked for me will work for these kids."

He kept his straight rows, he gave tests every Friday, and students (those who could) learned. Those who couldn't stayed home as often as possible. "After all," he commented, "We still have to have garbage collectors. If everybody gets a good education, who'll do the work?"

In traditional classes, you tell students to read a certain chapter and the next day you lecture or ask questions. By doing this you assume that all students learn in the same way. Of course, you know they don't, nor do they have the same interests. But this is the way it has been done. It's still the easy way.

The trend today is toward individualized instruction and learning. This means changed teacher behavior as well as changed student behavior. You must be competent in diagnosis and let students know what they need to learn, how they can

331

learn it, and how they can evaluate their progress. In addition to diagnostic procedures there must be organization and materials on various levels and interests. Students must be given options: different ways of approaching the tasks of learning.

Is there a way to individualize your instruction? Yes. Set up your own classroom and do an efficient job of teaching. When children get excited about learning, when they begin talking about what's going on in your class, other teachers will ask questions. Don't brag, don't belittle other's efforts, don't try to change them. Simply answer their questions honestly, show them if they are interested. Act as the catalyst for better practices. Every school needs someone to serve in this capacity. It may be uncomfortable at times, but it's the minds of the students you're battling for.

If you can, go to professional meetings, then come back and share what you learn. If you're asked to, lead an in-service workshop or serve on the committee to improve your school. If you read an exciting article in a professional magazine, pass it along. But be aware of the fact that you won't always be accepted. I remember spending a week at one of the most rewarding conferences on using films and other media in the classroom I've ever attended. I came home excited and full of ideas to pass on to my teachers. I even made plans and ordered a film to demonstrate with, only to be told by the county office that teachers didn't like so many meetings and I couldn't have one. (This same office had paid approximately $100 for my week—supposedly to get help to pass on to other teachers.)

How Does One Individualize a Classroom?

According to several sources (35, 8, 55, 105, 147), the basic ingredients necessary for individualizing instruction are:
1. Attitude: You must feel that the child is more important than the group or the chapters of a book. You must also be sold on the idea of individualizing to meet student needs.
2. Materials: You must have all kinds and levels of teacher-made and commercial materials, machines, and equipment.
3. Diagnosis: You must be a diagnostician. A medical doctor doesn't prescribe pills before he examines the patient. Neither should you. Find out where the learner is in relationship to subject matter or skills you want to present. (See chapter 2.)
4. Ways to implement individualization in the classroom:
   a. Levels of questions according to levels of understanding
   b. Contracts
   c. Modules
   d. Independent Study
   e. Learning packets, kits, etc.
   f. Programmed Instruction
   g. Learning Centers

h. Flexible Groupings: Large and small groups, skills group, peer groups, tutoring, interest groups, paraprofessionals, committee assignments, and so on.
5. Ways of Assessing Learning

The Learning Module

The learning module (35) is a set of activities set up a facilitate students' success in accomplishing some learning task. It usually consists of these elements:
1. Title: What is it?
2. Overview: Our goal and why we're doing it.
3. Terminal Objectives: What will student be able to do when he or she completes the work in the module?
4. Pretest: If he can already perform the task, he shouldn't waste time doing the module.
5. Enabling Activities: What the student should do to get where she's going. Series of activities designed to lead the student toward performance of objectives.
6. Posttest: Did he learn to perform? If so, go on to next module. If not, go back to number 5 for more activities until the student can demonstrate mastery.

Modules can be made on most any subject. The main value of modular work is that student does not have to go through the tasks if he is already proficient in the skills. All students do not need the same help, structure, or learning. Giving them the same has produced and continues to produce boredom, frustration, and disgust with school.

A Sample Module*

Title:	Ralph Bunche—Statesman
Overview:	The black race has produced some statesmen who have achieved world-wide fame. The purpose of this module is to become acquainted with one of the outstanding black American statesmen.
Terminal Objective:	The learner will list five facts that led to leadership qualities found in Ralph Bunche.
Enabling Objectives:	1. The learner will read the mimeographed sheet about Ralph Bunche and answer the questions at the bottom of it with 80 percent accuracy.
	2. The learner will take part in a discussion with the teacher about the life of Ralph Bunche.

* This module was made and used by Jerri Collier, a Georgia classroom teacher.

	3. The learner will list on paper five facts that led to leadership qualities that are found in Ralph Bunche with 90 percent accuracy.
Pre-Assessment:	List five facts that contributed toward making Ralph Bunche a good leader.
Enabling Activities	1. Read: a. Mimeographed sheet on Ralph Bunche and answer questions at the bottom.
	b. *Famous Black Americans,* by Carl Smith, pages 103–12.
	2. Listen: a. To student-teacher discussions on Ralph Bunche.
	b. Tape: "Ralph Bunche."
Post-Assessment:	3. View Film: "Ralph Bunche and the U.N."
	List five facts that contributed toward making Ralph Bunche a great leader.

Contracts

A contract might be described as a cluster of activities designed for a child to pursue individually. It should be on some skill where he or she needs work and should be appropriate to his level and degree of independence. A language arts contract could deal with finding key words in sentences, leading toward key ideas in paragraphs. The student contracts with the teacher on how many of the varied activities he/she wishes to do, and for what letter grade, by a designated time agreed on by both.

There are certain cautions which should be exercised in using contracts with students.

1. Contract should fit the needs of the child. What skill needs to be developed?
2. While paper and pencil tasks are appropriate, some activities should not involve them.
3. Provide for student choice at any level.
4. State instructions clearly and simply.
5. State in simple behavioral terms at the beginning of the contract how completing it will help the student and what he should be able to do.
6. Break tasks into a sequence of steps easy enough to accomplish and hard enough to challenge.
7. Open-ended tasks should be used so students go their own directions. Even slow students need this opportunity.
8. Provide for self-checking when appropriate.
9. Develop a serious attitude toward contracting and record keeping by the individual student.
10. Some students cannot handle individual independent work and will need more structure and guidance than others. Watch out for the following difficulties which you may need to deal with:
    a. rushing through tasks to get finished
    b. complaining

   c. talking and wasting time (consistently)
   d. excessive dawdling
   e. inattention to instructions or details
   f. looking at the clock excessively
   g. unfinished contract tasks
   h. sloppy and/or no record keeping of tasks performed
   i. copying from peers

Sample Contract: Affixes

Purpose: To acquaint the student with affixes and help him to understand how they change the meaning of a word.
To extend the students' vocabularies by adding meaning to base words.
To practice using affixes. (Student will do contract only if needed.)

Objectives: The student will learn to:
      recognize the form and meaning of prefixes.
      recognize the form and meaning of suffixes.
      understand how an affix can change the meaning of a word.
      use suffixes and prefixes with words to give new meaning.
      relate concepts learned to new situations.

Directions: After initial introduction of affixes by teacher, and after pretest to discover who (if any) needs additional help and practice on the skill of recognizing and/or using affixes, the teacher and student discuss the contract. Time for its completion is agreed upon and both student and teacher sign. Upon completion of contract (may ask for help if needed), student takes post test. Hopefully, he will perform successfully. If not, further steps must be taken to help him.

Grades:
    For grade of *C:* Exercises I, II, IV, V, VII.
    For grade of *B:* Exercises I-VIII.
    For grade of *A:* Total.

    I agree to complete this exercise on suffixes and prefixes by the following date.

    Name: ———————————————————
    Teacher's Name: ——————————————
    Date of Completion: ————————————
    Grade I plan to work for: ——————————

A. Working with Prefixes

    The prefix is a syllable at the beginning of a word. A prefix added to a word generally alters the aspect of the idea.
Below are listed some of the most used prefixes, together with their meaning and qualifying words.

Prefix	Meaning	Qualifying Word
ab	away from	absent
ambi, amphi	both	amphibian
ad	to	adhere
ante	before	anteroom
anti	against	antibody
auto	self	autobiography
be	by	beside
bi	two	bicycle
circum	around	circumference
com, con, co	together	combine
contra, counter	against	contraband
de	from, down	depart
dis	not, away	disagree
en	in	enroll
ex	out	export
hemi	half	hemisphere
hyper	above	hyperactive
hypo	under	hypodermic
il, ir	not	illegal
mis	wrong	misinform
multi	many	multitude
non	not	nonskid
op	against	oppose
out	over, surpass	outshine
para	beside	paragraph
per	through	pertain
poly	many	polysyllable
post	after	postdate
pre	before	pretest
pro	in front of, before	program
re	back	redo
semi	half	semicircle
sub	under	submarine
super	above	superintendent
syn, sym	together	sympathy
trans	across	transworld
ultra	above	ultramicroscopic
un	not	untried

Some Suggested Activities for Working with Prefixes

I. Place the prefix *un* at the beginning of the words and give their meanings.

_____settled   _____importance
_____happy   _____finished
_____interesting   _____learned
_____open   _____paralleled
_____loved   _____inhabited
_____able   _____satiated

Use another prefix which is interesting to you and work with it as you did with *un*.

II. Decide on the meaning of each of the words below by looking at the prefix.

postpaid_____   dehydrate_____
misspelled_____   automatic_____

semicircle_____   ultramodern_____
Interstate_____   transcontinental_____
antislavery_____   disablement_____

III. Check the words below. If they have a prefix, write *pre* in the blank space.

_____impossible	_____union	_____unafraid
_____vita	_____understand	_____disaster
_____incomplete	_____dishpan	_____foreground
_____incorrect	_____uncle	_____morbid
_____disobey	_____improve	_____rejoin
_____compensate	_____reappear	_____grandmother
_____remodel	_____misty	_____formal

B. Working with Suffixes

A suffix is a syllable added at the end of a word and usually changes the original word to a different class or kind. Some of the most often used suffixes are listed here.

able	capable of being
age	act or state of
al	relation to
ate (noun)	one who
ate (verb)	to make
ble, ible	capable of being
den, dom	state or condition
er	little, maker of
est	comparison
ful	capable of being
ian	relating to
ise, ize	to make
ism	act of
ly	like, in manner
less	without
ment	state or quality
ship	relationship
ster	one who
tion	state or condition
ward	direction of

IV. Write *er* and *est* after these words. Then use them in sentences.
old
long
short

V. Write the suffix *ly* after each word and give a meaning of each new word.
exact _____
quiet _____
careful _____
quick _____

slow _____
precise _____
adequate _____

VI. Write the meaning of the words below. Circle the suffix and underline base word.

painful _____
wonderful _____
improvement _____
unforgivable _____
slowly _____
randomly _____

wonderful _____
thoughtfully _____
manly _____
farmer _____
kingdom _____
lonely _____

VII. Add prefixes, suffixes, or both to the base words. Make as many words as possible by using the base words given below.
Example: *kind* kindly, kindness, unkind, unkindness, unkindly, kinder, kindest, unkindest, superkind, unkindliness, etc.

honest _____
tell _____
happy _____
port _____
employ _____

learn _____
space _____
believe _____
comfort _____
fire _____

VIII.   Use the Cloze procedure with affixes. Read the paragraph for context clues. Then look at the base words at the end of the paragraph. Can you decide which word belongs in which blank space and figure out what form of affix will make the meaning clear to someone else who reads the material? Fill in the blank spaces. Then check at the end of this contract to see how close you came to the author's words.

Jan Newman cocked her head to one side, stuck her finger in her cheek and (1)_____ signed. Her eyes sparkled (2)_____ as she listened (3)_____ to the final rehearsal. She had goaded them (4)_____, almost to the point of hate, during practice. She was like that. Her own intelligence, ambition, and (5)_____ challenged the most (6)_____ to do his best, even to stretch beyond (7)_____, (8)_____limits. "You were (9)_____. I'm proud of you," she told her (10)_____ choir members as they (11)_____ finished the last number and folded the music.
They gazed at her (12)_____. Was this their usual (13)_____, (14)_____ director complimenting them?
The base words: rest, satisfy, audible, perservere, brilliant, mercy, believes, sloth, youth, happy, tentive, seem possible, delight.

IX.   Make Your Own

The hardest and most important part of any learning is the task of using the ideas, words, concepts, or whatever you're attempting to learn. There is really no point to memorizing affixes and their meanings. The point is to use them to make your language, both spoken and written, more meaningful and interesting.

Would you like to show how well you know affixes, what they are and do, and how you can be creative in using them? If so, make some sentences, or write a story similar to the one above, and let your friends try to figure out what you mean.

Another task which you might enjoy is to take one of the books you are reading and rewrite some of the material in it. Use different affixes to change or extend meaning. Make the material negative. Use a few affixes to change the entire meaning. Have fun with this and then let your teacher enjoy it. Can she figure out what was there before you reshaped it?

Sample Contract for Language Arts

Title: Vocabulary Building

Objective: Student will be able to use correctly five new vocabulary terms when he finishes this contract.

Task I.   Examine closely the material in the five jars on the window ledge. Write the names of each on a piece of paper. Ask for help in spelling or look them up in the picture dictionary or the encyclopedia.

Task II.   Use your dictionary to find the meaning of the underlined words listed on the chart behind the jars. Write the sentences on your paper and for each underlined word, use a different word which means the same thing (a synonym).

Task III.   Think about some words that talk about the things in the jars, that describe what they look like, feel like, or smell like. Write down on your paper 5 words that describe the materials in each jar.

Your choice: Select two (more if you like) of the following things to do.

Task IV.   Change the sentences in Task II to make them negative.

Task V.   Find five words in your current library book which you think might stump your partner or the class. Write the words and make a check mark beside each one your partner knew. (Be sure that you know what they mean.)

Task VI.   Write a "nonsense" story or a sensible story using the words in Task I.

Task VII.   Write on your paper the words which have affixes. Identify the meaning of each. (Use dictionary or any other source.)

Task VIII.   If you don't know them, learn to spell the five new words.

Some Advantages of Contracts
1. Student has some say in how he schedules and uses his time.
2. Student faces his own needs.
3. Contract work permits self-discipline, in fact, demands it.
4. Student becomes self-initiated in learning tasks.
5. Student must learn to do critical thinking—important vs. unimportant.
6. Student learns to organize time and data.
7. Student must take part of the responsibility for evaluating his progress.
8. Student doesn't feel trapped in merry-go-round of materials he has no interest in. Can see a way through 3, 4, or 5 days in comparison to six weeks or a semester.

Programmed Instruction

Another popular way to get into individualization of instruction is through the use of programmed materials (37, 59, 72, 122). These come in many forms. One of the best instruments in the classroom is the tape recorder. With the advent of cassettes, this has become even easier to use. Programmed materials include:

A. Tapes for:
    1. giving instructions or directions
    2. lecture on any topic
    3. student performances—plays, reading stories, etc.
    4. reading textbooks
    5. drill
    6. guiding filmstrips and slide viewing
    7. music to study by
    8. to give tests
    9. record of pupil progress—record his oral readings at beginning of period, and some time later listen to the difference.

B. Teaching machines and all the materials which go with them
C. Workbooks, work sheets, study guides. Both teacher-made and commercial.
D. Films, filmstrips, slides, records, tapes—all which the children can learn to manipulate.
E. Creative activities and games.

Advantages of Programmed Learning

1. Small bits of information are presented at one time
2. Student can progress at his/her own rate (if he/she is correctly placed to begin with)
3. Instant feedback, both self-checking and sequenced
4. Repetition of skills
5. More efficient use of teacher time
6. Individualizes—student doesn't have to wait to be told what to do
7. Some types will motivate some students (such as machines for apathetic boys)
8. Student and teacher knows skills to be worked on
9. Student must learn to plan and organize his or her work and time
10. Some programmed materials tell him why he is right or wrong and send him back if he is wrong

Disadvantages of Programmed Learning

1. Student may waste time or go so fast that he or she doesn't really learn
2. Student may always choose and even redo easy materials
3. Work may become busy work
4. Monotonous
5. Mechanical, no rapport with teacher
6. Requires mountains of time and materials—teacher must plan and prepare

7. Student may copy neighbor's work
8. Record keeping

Grouping

Grouping has been around a long time: the traditional three reading groups, the so-called homogeneous groupings, and the tracks in secondary school. These were usually fixed groups and unyielding. In attempting to individualize, use is made of a more flexible organization which is constantly changing to meet the needs of the students. There are large groups for (1) giving directions or instructions, (2) information and announcements, (3) interest discussion groups, and (4) groups to view a film, to listen to a lecture, and so forth. However, the small group is the most effective way to really teach. That's where working on projects, learning and practicing of skills, and working in a society of peers takes place.

In smaller groups we can have: a one-to-one (tutoring) buddy system, (2) a group leader in small group teaching, and (3) paraprofessionals to help to meet individual needs.

Laps—Learning Activity Packets

Learning Activity Packets are just what the term implies—groups of highly motivating activities, sequenced and produced to lead the learner toward successful performance.

Learning Centers

Learning centers (games, study guides, activities used all through this book) are ideal ways for individualizing classroom activities. However, along with their advantages, like every other approach to the teaching-learning situation, these have built-in problems similar to programmed learning and contracts, which you must be aware of.

Contracts, LAPs, machines, and other programmed materials should be used in learning centers.

Some Other Problems in Individualizing Instruction*

1. Identification of the competency or skill we want student to get.

Making him or her aware that he or she needs to learn it.
Making him aware that he can learn it.
Making her aware that she has learned it.

---

* Based on information in sources 35, 55, 106, and 147.

2. Assessment of these competencies.

Do they learn any more or any better under this system than formerly?
How do we measure them? On performance, on knowledge, on both?
If they fail, is it the fault of the teacher, the materials, the student?
What happens in learning (between student and teacher) is not easily measured.

3. Time.

To have individual conferences with students and with their parents.
To diagnose daily.
To make materials or find them to fit individual needs.
To keep records, both student and teacher must do so.
To observe performance.
To let students plan, organize, and evaluate their own learning.

4. Pacing.

Ideally, student should self-pace and take as long as needed. Is this practical?
Will it work? What if he plays around?

5. Grading.

Do you keep the traditional letter or number grades?
Does a student who finished ten modules in one week deserve a better grade
than does the one who worked consistently and successfully but finished
only five?
Will pass-fail work and/or satisfy?
Parent-student-teacher conferences when work is completed; are these to be
desired or will student-teacher written report satisfy? Some kind of
evaluation is necessary and difficult.

Oral Reading in the Middle
School Program

With all the emphasis on group activity, study guides, and individualized
learning, what is the place of oral reading. Has it lost its importance?

While the subject of oral reading in the school program is often a controversial subject, no one will deny that it is still important. The problem has come
from so many classroom practices where Round Robin oral word-calling has produced non-readers. Weak students are embarrassed, frustrated, and ridiculed. Good
students are frustrated, bored, waste time and see no purpose for what they are
forced to do. Behavior problems result from both situations.

Can oral reading be relevant for students during this middle age of their school life? Can students understand needs, purposes and rewards? Can teachers engender enthusiasm for oral reading performance? The answer to each of these questions is yes.

One eighth grade teacher and her class discussed the characteristics of a good oral reader and then made an attractive chart of the things to remember. When students had an oral reading task, they would check the chart to remind them of good practices. Some of the characteristics which soon became automatic for them were:

1. can pronounce the words
2. reads fluently
3. understands what he reads
4. is poised and self-confident
5. enunciates clearly and loud enough
6. uses a variety and appropriateness of tone, pitch and rate
7. interprets as he reads (understands punctuation marks)
8. avoids personal offensive mannerism
9. uses good posture and
10. enjoys the activity.

When Should Oral Reading Be Used in the Classroom*

For diagnostic purposes. Mistakes made during oral reading may give the teacher a clue to the kinds of errors a student makes in silent tasks. One caution should be kept in mind here: there may be words he cannot pronounce yet know the meaning of in context. Some points for which the teacher should check as she listens are:

a. pronunciation_____does he miss little or big words?
  does he get initial sounds and miss others?
  does he read so fast that he slurs words?
b. punctuation_____does he overlook periods, question marks, commas, etc.?
c. fluency_____what is his rate of decoding?
  is he reading everything the same rate?
d. substitutions
e. reversals
f. omissions
g. insertions
h. regressions
i. self-confident_____does he attempt to pronounce unknown words or say I don't know?
j. understands what he reads

---

* Based on information from sources 37, 53, 71, 59B, 71, 121, 161.

Oral reading can lead to literary appreciation. A good teacher model is an asset here.

Self-assurance and poise. Social assurance and emotional development may be developed through activities involving oral reading. Students may share jokes, interesting stories they have heard or read in materials other than textbooks, choral reading, etc. If one is no good in sports or other physical activities, he may excel in situations involving drama, reading, and other classroom experiences of like nature. These sharings will not produce poise and self-confidence overnight, but with practice, most students will improve.

Vocabulary and comprehension can be enhanced through oral reading. Teach the abstract concepts of emotion by having students read a familiar sentence showing fear, hate, anger, love, happiness, etc. "Mary had a little lamb, It's fleece as white as snow," and "Mammy's little baby loves shortening, shortening, Mammy's little baby loves shortening bread," are two favorites of my students.

To improve speech. When reading something they like, teacher can guide their practice in making the sounds they might be having trouble with in the materials they're using.

To provide enjoyment for others.

To communciate ideas.

To improve listening habits.

Prerequisites for Good Oral Reading

Pre-study. Students should practice silently before reading orally. They must know the words and teacher may need to give direct help.

Material should be on comprehension level of student. If he can't understand it himself, he can't communicate a message to listeners.

Good audience situations. Usually only one person should have the material to be read. (Exceptions—plays, choral readings, etc.)

Materials for oral reading should be of interest to the students. Student needs to know and react to the purpose for the task.

Teacher gives help with words and/or concepts before oral reading, if needed.

Student knows meaning of punctuation marks—can interpret. If not, teacher must help.

Criticism from peers, if given, should not be personal. Reading, not the reader, should be evaluated. Good points as well as errors need commenting on by teacher.

Student should get to practice reading orally before doing so for the group. (One of the most successful oral reading lessons in a college reading improvement class was with the use of paperbacks. Students chose a selection from a stack of perhaps fifty to survey for possible reading. They were told to survey the book, find a passage to read orally and sell the book to their classmates. They scanned the books looking for interesting portions, chose one, and practiced reading silently. I was walking around the room to give help when needed. When they were satisfied that they could read efficiently, I had them all practice reading orally, at the same time. After two practices of reading, putting as much expression as possible into it, books were laid aside and they listened to each other. Students thoroughly enjoyed the activity and actually created enough interest to get some of the books taken home to read.)

Oral reading should be functional, a part of the total school program, and with a specific purpose which students know and consider worthwhile. Some specific reasons for oral reading performance might be:
   a. to illustrate a point
   b. to prove a point
   c. to compare different author viewpoints
   d. to read an announcement, the minutes of meetings, reports, etc
   e. to make tape recordings of different interpretations of some passage
   f. to make tape recordings to keep to show improvement over a period of concentrated effort
   g. in dramatizations of plays, choral readings, puppet shows, radio and TV shows
   h. for pure enjoyment. This one is too often overlooked.

Oral reading should be pleasurable. Though listed under functions for oral reading, this one should be listed in a category all by itself. The things we like to do, we will do. Reading is no different. A teacher who sets up the atmosphere where oral reading is pleasurable and rewarding will have students asking for the time to do it. (Examples: The Claus family, The Preamble to the Constitution, or let them write "The Legend of Sleepy Hollow" as a drama and perform it)

Middle-Year Students and Appreciation of Books

There is little research on how to influence middle-year students to appreciate good literature and to read more. Probably the biggest problem is to stimulate teachers to put forth more effort in developing the tastes of children with whom you work.
Some steps in improving taste in literature.
   1. Listening. (Give him something interesting to listen to.) Yes. Teachers should read to students in these middle years.
   2. Help child become an independent reader. (Teach him to read and let him browse among books.) The linguists are telling us that language is inherent. Our job is to bring it out and encourage students to expand and use it.
   3. Ownership of books. Encourage book clubs, get parents or PTA to sponsor book clubs, etc.
   4. Let child discover comics (if he hasn't already.) Leads to wider interest and motivation toward reading skill. Don't worry that it's the comics he's reading.

5. When student recognizes reading can do things for him, (help him to get this understanding) he'll respond more positively.
6. Highest level of improving taste—when reader recognizes reading with the realization of what it can mean in his life.
7. Don't give "dumb" questions on everything nor require dull book reports.
8. A warm receptive atmosphere where students and books are brought together by a teacher who cares.

Motivation and interest must be based on the nature of the students themselves.
Some ideas to try are:

a. read to them—music to accompany—discussion
b. act out stories and poetry—let them write adaptations
c. laughter may bring interest to poetry—try humorous
d. students select stories, poems and music themselves
e. recording student's readings
f. book reports—can be worthwhile if handled competently—children given chance to discuss, disagree and even to say they don't like it without fear of recrimination from teacher
g. teacher asks questions and students answer as a character in the story
h. "Hit parade" of books—let them read anything
i. goals and objectives perceived by students
j. reading without a title—guess title from contents—see how close they can come to author's title
k. culmination—writing about something
l. literature is more than names and dates—train students to detect false from true, hollow and gaudy from simple and profound
m. activity more important than memorization
n. flexibility, appreciation for student effort, and enthusiasm on part of teacher.

Taste in reading and literature is not transferable, but may grow as maturation occurs, opportunity permits, and experiences are guided.

Evaluation

This brings us to the most sticky problem of all. Just as it is in the traditional classroom, evaluation or assessment of student learning in the individualized atmosphere is complicated, often unfair, and necessary.

What happens when you measure learning by changed behavior?

What happens when you accept the definition of reading as a cognitive process (thinking)?

You see or hear a word. You get a mental image (if concept is in your experience), you ask a question. Is it like something else you know or have heard about? How much do you know about it? What concepts are in your experience? Do you break it apart, put it together, disagree, accept or reject? How can you use it? What does it have to do with the other things you know?

If we accept even a limited few of the attempts at definitions made in literature, and we do, then the task of teaching, guiding, and evaluating remains. How does one evaluate a process? How does one assess reading as a thought process? We know we can't measure the complicated process called thinking, only certain aspects of it. What aspects and what measures?

Since words appear to control and guide most phases of communication, words must be the tools of thought. In order to know, we must learn to say, to give labels to concepts or classes of experiences. Just as the teacher's concept of reading will effect his teaching practices, it will also determine how he evaluates. In the past many teachers have thought of evaluation as a test to see "how much this kid knows about what I've been teaching, and his score will depend upon his I.Q." Today, the trend, at least in some areas, is away from these two mistaken assumptions.

All tests are samples of behavior (Kingston). Any score is one score for one task for one day. It may be twenty points more or less tomorrow. Measurement of reading comprehension should be based on an attempt to determine how well a student can accomplish a task with a given selection of material. What does the task in the learning center require of the child? Can he perform successfully?

The aim of teaching reading is to develop proficiency in satisfying some specified reading purpose accurately and economically. Anderson (3, p. 206) suggests giving the questions, purposes and problems before reading. Then the reader knows why he should read and for what. Don't keep questions hidden, he advises. A student is more likely to do accurate and purposeful reading if he knows what he's looking for. Evaluation asks: Did he find what he was looking for? If so, he succeeded with the task.

Most of us concede that the measurement of reading as a thought process is complicated. We read. What happens? It depends upon our personal background, personality, experiences, interests, understandings, purposes, etc. It is a personal kind of response.

How do we know what a student has learned? When he can do something he couldn't do before. How do we know whether he can do this something? Let him do it.

Evaluation (1) should be continuous, assessing both teaching and learning. (2) Goals should be set. What is it we plan to teach and later measure? (3) How can this measuring be used to improve instruction? (4) What instruments will we use: formal, informal, or both? (5) How does the student handle what he attempts? We observe performance in operation, the uses being the final product.

Each of these steps plus the interpretation of scores depend upon human judgment.

What skills can adequately be measured? Lenner (92) suggests:

1. General verbal factors. Vocabulary and how it is used.
2. Comprehension of explicitly stated materials. Can he follow directions, get literal meanings, perform reference skills?
3. Comprehension of implicit or latent meaning. Can he draw inferences, predict outcomes, apply problem-solving techniques, etc. (reasoning)
4. An element that might be termed "appreciation." Can he detect mood, author's purpose, patterns of materials, etc.

Guilford (70, p. 176) says we can train and measure certain types of thinking. He talks about three types.

A. *Divergent productive thinking.* This involves elaboration upon information in different directions.

Examples: 1. Using a letter of the alphabet as the basis, draw an animal
2. Given a piece of thin flexible wood in art, make an object not normally made of wood, (Japanese fan.)
3. Name all the concepts you can related to precipitation.
4. Today's headlines read "Women's Lib Group Demands More Money for Less Work." Give a reply as Jane Adams, St. Paul, or Mahatma Ghandi might give.

B. *Convergent thinking.* This type of thinking is not as exciting but is easier to teach and measure than divergent. It calls for right answers.

Examples: 1. Underline the verbs in a paragraph.
2. What caused the Chicago fire? (a book answer)
3. After study, list the causes of the American Revolution. Also, what were the effects on this country?

C. *Evaluative or critical thinking.* The basic abilities in critical thinking are less certain, relate to different values, interests and structural set-up. The student sets up his criteria, his standards, his conditions in relation to all he knows, and his purpose for evaluation.

Examples: 1. Should students strike to get changes they want?
2. Should students have a say in their final grades?
3. What is wrong with the practice of cheating?

When student is given statement of relationships and several alternative conclusions, he must determine, by premises, which is sound. According to some standard which must be set up before he begins, he examines, he chooses and asks under what conditions would this work? Do the conditions exist? Is there a better way? Evaluation involves sensitivity to problems and common sense judgment.

In addition to kinds of task teachers set up, many other techniques can be and are used to assess ability of students. Standardized and teacher-made tests plus many informal measures can be listed. Here are some possibilities.

Let students write original work
Informal Reading Inventories
Anecdotal records
Cumulative records
Tape recordings (keep tapes for comparison)
Product progress reports (keep samples of work)
Observations
Checklists
Sociometric forms
Let students talk, agree, disagree, defend
Let students write summaries
Let students tell stories
Let students get involved in grouped learning
Ask student how he's doing?

Lab report folders
Attitude change or lack of it
Number of books voluntarily read
Questionnaires on student opinion

Oral reading may be appraised by the quality of student identification with author's words. His tone, phrasing and inflection will give interpretation of the sentences. Yet, as stated elsewhere in this book, inability to demonstrate comprehension thusly may be a function of restricted language, restricted experiences and limited intelligence or combination of these rather than function of reading difficulty.

Students' reactions to and success with study gives us another way of evaluating or assessing student comprehension. Can he succeed with the tasks set up by the study guides? These do not call for memorized set of answers for a test score, but measures of understanding of reading. The usual types of tests with literal questions measure memory and/or recall more than they measure understanding. Students can memorize many facts and answer questions correctly, yet not understand the concepts at all. Most anyone, even trainable, can memorize answers. It often shows more intelligence to ask a good question than to memorize an answer from someone else. Having questions in one's mind as a result of reading attests to the fact that cognitive processes are at work.

SUMMARY

I hear and I forget
I see and I remember
I do and I understand

If we've learned anything about educational practices in the last decade, surely it is the wisdom of this ancient Chinese proverb. How many hundreds of thousands of student hours have been spent in rote memory of now obsolete facts! How many students learned to hate school and anything to do with it because they didn't have the capacity to retain as well as their peers. And we must not forget the "born free and equal" bit. The present generation decided to label us phonies. Are they justified? The only real equality human beings have is the amount of time allotted to each of us per day.

If public education is to continue as an institution, the school of the 1980s must be "schooling for life." Indeed, if not for living as successful citizens in adulthood, what is our purpose? Therein lies the key: *success.* Who is to say what the word means? Success imposed by external forces, by pressures and powers of social reinforcers, patterns taught by behavior modification in organized authoritative classrooms, or success for individual learners who have chosen their own values from the storehouse they've studied about? Success in making and dealing with problem-solving decisions.

One of the magnetic qualities of early television was its humanness—the mistakes of actors and technicians, and the spontaneity of audiences. Today's canned pretaped polished performances (if they can be described in such terms) are not nearly so interesting for the average viewer. The freedom of actors to take a chance, to run the risk of errors, and to do it in their own unique fashions, has an analogy in today's educational communities. Students need the chance to discover, to experience, to grow, and from their learning under mature guidance, to choose their own life-style according to their own inclinations.

There are values, motivations, charisma, feelings, and intentions of individuals which may be a direct result of good classroom practices but which can never be expressed or measured in behavioral terms. One teacher can work students to the *nth* degree and they enjoy it. Another teacher can give a minimum of work, yet students complain. What's the difference? How is this difference measured? One teacher can sit down with a group of students and one textbook and do more teaching in one-half hour than another can do all day with all the modern gadgets and materials.

Montessori said it long ago. Set up the structure, get out of their way, and let them learn. Make yourself unneeded in the classroom and you're a success. After all, isn't learning a form of self-discipline?

Individualization is one way to overcome some of our traditional stumbling blocks to excellency, every student competing with himself to improve according to his own potential in the tasks he's chosen—asking guidance, direction, and approval of his efforts—and accepting his own unique limitations and strengths. He knows, he can do, and he understands why!

Activities for the Teacher

1. Using the materials from the unit you are now working on in class, write a module for one of your classes.
2. Write a contract for one of the groups in your class which needs special attention.
3. Share the above tasks with your peers. Does either of them need revising?
4. Try out these two activities on some students. Study the results. Did students react any differently than they do from the traditional lecture, recitation, and test approach?
5. If you are not presently working with students, take your choice of the reading/study skills listed in chapter 12 and using available materials in the Reading Center, Curriculum Materials Center, and the Library, write a sample module and contract which you will be able to use in the future. When you make your test on them, make and label samples of both divergent and convergent questions on the material covered.

APPENDIX
Six-Weeks Plan for Study Skills—Grades 7, 8, and 9

Subject, Class, or Section: Remedial Reading, Section 1   9:00-10:00 A.M.

	MONDAY	TUESDAY	WEDNESDAY	THURSDAY	FRIDAY
LESSON	Using Source Materials to find information	Getting Acquainted with the Textbook, Motivation	The Newspaper and What It Tells Us	Use of the Index in locating information. Also, complete newspaper work	Reading tables
OBJECTIVES		1. Purpose of the Table of Contents 2. Develop skill in using it 3. Teacher observation of student use for future reference	1. To familiarize students with sections, make-up and information to be found in newspapers 2. To get across the concept that newspapers are functional	1. To develop skill in using index a. alphabetical list b. use of key words c. cross references	1. Practice in skill of reading tables for understanding 2. Become familiar with relationships and references used tables
MATERIALS	All reference materials available: encyclopedias, atlas and biographies, card files, thesaurus, almanacs, maps, dictionaries, periodicals	overhead projector, transparency of one page of table, work sheets, copies of any textbook they will be using	newspapers from two or three cities or several papers from the same city study guides (some examples found in this text)	overhead projector, transparency of page to be studied, work sheets, textbooks	duplicated copies of table from texts, newspapers or magazines, study guides
PROCEDURE	1. Handle and examine these sources 2. Discuss the information on them 3. Do study sheets in groups 4. Check 5. Discuss if you see a need (students do not know how to use) 6. Summarize	1. Ask name of last year's science book (probably won't know) 2. Discuss book in hand, set purpose 3. Project page x 4. Discuss what is listed there and how 5. Do worksheets 6. Summarize	1. Cover walls with papers before class 2. Discuss project 3. Talk about free speech, fact vs. opinion, advertizing 4. Give them study sheets and the privilege to work alone or with some one 5. Won't finish	1. Review table of Contents. Look at Index. 2. Discuss projected page 3. Do study sheets 4. Help with any point which needs clarification 5. Watch for areas where students need further help.	1. Give worksheets and watch how they handle the task 2. Answer questions as they arise 3. Look for other kinds of tables, graphs and charts in textbooks or other materials 4. Discussion with class only if needed
REACTIONS					

Subject, Class, or Section:	Remedial Reading, Section 1	9:00-10:00 A.M.

	MONDAY	TUESDAY	WEDNESDAY	THURSDAY	FRIDAY
LESSON:	Give an Informal Inventory on Skills	Finish IRI on skills, or discuss if they finished	"Civilization Strikes Again" or some other story.	Following Directions	Meaning of words in Context
OBJECTIVES:	1. To find out how well they can use the skills worked on last week. 2. To check comprehension of this text	If no discussion needed, talk to them about their study habits, how being a good reader depends partly on them, lead into topic of concentration. Elicit definition.	It's about time to read, they may tell you. Use a story fairly easy to let them succeed, but one full of interest	1. To reinforce the importance of reading directions carefully 2. To introduce concept of categories 3. Group process	1. To emphasize how much help writers give us with new words 2. To practice using some of these helps.
MATERIALS:	duplicated copies of Informal Inventory on your textbooks	textbooks and IRI on Skills used yesterday Film: "How to Concentrate" (11 min) Coronet —in most school media centers	copies of story, questions to look at before or after reading (your choice) Or: no questions, just read for fun.	directions and worksheets (many exercises given in this text or make your own)	duplicated copies of work sheets with sentences or material based on people and things they are interested in, if possible. Dictionaries, if needed
PROCEDURE:	1. Tell them no grades on Inventory. Simply to find out if they need any more help on skills. 2. Can they locate information? Tell them to work as fast and as accurately as they can. 3. Time according to your group, or not.	1. Let them finish IRI on Skills if they didn't finish yesterday. 2. Discuss IRI if needed. 3. Talk about study-habits and concentration. 4. Show film 5. Discuss it, if needed or interest.	1. Quick brief motivation for chosen story 2. Silent reading 3. Questions can be discussed if they show any interest 4. Or perhaps just general discussion. 5. Let students lead discussion (Too many times we destroy by discussion)	1. Let students do categorizing task 2. Group into fours and compare results 3. Do pre-planned worksheet of following directions, perhaps make something which would be of interest to them. Did they follow directions?	1. Group students according to needs. 2. Give work tasks according to these groups. 3. Do some task on using words in context. (Pre-planned by you) Let them talk among themselves. 4. Might do a choral reading.
REACTIONS:					

Subject, Class, or Section:	Remedial Reading, Section 1	9:00-10:00 A.M.

	MONDAY	TUESDAY	WEDNESDAY	THURSDAY	FRIDAY
LESSON:	Following Directions in textbooks	Following Directions — students in charge	Following Directions continued	Study of affixes in the structure of words	Study of affixes continued —the suffix
OBJECTIVES:	1. To stress the importance of reading accurately in texts 2. To show that this entails understanding vocabulary 3. To review word attack skills from last week	1. To demonstrate to students that they can take responsibility for their own assignments in science 2. Practice in the skill of following directions 3. Group process 4. Re-emphasize the fact that vocabulary must be understood in reading directions	1. To give each student chance to participate 2. To make reading functional for students 3. To demonstrate teacher's confidence in them	1. To review concept that the make-up of words can aid in getting meaning 2. To teach meanings of a few invariant affixes 3. To give practice in using prefixes to derive meaning	1. To review prefix in getting meaning from structure 2. Meaning of suffix understood 3. Practice in using
MATERIALS:	*The Physical World,* textbook; or duplicated copies of experiments, copper wire, rusty nail, carbon rods, copper chloride, dry cells, beaker, water, two test tubes	These will depend upon the make-up of groups and how level of reading limits or enhances the chosen experiments	Again this will depend upon types of experiments attempted.	clocks, history and biology texts, work sheets, microscope	same as yesterday

MONDAY	TUESDAY	WEDNESDAY	THURSDAY	FRIDAY
PROCEDURE: 1. Set purpose and motivate 2. Discuss directions do quick scan for any words they may not know 3. If any, preteach 4. Read directions silently 5. Elicit from students step-by-step directions and list them on board 6. Perform experiment 7. Evaluate — review steps. Ask how would process be used in real life? Erase and let students write up Rewrite steps and let students check their work 8. Make assignment for next two days Group according to interests or needs. Choose from list, experiment	PROCEDURE: 1. Groups assigned yesterday will do their assignment today 2. Have them write steps on board just as you did. 3. They perform the experiment and explain it 4. Summarize orally then write it up 5. Check work 6. Two experiments today 7. Remind groups for tomorrow 8. Summarize	PROCEDURE: 1. Follow same procedure as previous two days. 2. Let groups present their experiments 3. Discuss 4. Attempt to find out if they are seeing any relationships which you've hoped to build in their minds. 5. Two or more experiments today 6. Summarize	PROCEDURE: 1. Pre-test for meanings of those chosen to work on today. If they know, don't. If not, 2. Discuss sentences used and see if they can get meaning from context. 3. Try structure 4. Use concrete objects to explain clocks for chrono, microscope for micro, etc. 5. Have students read some pre-chosen essay of textbook where the words are frequently used. 6. Use dictionary — give specified time to find as many words as possible with the affix. 7. Summarize & Assign	PROCEDURE: 1. Check homework, if any 2. Review meanings of prefix and those learned yesterday 3. Talk about the list of suffixes you have ready to give them. 4. Let students think of words they already know which use them 5. Summarize 6. Make up exercises for use with your students, depending upon level on which they work. 7. Assignment, if any
REACTIONS:	REACTIONS:	REACTIONS:	REACTIONS:	REACTIONS:

Subject, Class, or Section:	Remedial Reading, Section 1	9:00-10:00 A.M.

	MONDAY	TUESDAY	WEDNESDAY	THURSDAY	FRIDAY
LESSON:	Word Recognition	Word Recognition continued	Word Recognition continued	Word Recognition continued.	Use of the Dictionary
OBJECTIVES:	1. To help students see they know more about word analysis than they use. 2. To have them discover the generalization that syllables (clusters) are units of sound.	1. To review yesterday's lesson 2. To practice with syllables as sound units 3. To introduce very briefly scanning	1. Practice 2. To use larger technical words that may not be divided according to rules 3. Overlearn	1. To review skills of previous lessons. 2. to add words that can't be pronounced phonetically 3. To figure out word from context	1. Review 2. To acquaint the students with the varied forms of information in dictionary 3. To review or teach the concept of guide words 4. Many meanings vs. one.
MATERIALS:	list of small nonsense words, list of larger nonsense words, worksheets for categorizing tasks, humorous story about words (your choice)	lists of words harder than yesterday's work sheets for categorizing (many in this text), transparency of page of index of texts, or Encyclopedia Guide	Anything you have available — choose to meet needs of students. SRA kits, programmed workbooks, *Be a Better Reader*, teacher-made exercises.	dictionary, worksheets, lists of words taken from reading material	dictionaries, study sheets, transparency and overhead projector, lists of words, film strip, and film strip projector
PROCEDURE:	1. Either you read to them, or let students read article 2. Let them give words which the article made them think of 3. Discuss how words are approached for pronunciation. Try some nonsense words 4. Do worksheet: "What's in a Dictionary?"	1. Set purpose by reviewing yesterday's concepts. 2. Talk about structure and how it helps analyze words 3. Try long words for pronunciation and meaning 4. Do worksheet on subject (some given in this text) 5. Scan transparency to find unknown words 6. Summarize	1. What you do today will depend upon what you found to be the needs from the previous days. 2. Might practice with some difficult words from students' assignments in other classes. 3. Might do some vocabulary puzzles or other fun exercises.	1. Review structure of words, affixes, compounds, etc. 2. Add words with no phonetic parts and practice on. 3. Do a different kind of categorizing task. 4. Do some reading to get meaning from context. Verify by using dictionary.	1. Review syllabication 2. Give practice with words from other class materials 3. Survey dictionary 4. Discuss guide words 5. Practice fast scanning in dictionary using guide words 6. Do worksheet as you discuss film 7. Do exercise on multiple meanings
REACTIONS:					

Subject, Class, or Section:	Remedial Reading, Section 1	9:00-10:00 A.M.

MONDAY

LESSON:
Identifying main idea by finding key words

OBJECTIVES:
1. To have students learn or reinforce the skill of recognizing key words
2. To have students know the meaning of key words and main ideas
3. To introduce concept of kernel sentences

MATERIALS:
overhead projector, regular textbooks, study guides on texts, practice sheet on kernel sentences, (exercises given in this book)

TUESDAY

LESSON:
Key words, main ideas and topic sentences

OBJECTIVES:
1. To review yesterday's work
2. To introduce use of topic sentences
3. To teach concept that topic sentence may contain main idea
4. Relating to assignments

MATERIALS:
humorous story or other material to be read by teacher, study guides on levels of students or work sheets similar to those given in this text

WEDNESDAY

LESSON:
Relationships of words, sentences and paragraphs

OBJECTIVES:
1. Succinct review of key words, main idea and topic sentence
2. To teach the concept that relationships exist and key words help to see this relationship

MATERIALS:
work sheets for practice from texts, commercial kits, or teacher-made kits

THURSDAY

LESSON:
Study of "Changes in the Earth's Surface"

OBJECTIVES:
1. To practice the reading and study skills in science material
2. To motivate for further reading
3. To have students involved in group process consider problem - solving techniques

MATERIALS:
textbook with this material in it, or duplicated materials for each student
work sheets
materials for teacher to use in preteaching vocabulary

FRIDAY

LESSON:
"Changes in the Earth's Surface" continued

OBJECTIVES:
To complete the work and study began yesterday. Could not possibly finish it in one day

MATERIALS:
Same as yesterday

PROCEDURE:	PROCEDURE:	PROCEDURE:	PROCEDURE:	PROCEDURE:
1. Sentences on board with one unfamiliar key word. 2. Let students try to figure meaning 3. How did they know? Discussion of importance of key words in sentences and paragraphs. 4. Dramatize some key words. "Fire," "Help!" 5. Oral practice with some material 6. Written practice 7. Group or alone, do work sheets on expansion of kernel sentences. Discuss any differences. 8. Summarize and evaluate	1. Read short selections to them 2. Let them tell you main idea 3. Introduce idea that main ideas can be found anywhere in sentences of paragraphs. First, last, middle, both first and last, any sentence, or not at all and must be inferred. 4. Give study guides in different levels to fit needs of your group. Let them work then compare their answers. 5. Project any major differences and let class discuss 6. Use textbook and let them find main idea. Topic sentence. 7. Can they? summarize.	1. Review by doing exercises in texts 2. Discuss their findings. Do they all agree? 3. Discuss relationships of sentences to paragraphs and paragraphs to longer pieces. 4. Do exercises such as the ones given in this textbook on relationships of materials found in different content areas. 5. Check 6. Summarize	1. Using the words and ideas given for this lesson in this text, chapter 7, pre-teach some vocabulary for this unit. 2. Let students attempt to figure words first 3. Silent reading or assigned work from previous day. 4. Group or work alone and do specifically assigned work according to needs 5. Groups compare answers. Discussion if needed. 6. Summary and finish up work next session	1. To complete the study and work on "Changes in the Earth's Surface," summarize what they did the previous day, what they need to do today and let them get to work. 2. Be available if help is needed by any group of individual.
REACTIONS:	REACTIONS:	REACTIONS:	REACTIONS:	REACTIONS:

Subject, Class, or Section:	Remedial Reading, Section 1	9:00-10:00 A.M.

MONDAY

LESSON:
Map reading and introduction to Tarry Town

OBJECTIVES:
1. To practice the skill of reading maps
2. To reinforce and extend map skills
3. To give practice in functional setting
4. To motivate for the reading of "The Legend of Sleepy Hollow," or other story of your choosing.

MATERIALS:
maps of all kinds, movie projector, worksheets, film — "Reading Maps", from Encyclopedia Brittanica film library

PROCEDURE:
1. Have film set up when students enter Show it.
2. Discuss film and any points students may bring up
3. Review concepts of latitude and longitude.
4. Practice with individual maps and study guides
5. Evaluate and summarize
6. Mention Tarry Town. Is it a real place? Where? Have they ever heard of it?
7. Talk some about Ichabod Crane and ghosts

REACTIONS:

TUESDAY

LESSON:
"The Legend of Sleepy Hollow."

OBJECTIVES:
1. Silent reading practice
2. To give variety
3. To practice skills
4. To enjoy story

MATERIALS:
A book with the story in it dictionaries vocabulary sheets study guides, three levels of comprehension

PROCEDURE:
1. Preparation for reading. (Details in chapter 7)
2. Tell them you will be working on this story for three days because it is so much fun and we can do so many things with it.
3. Pre-teach some vocabulary.
4. Read silently. (If some have already read it, as they will, give them their tasks to work on.
5. All busy, with teacher moving quietly to help where needed.

REACTIONS:

WEDNESDAY

LESSON:
"The Legend of Sleepy Hollow" continued

OBJECTIVES:
same plus
1. analogy concept and figurative language introduced

MATERIALS:
same

PROCEDURE:
1. Very brief discussion on analogies and figurative language. (These students may have never heard of either one)
2. Take a little time for dialogue about what they have read. What is their reaction so far?
3. Let them use dictionary and textbook
4. Do study guides

REACTIONS:

THURSDAY

LESSON:
Complete the study of "The Legend of Sleepy Hollow,"

OBJECTIVES:
same plus
1. three levels of comprehension utilized with students

MATERIALS:
Questions on different levels of understanding.

PROCEDURE:
1. Group and get right down to work.
2. Give directions that they talk among themselves in their groups and agree on answers.
3. Full class discussion on points of disagreement.
4. Any additional work you want them to do as evidence of how they react to story.
5. Summarize and evaluation. How do students like the way this story was handled?

REACTIONS:

FRIDAY

LESSON:
Diagnostic Review

OBJECTIVES:
1. To determine whether students need further work on the skills and if so, what areas?
2. Can some be moved out?

MATERIALS:
Iowa Basic Skills, or SRA Achievement Batteries, or Teacher-made Informal Inventory of Skills (4-6 and 7-9 levels)

PROCEDURE:
1. Explain to them the reason for this test. To see how much they have improved from six weeks ago. Do they need further practice on some of the skills but not on others? (The level of test per student will depend upon how well he performs. Which level does he need to succeed?)
2. Give test
3. Grade test
4. Make analysis
5. Make future plans for each individual student.

REACTIONS:

NOTES

1. Albert J. Kingston, "The Measurement of Reading Comprehension," in Roger Farr, ed., *Measurement and Evaluation of Reading* (New York: Harcourt Brace Jovanovich, 1970), p. 233. Used with permission of NTC, Inc.

2. A. L. Gates, "Character and Purposes of the Yearbook," in *Reading in the Elementary School*, 48th Yearbook, Part II (Chicago: University of Chicago Press, 1949), p. 3. Used with permission of NSSE.

3. Edward L. Thorndike, "Reading as Reasoning: A Study of Mistakes in Paragraph Reading," *Journal of Educational Psychology* 8 (June 1917).

4. Albert J. Kingston, *A Conceptual Model of Reading Comprehension*, 10th Yearbook of the NRC (Milwaukee: Marquette University Press, 1967). Used with permission of NRC.

5. From *The Mind Builder*, by Richard W. Samson. Copyright © 1965 by Richard W. Samson. Reprinted by permission of the publishers, E. P. Dutton & Co., Inc.

6. Jules C. Abrams, "Neurological and Psychological Influences on Reading," in Helen K. Smith, ed., *Perception and Reading*, Vol. 12 (Newark, Del.: IRA, 1968), p. 63. Used with permission of IRA.

7. Ibid., p. 64.

8. Ibid., p. 63.

9. William S. Palmer, "Cognition in Reading: Modes and Strategies," in *Quest for Competency in Teaching Reading* (Newark, Del.: IRA, 1972), p. 174.

10. Ibid., p. 176. Used with permission of IRA.

11. A. J. Kingston, *A Conceptual Model*.

12. Harold L. Herber, *Teaching Reading in Content Areas*, © 1970. Reprinted by permission of Prentice-Hall, Inc., Englewood Cliffs, New Jersey.

13. George Spache, "Construct of Comprehension," in *Reading and Inquiry*, Vol. 10 (Newark: Del.: IRA, 1965).

14. Donald L. Cleland, "Construct of Comprehension," in *Reading and Inquiry*, vol. 10 (Newark, Del.: IRA, 1965).

15. I. E. Aaron, "An Informal Reading Inventory," *Elementary English* (November 1960); Emmett A. Betts, *Foundations of Reading Instruction* (New York: American Book Company, 1946); Marjory S. Johnson and Roy A. Kress, *Informal Reading Inventories* (Newark: Del.: IRA, 1965); William R. Powell, "Reappraising the Criteria for Interpreting Informal Reading Inventory," in D. DeBoer, ed., *Reading Diagnosis and Evaluation* (Newark, Del.: IRA, 1970).

16. G. L. Bond and M. A. Tinker, *Reading Difficulties: Their Diagnosis and Correction* (New York: Appleton-Century-Crofts, 1965). Used with permission of the publisher.

17. Edward B. Fry, *Reading Instruction for Classroom and Clinic* (New York: McGraw-Hill Book Company, 1972), p. 269.

18. A. J. Harris, *How to Increase Reading Ability* (New York: David McKay Company, 1970), p. 215.

19. Joy L. Keith, *Comprehension Joy* (Naperville, Ill.: Reading Joy, 1974), p. 18. Used with the permission of the author.

20. From *Remedial Techniques in the Basic School Subjects*, by Grace Fernald.

Copyright 1943, McGraw-Hill Book Company. Used with permission of McGraw-Hill Book Company.

21. Harold Herber, *Teaching Reading in Content Areas,* © 1970. Reprinted by permission of Prentice-Hall, Inc., Englewood Cliffs, New Jersey.

22. David Sturgill, unpublished story written for his Sixth Grade. Based on material from Walbank and Schrier, *Living World History,* 2nd ed., Scott, Foresman and Worldbook Encyclopedia (Chicago: Field Enterprises Educational Corp., 1972). Used with permission of the author.

23. John Bormuth, "The Cloze Readability Procedure," in *Elementary English* XVV (April 1968), p. 429–36; A. J. Kingston and W. W. Weaver, "Feasibility of Cloze Technique for Teaching and Evaluating Culturally Disadvantaged Beginning Readers," in *Journal of Social Psychology* (December 1970), pp. 205–14; Eugene Jongsma, *The Cloze Procedure as a Teaching Technique* (Newark, Del.: IRA, 1971); Miles V. Zintz, *Corrective Reading,* 2nd ed. (Dubuque, Iowa: William C. Brown, 1972), p. 50; Wilson L. Taylor, "Cloze Procedure: A New Tool for Measuring Readability," in *Journalism Quarterly* 30 (Fall 1953), p. 416.

24. Idea based on information in Justin Fishbein, "Understanding Understanding— And What You Can Do About It," Workshop, Appalachian Reading Symposium: Boone, N.C. (November 1973).

25. Adaptation of SQ3R method in *Effective Study,* 4th edition by Francis P. Robinson. Copyright © 1941, 1946 by Harper & Row, Publishers, Inc. Copyright © 1961, 1970 by Francis P. Robinson. By permission of the publishers.

26. Olive S. Niles, *Improvement of Basic Comprehension Skills: An Attainable Goal in Secondary Schools.* Monograph on Secondary Education No. 6381 (New York: Scott Foresman, 1964).

27. Harold L. Herber, *Teaching Reading in Content Areas,* © 1970. Reprinted by permission of Prentice-Hall, Inc., Englewood Cliffs, New Jersey.

28. Virgie M. McIntyre, "Reading Graphic Materials in Secondary Schools," in Richard Culyer, ed., *Assuring Every Child the Right to Read,* Conference Proceedings of Fourth Annual Conference (Winston-Salem: NCC of IRA, 1972).

29. Adapted from Edwin P. Grobe, *300 Word Games for English Classes* (Portland, Me: Weston Walch, 1973).

BIBLIOGRAPHY

1. Aaron, I.E. "An Informal Reading Inventory." *Elementary English,* November 1960.
2. Abrams, Jules C. "Neurological and Psychological Influences on Reading." In Helen K. Smith, ed., *Perception and Reading,* vol. 12. Newark, Del.: IRA, 1968.
3. Anderson, A. W. "Directed Reading Comprehension." *Reading Teacher* 13 (February 1960), pp. 206–11.
4. Anderson, I. H. and Dearborn, W. F. *The Psychology of Teaching Reading.* New York: The Ronald Press Company, 1952.
5. Andrews, Theodore E., ed. "Florida International University." *Multistate Consortium on Performance-Based Teacher Education,* vol. 2, no. 5, (November 1973).
6. Arbuthnot, M. H. *The Arbuthnot Anthology.* Chicago: Scott, Foresman & Co., 1953.
7. Bannatyne, Alex. "The Transfer from Modality Perceptual to Modality Conceptual." *Perception and Reading.* Newark, Del.: IRA, 1968.
8. Barbe, Walter D. *Personalized Reading Instruction.* Englewood Cliffs, N.J.: Prentice-Hall, 1961.
9. Barrett, T. C., ed. *The Evaluation of Children's Reading Achievement* (Perspectives). Newark, Del.: IRA, 1967.
10. ———. "Taxonomy of Reading Comprehension." *Reading 300 Monograph.* Lexington, Mass.: Ginn & Co., 1972.
11. Benger, Kathlyn. "The Relationships of Perception, Intelligence and Grade DNE Reading Achievement." *Perception and Reading,* vol. 12. IRA Conference Proceedings, 1968.
12. Bennett & Malloy. *Cavalcade of Poems.* Scholastic Magazine, Inc. 1968.
13. Berg, Paul Conrad. "Psychology of Reading Behavior." *Psychology of Reading Behavior,* 18th Yearbook, IRA.
14. Bert, Paul and Rentel, Victor M. "Improving Reading Skills." *Journal of Reading* (April 1966).
15. Bessel, Arthur. "Piaget and Grades K-6." *Elementary English* (February 1972).
16. Betts, Emmett A. "Reading is Thinking." *The Reading Teacher,* (December 1961).
17. ———. *Foundations of Reading Instruction.* New York: American Book Co., 1957.
18. Bloom, B. S., ed. *Taxonomy of Educational Objectives.* New York: David McKay Co., 1956.
19. Bloomfield, L. *Language.* New York: Henry Holt & Co., 1933.
20. Bond, G. L. and Tinker, M. A. *Reading Difficulties: Their Diagnosis and Correction.* New York: Appleton-Century-Crofts, 1965.
21. Botel, M. *How to Teach Reading.* Chicago: Follett Publishing Co., 1962.
22. Bracken, Dorothy K. "The Teacher's Function in Developing Listening Skills." *Quest for Competency in Teaching Reading,* 1972.
23. Brown, J. I. *Efficient Reading.* Boston: D. C. Heath & Co., 1962.

24. Bruner, Jerome S. *Toward a Theory of Instruction.* Cambridge: Harvard University Press, 1967.

25. _____. *The Process of Education.* Cambridge: Harvard University Press. 1961.

26. Burrows, A. T. *Teaching Children in the Middle Grades.* Boston: D. C. Heath & Company, 1962.

27. Carlsen, G. Robert. *Books & the Teen Age Reader.* New York: Bantam Books, 1967.

28. Carter, H. L. and McGinnis, Dorothy. *Teaching Individuals to Read.* Boston: D. C. Heath & Co., 1962.

29. Chall, J. S. *Learning to Read: The Great Debate.* New York: McGraw-Hill, 1967.

30. Chomsky, Carol. "Stages in Language Development and Reading Exposure." *Harvard Educational Report,* vol. 42 (February 1972).

31. Clayton, Thomas. "What is Learning?" *Teaching & Language—A Psychological Perspective.* Englewood Cliffs, N.J.: Prentice-Hall, 1965.

32. Cleland, Donald L. "Construct of Comprehension." *Reading & Inquiry,* vol. 10 (1965).

33. Conference on Reading. University of Chicago. *Reading: Seventy-five Years of Progress.* Chicago: The University of Chicago Press, 1966.

34. Cordts, A. D. *Phonics for the Reading Teacher.* New York: Holt, Rinehart & Winston, Inc., 1965.

35. Davis, Michael, ed. *Personalizing Instruction Through Competency-Based Teacher Education.* Symposium on CBTE. Western Carolina University, Cullowhee, N.C. (April 1973).

36. Davis, Nancy B. *Basic Vocabulary Skills.* New York: McGraw-Hill, 1969.

37. DeBoer, John and Dallman, Martha. *The Teaching of Reading.* New York: Holt, Rinehart & Winston, Inc., 1965.

38. Dechant, E. V. *Improving the Teaching of Reading.* Englewood Cliffs, N.J.: Prentice-Hall, 1964.

39. Dawson, M. A., ed. *Developing Comprehension/Critical Reading.* (Selected IRA Reprints.) Newark, Del.: IRA, 1968.

40. Deighton, Lee. *Vocabulary Development in the Classroom.* New York: Bureau of Publications, Teachers College, Columbia University, 1959.

41. DeVitis, A. A. and Warner, J. R. *Words in Context: A Vocabulary Builder.* New York: Appleton-Century-Crofts, 1966.

42. Dewey, John. *How to Think.* Boston: D.C. Heath, 1933.

43. Dolch, E. W. *Psychology and Teaching of Reading.* Champaign, Ill.: The Garrard Press, 1951.

44. _____. "How to Diagnose Children's Reading Difficulty by Informal Classroom Techniques." *Reading Teacher* 6 (1953).

45. Durkin, D. and Miel, Alice. *Phonics and the Teaching of Reading.* New York: Bureau of Publications, Columbia University, 1962.

46. Durkin, D. *Teaching Them to Read.* Boston: Allyn & Bacon, 1970.

47. Durr, W. K. *Reading Instruction: Dimensions and Issues.* Boston: Allyn & Bacon, 1967.

48. Durrell, D. D. *Improving Reading Instruction.* Tarrytown-on-Hudson, N.Y.: World Book Company, 1956.

49. _____. "Individual Differences and Their Implications with Respect to Instruction of Reading." NSSE, vol. 36, chap. XI.

50. Early, M. J., ed. *Reading Instruction in Secondary Schools,* (Perspectives). Newark, Del.: IRA, 1964.

51. Ekwell, E. . *Locating and Correcting Reading Difficulties*. Columbus, Ohio: Charles E. Merrill, 1970.

52. Elkind, David. "Misunderstanding about How Children Learn." *Today's Education* (March 1972).

53. Fader, Daniel. *Hooked on Books*. New York: Putnam & Sons, 1966.

54. Fernald, G. M. *Remedial Techniques in Basic School Subjects*. New York: McGraw-Hill, 1943.

55. Figurel, J. Allen, ed. "Individualized Instruction in the Classroom." *Improvement of Reading Through Classroom Practice*. Proceedings of Annual Convention, IRA, 1964.

56. Fishbein, Justin. "Understanding Understanding—And What You Can Do About It," Lecture. Appalachian Reading Symposium, Appalachian State University, Boone, N.C., November 1973.

57. Frazier, Alexander. "Individualized Reading: More Than New Forms & Formulas." *Elementary Education* 39 (December 1962).

58. Fries, C. C. *Linguistics and Reading*. New York: Holt, Rinehart & Winston, 1962.

59. Fry, Edward *Teaching Machines and Programmed Instruction, An Introduction*. New York: McGraw-Hill, 1963.

60. Gage, N. L., ed. *Handbook of Research on Teaching*. Chicago: Rand McNally & Company, 1963.

61. Gagne, Robert M. *The Conditions of Learning*. New York: Holt, Rinehart & Winston, 1965.

62. Gallant, R. *Handbook in Corrective Reading*. Columbus, Ohio: Charles E. Merrill, 1970.

63. Gans, Roma. *Common Sense in Teaching Reading*. Indianapolis: Bobbs-Merrill Co., 1963.

64. Gates, A. L. "Character and Purposes of the Yearbook." *Reading in the Elementary School*. 48th Yearbook of NSSE, Part II. Chicago: University of Chicago Press, 1949.

65. _____. *Teaching Reading*. Washington, D.C.: NEA, 1942.

66. Glasser, William. *Schools Without Failure*. New York: Harper & Row, 1969.

67. Goodman, K. S. *Psycholinguistic Nature of the Reading Process*. Detroit: Wayne State University Press, 1968.

68. Gray, W. S. *Improving Reading in all Curriculum Areas*. Chicago: Scott, Foresman & Company, 1956, pp. 8–24.

69. Grobe, Edwin P. *300 Word Games and Activities for English Class*. Portland, Me: Walch, 1973.

70. Guilford, J. P. "Frontiers in Thinking That Teachers Should Know About." *The Reading Teacher,* (February 1960): 176.

71. Hall, Mary Anne. *Teaching Reading as Language Experience,* 2nd ed. Columbus, Ohio: Charles E. Merrill, 1975.

72. Harris, A. J. *How to Increase Reading Ability*. New York: David McKay Company, 1970.

73. _____, ed. *Readings on Reading Instruction*. New York: David McKay, 1963.

74. Heilman, A. W. *Phonics in Proper Perspective,* 2nd ed. Columbus, Ohio: Charles E. Merrill, 1975.

75. Herber, H. D. *Teaching Reading in the Content Areas*. Englewood Cliffs, N.J.: Prentice-Hall, 1970.

76. Hildreth, Gertrude. "Some Principles of Learning Applied to Reading." *Readings on Reading Instruction*. New York: David McKay, 1963.
77. Holt, J. *How Children Fail*. New York: Pitman Publishing Corporation, 1964.
78. Huey, E. B. *The Psychology and Pedagogy of Reading*. Cambridge, Mass.: M.I.T. Press, 1968.
79. Huck, Charlotte S. and Kuhn, Doris Y. *Children's Literature in the Elementary School*. New York: Holt, Rinehart & Winston, 1968.
80. Irving, Washington. "The Legend of Sleepy Hollow." *Adventures Ahead*. New York: Harcourt, Brace & World.
81. Israel, Saul; Roemer, Norman H. and Durend, Loyal. *World Geography Today*. New York: Holt, Rinehart & Winston, 1963.
82. Johnson, M. S. and Kress, R. A. *Informal Reading Inventories*. (Reading Aids Series). Newark, Del.: IRA, 1965.
83. Joyce, Bruce R. and Hartoonian, Berg. *The Structure of Teaching*. Chicago: SRA, 1967.
84. Kingston, A. J. *A Conceptual Model of Reading Comprehension*. 10th Yearbook of the NCR. Milwaukee: Marquette University Press, 1967.
85. Karlin, R. *Teaching Reading in High School*. Indianapolis, Bobbs-Merrill Company, 1963; "A Three-Pronged Attack on Vocabulary Development." J. A. Figurel, ed. *Proceedings of Annual Convention*, IRA, 1968.
86. Kephart, N. *The Slow Learner in the Classroom*. Columbus, Ohio: Charles E. Merrill, 1961.
87. Keith, Joy. *Comprehension Joy*. Naperville, Ill.: Reading Joy, 1974.
88. Kipp, Helen B. "The Development of Thinking and Concepts." *Interpreting Language: An Essential of Understanding*. A Research Bulletin of the National Conference on Research in English.
89. Kress, Roy A. and Johnson, Marjorie. *Informal Reading Inventories*. Newark, Del.: IRA, 1965.
90. Lefevre, C. A. *Linguistics and the Teacher of Reading*. New York: McGraw-Hill, 1964.
91. Lefler, Hugh T. *North Carolina: History, Geography, Government*. New York: Harcourt, Brace & World, 1966.
92. Lenner, Roger T. "What Can Be Measured?" Roger Farr, ed. *Measurement and Evaluation of Reading*. New York: Harcourt, Brace and World, 1970.
93. Mackworth, J. F. *Reading Research Quarterly*, vol. 3 (Summer 1972).
94. MacLachlan, McNeill, Bell. "Matter and Energy." *The Foundations of Modern Physics*.
95. Marksheffel, N. D. *Better Reading in the Secondary School: Principles and Procedures for Teachers*. New York: The Ronald Press, 1966.
96. Mazurkiewicz, A. J. *New Perspectives in Reading Instruction*. New York: Pitman Publishing Corporation, 1964.
97. McIntyre, Virgie M. "Reading Graphic Materials in Secondary School." Richard Culyer III, ed. *Assuring Every Child the Right to Read*. Proceedings of Fourth Annual Conference, NCCIRA.
98. McCullough, Constance. "Components of a Reading Program for the Intermediate Grades." *Quest for Competency in Teaching Reading*. Newark, Del.: IRA, 1972.
99. McCarthy, D. "Language Development in Children." *Manual of Child Psychology*, 2nd ed. New York: John Wiley & Sons, 1954.

100. McClung, Robert. *Horseshoe Crab*. New York: Morrow, 1967.

101. Monroe, Marian and Roberts, Bernice. *Foundations for Reading*. New York: Scott, Foresman, & Company, 1964.

102. Munsinger, Harry. *Fundamentals of Child Development*. New York: Holt, Rinehart & Winston, 1971.

103. National Society for the Study of Education. Forty-eighth Yearbook, 1961, *Reading in the Elementary School*. Sixtieth Yearbook, 1961, *Development in and Through Reading*. Sixty-seventh Yearbook, 1968, *Innovation & Change in Reading Instruction*. Chicago: University of Chicago Press.

104. Niles, Olive S. *Improvement of Basic Comprehension Skills: An Attainable Goal in Secondary Schools*. Monograph on Secondary Education #6381. New York: Scott Foresman, 1964.

105. Niles, Olive S. and Early, Margaret J. "Adjusting to Individual Differences in English." *Journal of Education* 138. Boston: Boston University, School of Education.

106. Otto, W. and Smith, R. J. *Administering the School Reading Program*. Boston: Houghton Mifflin, 1970.

107. Palmer, William S. "Cognition in Reading: Modes & Strategies." *Quest for Competency in Teaching Reading*. Newark, Del.: IRA, 1972.

108. Pauk, William. "Techniques for Textbook Study." *Reading Improvement* (Spring 1969).

109. Piaget, Jean. *The Language & Thought of the Child*. Translated by M. Gagain. New York: Harcourt, Brace & Company, 1932.

110. Pilgrim, Geneva H. and McAllister, Mariana K. *Books, Young People and Reading Guidance*. New York: Harper & Row, 1968.

111. *Reading Research Quarterly*. Summer 1968 to Summer 1974.

112. Robinson, H. A. and Rauch, S. J. *Guiding the Reading Program, A Reading Consultants Handbook*. Chicago: SRA, 1965.

113. Robinson, H. M. *Why Pupils Fail in Reading*. Chicago: University of Chicago Press, 1946.

114. Russell, David. *Children's Thinking*. Boston: Ginn & Co., 1956.

115. Russell, D. H. and Russell, E. F. *Reading Aids through the Grades*. New York: Columbia University Press, 1961.

116. Samson, Richard W. "What is Thinking?" *The Mind Builder*. New York: Dutton, 1965.

117. Sanders, Norris. *Classroom Questions—What Kinds?* New York: Harper & Row, 1966.

118. Sandoz, Mari. "Winter Thunder." *From Insights: Themes in Literature*.

119. Schank, Roger C. "Conceptual Dependency: A Theory of National Language Understanding." *Cognitive Psychology* 3, no. 4 (October 1972).

120. Schick, George B. and Schmidt, Bernard. *A Guide Book for the Teaching of Reading*. Chicago: Psychotechnics Press, Psychotechnics, Inc., 1966.

121. Schubert, D. G. and Torgerson, T. L., eds. *Readings in Reading: Practice, Theory and Research*. New York: Thomas Y. Crowell, 1968.

122. _____. *Improving Reading in the Elementary School*. Dubuque, Iowa: William C. Brown, 1972.

123. Shostak, Jerome. *Vocabulary Workshop*. New York: Oxford Book Company, 1961.

124. Shugre, Michael. *How the "New English" Will Help Your Child*. New York: Association Press, 1966.

125. Smith, Nila B. *Reading Instruction for Today's Children.* Englewood Cliffs, N.J.: Prentice-Hall, 1963.

126. _____, ed. *Current Issues in Reading.* Newark, Del.: IRA, 1968.

127. Smith, Rodney P. "A Review of Selected Research in Language Arts Reported in 1971." *Journal of Reading Behavior* 4, no. 2, (Spring 1972).

128. Smoke, K. L. "An Objective Study of Concept Formation." *Psychological Monograph* LXVII, no. 4 (1932).

129. Spache, Evelyn B. *Reading Activities for Child Involvement.* Boston: Allyn & Bacon, 1973.

130. Spache, George D. and Spache, Evelyn. *Reading in the Elementary School.* Boston: Allyn & Bacon, 1969.

131. Spache, George D. and Berg, Paul. *The Art of Efficient Reading.* New York: Macmillan Co., 1955.

132. Spache, George D. "Contributions of Allied Fields to the Teaching of Reading," *Innovation & Change in Reading Instruction.* NSSE, 67th Yearbook.

133. _____. "Construct of Comprehension." *Reading & Inquiry* 10 (1965).

134. Staiger, Ralph and Sohn, David A., eds. *New Directions in Reading.* New York: Bantam Books, 1967.

135. Stauffer, R. G., ed. *The First Grade Reading Studies: Findings of Individual Investigations,* Newark, Del.: IRA, 1967.

136. _____. *Teaching Reading as a Thinking Process.* New York: Harper & Row, 1968.

137. _____. *Directing Reading Maturity as a Cognitive Process.* Evanston, Ill.: Harper & Row, 1968.

138. Strang, Ruth. *Learning to Read—Insights for Education.* Ontario Institute for Studies in Education, Toronto, 1970.

139. Strang, R.; McCullough, C. M.; and Traxler, A. E. *The Improvement of Reading,* New York: McGraw-Hill, 1967.

140. Termen, S. and Walcutt, C. C. *Reading: Chaos and Cure.* New York: McGraw-Hill, 1958.

141. Thomas, Ellen L. and Robinson, H. Allan. *Improving Reading in Every Class.* Boston: Allyn & Bacon, 1972.

142. Thorndike, Edward L. "Reading as Reasoning: A Study of Mistakes in Paragraph Reading." *Journal of Educational Psychology* 8 (June 1917).

143. _____. "The Psychology of Thinking in the Case of Reading" *Psychological Review* 14, no. 5 (1917).

144. Torrance, E. Paul and Myers, R. E. *Creative Learning & Teaching.* New York: Dodd, Mead, 1970.

145. Travers, Robert M. W. *Essentials of Learning.* New York: Macmillan, 1967.

146. Trela, T. M. *Fourteen Remedial Reading Methods.* Palo Alto, Calif: Fearon Publishers, 1969.

147. Tyler, F. T. (Committee Chairman) *Individualized Instruction.* NSSE, 61st Yearbook, Part I. New York: Scholastic Magazine, 1962.

148. Umans, S. *New Trends in Reading Instruction.* New York: Teachers College Press, Columbia University, 1963.

149. Veatch, J. *Individualizing Your Reading Program.* New York: G. P. Putnam, 1959.

150. Vygotsky, Lev. S. *Thought and Language.* Cambridge, Mass.: MIT Press, 1962.

151. Walcutt, C. C. (with Joan Lamport and Glenn McCracken) *Teaching Reading.* New York: Macmillan Co., 1974.

152. Wallen, Normal, and Travers, Robert. "Analysis and Investigation of Teaching Methods." N. L. Gage, ed. *Handbook on Research on Teaching*. New York: Macmillan Co., 1960.

153. Wanat, Stanley F. "Language Acquisition: Basic Issues." *The Reading Teacher* (November 1971).

154. Warner, Sylvia Ashton. *Teacher*. New York: Simon & Shuster, 1963.

155. Wiener, M. and Cromer, V. "Reading and Reading Difficulty: A Conceptual Analysis." *Harvard Educational Review* 37, no. 2 (Fall 1967): pp. 620–43.

156. Weiss, M. J. *Reading in the Secondary Schools*. New York: The Odyssey Press, 1961.

157. Winkler, Charles. "Reading in the Content Area." *Translating Theory into Practice*. Proceedings from 3rd Annual Conference, NCC of IRA. Charlotte, N.C., 1971.

158. Wilson, R. M. *Diagnostic and Remedial Reading*. Columbus, Ohio: Charles E. Merrill, 1967.

159. World Book Encyclopedia. "Literature for Children." New York: Field Enterprise Education Corp., 1968.

160. Witty, P. A. *Teaching of Reading: A Developmental Process*. Boston: D. C. Heath, 1966.

161. Zintz, M. V. *Corrective Reading*. Dubuque, Iowa: William C. Brown, 1971.

Index

Painting,
    on glass, 297
    with wax, 293
Paired associates, 59
Palmer, W.S., 5, 46
Pantomime, 51
Paragraph sense, 83, 97
    (*see also* Main ideas; Sequence)
Paraphrasing,
    (*see* Summarizing)
Past experiences, 65, 134
Pauk, W., 111
Pejoration, 69
Perception, 32, 47
Personification, 64
Pfirmann, A.C., 160
Phoneme, 56
Phonic analysis, 56
Phonics survey test, 12-20
Phonologist, 13
Phonovisual, 133
Physics,
    language of, 98
Piaget, J., 47
Pilgrim's Progress, 27, 32
Pledge to the Flag, 3, 104
Port-manteau, 69
Potential, 25
PQRST, 265
Preamble to the Constitution, 289, 345
Precipitation, 112
Predicting meaning, 142, 145
Prefixes,
    (*see* Affixes)
Preteach vocabulary, 73, 138, 147
Prince and The Pauper, The, 27, 32
Principles of learning, 225
Projection charts, 205-6
Programmed reading, 115, 133
    advantages and disadvantages, 340
    materials for vocabulary
        development, 61
Propaganda techniques, 124-27
Psalm 121, 31, 33
Psycholinguist, 13
Psychology of learning, 225
Puppets to teach vocabulary, 51
Purpose for reading, 6, 145, 231, 347
    questions to set, 136
Pushcart War, The, 29, 32

Puzzles,
    to reinforce vocabulary, 187
    to teach vocabulary, 59, 75
Pygmalion in the Classroom, 131, 161

Questions,
    convergent, 121
    divergent, 121
    evaluative, 145
    inferential, 26, 144
    literal, 14, 26, 128, 136, 151
    to set purpose, 87
    yes and no, 119
Quotations,
    for motivation, 109
    for reference skills, 278

Rate of reading, 82, 266
Readability,
    scales of, 41-43
Readiness, 81, 146
Reading,
    and math, 152-62
    approaches for teaching, 131
    atmosphere for, 4, 18
    choral, 55, 288
    creative, tasks for, 89, 121, 177,
        220, 239, 240
    critical skills, 266
    definitions, 1, 5, 140, 228
    developmental, 5, 83, 122, 249
    evaluative, 285
    in a revolutionary society, 331
    in science, 146, 352
    oral, 309, 342
    purposes for, 6, 136, 145, 231, 347
    skills listed, 264
    strategies, 115-16
    student perception of, 9
    teacher perception of, 10
    teacher to student, 59
    ten specific strategies for
        remedial, 115
Reading Teacher, The, 279
Reasoning, 11, 48
Rebus, 132
Recall,
    a part of comprehension, 273
    depends upon, 275
    practice with, 180, 274
    skills of, 6, 265, 365